MC

Microsoft Certified
Azure AI Fundamentals

Study Guide

MC

Microsoft Certified
Azure AI Fundamentals

Study Guide

EXAM AI-900

ADORA NWODO

SYBEX®
A Wiley Brand

Library of Congress Cataloging-in-Publication Data applied for:

Paperback ISBN: 9781394352753
ePDF ISBN: 9781394352777
ePub ISBN: 9781394352760

Cover Design: Wiley
Cover Image: © Jeremy Woodhouse/Getty Images

Set in Sabon LT Std 9.5/12 pt by Lumina Datamatics

To my mum, Onyinyechi Nwodo.

Acknowledgments

Writing this book has been an incredibly rewarding journey, and I am deeply grateful to everyone who supported me along the way.

First, I want to thank the amazing team at Wiley for believing in this project and guiding it from concept to completion. Your editorial insights, production expertise, and unwavering support helped shape this book into what it is today.

To my family, thank you for your endless encouragement, love, and prayers. Your belief in me is the foundation I stand on.

To my friends, thank you for cheering me on, checking in when I went quiet, and celebrating every milestone with me.

And to my team, thank you for holding things down so I could focus on writing. Your dedication, flexibility, and support mean more than words can express.

This book is for everyone who dreams of learning, growing, and building with AI. I hope it takes you one step closer to your goals.

About the Author

Nenne Adaora Nwodo professionally known as Adora Nwodo is a multi-award winning Engineering Manager. She currently works at the intersection of Cloud Engineering and Developer Platforms. She is passionate about Cloud and Emerging Technologies. With a First Class Computer Science degree from the University of Lagos, Adora has a strong Software Engineering background. Adora enjoys building innovative technology on the cloud.

Apart from building and advocating for mixed reality technologies, Adora is a Digital Creator and the Founder of NexaScale, a social enterprise aimed at fostering the growth and development of technology enthusiasts by providing resources and opportunities for project building and work experience—helping them start and scale their careers. She has courses online that teach people about infrastructure automation; she has also published multiple articles on Software Engineering, Productivity & Career Growth on her blog, AdoraHack. She also has a YouTube channel for AdoraHack where she posts tech content that could be useful to Software Developers.

Adora is the author of six cloud engineering books, including *Beginning Azure DevOps*, a book published by Wiley. She is extremely passionate about the developer community and is driving inclusion for women in technology. She co-organizes community events for unStack Africa, contributes to Open Source, and speaks at technology conferences worldwide.

About the Technical Editor

Doug Holland is the Founder and Principal Software Engineer at Intrepid Reality. He holds a master's degree in software engineering from Oxford University and has been recognized for his technical leadership as a Microsoft MVP and Intel Black Belt Developer. Before founding Intrepid Reality, Doug's career spanned almost 25 years at companies such as Microsoft Corporation, Intel Corporation, and Hewlett Packard.

Contents at a Glance

Contents

Introduction

Purpose and Structure of the Exam

The AI-900 exam, also known as the Microsoft Azure AI Fundamentals exam, is designed to test your basic understanding of artificial intelligence (AI) and how it works in the context of Microsoft Azure. The purpose of this exam is to make sure you have a solid foundation in AI concepts, even if you don't have a technical background. It's meant for people who are new to AI or those who want to validate their knowledge of AI and how it's used in Azure. This exam is not about deep technical skills or coding; instead, it focuses on understanding the big picture of AI, including its benefits, challenges, and common use cases.

The exam is structured to cover a range of topics related to AI and machine learning, but it's not overly complicated. It typically includes around 40–60 questions, and you'll have 45 minutes to complete it. The questions are multiple choice, and they test your knowledge of AI concepts, Azure AI services, and how AI can be applied in real-world scenarios. The exam is designed to be approachable, so even if you're just starting out with AI, you can feel confident going into it as long as you've prepared well.

One of the key things to understand about the AI-900 exam is that it's not just about memorizing facts. Instead, it's about understanding how AI works and how it can be used to solve problems. For example, you'll need to know what machine learning is, how it differs from traditional programming, and how Azure services like Azure Machine Learning or Cognitive Services can be used to build AI solutions. The exam also covers ethical considerations in AI, such as fairness, privacy, and transparency, which are important topics in today's world.

This is a great starting point for anyone interested in AI, whether you're a student, a business professional, or someone looking to switch careers. It's designed to be accessible, and it gives you a solid foundation in AI concepts and Azure tools, and it can be a stepping stone to other Azure role-based certifications like Azure Data Scientist Associate or Azure AI Engineer Associate. When you pass this exam, you'll gain a valuable certification, but you'll also have a better understanding of how AI is shaping the future of technology.

Key Skills Measured in the Exam

The AI-900 exam focuses on testing your understanding of key AI concepts and how they are applied using Microsoft Azure services. One of the main areas it covers is Artificial Intelligence workloads and considerations, which makes up about 15–20% of the exam. This includes understanding what AI is, how it can be used in different industries, and the ethical considerations that come with building and deploying AI systems. You'll need to know about fairness, reliability, privacy, and transparency, and why these principles are important when working with AI.

Another significant part of the exam, making up 20–25%, is the fundamental principles of machine learning on Azure. This section tests your knowledge of basic machine learning concepts, such as supervised, unsupervised, and reinforcement learning. You'll also need to understand how machine learning models are trained and evaluated, and how Azure Machine Learning can be used to build and deploy these models. While you don't need to know how to code, you should be familiar with the tools and services Azure provides for machine learning.

The exam also covers computer vision workloads on Azure, which accounts for 15–20% of the test. This includes understanding how Azure services like Computer Vision and Custom Vision can be used to analyze images and videos. You'll need to know about common use cases, such as object detection, facial recognition, and image classification, and how these can be applied in real-world scenarios.

Another 15–20% of the exam focuses on Natural Language Processing (NLP) workloads on Azure. This section tests your knowledge of how Azure services like Text Analytics, Translator, and Speech can be used to process and analyze text and speech data. You'll need to understand common NLP tasks, such as sentiment analysis, language translation, and speech-to-text conversion, and how these can be used to improve business processes.

Finally, the exam includes generative AI workloads on Azure, which also makes up 15–20% of the test. This section covers the basics of generative AI, including how it can be used to create new content, such as text, images, or even code. You'll need to understand how Azure services like OpenAI can be used to build generative AI solutions and the potential applications of this technology in areas like content creation, customer support, and more.

How to Use This Study Guide Effectively

To get the most out of this study guide, it's important to approach it with a clear plan. Start by reading this introduction to understand the structure of the AI-900 exam and what it covers. This will give you a good idea of what to expect and how to focus your study time. The guide is designed to walk you through each topic step by step, so take your time with each chapter. Don't rush through the material; instead, make sure you fully understand the concepts before moving on to the next section.

As you go through the chapters, take advantage of the practical examples and visual aids provided. These are there to help you connect the concepts to real-world scenarios, making it easier to remember and apply what you've learned. If you come across something you don't understand, don't skip over it. Go back, reread the section, or use additional resources if needed. The goal is to build a strong foundation, so it's okay to spend extra time on topics that are new or challenging for you.

The practice questions at the end of the guide are one of the most valuable tools for your preparation. Use them to test your knowledge and identify areas where you might need more review. Treat these review questions like the real exam; time yourself and try to answer the questions without looking at the answers. This will help you get comfortable with the format and build your confidence. After each practice session, review your answers and read the explanations to understand why the correct answers are right and why the others are wrong.

Finally, make a study schedule that works for you. Set aside regular time each day or week to work through the guide, and stick to it. Consistency is key when preparing for an exam like this. If you follow the guide step by step, take advantage of the practice materials, and stay consistent with your study habits, you'll be well-prepared to pass the AI-900 exam and gain a solid understanding of Azure AI fundamentals.

Exam Preparation Strategies and Tips

Preparing for the AI-900 exam doesn't have to be overwhelming if you approach it with the right strategies. First, start by understanding the exam objectives and what topics are covered. This will help you focus your study time on the areas that matter most. The study guide breaks down each topic into manageable sections, so take it one chapter at a time. Don't try to cram everything at once; instead, set a realistic study schedule that allows you to cover the material thoroughly without feeling rushed.

As you study, make sure to actively engage with the content. This means taking notes, summarizing key points in your own words, and testing yourself as you go. The practice questions in the guide are helpful for this. Use them to check your understanding and identify any weak areas. If you find yourself struggling with a particular topic, go back and review it until you feel confident. Remember, the goal isn't just to memorize facts but to truly understand how AI concepts work and how they're applied in Azure.

Another important tip is to simulate the exam environment when you practice. Set aside time to take the mock exams under real exam conditions, timed and without distractions. Figure I.1 shows what the mock exams (or practice assessment) look like. You can set a timer yourself as you take the test. This will help you get used to the pressure of the actual test and improve your time management skills. After each practice session, review your answers carefully. Pay attention to the explanations for both correct and incorrect answers, as this will deepen your understanding of the material.

Don't also forget to take care of yourself during the preparation process. Studying for an exam can be stressful, so make sure to take breaks, get enough sleep, and stay hydrated. A clear mind will help you absorb the material better and perform well on exam day. If you follow these strategies and use the study guide effectively, you'll be well-prepared to tackle the AI-900 exam with confidence.

FIGURE I.1 AI-900 practice assessment.

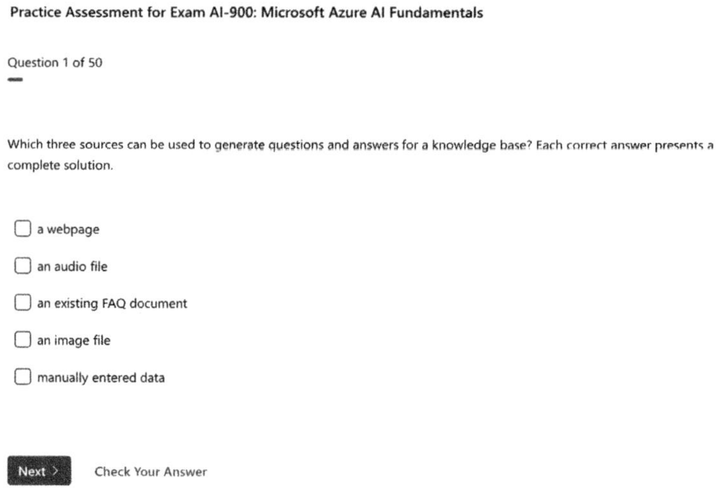

Practice Assessment for Exam AI-900: Microsoft Azure AI Fundamentals

Question 1 of 50
—

Which three sources can be used to generate questions and answers for a knowledge base? Each correct answer presents a complete solution.

☐ a webpage

☐ an audio file

☐ an existing FAQ document

☐ an image file

☐ manually entered data

Next >   Check Your Answer

How This Book Is Organized

This book consists of 13 chapters plus supplementary information: a glossary, this introduction, and the assessment test after the introduction. The chapters are organized as follows:

Chapter 1, "Overview of AI Concepts and Workloads"

Chapter 2, "Responsible AI in Azure"

Chapter 3, "Core Concepts of AI Models and Solutions"

Chapter 4, "Introduction to Machine Learning Concepts"

Chapter 5, "Machine Learning in Azure"

Chapter 6, "Introduction to Computer Vision"

Chapter 7, "Azure Tools for Computer Vision"

Chapter 8, "Introduction to Natural Language Processing (NLP)"

Chapter 9, "Azure Tools for NLP Workloads"

Chapter 10, "Introduction to Generative AI"

Chapter 11, "Azure OpenAI Service"

Chapter 12, "AI Agents in Azure"

Chapter 13, "AI Use Cases and Industry Applications"

Chapter Features

Each chapter begins with a list of the objectives that are covered in that chapter. The book doesn't necessarily cover the objectives in order. Thus, you shouldn't be alarmed at the ordering of the objectives within the book.

At the end of each chapter, you'll find a couple of elements you can use to prepare for the exam:

Exam Essentials   This section summarizes important information that was covered in the chapter. You should be able to perform each of the tasks or convey the information requested.

Review Questions   Each chapter concludes with 20 review questions. You should answer these questions and check your answers against the ones provided for the book. If you can't answer at least 80% of these questions correctly, go back and review the chapter, or at least those sections that seem to be giving you difficulty.

The review questions, assessment test, and other testing elements included in this book are *not* derived from the actual exam questions, so don't memorize the answers to these questions and assume that doing so will enable you to pass the exam. You should learn the underlying topic, as described in the text of the book. This will let you answer the questions provided with this book *and* pass the exam. Learning the underlying topic is also the approach that will serve you best in the workplace—the ultimate goal of a certification like this one.

To get the most out of this book, you should read each chapter from start to finish and then check your memory and understanding with the chapter-end elements.

Bonus Digital Content

This book is accompanied by an online learning environment that provides several additional elements. Items available among these companion files include the following:

Practice tests   All of the questions in this book appear in our proprietary digital test engine—including the 25-question assessment test at the end of this introduction and the 160 questions that make up the review question sections at the end of each chapter. In addition, there is a 65-question bonus exam.

Electronic "flashcards" The digital companion files include 65 questions in flashcard format (a question followed by a single correct answer). You can use these to review your knowledge of the exam objectives.

Glossary The key terms from this book, and their definitions, are available as a fully searchable PDF.

Interactive Online Learning Environment and Test Bank

You can access all these resources at www.wiley.com/go/sybextestprep.

Conventions Used in This Book

This book uses certain elements to help you quickly identify important information and to avoid confusion:

 A note indicates information that's useful or that can save you time and frustration.

Sidebars

A sidebar is like a note but longer. The information in a sidebar is useful, but it doesn't fit into the main flow of the text.

Microsoft Azure AI Fundamentals AI-900 Exam Objectives

This table provides the extent, by percentage, which each subject area is represented on the actual examination.

Subject Area	% of Exam
Describe Artificial Intelligence workloads and considerations	15–20
Describe fundamental principles of machine learning on Azure	20–25

Subject Area	% of Exam
Describe features of computer vision workloads on Azure	15–20
Describe features of Natural Language Processing (NLP) workloads on Azure	15–20
Describe features of generative AI workloads on Azure	15–20
Total	100

Exam objectives are subject to change at any time without prior notice and at Microsoft's sole discretion. Please visit Microsoft's website for the most current listing of exam objectives.

Objective Map

OBJECTIVE	CHAPTER
Domain 1: Describe Artificial Intelligence workloads and considerations	1, 2, 12, 13
Subdomain 1a: Identify features of common AI workloads	1, 12, 13
1-1 Identify computer vision workloads	1, 13
1-2 Identify natural language processing workloads	1, 12, 13
1-3 Identify document processing workloads	1
1-4 Identify features of generative AI workloads	1
Subdomain 1b: Identify guiding principles for responsible AI	2
1-5 Describe considerations for fairness in an AI solution	2
1-6 Describe considerations for reliability and safety in an AI solution	2
1-7 Describe considerations for privacy and security in an AI solution	2

OBJECTIVE	CHAPTER
1-8 Describe considerations for inclusiveness in an AI solution	2
1-9 Describe considerations for transparency in an AI solution	2
1-10 Describe considerations for accountability in an AI solution	2
Domain 2: Describe fundamental principles of machine learning on Azure	3–5
Subdomain 2a: Identify common machine learning techniques	3, 4
2-1 Identify regression machine learning scenarios	3, 4
2-2 Identify classification machine learning scenarios	3, 4
2-3 Identify clustering machine learning scenarios	3, 4
2-4 Identify features of deep learning techniques	3, 4
2-5 Identify features of the Transformer architecture	3, 4
Subdomain 2b: Describe core machine learning concepts	3, 4
2-6 Identify features and labels in a dataset for machine learning	3, 4
2-7 Describe how training and validation datasets are used in machine learning	3, 4
Subdomain 2c: Describe Azure Machine Learning capabilities	3, 5
2-8 Describe capabilities of automated machine learning	3, 5
2-9 Describe data and compute services for data science and machine learning	3, 5
2-10 Describe model management and deployment capabilities in Azure Machine Learning	3, 5
Domain 3: Describe features of computer vision workloads on Azure	6, 7, 13
Subdomain 3a: Identify common types of computer vision solution	6, 7, 13
3-1 Identify features of image classification solutions	6, 7, 13

Assessment Test

1. A healthcare technology company is developing a comprehensive AI system for patient care that must (1) analyze medical images to detect abnormalities, (2) process patient feedback in natural language to assess satisfaction, (3) predict patient readmission risk based on historical data, and (4) generate personalized treatment summaries for doctors. Based on the AI concepts covered in this chapter, which combination of AI technologies would be most appropriate for this multi-faceted system?

    A. Computer Vision, Natural Language Processing, Expert Systems, Knowledge Mining

    B. Computer Vision, Natural Language Processing, Predictive Analytics, Generative AI

    C. Deep Learning, Reinforcement Learning, Machine Learning, Expert Systems

    D. Computer Vision, Expert Systems, Knowledge Mining, Reinforcement Learning

2. A company wants to automatically detect and anonymize personally identifiable information (PII) such as email addresses and physical addresses in customer service transcripts before using them to train an AI model. Which Azure tool is specifically designed for this purpose?

    A. InterpretML

    B. Fairlearn

    C. Presidio

    D. Azure AI Content Safety

3. A multinational company is developing a voice recognition system for customer service that must work across diverse global markets. During testing, they discover the system has higher error rates for speakers with non-Western accents and struggles with regional dialects. Additionally, the system fails to provide accessible alternatives for users with speech impairments. Which Responsible AI principle is primarily violated, and what comprehensive approach should be taken using Azure services?

    A. Fairness; use Fairlearn to measure demographic parity across accent groups and reweight training data

    B. Privacy; implement Confidential Computing to protect voice data and use encryption for all audio processing

    C. Inclusiveness; use Azure AI Language's multilingual support, expand training data diversity, and integrate accessibility features

    D. Reliability; improve error handling mechanisms and implement continuous monitoring with Azure Monitor

4. A multinational pharmaceutical company is developing an AI model to predict drug interactions using their proprietary research data spanning 20 years. The model must meet strict regulatory compliance requirements, provide full transparency in decision-making for regulatory audits, and achieve the highest possible accuracy for patient safety. The company has significant computational resources and a team of data scientists. However, they discover that no existing pretrained models adequately handle their specific molecular data formats and regulatory constraints. What approach should they pursue and why?

   A. Use a pretrained chemistry model and fine-tune it extensively to meet their specific requirements

   B. Build a custom model from scratch with complete control over architecture, data, and compliance features

   C. Combine multiple pretrained models in an ensemble approach to improve accuracy

   D. Use transfer learning with a general-purpose deep learning model and adapt it for pharmaceutical data

5. A healthcare technology company has deployed an AI diagnostic model in production and wants to ensure it maintains high performance over time. The model analyzes medical images to detect early signs of disease. Which monitoring and maintenance activities should they implement to ensure continued reliability? (Choose all that apply.)

   A. Monitor model response times and error rates using Azure Monitor

   B. Set up automated retraining pipelines with new medical image data

   C. Implement data drift detection to identify changes in incoming image characteristics

   D. Maintain static model parameters to ensure consistent predictions

6. A data scientist notices their model achieves 99% accuracy on training data but only 65% accuracy on the test set. The training and validation error curves show a large gap that increases over time. Which combination of techniques would best address this issue?

   A. Increase model complexity and add more features

   B. Apply regularization, dropout, and cross-validation

   C. Use min-max scaling and one-hot encoding

   D. Implement stratified splitting and feature engineering

7. When preparing categorical data for machine learning algorithms, which encoding techniques should be considered? (Choose all that apply.)

   A. Label encoding for ordinal categories

   B. One-hot encoding for non-ordinal categories

   C. Target encoding with regularization

   D. Feature scaling for categorical variables

8. What is the primary purpose of Azure AutoML?

    A. To automate model selection, training, and evaluation for users without deep data science knowledge

    B. To manage Azure storage accounts and data lakes

    C. To provide GPU compute resources for deep learning

    D. To create REST API endpoints for deployed models

9. A manufacturing company is implementing a comprehensive deep learning solution for quality control using computer vision. Which Azure ML capabilities and considerations should they implement for optimal performance and management? (Choose all that apply.)

    A. GPU-based compute clusters for training neural networks on image data

    B. Model versioning and registration for tracking different model iterations

    C. Real-time endpoints with AKS for production deployment with auto-scaling

    D. Data drift detection to monitor changes in product images over time

10. A medical facility wants to digitize thousands of handwritten patient intake forms to make them searchable and reduce manual data entry. The forms contain various handwriting styles and may have coffee stains or wrinkles. Which computer vision approach would be most suitable?

    A. Optical Character Recognition (OCR) with robust preprocessing techniques

    B. Facial analysis to identify patients from photos on forms

    C. Object detection to locate form fields and checkboxes

    D. Image classification to categorize forms by department

11. Which of the following are core tasks within computer vision? (Choose all that apply.)

    A. Image classification for labeling entire images

    B. Natural language processing for text generation

    C. Object detection for locating multiple items in images

    D. Optical Character Recognition (OCR) for extracting text from images

12. Your company needs to extract text from handwritten notes and multi-column documents with high accuracy. Which Computer Vision feature provides the best results?

    A. Legacy OCR endpoint

    B. Tagging and categorization

    C. Read API

    D. Object detection

13. Which factors should be considered when implementing a production Face Service solution for employee authentication? (Choose all that apply.)

   A. Regular deletion of face data based on retention policies

   B. Using managed identity instead of API keys for authentication

   C. Implementing person groups with proper training workflows

   D. Monitoring model performance across demographic groups

14. A company wants to analyze customer feedback to determine if reviews are positive, negative, or neutral. They have limited labeled training data but need quick implementation. Which sentiment analysis approach should they choose?

   A. Train a custom neural network from scratch

   B. Use lexicon-based sentiment analysis with predefined word scores

   C. Implement a complex transformer model

   D. Build a statistical n-gram model

15. Which components are essential for building an effective chatbot system? (Choose all that apply.)

   A. Natural Language Understanding (NLU) for intent recognition

   B. Entity extraction to identify key information

   C. Dialogue management for context tracking

   D. Image classification capabilities

16. A company wants to analyze customer feedback emails to determine if they are positive, negative, or neutral. Which Azure AI Language Service feature should they use?

   A. Key phrase extraction

   B. Entity recognition

   C. Sentiment analysis

   D. PII detection

17. When implementing Azure Cognitive Search with AI enrichment pipelines, which components are essential for transforming unstructured documents into searchable content? (Choose all that apply.)

   A. Skillsets with prebuilt or custom AI models

   B. Indexers to connect data sources to the pipeline

   C. Search indexes to store enriched data

   D. Neural machine translation models

18. A financial services company is implementing a conversational AI assistant that must provide accurate, up-to-date information about regulatory changes. They're concerned about the model generating outdated or incorrect information. Which approach would best address this challenge?

   A. Increase the model's parameter count to improve memory

   B. Use higher temperature settings for more creative responses

   C. Implement Retrieval-Augmented Generation (RAG) with external knowledge sources

   D. Fine-tune the model on historical financial data only

19. Which are key components of transformer-based large language models that make them effective for text generation? (Choose all that apply.)

   A. Self-attention mechanisms

   B. Parallel processing of text sequences

   C. Sequential word-by-word processing

   D. Ability to capture long-range dependencies

20. A healthcare organization needs to implement content filtering for their Azure OpenAI deployment that permits medical descriptions while maintaining strict controls on other content types. What should they configure?

   A. Provisioned Throughput Units with custom scaling

   B. Custom content filtering thresholds through Azure portal

   C. GPT-4o multimodal processing limits

   D. Azure AI Search integration policies

21. Which Azure OpenAI models are specifically designed for multimodal capabilities? (Choose all that apply.)

   A. GPT-4o

   B. text-embedding-3

   C. GPT-4 Turbo with Vision

   D. GPT-3.5-Turbo

22. An enterprise needs to implement an AI agent that can analyze customer complaints, retrieve relevant company policies, generate appropriate responses, and escalate complex issues. Which combination of Azure AI agent capabilities would be most essential for this implementation?

   A. Function calling for escalation, agent memory for context, and basic reflex responses

   B. Natural language understanding, knowledge grounding with RAG, function calling, and utility-based decision-making

   C. Simple reflex responses, basic data storage, and manual oversight controls

   D. Image processing capabilities, speech recognition, and automated workflows

23. An organization is implementing AI agents that will handle sensitive customer data and make autonomous decisions. Which responsible AI measures should be implemented to ensure ethical and safe operation? (Choose all that apply.)

   A. Content filtering systems that scan prompts and responses for harmful material

   B. Role-based access controls limiting who can modify agent prompts and data sources

   C. Retrieval-augmented generation to ground responses in verifiable documents

   D. Continuous telemetry tracking content safety triggers and hallucination rates

24. A healthcare organization wants to analyze patient data to identify those at high risk for readmission after surgery. Which Azure service would be most appropriate for this predictive analytics use case?

   A. Azure Bot Service for patient communication

   B. Azure Machine Learning for risk prediction models

   C. Azure Digital Twins for hospital modeling

   D. Azure IoT Hub for medical device monitoring

25. A global financial institution wants to implement a comprehensive AI solution for fraud detection, customer service, and regulatory compliance. Which Azure capabilities should they integrate to address all these requirements? (Choose all that apply.)

   A. Azure Anomaly Detector for real-time fraud pattern detection

   B. Azure Bot Service with multilingual capabilities for customer support

   C. Azure Confidential Ledger for immutable decision audit trails

   D. Azure Custom Vision for document processing automation

Answers to Assessment Test

1. **B.** This comprehensive system requires multiple specialized AI technologies working together. Computer Vision is needed to analyze medical images and detect abnormalities (requirement 1). Natural Language Processing handles the processing of patient feedback in natural language (requirement 2). Predictive Analytics uses historical patient data to forecast readmission risk (requirement 3). Generative AI creates personalized treatment summaries by generating new content based on patient data and medical knowledge (requirement 4). Option A incorrectly suggests Expert Systems for prediction and Knowledge Mining for content generation. Option C uses overly broad categories and includes Reinforcement Learning, which isn't suitable for any of these specific requirements. Option D incorrectly applies Expert Systems and Knowledge Mining to tasks better suited for predictive analytics and content generation. For more information, please see Chapter 1, "Overview of AI Concepts and Workloads."

2. **C.** Microsoft Presidio is specifically designed to enhance data privacy by automating the detection and anonymization of sensitive information across structured and unstructured datasets. It uses pattern recognition (Regex), natural language entity recognition (NER), and context-aware anonymization to identify and mask PII like names, email addresses, medical records, and physical addresses. Presidio supports multiple anonymization techniques including masking, encryption, and tokenization while ensuring compliance with GDPR, HIPAA, and CCPA. InterpretML focuses on model explainability, Fairlearn addresses bias detection, and Azure AI Content Safety filters harmful content rather than anonymizing PII. For more information, please see Chapter 2, "Responsible AI in Azure."

3. **C.** Inclusiveness ensures AI systems serve diverse populations equitably, accounting for differences in language, culture, ability, and background. The described issues—higher error rates for non-Western accents, dialect recognition problems, and lack of accessibility for speech impairments—directly violate inclusiveness principles. Azure AI Language supports over 100 languages and dialects, helping address accent and dialect challenges. The comprehensive approach requires expanding training data to include diverse speech patterns, implementing accessibility features like alternative input methods for users with speech impairments, and ensuring cultural adaptability. While fairness (option A) addresses bias, the core issue is broader inclusiveness. Privacy (option B) and reliability (option D) don't address the fundamental accessibility and cultural representation problems. Inclusive design demands proactive accommodation of marginalized groups rather than treating diversity as an afterthought. For more information, please see Chapter 2, "Responsible AI in Azure."

4. **B.** Building a custom model from scratch is the most appropriate approach for this scenario due to several critical factors. First, the company has proprietary data formats that pretrained models cannot adequately handle, requiring specialized architecture design. Second, regulatory compliance in pharmaceuticals demands full transparency and interpretability in AI decision-making, which custom models provide through complete control over algorithms and parameters. Third, the company has the necessary resources

xxxviii   Answers to Assessment Test

(computational power, data scientists, and financial capacity) to invest in custom development. Finally, patient safety requires the highest possible accuracy, which can be achieved through domain-specific optimization that custom models allow. While pretrained models offer speed and cost benefits, they cannot meet the specialized requirements of pharmaceutical regulatory compliance, data format compatibility, and the level of transparency needed for drug interaction predictions where human lives are at stake. For more information, please see Chapter 3, "Core Concepts of AI Models and Solutions."

5. **A, B, C.** Effective model maintenance requires comprehensive monitoring and updating strategies. Monitoring response times and error rates (A) helps detect performance degradation before it affects patient care. Automated retraining pipelines (B) ensure the model stays current with new medical data and emerging disease patterns. Data drift detection (C) is crucial in healthcare where imaging technology, protocols, or patient populations may change over time. Option D is incorrect because maintaining static parameters would prevent the model from adapting to new patterns, medical advances, or changing conditions—the opposite of what's needed for long-term reliability. Healthcare AI systems must continuously evolve through regular updates, bias testing, and version control to maintain accuracy, safety, and fairness across different patient demographics. For more information, please see Chapter 3, "Core Concepts of AI Models and Solutions."

6. **B.** The large gap between training and test performance indicates overfitting, where the model memorizes training data rather than learning generalizable patterns. Regularization constrains model complexity, dropout prevents over-reliance on specific neurons, and cross-validation provides better validation estimates. Increasing complexity would worsen overfitting, while scaling and encoding address different data preparation issues. For more information, please see Chapter 4, "Introduction to Machine Learning Concepts."

7. **A, B, C.** Label encoding assigns integers to categories and works well for ordinal data with natural ordering. One-hot encoding creates binary columns for each category and is safer for non-ordinal data to avoid implying false relationships. Target encoding replaces categories with target variable means but requires regularization to prevent overfitting. Feature scaling applies to numerical data, not categorical variables. For more information, please see Chapter 4, "Introduction to Machine Learning Concepts."

8. **A.** Azure AutoML is designed to make machine learning more accessible by automating many of the complex steps required to build and train models. It helps users without extensive data science backgrounds by automatically handling algorithm selection, hyperparameter tuning, and model evaluation, allowing them to focus on defining the problem and providing data rather than technical implementation details. For more information, please see Chapter 5, "Machine Learning in Azure."

9. **A, B, C, D.** Deep learning computer vision solutions require GPU compute clusters for efficient training on image data due to the computational intensity of neural networks. Model versioning and registration are essential for tracking iterations and managing different versions of quality control models. Real-time endpoints with AKS provide the scalability and low-latency inference needed for production manufacturing environments. Data drift detection is crucial for monitoring changes in product variations, lighting conditions, or

camera setups that could affect model performance over time. For more information, please see Chapter 5, "Machine Learning in Azure."

10. A.   OCR is specifically designed to extract text from images and convert it into machine-readable data, making it ideal for digitizing handwritten forms. Modern OCR systems can handle various challenges like different handwriting styles, lighting conditions, and document distortions such as wrinkles or stains. The robust preprocessing techniques help improve accuracy by adjusting brightness, reducing noise, and enhancing text visibility before character recognition occurs. For more information, please see Chapter 6, "Introduction to Computer Vision."

11. A, C, D.   The core computer vision tasks include image classification (assigning labels to entire images based on content), object detection (locating and identifying multiple objects within images using bounding boxes), and OCR (converting text in images into machine-readable data). Natural language processing is a separate AI domain focused on understanding and generating human language, not visual data processing. For more information, please see Chapter 6, "Introduction to Computer Vision."

12. C.   The Read API uses modern neural networks and handles complex layouts, cursive handwriting, and multiple languages with far greater accuracy than the legacy OCR endpoint. It also supports asynchronous processing for better performance. Legacy OCR works best only on clear, high-contrast scans and struggles with complex layouts. For more information, please see Chapter 7, "Azure Tools for Computer Vision."

13. A, B, C, D.   All options are critical for production Face Service implementations. Regular data deletion ensures GDPR compliance and responsible AI practices. Managed identity provides secure authentication without exposing credentials. Person groups enable the one-to-many identification needed for employee authentication. Monitoring across demographics ensures fairness and addresses potential bias issues, which is essential for responsible AI deployment. For more information, please see Chapter 7, "Azure Tools for Computer Vision."

14. B.   Lexicon-based approaches use predefined dictionaries where words have sentiment scores and work well without requiring training data, making them ideal for quick prototypes or when labeled data is limited. While they have limitations with context and sarcasm, they provide a transparent method that can be implemented quickly for basic sentiment analysis tasks. For more information, please see Chapter 8, "Introduction to Natural Language Processing (NLP)."

15. A, B, C.   Effective chatbots require NLU to identify user intents (like "book a flight"), entity extraction to pull out key information (dates, locations, names), and dialogue management to maintain context across conversation turns so the bot can handle follow-up questions. Image classification is not a core component of text-based chatbot systems, though it might be useful in specialized multimodal applications. For more information, please see Chapter 8, "Introduction to Natural Language Processing (NLP)."

16. C.   Sentiment analysis is the Azure AI Language Service feature that evaluates whether text is positive, negative, or neutral, making it perfect for analyzing customer feedback emails. Key phrase extraction identifies important phrases, entity recognition finds named entities like people or places, and PII detection locates sensitive personal information, but none of these determine emotional tone or sentiment. For more information, please see Chapter 9, "Azure Tools for NLP Workloads."

17. A, B, C.   AI enrichment pipelines require skillsets (collections of AI models for text analytics, entity recognition, etc.), indexers to connect data sources like Blob Storage to the pipeline, and search indexes to store the enriched, searchable data. Neural machine translation models are specific to Azure Translator Service and not core components of Cognitive Search enrichment pipelines, which focus on making documents searchable rather than translating them. For more information, please see Chapter 9, "Azure Tools for NLP Workloads."

18. C.   Retrieval-Augmented Generation (RAG) combines generative models with external knowledge sources, allowing the system to retrieve current information from regulatory databases or documentation before generating responses. This approach helps ensure accuracy and currency of information rather than relying solely on potentially outdated training data. Increasing parameters or temperature doesn't address accuracy concerns, and fine-tuning only on historical data wouldn't provide current regulatory information. For more information, please see Chapter 10, "Introduction to Generative AI."

19. A, B, D.   Transformer-based LLMs use self-attention mechanisms that allow each word to "pay attention" to every other word in the sequence, parallel processing that analyzes all words simultaneously rather than sequentially, and the ability to capture long-range dependencies regardless of how far apart words appear in text. Sequential processing is characteristic of older RNN architectures, not transformers, which process entire sequences in parallel. For more information, please see Chapter 10, "Introduction to Generative AI."

20. B.   Azure OpenAI includes a content filtering system that scans prompts and responses for inappropriate content. Administrators can customize thresholds and allowed categories through the Azure portal or management APIs. A healthcare chatbot might permit medical descriptions of human anatomy that would normally be filtered as sexual content, while maintaining strict controls on other categories. For more information, please see Chapter 11, "Azure OpenAI Service."

21. A, C.   GPT-4o and GPT-4 Turbo with Vision are multimodal models that can process both text and images. GPT-4o can also handle short audio clips, making it truly multimodal. text-embedding-3 is specialized for converting text to vectors, and GPT-3.5-Turbo is text-only. These multimodal capabilities allow a single model to read photographs, interpret images, and generate context-aware responses. For more information, please see Chapter 11, "Azure OpenAI Service."

22. B.   This complex scenario requires multiple sophisticated capabilities: natural language understanding to interpret customer complaints, knowledge grounding with RAG to retrieve relevant company policies and ensure accurate responses, function calling to interact with external systems for escalation, and utility-based decision-making to evaluate different response options and choose the most appropriate course of action. This combination enables the agent to handle the complete workflow intelligently. For more information, please see Chapter 12, "AI Agents in Azure."

23. A, B, C, D.   Comprehensive responsible AI implementation requires multiple layers: content filtering to prevent harmful outputs, role-based access controls for governance, RAG to reduce hallucinations by grounding responses in factual data, and continuous monitoring through telemetry to track safety metrics and performance. These measures work together to create a robust framework for ethical and safe AI agent deployment. For more information, please see Chapter 12, "AI Agents in Azure."

24. B.   Azure Machine Learning helps hospitals analyze patient records to find patterns and identify patients at risk for conditions like readmissions, diabetes, or heart problems. These predictive systems examine lab results, vital signs, medication history, and lifestyle information to move from reactive care to proactive care, allowing care teams to provide extra support and prevent unnecessary hospital stays. For more information, please see Chapter 13, "AI Use Cases and Industry Applications."

25. A, B, C.   This comprehensive financial scenario requires Azure Anomaly Detector to identify unusual transaction patterns that may indicate fraud, Azure Bot Service with multilingual support (via Azure Translator) for global customer service, and Azure Confidential Ledger to maintain unchangeable records of AI-influenced decisions for regulatory compliance and audit purposes. While Azure Custom Vision could process documents, it's not specifically mentioned as a core requirement for fraud detection, customer service, or regulatory compliance in financial services. For more information, please see Chapter 13, "AI Use Cases and Industry Applications."

Chapter

1

Overview of AI Concepts and Workloads

MICROSOFT CERTIFIED: AZURE AI FUNDAMENTALS (AI-900) EXAM OBJECTIVES COVERED IN THIS CHAPTER:

✔ **Domain 1: Describe Artificial Intelligence workloads and considerations**

- Subdomain 1a: Identify features of common AI workloads

  - 1-1 Identify computer vision workloads

  - 1-2 Identify natural language processing workloads

  - 1-3 Identify document processing workloads

  - 1-4 Identify features of generative AI workloads

This chapter discusses the foundational concepts of artificial intelligence (AI) and the various types of AI workloads that are commonly used in modern technology and business. You'll learn about the core principles of AI, including how it differs from machine learning and deep learning, and explore the role of AI in solving real-world problems. The chapter also introduces the concept of client-server applications in AI, explaining how data flows between clients and servers and why scalability and performance are critical in AI systems.

Additionally, this chapter covers the importance of cloud computing in AI, particularly how Azure provides solutions for AI workloads. You'll learn about specific AI use cases, such as content moderation and personalization, and understand how these workloads are applied in industries like social media, e-commerce, and more. Finally, the chapter dives into knowledge mining and document intelligence, and explains how AI can extract information from unstructured data and the Azure services that support these processes.

By the end of this chapter, you'll have a solid understanding of the key AI concepts and workloads that are essential for the AI-900 exam, as well as how these technologies are implemented in Azure.

Introduction to Artificial Intelligence

The world is changing, and there are many opportunities for innovation and progress driven by emerging technologies. As we move through a time of rapid change, AI has become a key player and is currently transforming industries, improving how we interact with machines, and giving us new solutions to complex problems in everyday life.

At its core, artificial intelligence refers to the capacity of computers or other machines to exhibit or simulate intelligent behavior by performing tasks that, when executed by humans, require cognitive functions such as learning, reasoning, problem-solving, perception, and understanding natural language.

As shown in Figure 1.1, AI is a broad concept that includes different types of intelligence, each becoming more specialized. We start with the general idea of AI, which aims to simulate human-like intelligence and enables machines to understand and process data.

The first specialized form of AI is Machine Learning (ML). ML allows machines to learn from data without being explicitly programmed, and this allows machines to make predictions and decisions based on patterns they find in the data. Within ML, there are

FIGURE 1.1   Core concepts of artificial intelligence.

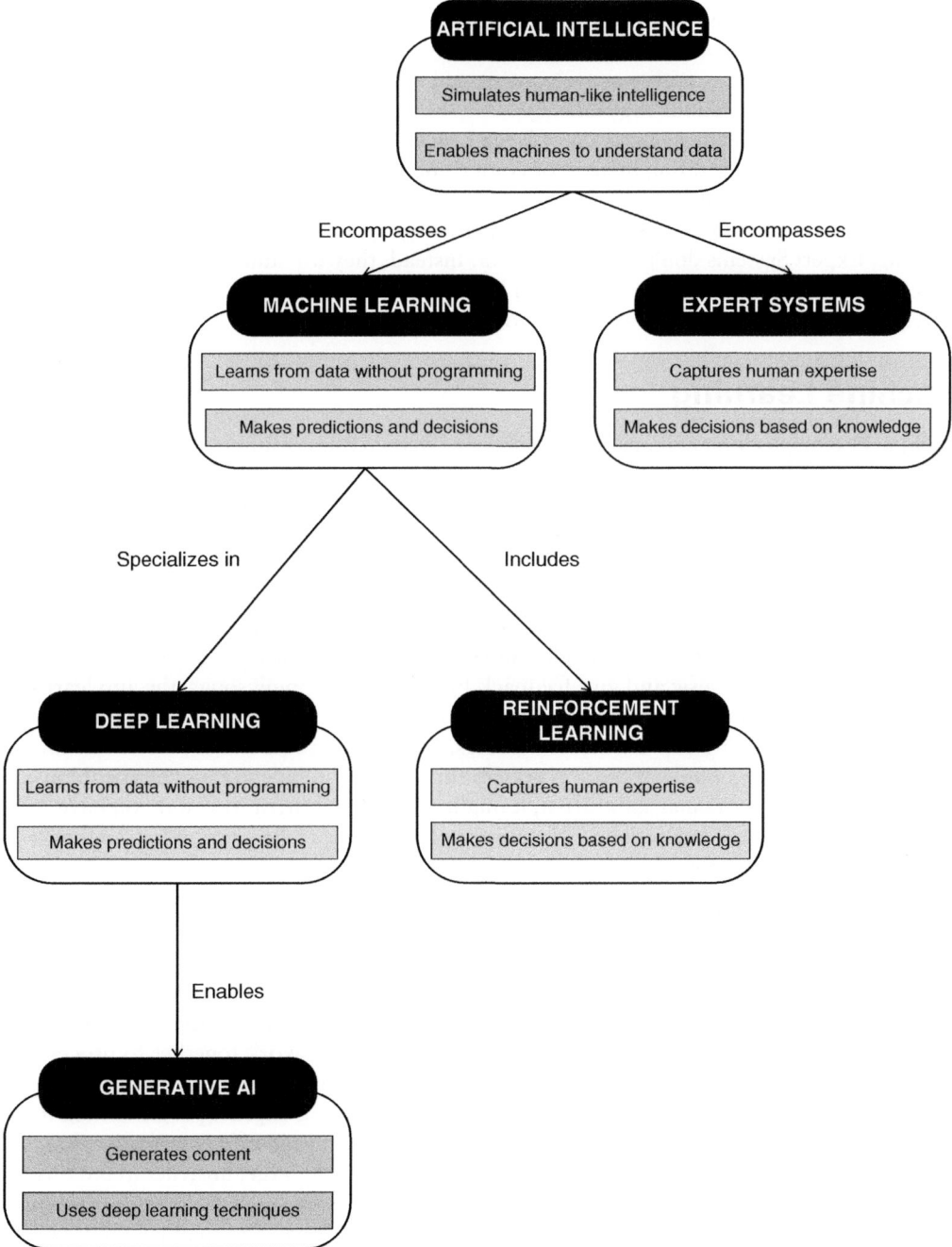

further specializations. Deep Learning is one such area, which uses complex neural networks to process large amounts of data and make more accurate predictions and decisions. It plays a major role in areas like speech recognition, image analysis, and self-driving cars. Another area within ML is Reinforcement Learning, where machines learn to make decisions through trial and error, interacting with an environment and receiving feedback via rewards or penalties based on the actions they take.

Generative AI is a further extension of Deep Learning. It focuses on creating new content, such as writing text, generating images, or composing music, by learning from data and using deep learning techniques.

On the other side, Expert Systems are another category under AI. Unlike Machine Learning, Expert Systems don't learn from data. Instead, they use human expertise and predefined rules to make decisions based on knowledge.

Let's look at the core concepts in a bit more detail.

Machine Learning

Machine Learning is a type of artificial intelligence that enables computers to learn from data and improve their performance over time, without being explicitly programmed. Instead of following a set of instructions, a machine learning model analyzes large amounts of data, identifies patterns, and makes predictions or decisions based on those patterns. As it processes more data, the model "learns" and becomes more accurate, much like how humans improve their skills with practice.

To explain this in a simple way, imagine you have a music streaming app that suggests new songs for you. At first, the app might not suggest the best songs, but as you and millions of other users listen to music and give feedback by liking or skipping songs, the app learns what different types of people enjoy. Over time, it gets better at suggesting songs you might like based on patterns it discovers across all users, not just your individual preferences and listening history. For example, if the app notices that users who like jazz and classical music also tend to enjoy a particular indie artist, it might suggest that artist to you if you have similar tastes. The more data it collects from its entire user base, the better it becomes at making accurate suggestions for everyone.

Deep Learning

Deep Learning is a specialized area of ML that uses neural networks with many layers to process large amounts of data and make highly accurate predictions or decisions. The idea is inspired by the structure of the human brain, where neurons work together to process information. Deep learning models are capable of automatically identifying patterns in complex data such as images, audio, and text without requiring explicit programming for every task. This ability to learn from vast amounts of data and identify patterns is what makes deep learning powerful in solving problems that involve large, unstructured datasets.

To put this in a real-life concept for you to grasp better, let's assume that you're teaching a computer to recognize different types of animals in photos. Instead of manually telling

FIGURE 1.2   Neural networks.

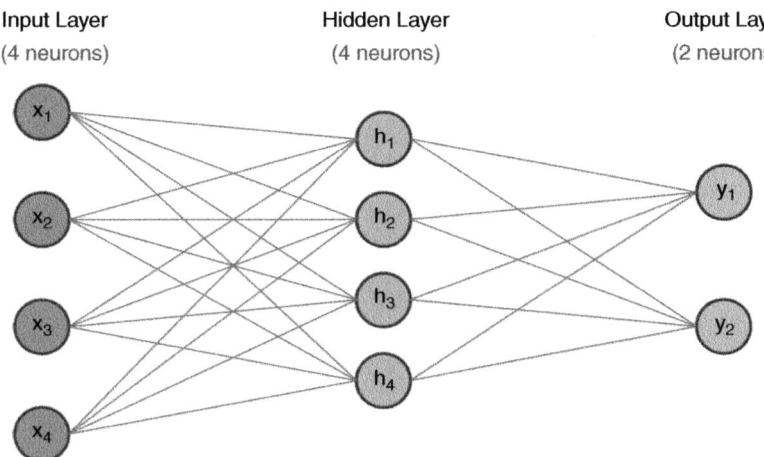

the computer what each animal looks like, deep learning allows the computer to look at thousands of pictures of animals and "learn" by itself. It starts by looking for basic features like shapes and colors, then combines these features to understand more complex patterns like fur patterns or the shape of an animal's ears. Over time, the system gets better at recognizing animals in new photos, even those it has never seen before. This process, where the computer builds up its understanding step by step, is deep learning in action.

For context, a neural network is like a system of many interconnected nodes, or "neurons," that work together to process information (see Figure 1.2). These neurons are arranged in layers: the first layer receives the input data, the middle layers process that data, and the final layer produces the output. Each neuron in the network is responsible for looking at a small part of the information, such as identifying a specific feature in an image or a word in a sentence. As the data moves through the layers, the neurons adjust their responses based on the patterns they learn from the data. Think of it like a group of people working together to solve a problem. Each person in the group looks at the problem from a different angle and shares their findings with the others. The more they collaborate and learn from each other, the better they get at solving the problem. In a neural network, the more data it processes, the better it gets at recognizing patterns, making decisions, and producing accurate results.

Natural Language Processing

Natural Language Processing (NLP) is a field of artificial intelligence that focuses on the interaction between computers and human language. NLP enables machines to understand, interpret, and generate human language in a way that is both meaningful and useful. This involves breaking down text or speech into smaller, understandable parts, such as words and phrases, and then analyzing their structure, meaning, and context. NLP powers many of the systems we use every day, from translation tools to chatbots, by allowing computers to handle complex language tasks like answering questions, summarizing text, or recognizing sentiment. Think of how AI systems like ChatGPT or Microsoft's Copilot process the prompts and questions you type to them. When you ask a question, like "What's the weather like today?," the system uses natural language processing to break down your words, understand what you're asking, and find the right answer. It has to figure out that you're asking about the weather and that "today" means the current day. Then, it looks up the weather and responds with the correct information.

Computer Vision

Computer Vision is a field of artificial intelligence that enables computers to interpret and understand visual information from the world, such as images or videos. Through computer vision, machines can analyze and extract meaningful data from pictures, identifying objects, faces, and even activities. This technology involves complex algorithms that allow a computer to "see" and process visual data much like how humans use their eyes to observe and interpret the environment. Applications of computer vision include facial recognition, object detection, medical imaging, and autonomous driving, where systems must make decisions based on what they "see."

To explain this with a simple example, think about how a photo-sharing app can automatically tag your friends in pictures. When you upload a photo, the app uses computer vision to "look" at the faces in the picture, compare them to the ones it has learned about before, and then suggest names for each person. The app doesn't need you to manually label each face every time because it can recognize who's in the picture based on its understanding of the visual features. This ability to "see" and understand images is the essence of computer vision in action.

Robotics and Autonomous Systems

Robotics and Autonomous Systems combine artificial intelligence with physical machines to create systems that can perform tasks on their own, without needing direct human control. These systems use sensors, actuators, and AI algorithms to perceive their environment, make decisions, and take actions based on what they learn. Robotics focuses on the creation and design of machines that can carry out physical tasks, while autonomous systems go a step further by enabling these machines to make decisions independently and adapt to changing conditions. Applications range from factory robots and drones to self-driving cars, where these systems can operate in complex, real-world environments with minimal human intervention.

This field has seen remarkable advances in recent years. Companies like Boston Dynamics have developed robots that can run, jump, and navigate complex terrain with agility that rivals human movement. Meanwhile, humanoid robots like Tesla's Optimus are being designed to perform everyday tasks in homes and workplaces, potentially revolutionizing how we think about automation in our daily lives. These breakthroughs demonstrate how rapidly robotics technology is evolving from laboratory experiments to practical applications.

One example of this is a self-driving car. The car uses sensors like cameras, radar, and LIDAR to see the road, detect obstacles, and understand traffic conditions. The system then makes decisions, such as when to turn, stop, or accelerate, based on the information it gathers. The car can navigate through the streets all on its own, without needing you to steer or press the gas pedal.

Expert Systems and Knowledge Representation

Expert Systems and Knowledge Representation involve designing computer programs that mimic the decision-making abilities of human experts by using structured collections of rules and information. These systems store specialized knowledge through if-then rules, semantic networks, or other formal representations, so that a computer can apply it to new problems. This method of encoding information, known as knowledge representation, allows the system to analyze complex data and provide expert-level advice or solutions. These expert systems basically take what experts know and package it in a way that computers can use to solve problems in areas like medical diagnosis, financial planning, or customer service. For example, consider a troubleshooting tool for your home internet connection. Instead of a technician being available all the time, the system uses a set of rules gathered from expert technicians. When you describe your problem, say, "I can't connect to the internet," the tool asks you a series of questions and then suggests possible fixes based on its stored knowledge. It might tell you to check your cables, restart your modem, or adjust your settings. It used an expert systems implementation to do this.

Reinforcement Learning

Reinforcement Learning is a type of machine learning where a system (called an agent) learns to make decisions by interacting with its environment. Instead of being told exactly what to do, the agent tries different actions and gets feedback. This feedback can be a reward for making a good choice or a penalty for a bad one. Over time, the agent learns which actions lead to better outcomes and improves its behavior based on experience. An example is teaching a robot to move through a maze. The robot starts with no knowledge of the maze and takes random steps. If it moves closer to the exit, it gets a reward. If it hits a wall or moves further from the exit, it gets a penalty. The robot keeps trying different paths, learning from the feedback, and over time, it figures out the best way to navigate the maze and maximizes its rewards by finding the shortest path.

The Role of AI in Modern Technology and Business

In business, AI is changing the way companies interact with customers. Chatbots, for example, are powered by AI to provide instant customer service, answering questions and resolving issues 24/7. AI also helps in personalizing customer experiences, such as recommending products based on past purchases or browsing history. These systems analyze vast amounts of customer data to identify preferences and behaviors, and this leads to a tailored experience for customers that increases satisfaction and sales. AI also helps businesses anticipate customer needs, simplify operations, and stay ahead of competitors by making smarter decisions based on data.

A real-life example of AI in action is the recommendation system used by streaming services like Netflix or YouTube. These platforms use AI to suggest movies and shows based on your watching habits, learning over time what types of content you enjoy. The more you watch, the more the system understands your preferences, improving the suggestions it gives. Other AI-driven tools like Google Maps also help people navigate by analyzing real-time traffic data to suggest the fastest route. These examples show how AI is used in our everyday life and how it enhances convenience and efficiency through smart technology that adapts to our behavior.

Types of AI Workloads in Azure

An AI workload is a way to describe a system that uses artificial intelligence to perform tasks like predicting future events, classifying data, or even creating new content. In the context of the Well-Architected Framework (Microsoft's set of best practices for building secure, reliable, efficient, and cost-effective cloud systems), these workloads are designed to handle predictive, discriminative, or generative tasks. The Azure Well-Architected Framework gives us five core pillars (Reliability, Security, Cost Optimization, Operational Excellence, and Performance Efficiency) that guide how AI systems should be designed and implemented in the cloud. This means that instead of relying on fixed rules, AI workloads mix code and data into models that can adapt and learn over time, even when fixed outcomes are impractical, all while adhering to these architectural principles.

One common AI workload is predictive analytics, which falls under discriminative AI. Discriminative AI uses models to find patterns in past data and make predictions about what might happen next. For example, a business might analyze previous sales to forecast future demand. These models classify and predict based on the training they receive from historical data, helping companies to turn large sets of data into useful information for business decision-making.

Another key workload is recommendation systems, which also belong to the realm of discriminative AI. These systems learn from users' past behaviors to suggest products or content that might interest them. Whether it's an online store suggesting items you might like based on your browsing history or a streaming service offering movies similar to the ones you watched, recommendation systems make everyday experiences more personal and efficient. They work by analyzing patterns in user behavior and matching them with similar trends observed in the data.

In contrast, generative AI is focused on creating new content rather than just classifying or predicting based on existing data. Generative models can produce articles, stories, artwork, and even synthetic data to balance out datasets. While discriminative models help in making decisions or predictions from given inputs, generative models add the ability to innovate and create, offering entirely new experiences that traditional systems cannot provide. Both approaches expand the capabilities of AI workloads across different industries, making tasks more adaptable and responsive to complex real-world needs.

On Azure, implementing these AI workloads is supported by an integrated set of tools and services that simplify data management, model building, and deployment. Services like Azure Machine Learning and Azure Synapse Analytics enable the creation of predictive models and recommendation systems, while tools like the Azure OpenAI Service support generative tasks. Azure's environment helps organizations connect various data sources, manage large volumes of data, and continuously update models to handle challenges like compute costs, security, and evolving requirements.

Client-Server Applications in AI

Client-server architecture is a way of organizing how computers work together in AI systems. In this model, the client is the part that interacts with the user, such as a web browser or mobile app, while the server is a more powerful computer that handles heavy processing. The client sends requests to the server, which then runs the complex AI tasks like analyzing data or making predictions. Once the server completes these tasks, it sends the results back to the client, which displays the information to the user. This separation allows the heavy computational work, such as data analysis and model training, to be done on the server, while the client remains simple and responsive for the user.

This architecture is important for devices such as mobile phones, tablets, smart watches, or IoT devices, which have minimal computing resources and instead rely upon cloud-based AI infrastructure. Rather than requiring each user to have a high-performance computer capable of running complex AI models, users can access advanced AI capabilities through lightweight clients that connect to powerful servers in the cloud. This model enables AI features like voice recognition on a smart watch, real-time language translation on a smartphone, or predictive maintenance alerts from industrial IoT sensors, all without the individual devices needing the processing power to run these sophisticated algorithms locally. It also makes updating and maintaining the AI system easier, since improvements or changes can be made on the server side and automatically benefit all users.

When a user interacts with an AI system, like asking a question or uploading an image, the client (such as a mobile app or website) sends this data to the server over the internet. The server, which hosts the AI models, processes the data by running it through algorithms to generate a response or perform a task. Once the processing is complete, the server sends the result back to the client, which then displays it to the user. This back-and-forth flow of data illustrated in Figure 1.3 happens quickly, often in seconds, allowing users to interact with AI systems in real time without needing to know about the complex computations happening behind the scenes.

Imagine using a tool modeled like this or any one of your favorite generative AI tools at peak time and getting an "Unavailable" message as opposed to the answer you were

FIGURE 1.3 Client-server applications in AI.

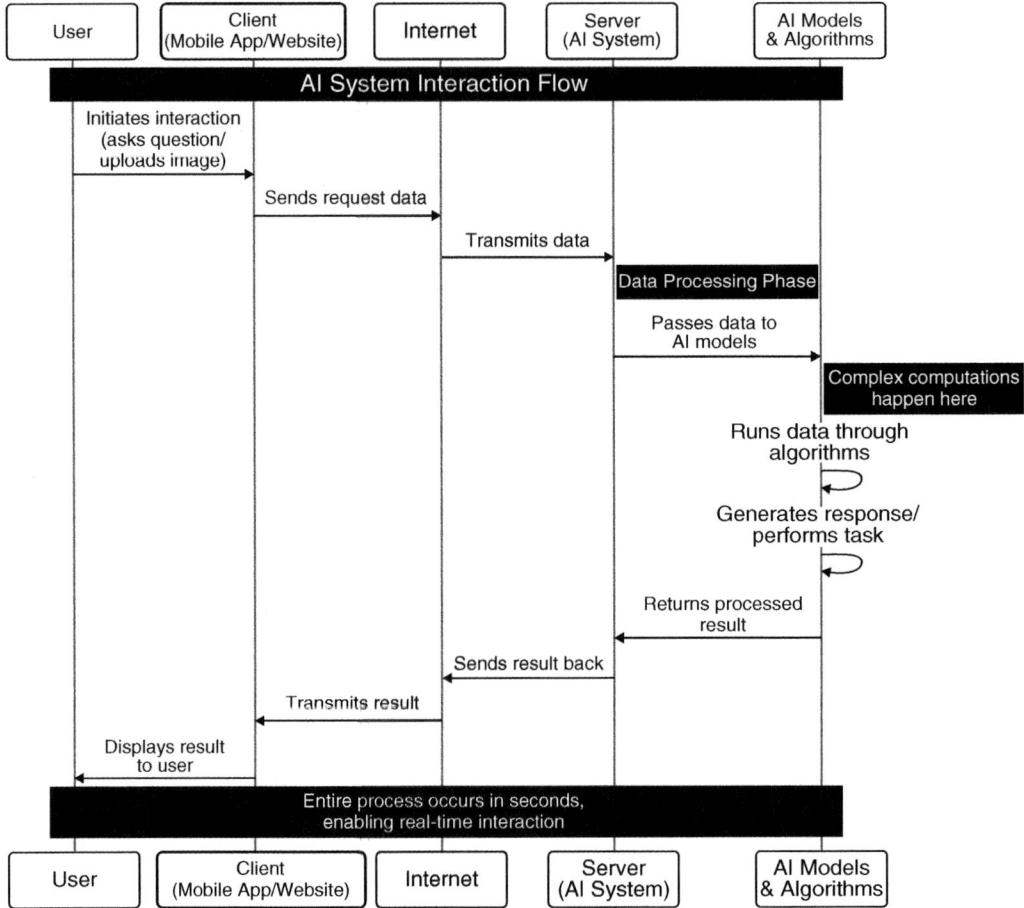

looking for. This frustrating scenario highlights the importance of scalability in client-server AI systems. Scalability ensures that as more users connect and request services, the server can handle the extra load without slowing down or failing. When a system is designed to be scalable, it means it can grow and adapt to meet higher demand, making sure that the experience remains smooth even when many people are using the service at once.

Performance is just as crucial in these systems, as it affects how quickly and accurately the AI responds to your requests. A high-performance client-server AI system processes complex tasks fast and delivers results in a timely manner, which is key for user satisfaction. If the system is slow or unresponsive, users may lose trust in the service, especially during busy times when quick responses are needed.

Cloud Concepts for AI

Cloud computing has become very important in modern technology, and its relevance to artificial intelligence cannot be overstated. It is the delivery of computing services (such as storage, processing power, and networking) over the internet, often referred to as "the cloud." For AI, this means access to vast computational resources without the need for expensive on-premises infrastructure. AI workloads, which often require significant processing power and data storage, can be efficiently managed in the cloud. This allows organizations, from startups to large enterprises, to experiment, develop, and deploy AI solutions at scale without the upfront costs of building and maintaining their own hardware. In essence, the cloud acts as an enabler, and it makes AI more accessible and practical for a wide range of applications.

One of the most compelling benefits of using cloud services for AI workloads is scalability. AI projects often start small but can quickly grow in complexity, and as they evolve, they will require more resources. Cloud platforms have plans that allow businesses to scale their computing power up or down based on demand, and this ensures that they only pay for what they use. This flexibility is very valuable for AI, where training models can require enormous amounts of data and processing time. Additionally, cloud services often come with built-in tools and frameworks specifically designed for AI development, such as pretrained machine learning models, data labeling services, and automated machine learning (AutoML) capabilities. These tools accelerate development and also lower the barrier to entry for those who may not have deep expertise in AI.

Another advantage of using the cloud for AI is the ability to collaborate and innovate more effectively. Cloud platforms enable teams to work on AI projects from anywhere in the world, and they will be able to access shared resources and datasets in real time. This creates more opportunities for collaboration among data scientists, engineers, and business stakeholders, leading to faster iteration and better outcomes. This also makes it possible for researchers across different locations to collaborate too.

When it comes to cloud providers, Microsoft Azure stands out as a powerful platform for AI solutions. Azure has a comprehensive suite of AI services, from cognitive APIs for vision, speech, and language processing to advanced machine learning tools like Azure Machine Learning. Azure also has powerful infrastructure for training and deploying AI models, including GPU-enabled virtual machines and Kubernetes-based orchestration. Using Azure for AI also means that you have seamless integration with other products in the Microsoft ecosystem, such as Power BI and Dynamics 365, and through this, you can embed AI into existing business workflows to grow your business or improve customer experience.

Cloud-based systems such as Azure are popular for running AI, but other types of systems exist to meet different needs. Edge AI processes data right on devices like smartphones or sensors so that responses come in real time without needing the cloud. Distributed systems spread tasks over many servers to handle more work, while on-premises setups keep AI systems within a company to control sensitive data more closely.

Hybrid models combine cloud and edge computing to improve speed and lower costs. Federated learning trains AI across many devices without sharing raw data. This is useful for industries that must protect privacy, such as healthcare. Each architecture has its benefits, and platforms like Azure integrate with these approaches (e.g., Azure IoT Edge for edge computing).

AI Workloads in Content Moderation and Personalization

Content moderation has become one of the most critical and challenging tasks for social media platforms and online communities. With billions of users generating posts, images, and videos every day, the volume of content continues to increase, and AI serves as a way to automate the process for large volumes of content. Machine learning models, trained on vast datasets of labeled content, can automatically detect harmful material such as hate speech, graphic violence, or misinformation. For example, AI systems analyze text for toxic language using natural language processing (NLP), scan images for explicit content via computer vision, and flag deepfakes by identifying inconsistencies in audiovisual patterns. Social media platforms like Facebook and Instagram rely on these tools to maintain safer digital spaces. However, AI isn't perfect. Context matters. Sarcasm, cultural nuances, or emerging slangs can stump even advanced algorithms. To address this, many platforms use a hybrid approach: AI handles the initial filtering, and humans review edge cases. Azure supports these efforts with services like Azure Content Moderator, part of its Cognitive Services suite, which has prebuilt models for text, image, and video moderation.

Now, let's also take a look at AI personalization. Some examples are Netflix suggesting your next binge-worthy show and Spotify crafting a playlist that fits your current mood. Personalization relies on algorithms that analyze user behavior (clicks, searches, purchase history, and even dwell time on a webpage) to predict preferences. E-commerce companies use collaborative filtering, a technique that matches your habits with similar users, to recommend products you're likely to buy. Streaming services use deep learning to dissect patterns in your viewing history and adjust recommendations in real time. But personalization goes beyond entertainment. News apps curate articles based on your interests, fitness and nutrition apps adapt workouts and meals to your progress and diet, and even healthcare platforms tailor wellness plans using AI. Azure has Azure AI Personalizer, a cloud service that uses reinforcement learning to dynamically optimize user experiences.

While AI does innovative things, it also raises complex ethical dilemmas. In content moderation, biases embedded in training data can lead to over-censorship or under-detection. For example, an algorithm trained predominantly on English-language content might struggle with dialects or non-Western cultural contexts, unfairly flagging harmless posts. Personalization algorithms can also create "filter bubbles," which isolates users in echo chambers that reinforce their existing beliefs, a phenomenon linked to societal polarization. Privacy is another concern: To personalize experiences, AI systems often collect granular data, and there's the risk of misuse or data breaches. Microsoft, however, addresses some of these issues through frameworks like Responsible AI, which emphasizes fairness, accountability, and transparency. Tools such as Microsoft Fairlearn help developers detect and mitigate bias in models. Yet technology alone isn't the solution. Ethical AI requires ongoing human involvement, diverse training data, and clear policies to balance automation with empathy. For instance, should an AI censor a post critiquing a political leader, or does that infringe on free speech? There are no easy answers, but the conversation must involve technologists, ethicists, and communities to ensure AI serves humanity, not the other way around.

Knowledge Mining and Document Intelligence Workloads

Knowledge mining is the practice of transforming unstructured data, like emails, social media posts, PDFs, images, and videos, into organized and searchable information. Here are some examples of how organizations can use knowledge mining:

- **Manufacturing:** A manufacturing company might use knowledge mining to analyze decades of maintenance logs and sensor data to predict equipment failures. This process helps identify patterns that indicate when machines might need repairs, and this could allow the company to perform maintenance before a breakdown occurs.

- **Education:** A university could mine research papers and student feedback to identify gaps in curriculum design. As a result, the institution might be able to see patterns that can help them improve course offerings and enhance educational programs.

- **Retail:** A retail business can mine customer reviews and online chats to better understand what shoppers like and dislike. This helps the company refine its product selection and customer service by highlighting popular trends and areas needing improvement.

- **Finance:** A financial company might sort through market reports and news articles to assess risks and opportunities in investments. This can help the firm to make more informed decisions by discovering patterns that indicate shifts in market conditions.

- **Media:** This is also useful to content creators or media companies because they could analyze viewer comments and social media reactions (likes and dislikes) to guide the creation of content that truly connects with their audience so that they can tailor their content and schedule to better meet viewer interests and preferences.

The key lies in combining different intelligent services like NLP to understand text, computer vision to interpret images, and machine learning to spot trends. Azure has services designed to simplify knowledge mining and document intelligence, and they are listed below:

- Azure AI Search uses built-in AI to index content, extract entities (such as names, dates, or locations), detect languages, and generate summaries. This transforms cluttered data repositories into searchable knowledge bases and allows users to query complex information efficiently.

- Azure AI Services expands these capabilities with prebuilt models tailored for document processing. It automates tasks like extracting text, tables, and key fields from invoices, contracts, or handwritten notes. This reduces manual effort in industries like finance, where accurate data extraction from forms is critical.

- With Azure Machine Learning, organizations can train custom models. These models address unique or industry-specific scenarios, such as identifying compliance risks in regulatory documents or detecting anomalies in manufacturing reports.

- Azure AI Bot Service connects data with end users by creating conversational interfaces. Bots powered by Azure AI Search and document intelligence allow employees to query data using natural language. For instance, a customer support team could ask a bot to retrieve warranty details from a scanned contract, simplifying access to critical information without technical expertise.

Summary

This chapter covered an introduction to artificial intelligence and explained its main ideas and tasks. It showed what AI is and how it is different from machine learning and deep learning. It talked about how machine learning helps computers learn from data and how deep learning uses networks of connected units to solve harder tasks such as recognizing images and voices. The chapter also looked at natural language processing for understanding human speech, computer vision for making sense of images, robotics for performing physical tasks, expert systems that use set rules and human knowledge, and reinforcement learning where systems learn by trying and receiving rewards.

This chapter also explored how cloud services like Azure support these AI tasks. It described common tasks such as predictive analytics that use past data to make guesses about the future and recommendation systems that suggest items based on user behavior. The chapter explained how client-server design separates the heavy work of data processing from the user interface. It also discussed how cloud computing helps manage large amounts of data and makes it easier to grow the system when needed.

Exam Essentials

Understand the core ideas of AI.   Learn what artificial intelligence is and how it differs from machine learning, deep learning, and reinforcement learning.

Recognize common AI workloads.   Know how predictive analytics, recommendation systems, and generative AI work to solve real-world problems.

Learn about key AI services.   Understand how natural language processing, computer vision, robotics, and expert systems help computers mimic human tasks.

Understand the role of client-server and cloud concepts in AI.   Know how systems like Azure support AI by managing data, scaling performance, and hosting models.

Understand knowledge mining and document intelligence.   Learn how unstructured data is turned into organized, searchable information using Azure tools.

Review Questions

1. Imagine you are tasked with designing an AI system for a retail company. The system should predict future sales based on past purchase data and seasonal trends. Which AI workload would best handle this task?

    A. Generative AI

    B. Predictive Analytics

    C. Natural Language Processing

    D. Expert Systems

2. A university is looking to improve its curriculum by analyzing decades of research papers and student feedback. Which type of AI workload would be most appropriate for turning these unstructured data sources into organized, searchable information?

    A. Knowledge Mining

    B. Reinforcement Learning

    C. Deep Learning

    D. Recommendation Systems

3. Consider an online streaming service that wants to offer personalized movie suggestions to its users. The service must learn from each user's viewing history and adjust its recommendations over time. Which Azure service is best suited for this kind of workload?

    A. Azure Machine Learning

    B. Azure Cognitive Services—Text Analytics

    C. Azure OpenAI Service

    D. Azure AI Personalizer

4. A self-driving car must decide in real time how to navigate through busy streets using sensor data from cameras, radar, and LIDAR. Which AI approach would allow the car to learn from its environment through trial and error?

    A. Deep Learning

    B. Expert Systems

    C. Reinforcement Learning

    D. Knowledge Mining

5. Imagine you are designing an AI tool to automatically generate creative marketing content. The system should be able to write text that mimics human language styles. Which AI workload is best suited for this purpose?

    A. Generative AI

    B. Predictive Analytics

C. Natural Language Processing

D. Expert Systems

6. A financial firm wants to use AI to analyze market reports and news articles to identify shifts in market conditions. What is the primary purpose of this AI workload?

A. To generate new market forecasts from scratch

B. To extract and organize useful information for decision-making

C. To create personalized financial advice based on customer data

D. To directly control trading algorithms without human oversight

7. An agricultural advisory platform offers farmers recommendations on crop management by using historical weather data and expert guidelines. The system relies on a set of rules created by agricultural experts. What type of AI workload is this?

A. Expert Systems

B. Predictive Analytics

C. Generative AI

D. Natural Language Processing

8. A media company is looking to improve its content strategy by analyzing viewer comments and social media reactions. Which AI workload will best help them understand audience behavior and tailor their content accordingly?

A. Knowledge Mining

B. Computer Vision

C. Recommendation Systems

D. Expert Systems

9. An enterprise is considering using a hybrid cloud approach for its AI workloads. This approach combines cloud services with on-premises infrastructure. What is the main benefit of using a hybrid model in this context?

A. It reduces the need for any security measures

B. It allows the organization to keep sensitive data in-house while still leveraging cloud scalability

C. It is the cheapest option available

D. It eliminates the need for continuous system updates

10. In the context of client-server architecture in AI systems, why is it beneficial to separate the heavy computational work from the user interface?

A. It allows every user to have their own high-performance server

B. It makes it easier to update the system and manage complex tasks on a centralized server

C. It reduces the overall cost of cloud storage

D. It eliminates the need for any human oversight

11. An AI developer is building a system that automatically tags images with labels like "cat," "dog," or "car" by analyzing the image content. What is most appropriate for this image-based task?

   A. Computer Vision

   B. Expert Systems

   C. Reinforcement Learning

   D. Predictive Analytics

12. Imagine you are tasked with designing an AI system for a smart home. The system needs to understand voice commands, predict energy usage, and even suggest ways to reduce power consumption. Which core AI concept should you start by understanding to design this system effectively?

   A. Artificial Intelligence as a whole

   B. Only Deep Learning

   C. Only Reinforcement Learning

   D. Only Natural Language Processing

13. You are working on an AI-powered customer support chatbot that needs to understand and respond to customer queries in plain language. Which technology best enables the system to interpret customer messages and generate meaningful replies?

   A. Deep Learning

   B. Natural Language Processing

   C. Reinforcement Learning

   D. Knowledge Mining

14. A manufacturing company needs an AI system that can predict equipment failures by analyzing decades of maintenance logs and sensor data. Which AI workload would be most effective in achieving this goal, and why?

   A. Expert Systems, because they use fixed rules for decision-making

   B. Generative AI, because it creates new data

   C. Predictive Analytics, because it forecasts future events based on past data

   D. Computer Vision, because it can analyze images of equipment

15. An organization needs to build, train, and deploy custom AI models to handle industry-specific tasks. They decided to use Azure services for this purpose. Which Azure service is specifically designed to support these activities?

   A. Azure Cognitive Services

   B. Azure Machine Learning

   C. Azure OpenAI Service

   D. Azure Bot Service

16. A tech startup wants to improve its AI system's performance by ensuring that it can handle an increasing number of users without slowing down. They plan to use cloud services to achieve this. What is the primary benefit of cloud computing in the context of AI workloads?

A. It allows the system to work offline

B. It makes it possible to quickly scale resources based on demand

C. It eliminates the need for data security

D. It removes the need for any system updates

17. A large organization wants to extract useful information from unstructured documents such as emails, PDFs, and images stored in various repositories. Which AI workload and associated Azure service would best help in organizing and making this data searchable?

A. Reinforcement Learning and Azure Bot Service

B. Knowledge Mining and Azure AI Search

C. Generative AI and Azure OpenAI Service

D. Predictive Analytics and Azure Synapse Analytics

18. A multinational company wants to build an AI solution that uses both cloud computing and edge devices to process data efficiently while keeping sensitive information secure. Which architectural approach would best address these needs, and how does it benefit the company?

A. Pure cloud computing, as it offers unlimited resources

B. Pure on-premises computing, to maintain full control of data

C. A hybrid model that combines cloud and edge computing

D. Federated learning without any cloud integration

19. An IT helpdesk troubleshooting tool asks users a series of questions about their computer issues and then provides suggestions based on a set of established rules. Which approach does this tool use?

A. Reinforcement Learning

B. Expert Systems

C. Natural Language Processing

D. Knowledge Mining

20. Imagine you are developing an AI system for a smart city. The system must analyze real-time sensor data to adjust traffic light timings and improve traffic flow. Which learning method is most appropriate for this dynamic task?

A. Deep Learning

B. Reinforcement Learning

C. Expert Systems

D. Generative AI

Chapter

2

Responsible AI in Azure

MICROSOFT CERTIFIED: AZURE AI FUNDAMENTALS (AI-900) EXAM OBJECTIVES COVERED IN THIS CHAPTER:

✔ **Domain 1: Describe Artificial Intelligence workloads and considerations**

  ▪ Subdomain 1b: Identify guiding principles for responsible AI

    ▪ 1-5 Describe considerations for fairness in an AI solution

    ▪ 1-6 Describe considerations for reliability and safety in an AI solution

    ▪ 1-7 Describe considerations for privacy and security in an AI solution

    ▪ 1-8 Describe considerations for inclusiveness in an AI solution

    ▪ 1-9 Describe considerations for transparency in an AI solution

    ▪ 1-10 Describe considerations for accountability in an AI solution

As we build AI systems that shape industries, influence decisions, and interact with people across the globe, ethical considerations must stand at the heart of their design. Responsible AI ensures these technologies are developed and deployed in ways that are fair, transparent, and safe, aligning not only with legal standards but also with societal values. This chapter introduces Microsoft's six core principles of Responsible AI (fairness, reliability, privacy, inclusiveness, transparency, and accountability) and explains how they address critical challenges such as bias, discrimination, and unintended harm. When AI is grounded in these principles, we create systems that earn trust and drive positive outcomes for everyone.

The chapter also takes a closer look at how Azure's tools and services turn these principles into practice. You'll learn how Fairlearn helps identify and reduce bias in AI models, how Confidential Computing safeguards sensitive data, and how Azure Machine Learning provides transparency into decision-making processes. These tools empower developers to build solutions that are not only innovative but also ethical and inclusive. Balancing technical expertise with a commitment to responsibility, this chapter equips you to navigate the complexities of real-world AI deployments while prioritizing integrity and human impact.

Importance of Responsible AI Principles

Responsible AI is about building systems that not only solve problems but do so in ways that respect human dignity, fairness, and societal values. It's a commitment to creating AI that doesn't just work, it works *for* people, safeguarding their rights and promoting trust. This approach involves a commitment to several core principles that guide the entire process, from the initial idea and data collection to the final deployment and ongoing maintenance of the technology. The principles are: fairness, reliability, privacy, inclusiveness, transparency, and accountability. See Table 2.1 for a responsible AI comparative matrix.

Fairness stands as the first principle, demanding that AI systems treat everyone equitably, free from hidden biases that could skew outcomes. Imagine a hiring tool that screens job applicants, fairness ensures it doesn't favor candidates based on gender, race, or background but evaluates skills and experience alone. Biases can creep in through flawed data or design

TABLE 2.1 Responsible AI: Comparative Matrix

Principle	Responsible implementation	Irresponsible implementation
Fairness	Testing algorithms across diverse demographic groups and adjusting to ensure balanced outcomes	Using biased historical data without correction, leading to discriminatory results
Reliability	Rigorous testing in diverse scenarios, continuous monitoring, and fail-safe mechanisms	Limiting testing and deployment without ongoing monitoring for performance degradation
Privacy	Data minimization, explicit consent, purpose limitation, and strong security controls	Excessive data collection and use beyond stated purpose without proper safeguards
Inclusiveness	Designing for diverse users, accessibility features, and culturally sensitive approaches	Designing for a limited user profile without considering diverse needs and abilities
Transparency	Explainable algorithms with clear documentation on capabilities, limitations, and decision factors	"Black box" systems with no explanation of decision-making processes or factors
Accountability	Clear governance structure, designated roles, audit trails, and paths for redress	Unclear ownership of outcomes with no process for addressing harms or taking responsibility

choices, leading to unfair advantages or disadvantages. Responsible AI actively seeks out and corrects these imbalances, striving for decisions that reflect true equality. As Table 2.1 illustrates in its row for fairness, a responsible approach involves testing algorithms across diverse demographic groups and adjusting them to ensure balanced outcomes. In contrast, an irresponsible approach might rely on biased historical data, causing discriminatory selections and perpetuating inequities.

Reliability comes next, which is about the need for AI systems to perform consistently and accurately in a variety of real-world conditions. Think of a self-driving car navigating different roads and weather scenarios; reliability demands that it functions safely whether it's on a busy highway or a quiet neighborhood street. Achieving this requires thorough testing, continuous monitoring, and regular updates to address emerging problems.

Privacy, the third principle, acts as a shield for personal data in an age where information is currency. AI systems often rely on vast amounts of data; data is what drives AI and enables it to learn. Privacy ensures this data isn't exploited, mishandled, or exposed. Techniques like anonymization, which strips away identifiable details, or encryption, which scrambles data into unreadable code, become essential tools. Responsible AI respects the boundary between innovation and intrusion, and ensures that technology never compromises individual confidentiality.

Inclusiveness stands at the heart of making sure AI works for everyone, not just a privileged few. Picture a voice assistant that must understand accents from around the world or a website that offers text-to-speech options for visually impaired users. Inclusiveness means recognizing the diversity of human experiences and proactively designing AI to accommodate them. As shown in Table 2.1, a responsible stance on inclusiveness involves broad user testing, accessibility features, and ongoing refinement to serve varied communities. An irresponsible approach might ignore these considerations, leaving entire groups underserved or excluded from the benefits of AI innovations.

Transparency reveals AI's decision-making and replaces mystery with clarity. When a bank's AI denies a loan application, transparency means explaining *why*: was it a low credit score, insufficient income, or an error in the data? Users deserve to understand how decisions affecting their lives are made. This principle rejects "black box" systems and advocates for interpretable models and clear communication. Transparency builds trust, turning AI from an inscrutable force into a collaborator.

Accountability ties responsibility to every AI system, ensuring humans, not algorithms, answer for outcomes. If an AI-powered hiring tool discriminates against certain candidates, accountability means the developers and organizations behind it address the harm. This principle establishes governance frameworks, audit trails, and redress mechanisms, and ensures that mistakes are corrected and lessons learned. It reminds us that technology is a tool shaped by human hands, and those hands must guide it ethically.

These principles form a blueprint for ethical AI. They acknowledge that innovation without responsibility risks harm, whether through biased algorithms, privacy breaches, or systems that fail when they're needed most. Microsoft, for instance, embeds these ideals into tools like Azure Machine Learning and has features like fairness metrics and interpretability dashboards to help developers align with ethical standards. But why do these principles matter beyond compliance? *They build trust.* When people understand how AI works and see it acting fairly, they're more likely to embrace it. Businesses, too, benefit. Ethical AI avoids legal pitfalls, promotes customer loyalty, and drives sustainable growth. A hospital using AI to diagnose diseases, for example, gains credibility when patients know the system is both accurate and unbiased.

Societal and Business Impacts of Adopting Responsible AI Practices

The societal and business impacts of adopting Responsible AI practices are both profound and far-reaching. On the societal front, when AI respects privacy, minimizes bias, and operates transparently, people grow to trust these systems and become more willing to embrace new technological solutions. This trust is vital for addressing large-scale challenges such as healthcare, education, and environmental conservation, where AI can make a meaningful difference if people feel confident in its reliability and fairness.

For businesses, responsible development leads to stronger reputations, reduced legal risks, and healthier relationships with customers and regulators. When companies openly demonstrate their commitment to ethics and social responsibility, they can promote loyalty and inspire broader collaboration across industries.

Fairness in AI Solutions

Fairness in AI means designing systems that treat everyone equitably and do not favor one group over another. It is about ensuring that algorithms make decisions solely based on relevant factors, such as skills or qualifications, rather than on characteristics like race, gender, or socioeconomic background. For instance, when an AI-powered hiring tool screens job applicants, fairness requires that the tool evaluates candidates on their abilities and experience, rather than perpetuating biases found in historical data. This focus on fairness helps to mitigate the risk of skewed outcomes that could lead to discrimination or unequal opportunities, ultimately striving to ensure that every decision reflects true equality.

Unfairness in AI occurs when these systems produce outcomes that reinforce existing biases or create new forms of discrimination. Imagine a facial recognition system that misidentifies individuals from underrepresented communities more frequently than others, or a loan approval algorithm that denies credit based on an applicant's residential area, which might be correlated with race or economic status. Such unfair outcomes harm individuals by denying them opportunities, and they also perpetuate broader societal inequities. Unfair AI systems can undermine public trust in technology and worsen systemic discrimination, making the pursuit of fairness a crucial objective.

Addressing fairness in AI is a challenge that requires a deep understanding of both technical and social dimensions. Biases can enter the system from the data used to train it or from the design choices made during development. It can also emerge over time as the AI system interacts with new data and diverse user groups. This is why ensuring fairness is not a one-time effort but a continuous process of identifying and mitigating potential harms. Tradeoffs often need to be made, where improving fairness in one aspect might affect other performance metrics. It is essential to be explicit about these tradeoffs and document the assumptions and priorities that guide the design and operation of the system.

Addressing fairness in AI is a challenge that requires a deep understanding of both technical and social dimensions. As shown in Figure 2.1, this process involves structured steps such as identifying potential biases (e.g., emergent patterns, population shifts) and implementing mitigations through data preprocessing, algorithmic constraints, or fairness optimization. The figure also emphasizes monitoring in production, where performance impacts, fairness definitions, and design justifications are continuously evaluated to detect issues like performance drift or new biases emerging from user feedback. For example, disparate impact analysis and fairness metrics evaluation, key components of the framework in Figure 2.1, ensure that group outcomes are compared systematically to avoid skewed results.

FIGURE 2.1 Continuous fairness process cycle in AI.

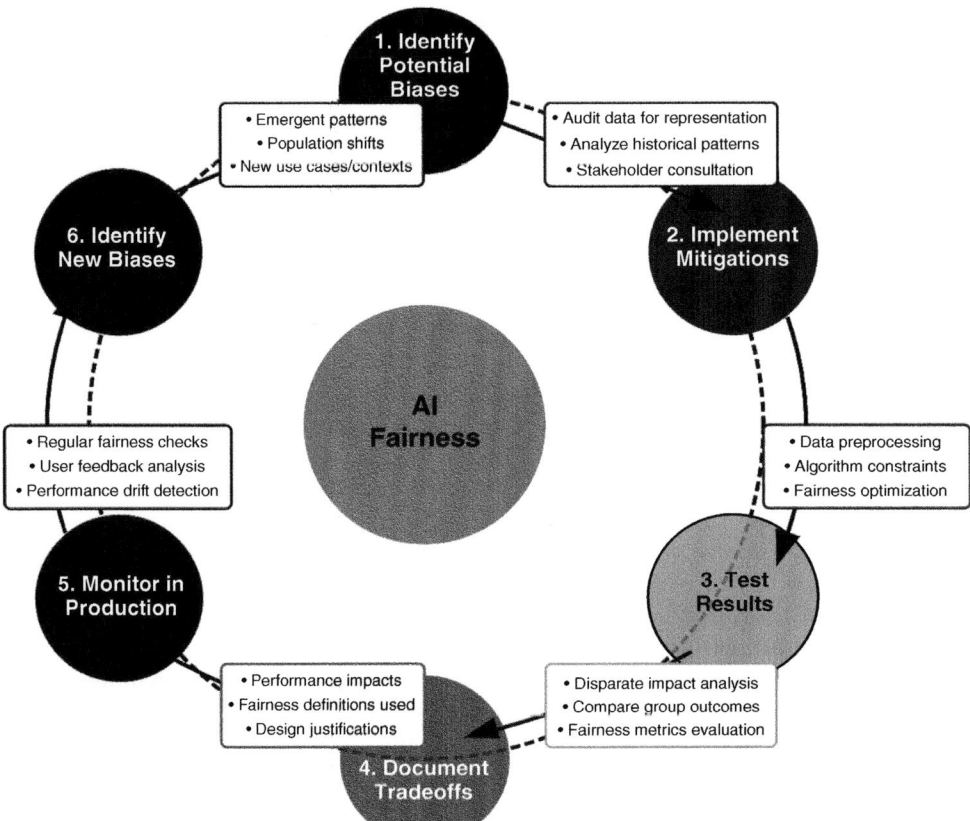

There are several techniques available to detect and mitigate bias in AI models, and these methods often begin with a careful examination of the data itself. A starting point is ensuring that the data sampling process accurately reflects the diversity of the population that the model will serve. For instance, if a dataset for a credit scoring system contains a disproportionate number of samples from high-income groups, the resulting model may unjustly disadvantage applicants from lower-income backgrounds. Techniques such as stratified sampling, oversampling underrepresented groups, or reweighting the data help balance this representation and ensure that the model learns from a more equitable sample. Fairness metrics like demographic parity, equal opportunity difference, and disparate impact ratios are then used to quantitatively evaluate whether the system's outcomes are biased. These metrics provide a numerical basis to measure and compare the fairness of different models, and this allows teams to identify potential biases and determine the necessary adjustments.

In addition to refining the data, there are algorithmic methods designed to reduce bias during the training phase of AI models. One popular approach is adversarial debiasing, where an additional model is used to detect correlations between sensitive attributes and the predictions made by the main model, thus encouraging the system to focus on relevant features instead. Another effective strategy is incorporating fairness constraints directly into the model's loss function. By doing so, the optimization process is guided to balance both predictive accuracy and fairness, even if that means making tradeoffs between the two. You can also use Fairlearn (`https://github.com/fairlearn/fairlearn`), a Python package that helps teams assess and improve the fairness of machine learning models, by providing a suite of tools that evaluate how different fairness metrics hold up under various scenarios and suggesting adjustments to the model to enhance equitable performance.

Beyond these technical approaches, there are practical toolkits that assist teams in systematically addressing bias throughout the AI development lifecycle. The Microsoft research team, for example, created the AI Fairness Checklist (`https://www.microsoft.com/en-us/research/project/ai-fairness-checklist`), a guide that prompts developers to consider fairness at every stage, from envisioning the system and scrutinizing its architecture to defining datasets and setting fairness criteria. This checklist encourages teams to document assumptions, weigh tradeoffs, and engage diverse stakeholders to find potential fairness-related harms that might not be apparent during the initial stages of development.

Reliability and Safety in AI Solutions

Reliability refers to the ability of an AI system to perform its intended functions consistently and accurately under varying conditions. It requires powerful error-handling mechanisms to manage unexpected inputs, data anomalies, or system failures. For instance, a natural language processing system must detect and flag ambiguous queries rather than generating incorrect or misleading responses. Reliability also demands rigorous validation during development, such as stress testing under extreme scenarios, to ensure the system behaves predictably even when faced with incomplete or noisy data.

Figure 2.2 is an example of how an AI-driven chat interface can demonstrate reliability by consistently providing correct or relevant answers. The image shows several user questions and the system's responses, each labeled according to its accuracy or the context needed. For instance, when the user asks about the capital of France, the system confidently and accurately responds with "Paris," indicating that it has retrieved factual information correctly. In another question, it clarifies that Gondor is a fictional kingdom from J.R.R. Tolkien's works, highlighting the importance of distinguishing real-world facts from fictional contexts. Finally, when asked why the sky is green, the system provides a more nuanced response, indicating uncertainty and inviting further clarification.

This scenario illustrates reliability in AI because it shows how the system can handle a variety of questions, some factual, some fictional, and some ambiguous, while maintaining

FIGURE 2.2   AI reliability in LLM conversations.

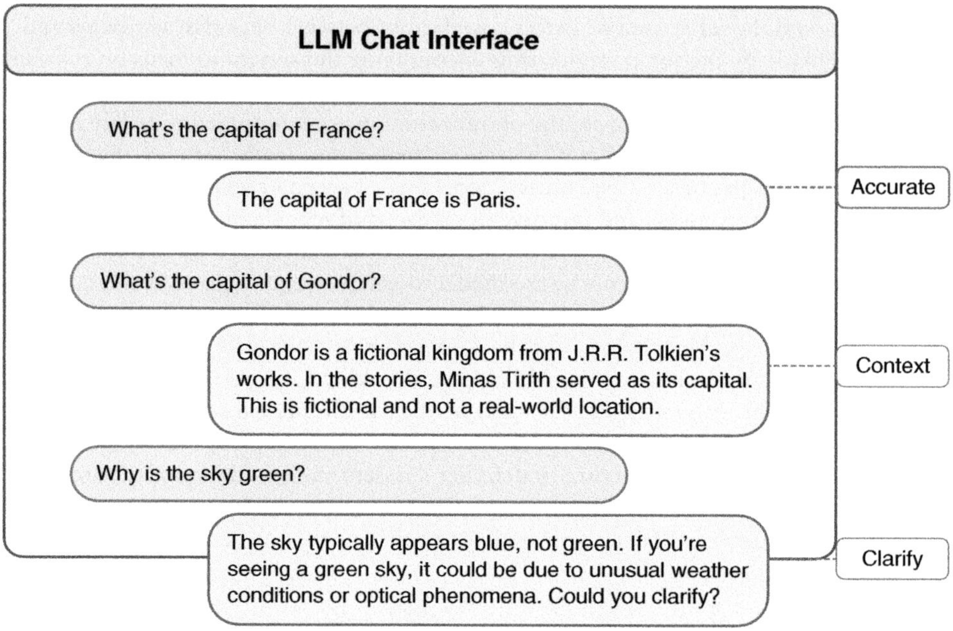

consistent behavior. A reliable AI model not only delivers accurate information but also knows when to prompt the user for more details if the question is unclear. In doing so, it helps prevent misunderstandings and misinterpretations.

Safety ensures that AI systems operate without causing harm to users, environments, or other systems. This involves designing algorithms with built-in safeguards to prevent catastrophic failures. For example, an autonomous vehicle's AI must prioritize collision avoidance over speed optimization, even in unpredictable traffic conditions. Key requirements like robustness, error handling, and traceability ensure these systems remain trustworthy under pressure.

Robustness ensures AI systems perform reliably under unexpected or challenging conditions. Think of it as building an immune system for AI: just as the body adapts to new germs, robust AI adapts to adversarial attacks (like manipulated inputs designed to trick it), data drift (when real-world data changes over time), or rare edge cases (unusual scenarios not seen during training). For instance, a facial recognition system must still identify a person accurately even if the lighting is poor or the image is slightly distorted. Robustness is achieved through rigorous testing, diverse training data, and techniques like adversarial training, where AI learns to ignore misleading inputs.

Error handling involves strategies to detect and resolve mistakes before they escalate. When an AI system encounters a problem such as flawed data, software glitches, or ambiguous requests, it should detect the issue, minimize harm, and recover smoothly. Using the same facial recognition system as an example, if the software's camera feed becomes momentarily scrambled, the system needs to log the error, avoid making false identifications, and prompt a brief re-scan.

Traceability creates accountability by documenting how decisions are made. Transparent records of inputs, processes, and outputs allow developers to audit outcomes and refine systems. Let's go back to our facial recognition system again. Here, traceability allows developers to see exactly which images were processed, how those images were preprocessed, which algorithm version made the identification, and what the final output was. This detailed log means that if a person is misidentified, one can review the entire decision-making process to understand whether the error was caused by poor lighting, a glitch in image processing, or even a flaw in the underlying model.

Azure's AI services include tools designed to embed responsibility directly into AI workflows. Here's a closer look at key offerings:

- **Azure AI Content Safety:** This service scans text, images, and videos for harmful content such as hate speech, violence, or explicit material and ensures that AI outputs align with ethical guidelines. For example, a social media moderation tool using this API automatically flags toxic comments or inappropriate images before they go live. It uses customizable severity scores, allowing businesses to set thresholds based on their policies.

- **Azure AI Document Intelligence:** Beyond extracting text from documents, it ensures ethical handling of sensitive data. For instance, it can redact personally identifiable information (PII) like Social Security numbers or medical records during processing, preventing accidental exposure.

- **Fairlearn:** Fairlearn detects and mitigates bias in AI models. It evaluates fairness metrics (e.g., demographic parity) and suggests adjustments, such as reweighting training data to reduce disparities.

- **InterpretML:** This tool explains how AI models make decisions and makes "black box" systems transparent. For example, InterpretML can show that a hospital readmission model prioritizes "age" and "previous diagnoses" over less relevant factors.

- **Responsible AI Dashboard:** A unified interface in Azure Machine Learning, this dashboard combines data analysis, fairness assessment, error analysis tools, and more to provide a holistic view of AI model behavior. It integrates with Azure Machine Learning's Python SDK, CLI, and studio, enabling developers to explore dataset distributions, evaluate model fairness across diverse groups, and diagnose how errors are distributed. The dashboard includes tools like model interpretability, revealing which features drive predictions at both aggregate and individual levels, and counterfactual analysis, which tests how tweaking inputs could alter outcomes.

- **Azure AI Personalizer:** While enabling personalized user experiences, this service adheres to ethical guidelines by avoiding manipulative practices. For example, a news app using Personalizer can recommend articles without creating "filter bubbles" by balancing user preferences with diverse content. It also allows users to opt out of data collection, respecting privacy.

- **Azure AI Language:** This includes features like PII detection and conversational language understanding that prioritize ethical data use. For instance, a chatbot using this service can automatically anonymize user names or addresses in transcripts, ensuring compliance with regulations like GDPR.

Privacy and Security Considerations

Privacy in AI means keeping sensitive information safe throughout a system's entire lifecycle. One big challenge is data anonymization, which removes personal details like names, addresses, or other identifying information from datasets so that AI can learn without exposing private information. While some AI systems are trained on medical records, access to personally identifiable information (PII) can be controlled through careful data preparation. As an example, an AI system designed to detect cancer in medical imaging needs only a set of training images but does not need to know which patient each image came from. The system can learn to identify cancerous patterns without accessing names, birth dates, or other personal details that could identify individuals.

AI systems face special threats too. For example, model inversion attacks can use a system's outputs to rebuild training data, like recreating a person's facial image from a facial recognition model's scores. Adversarial attacks add very small changes to images, such as a stop sign, that can cause a system to misclassify them. Data poisoning happens when attackers add biased examples to the training data to change how a model behaves. Even simple metadata, like the patterns of API use, can sometimes reveal sensitive details about a model's design or training data.

Protecting sensitive data in AI workflows uses several advanced methods. Differential privacy adds a bit of random noise to the data or results so that one person's information does not change the overall outcome much. Encryption protects data both when it is moving and when it is stored, so that even if someone gets the data, they cannot read it without the right key. Other methods like secure multiparty computation and homomorphic encryption let multiple parties work with data in an encrypted form without showing the underlying details.

Azure has built a strong foundation for privacy and security through services like Confidential Computing. This service creates secure, isolated environments where sensitive data can be processed while remaining encrypted, even during computations. It means that when AI systems run on Azure, the data is protected from unauthorized access, ensuring that personal information stays private throughout processing.

Azure also has a range of security tools and monitoring capabilities that work together to safeguard data at every stage. For instance, data is encrypted both while stored and during transit, so even if someone were to intercept it, they wouldn't be able to read the information without the proper keys. Azure's Security Center continuously monitors workloads and alerts users to potential threats, making it easier to manage and mitigate risks before they affect operations.

Additionally, Azure services help organizations comply with various privacy regulations and build trust with users. The integrated suite of tools allows businesses to control who accesses data, perform regular security assessments, and audit their systems for any vulnerabilities.

Inclusiveness in AI Solutions

Inclusiveness in AI is about designing systems that serve diverse populations equitably, accounting for differences in language, culture, ability, and background. It ensures technologies are accessible to marginalized groups, such as individuals with disabilities (e.g., visual or hearing impairments) or those from underrepresented regions. For example, a voice assistant must recognize accents and dialects beyond "standard" speech patterns, while image recognition tools should accurately identify diverse skin tones, ages, and cultural attire. Inclusiveness also demands cultural adaptability, which means avoiding biases in content recommendations or mistranslations in language models that might alienate non-Western users. At its core, it challenges developers to question assumptions about "typical" users and prioritize underrepresented voices in data collection, testing, and design.

Why Inclusiveness Matters

Exclusionary AI perpetuates inequality, which deepens divides in access to healthcare, education, and economic opportunities. For instance, a diagnostic tool trained primarily on data from one demographic might misdiagnose conditions in others, while a job-matching AI that overlooks nontraditional career paths could disadvantage neurodiverse candidates. Inclusive design, however, unlocks broader societal benefits: speech-to-text tools empower the hearing impaired, multilingual chatbots bridge language barriers, and culturally aware algorithms promote global collaboration. Beyond ethics, inclusivity makes innovation possible for several reasons. For example, diverse datasets reduce blind spots, which improves the power of models and also promotes user satisfaction. When inclusiveness is embedded into AI, developers will comply with accessibility standards (e.g., WCAG) and also build trust, which makes sure that the technology in question uplifts rather than excludes.

Designing Inclusive AI Systems with Azure

Creating inclusive AI systems begins by addressing dataset bias, a challenge highlighted in Microsoft's *Inclusive AI* guide (`https://inclusive.microsoft.design/ tools-and-activities/InPursuitofInclusiveAI.pdf`), where homogenous training data excludes underrepresented groups. Azure tackles this through multilingual support and cultural adaptability, enabled by tools like Azure AI Language, which supports over 100 languages and dialects. For instance, its translation API avoids gendered assumptions (e.g., defaulting "doctor" to male), aligning with the guide's emphasis on breaking harmful associations. Similarly, Azure Cognitive Services offers region-specific models, ensuring image recognition accounts for diverse cultural attire or skin tones, and these are critical for avoiding exclusionary outcomes like misclassifying non-Western clothing.

To ensure cultural adaptability, the guide stresses balancing automation with human input. Azure's Personalizer service exemplifies this by tailoring recommendations without reinforcing filter bubbles. For example, a streaming platform using Personalizer can blend user preferences with culturally diverse content, avoiding the "dinosaur gift loop" metaphor from the guide, where algorithms endlessly recycle past choices. This aligns with the document's call to "balance intelligence with discovery," ensuring AI systems evolve dynamically rather than stagnating in biased feedback loops.

Azure's accessibility-focused tools directly address physical and cognitive diversity. Azure Cognitive Services for Vision includes alt-text generation for images, aiding visually impaired users, while Speech-to-Text accommodates speech disorders and accents, reflecting the guide's push to "recognize exclusion" in interaction design. For developers, Fairlearn integrates with Azure Machine Learning to audit models for fairness gaps, such as underrepresenting non-binary genders in training data.

The *Inclusive AI* guide highlights the need for diverse teams to identify biases early. Azure supports this with the Responsible AI Dashboard, which combines fairness metrics, error analysis, and interpretability tools. Services like Azure AI Content Safety scan outputs for harmful language, which protects marginalized users and reflects the document's push to "cultivate diversity with privacy and consent."

Transparency and Accountability in AI Solutions

Transparency in AI ensures that decisions made by models are understandable to users and stakeholders. It encompasses *interpretability* (how a model works internally) and *explainability* (providing human-readable reasons for outputs). For example, a loan approval AI should explain why an application was rejected, such as low credit scores or insufficient income. Accountability ties transparency to responsibility, and this ensures that developers and organizations can audit decisions, correct errors, and address harms.

Techniques for Model Interpretability and Auditing

Techniques for model interpretability help break down complex AI decisions into simple, understandable parts. Tools like SHAP (SHapley Additive exPlanations) assign a clear value to each input feature, showing how much each one contributes to a specific prediction. For example, SHAP might reveal that "income" contributes 60% to a loan approval decision. LIME (Local Interpretable Model-agnostic Explanations) works by approximating the model's behavior for individual cases, offering a closer look at which features matter most for that particular decision.

This level of clarity is essential not only for debugging but also for ensuring fairness in AI systems. When developers understand how and why a model makes its decisions, they can spot if certain features are having too much influence or if unwanted biases are creeping in. For instance, if a model disproportionately weighs a factor like age or ethnicity in ways that could lead to discrimination, interpretability tools provide the evidence needed to adjust the model and make it more equitable.

Auditing adds another critical layer by keeping a detailed record of the model's development and usage. This involves using version control to track model changes over time and maintaining audit logs that record inputs, outputs, and user interactions. For example, a healthcare AI system's audit trail might reveal that outdated training data led to a drop in diagnostic accuracy, prompting the need for retraining.

Azure Machine Learning's Transparency Tools

Azure Machine Learning has tools that help ensure AI models are both understandable and accountable. These tools reveal how models make decisions, monitor their performance over time, and maintain a detailed record of data flows for thorough auditing. Here are some of the key tools and how they work:

- **InterpretML:** This tool generates both global and local explanations for AI model decisions by using methods such as SHAP and LIME. It visualizes the impact of each feature on the model's predictions, showing, for example, which factors contribute most to a loan approval or a healthcare diagnosis. This detailed breakdown helps developers and regulators see the inner workings of the model, identify potential biases, and ensure that decisions align with ethical standards.

- **Responsible AI Dashboard:** The dashboard combines various monitoring tools into a single, easy-to-use interface. It brings together fairness metrics, error analysis, and interpretability reports so that teams can quickly assess how their models perform across different groups and in different scenarios. By having all these insights in one place, it becomes easier to track performance, detect issues early, and make informed adjustments to the model.

- **ModelDataCollector:** The ModelDataCollector is part of the Azure Machine Learning SDK. This tool/class captures detailed logs of inputs and outputs during model deployment. By recording how data flows through the system, it enables teams to conduct post hoc audits, trace decisions back to their source, and verify that the system is operating as intended. This transparency is crucial when investigating any anomalies or unexpected behavior in the model, as it provides a clear record of what data was processed and how.

- **Azure Monitor:** Azure Monitor tracks key performance metrics and monitors data drift (when the input data starts to change over time). It continuously checks that the model maintains its expected level of performance and alerts teams if any degradation is detected. This proactive monitoring allows for timely interventions, ensuring that the model remains reliable and secure even as conditions evolve.

Azure Responsible AI Tools and Services

Azure has a comprehensive suite of tools to embed responsibility across AI development, deployment, and governance. Below are key services highlighted in Microsoft's resources.

Microsoft's Responsible AI Standard

Microsoft's Responsible AI Standard is a framework developed to guide the design, development, and deployment of AI systems that reflect ethical values and address society's needs. Recognizing a policy gap where laws and norms had not yet caught up with the rapid evolution of AI, Microsoft created this standard to offer clear, actionable guidance for product teams. It is built around six core principles we discussed in this chapter (fairness, reliability, privacy, inclusiveness, transparency, and accountability), and it ensures that AI systems not only solve problems effectively but also do so in ways that respect human rights and promote societal well-being.

The standard lays out specific goals and requirements for each of these principles. For example, under accountability, teams are required to conduct thorough impact assessments early in the development process, document potential risks, and set up oversight mechanisms to manage adverse impacts. Transparency goals mandate that every decision made by an AI system be clearly documented and explained, allowing stakeholders to understand the inputs, processes, and outputs. Meanwhile, reliability and safety requirements focus on setting acceptable error rates, defining operational ranges, and ensuring the system remains robust under various conditions. Privacy and security are maintained by adhering to Microsoft's internal standards, such as data anonymization, encryption, and secure processing protocols, ensuring that sensitive information is consistently protected throughout the system's lifecycle.

Importantly, the Responsible AI Standard is designed as a living document, and it evolves with new research, technological advances, and legal developments. Microsoft actively invites feedback from industry, academia, civil society, and government to refine and improve the framework, promoting a global dialogue around ethical AI practices.

AI Impact Assessment Guide

The AI Impact Assessment Guide is a framework designed to help teams evaluate the ethical, legal, and societal risks of deploying an AI system before it goes live. This guide serves as an early warning system, encouraging developers to pause and reflect on the potential impacts of their AI solution on people, organizations, and society at large. By asking a series of targeted questions, the guide helps teams identify areas where the system might cause harm, such as bias, privacy breaches, or unfair treatment of certain groups.

Using the guide involves filling out a detailed checklist that covers various aspects of the AI system, from its intended purpose and the nature of the data it uses, to how it will be monitored and updated over time. The guide prompts teams to document key assumptions, measure performance against ethical standards, and set up oversight processes. This rigorous approach ensures that all potential risks are identified early on and that there is a clear plan in place to address them. For example, teams might use the guide to determine whether their data accurately represents the population it will serve or to assess whether the model's decision-making process aligns with fairness and transparency requirements.

AI Impact Assessment Template

The AI Impact Assessment Template is a structured tool developed by Microsoft to help teams evaluate the potential effects of an AI system on people, organizations, and society. It guides users through various sections such as system information, purpose, intended uses, and stakeholder analysis. For example, teams start by describing the system in plain language, listing key features, and identifying where and how the system will be used. This structured approach ensures that all the relevant details are captured early on, allowing for a clear understanding of the system's context and its potential impacts.

By working through the template, developers are prompted to assess risks and benefits for different stakeholder groups, document assumptions, and identify potential harms such as biases or unintended negative outcomes. It includes specific questions and checklists that encourage teams to consider aspects like data requirements, fairness, and operational contexts. This rigorous process not only helps in pinpointing areas where the system might need improvements but also sets the stage for ongoing evaluation and updates as new risks emerge or as the system's use evolves.

The template is a key part of Microsoft's Responsible AI framework (`https://www.microsoft.com/en-us/ai/principles-and-approach`), and it connects the practical steps of risk assessment with broader ethical goals. It requires collaboration among engineers, designers, data scientists, and other stakeholders to ensure that the impact assessment is thorough and well-documented.

Threat Modeling

Threat modeling is a proactive process that helps identify and address security risks in AI systems before they are exploited. At Microsoft, this approach is integrated into the development lifecycle of AI solutions to ensure that potential threats, such as adversarial attacks, data poisoning, or unauthorized data access, are considered and mitigated early on. By using structured frameworks like Microsoft's STRIDE model (which stands for Spoofing, Tampering, Repudiation, Information Disclosure, Denial of Service, and Elevation

FIGURE 2.3   STRIDE framework for AI system security.

Threat Category	AI-Specific Threats	Mitigations
S–Spoofing	• Identity spoofing in AI APIs • Fake user data submission • Deepfake content generation	• Strong authentication • Content verification systems • API security measures
T–Tampering	• Training data poisoning • Model weight manipulation • Adversarial examples	• Data validation pipelines • Model integrity verification • Adversarial training
R–Repudiation	• Missing audit trails • Insufficient logging of AI decisions • Untraceable AI actions	• Comprehensive logging • Decision provenance tracking • Immutable audit trails
I–Information Disclosure	• Model inversion attacks • Training data extraction • Membership inference	• Differential privacy • Access controls • Secure enclaves
D–Denial of Service	• Resource exhaustion attacks • API flooding • Computational resource depletion	• Rate limiting • Resource monitoring • Scalable infrastructure
E–Elevation of Privilege	• Prompt injection attacks • System command execution • Authentication bypassing	• Input sanitization • Principle of least privilege • Secure API design

of Privilege), teams can analyze every component of an AI system, from data collection and model training to deployment and user interaction. See Figure 2.3.

In the context of AI at Microsoft, threat modeling is closely tied to the Secure Development Lifecycle (SDL). This process helps in mapping out potential attack vectors, and it also helps in designing countermeasures to prevent, detect, and respond to security incidents. For example, threat modeling might reveal vulnerabilities in how sensitive data is handled or how model outputs could be manipulated.

Fairlearn

Fairlearn (`https://fairlearn.org`) is an open-source Python toolkit that helps data scientists and machine learning engineers assess and mitigate bias in their models. It has a set of fairness metrics and algorithms that allow teams to measure how different demographic groups are affected by a model's predictions. For example, Fairlearn can calculate metrics like demographic parity or equal opportunity difference, which reveal whether a model is disproportionately favoring or disadvantaging certain groups.

Responsible AI Dashboard

The Responsible AI Dashboard is an interface within Azure Machine Learning that consolidates several key tools designed to help developers monitor and improve AI systems. One major feature is error analysis, which allows teams to examine how errors are distributed across the dataset and identify specific scenarios where the model might be underperforming. This feature gives developers detailed insight into which inputs lead to incorrect predictions, making it easier to diagnose issues and adjust the model accordingly.

Another important capability is model interpretability. This tool breaks down the decision-making process of an AI model by visualizing the impact of different features on the output. It provides a clear, visual representation of how each input contributes to a particular prediction, helping stakeholders understand the internal logic of the model.

The dashboard also includes counterfactual what-if analysis, which allows users to simulate changes in input features and observe how these alterations would affect the model's predictions. This "what-if" feature supports scenario planning and risk assessment by revealing potential vulnerabilities or unexpected behaviors.

InterpretML

InterpretML is an open-source toolkit developed by Microsoft to help make AI models more understandable. It uses techniques like SHAP and LIME to provide both global explanations and local explanations that reveal why a model made a specific prediction. For example, in a hospital readmission model, InterpretML can illustrate that factors such as "age" and "previous diagnoses" have a strong influence on predictions. This breakdown of decision-making processes turns the "black box" of AI into something that developers, auditors, and regulators can review and understand. More information about InterpretML can be found at `https://interpret.ml/`.

One of the major benefits of using InterpretML is its ability to generate intuitive visualizations that highlight the contribution of different features. These visual tools help teams quickly identify which inputs are driving model decisions, making it easier to spot potential issues or biases. In addition to visual explanations, InterpretML supports detailed local interpretability. This means that for any individual prediction, users can see explanations of the factors that influenced that specific outcome.

Counterfit

Counterfit is an open-source tool that tests the strength of AI models by simulating targeted attacks. It works by making small, controlled changes to input data, such as adding a bit of noise to an image, to see if the model still produces the correct output. This process helps reveal weak spots in the model where even tiny changes could cause errors.

Counterfit is also designed to integrate with broader AI development tools, like those available in Azure Machine Learning. Using Counterfit, developers can measure how sensitive a model is to minor modifications. For instance, if a facial recognition system is given an image with slightly altered brightness or contrast, Counterfit can show whether the

FIGURE 2.4   Presidio detection flow.

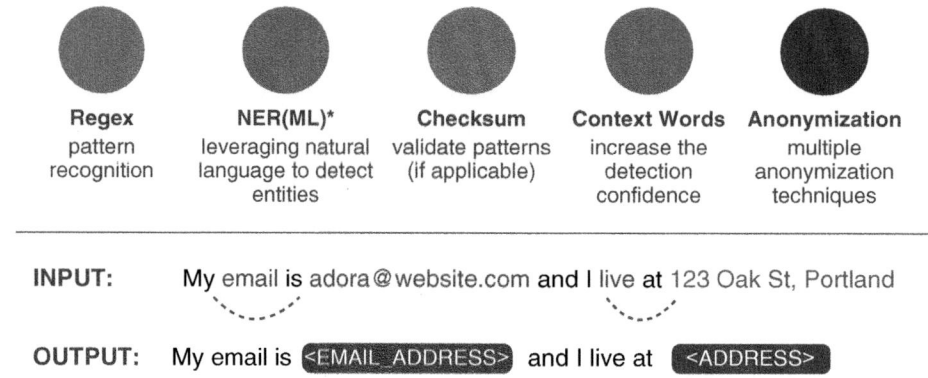

system continues to correctly identify the person. This technical approach helps pinpoint specific vulnerabilities that might go unnoticed during standard testing.

Presidio

Microsoft Presidio (see Figure 2.4) enhances data privacy in AI systems by automating the detection and anonymization of sensitive information (e.g., names, IDs, medical records) across structured and unstructured datasets. It uses Regex for pattern recognition (e.g., email addresses, physical addresses), NER (ML) to detect entities in natural language, and Checksum validation to verify data integrity where applicable. By applying Context Words Anonymization, Presidio increases detection confidence and dynamically anonymizes contextually sensitive data, as illustrated in Figure 2.4 with the replacement of email and address fields. The framework supports multiple anonymization techniques such as masking, encryption, and tokenization, ensuring compliance with GDPR, HIPAA, and CCPA while retaining data utility for tasks like model training or research analytics.

Microsoft Defender for Cloud

For AI scenarios, Defender for Cloud integrates with services like Azure Machine Learning, and applies machine learning–driven analytics to identify anomalies and prioritize risks. It enforces compliance with standards like GDPR or ISO 27001 through automated benchmarks and remediation steps, and ensures that sensitive data in AI workflows are handled securely.

Microsoft SEAL

Microsoft SEAL (Simple Encrypted Arithmetic Library) is an open-source homomorphic encryption library that enables computations on encrypted data without decryption, preserving privacy in applications, as well as AI and machine learning workflows. SEAL implements fully homomorphic encryption (FHE) using lattice-based cryptographic schemes, specifically the Brakerski-Fan-Vercauteren (BFV) scheme for integer arithmetic and the Cheon-Kim-Kim-Song (CKKS) scheme for approximate arithmetic on real numbers. These encryption methods allow mathematical operations like addition and multiplication to be performed directly on encrypted data, with the results remaining encrypted until explicitly decrypted by authorized parties. It can integrate with Azure Machine Learning to empower developers to build secure AI solutions where third parties (e.g., cloud providers) cannot access inputs or results.

Microsoft Purview

Microsoft Purview enables unified data governance and compliance across hybrid ecosystems, and this is critical for managing AI data sources and workflows. It automates data discovery, classification, and lineage tracking, which maps sensitive information across Azure, on-premises, and third-party platforms. For AI, Purview ensures models use compliant, high-quality data by applying sensitivity labels and enforcing access policies. It also provides visibility into how AI systems process data, auditing transformations from raw inputs to model outputs as a result of its integration with Azure Machine Learning and Synapse Analytics.

Azure Policy

Policy as Code keeps cloud environments secure and compliant by defining rules as programmable templates. Azure Policy uses this approach to automate governance. When it comes to responsible AI, Azure Policy ensures AI systems follow ethical guidelines by enforcing standards like encrypting sensitive data, restricting model access to authorized roles, or enabling audit trails to trace decisions. For instance, security teams and engineers can write policies that will block deployment of AI models that lack transparency documentation or enforce geographic data storage rules to meet privacy laws.

Azure AI Content Safety

Content is now a cornerstone of AI interactions. Azure AI Content Safety ensures these exchanges remain responsible by detecting and filtering harmful or inappropriate material (e.g., hate speech, violence) in text and images using machine learning models. Integrated via APIs, it scans AI-generated or user-provided content in real time, assigning severity scores to flag risks. For responsible AI, it enforces ethical standards by preventing misuse of models and aligns with compliance frameworks through audit-ready logs.

PyRIT

PyRIT (Python Risk Identification Toolkit) is an open-source framework developed by Microsoft to systematically identify and address risks in generative AI systems. It automates the evaluation of potential harms, such as unintended biases, security gaps, or unsafe outputs, by simulating scenarios to test model behavior under various conditions. The toolkit simplifies risk assessment workflows, enabling developers to pinpoint vulnerabilities early in the development lifecycle, such as flaws in training data or weaknesses in output filtering.

What Is AI Red Teaming?

AI Red Teaming is a methodical practice that is vital for building trustworthy AI that aligns with ethical standards and functions reliably in real-world applications. Here, specialists intentionally mimic real-world attacks or misuse to find weaknesses in AI systems before they go live. Unlike standard security checks, it targets AI-specific risks, such as systems producing unfair or harmful results, exposing sensitive data, or having insecure interfaces. Teams rigorously test the AI by challenging its inputs, altering its training data, or overwhelming its safety measures to expose flaws in security, ethics, or reliability. The findings help developers strengthen the system's defenses, refine safety protocols, and update governance rules to ensure fairness, transparency, and safety.

Human-AI Experience Toolkit

The Human-AI Experience Toolkit (HAX) is a Microsoft framework designed to improve how humans interact with AI systems by prioritizing usability, transparency, and trust. It provides guidelines and tools to help developers and designers create AI applications that are intuitive, explainable, and aligned with user needs. The toolkit emphasizes user-centered design and has checklists and patterns to address challenges like unclear decision-making or over-reliance on automation.

Inclusive Design

Inclusive Design is a methodology that creates products, services, and systems accessible to the widest range of users by addressing diverse needs from the outset. It focuses on identifying and removing barriers that exclude people, whether due to disability, language, culture, age, or situational limitations, and ensure that solutions work for everyone. In AI, this means building interfaces and workflows that adapt to varied abilities and designing models to avoid biases that marginalize groups. Tools like Microsoft's Inclusive Design Toolkit provide frameworks to embed empathy into development, such as prioritizing flexibility, simplicity, and multimodal interactions.

EconML

EconML is an open-source Python library by Microsoft that applies causal machine learning to estimate the real-world impact of decisions, policies, or interventions. EconML focuses on cause-and-effect relationships, using methods like Double Machine Learning and Meta-Learners to isolate the true effect of a variable while controlling for confounding factors. It integrates with ML frameworks like scikit-learn to handle complex, high-dimensional data, enabling businesses and researchers to answer questions like "How will this policy affect different groups?" or "Which customers respond best to discounts?"

Summary

This chapter covered the fundamentals of Responsible AI in Azure, focusing on how to build systems that are fair, reliable, private, inclusive, transparent, and accountable. It explained how these principles help to prevent bias, ensure consistent performance, protect sensitive data, and make AI decisions understandable to users. The chapter also introduced various Azure tools and techniques such as Fairlearn, Confidential Computing, and the Responsible AI Dashboard, that help developers integrate ethical guidelines into every step of the AI development process, from data collection to deployment and auditing.

Exam Essentials

Understand the Responsible AI principles.   Learn what fairness, reliability, privacy, inclusiveness, transparency, and accountability mean for AI systems and why they matter.

Tackle ethical challenges in AI.   Recognize issues like bias, data privacy, and inconsistent performance, and learn how careful design and technical methods can solve these problems.

Use Azure tools for Responsible AI.   Identify key Azure services such as Fairlearn, Confidential Computing, the Responsible AI Dashboard, and InterpretML, and see how they support ethical AI practices.

Ensure transparency and accountability.   Understand how clear logs, model explanations, and ongoing monitoring help explain AI decisions and hold developers responsible.

Promote inclusive and secure AI systems.   Learn how designing for diverse users and performing security checks like AI impact assessments and threat modeling help serve all users while protecting data.

Review Questions

1. A company builds an AI hiring tool that shows different results for similar candidates based on gender. Which Responsible AI principle should be applied to fix this?

   A. Fairness

   B. Reliability

   C. Privacy

   D. Inclusiveness

2. A financial institution deploys an AI loan approval system, but customers complain that the reasons for loan denials are unclear. Which step should be taken to resolve this issue using Azure tools?

   A. Increase the speed of data processing

   B. Use InterpretML to explain model decisions

   C. Encrypt all customer data

   D. Limit the number of loan applications

3. A startup is launching an AI chatbot on Azure. During testing, they find that the chatbot often misinterprets ambiguous questions. Which Responsible AI principle is most relevant, and what technique should be applied?

   A. Inclusiveness (Expand language support)

   B. Reliability (Improve error handling and prompt clarification)

   C. Privacy (Encrypt the conversation data)

   D. Accountability (Increase audit logs)

4. An e-commerce platform uses AI to personalize product recommendations. However, a review reveals that the system often shows similar types of products, limiting user exposure to diverse options. Which principle and approach should be applied?

   A. Fairness (Adjust bias detection)

   B. Reliability (Enhance performance testing)

   C. Inclusiveness (Broaden content diversity)

   D. Accountability (Implement stronger audit trails)

5. A company has deployed an AI system that provides customer support through a chat interface. Users have complained that the chatbot's responses are vague, and there is no clear indication of how decisions are made. What measure should the company take to improve the system's understandability?

   A. Integrate the Responsible AI Dashboard with interpretability features

   B. Increase data encryption for all customer interactions

   C. Focus on enhancing the system's reliability by adding more training data

   D. Use Fairlearn to adjust the system's bias

6. A fraud detection AI system is showing high sensitivity to small changes in input data, leading to false alarms. Which aspect of the system should be improved, and what steps should be taken?

   A. Enhance reliability by refining the training data and increasing tests under varied scenarios

   B. Increase privacy by encrypting all incoming data

   C. Improve fairness by using bias detection tools

   D. Boost transparency by adding detailed model logs

7. A software company wants to ensure that all modifications made to their AI model, including updates and fixes, are well-documented for future audits and accountability. Which practice should they adopt, and why is it important?

   A. Implement strong encryption for all internal communications

   B. Use audit trails combined with version control to record every change

   C. Focus on enhancing model speed and reducing latency

   D. Increase system transparency by publishing internal documentation

8. A retail company has deployed an AI system to manage discount offers based on customer purchasing patterns. However, the marketing team finds it difficult to understand how the system arrives at its decisions, leading to mistrust and misinterpretation of the offers. What step can the team take to improve clarity and trust?

   A. Implement stronger encryption to protect customer data

   B. Focus on increasing the volume of data processed

   C. Rebalance the training data to eliminate bias

   D. Use InterpretML to break down how different features influence the decisions

9. A tech company is planning to roll out a major update to its AI system used for customer sentiment analysis. The update aims to improve performance, but the team is unsure how the changes might affect the overall behavior of the system. Which process should the team follow to monitor the impact of these updates over time?

   A. Increase the frequency of user feedback surveys

   B. Conduct regular AI impact assessments combined with version control tracking

   C. Implement stronger encryption protocols during updates

   D. Focus on enhancing system reliability by increasing hardware resources

10. A social media platform deploys an AI content filtering system that is showing signs of bias by disproportionately filtering content from certain groups. The development team needs to address this issue to maintain fairness and trust. Which tool and process should they implement to mitigate bias effectively?

    A. Increase data collection from diverse sources

    B. Apply Fairlearn to measure and reduce bias in the model

    C. Switch to a different cloud service provider

    D. Remove the content filtering feature entirely

11. A government agency uses AI to monitor public safety, but citizens are concerned about how decisions are made. What is the best solution to increase public trust in the system?

A. Increase the system's processing power

B. Restrict the system to internal use only

C. Implement audit trails and use the Responsible AI Dashboard

D. Use Fairlearn to balance data

12. An AI-powered customer service system shows unpredictable behavior when faced with novel user inputs. What is the most suitable measure to improve its performance?

A. Increase data encryption levels

B. Enhance reliability by updating and testing the training dataset

C. Publish the source code for public review

D. Limit the types of user queries

13. An AI system deployed for monitoring network security is flagged for inconsistent behavior when encountering rare data patterns. Which approach should the security team adopt to address this?

A. Enhance reliability by retraining the model with additional edge cases

B. Focus on privacy by encrypting all network data

C. Improve transparency by showing detailed decision logs

D. Increase inclusiveness by incorporating user feedback

14. An AI system used in a smart home application must decide on energy usage recommendations. Users are concerned that they cannot understand the reasons behind these suggestions. Which step would best improve the situation?

A. Use Confidential Computing to secure data

B. Deploy InterpretML to provide clear, detailed explanations

C. Expand the dataset with more sensor data

D. Increase system speed for faster processing

15. A transportation company uses AI for route optimization in its fleet. Drivers have reported that the recommendations often do not account for local traffic patterns, causing delays. Which responsible AI principle should the team address, and what is a recommended solution?

A. Privacy (Use encryption for GPS data)

B. Reliability (Update the model with real-time traffic data)

C. Fairness (Ensure the algorithm treats all routes equally)

D. Transparency (Publish the route selection process)

16. A media company employs an AI system to generate personalized content recommendations. However, feedback shows that users from non-Western regions receive less relevant content. What should be done to address this issue?

    A. Enhance inclusiveness by integrating regional content and local languages

    B. Improve reliability by speeding up content processing

    C. Increase transparency by sharing the algorithm details

    D. Focus on privacy by anonymizing user data

17. A hospital deploys an AI system to extract information from patient records. To ensure compliance with privacy laws, they need to automatically remove or mask sensitive data like names and Social Security numbers. Which Azure tool should they use?

    A. InterpretML

    B. Confidential Computing

    C. Presidio

    D. Microsoft SEAL

18. A company must maintain unified data governance and compliance across multiple data sources used in its AI applications. Which Azure service provides the necessary data discovery, classification, and lineage tracking?

    A. Microsoft Purview

    B. Azure AI Content Safety

    C. InterpretML

    D. Presidio

19. A startup working on a generative AI model needs to evaluate risks such as unintended biases and unsafe outputs before deployment. Which tool is specifically designed to help identify these risks?

    A. AI Impact Assessment Template

    B. PyRIT (Python Risk Identification Toolkit)

    C. Responsible AI Dashboard

    D. Azure AI Document Intelligence

20. An organization wants to simulate real-world attacks on its AI system to identify vulnerabilities before deployment. What practice should they undertake?

    A. Use AI Red Teaming

    B. Implement Azure Policy for governance

    C. Conduct regular user surveys

    D. Increase data redundancy

Chapter 3

Core Concepts of AI Models and Solutions

MICROSOFT CERTIFIED: AZURE AI FUNDAMENTALS (AI-900) EXAM OBJECTIVES COVERED IN THIS CHAPTER:

✔ **Domain 2: Describe fundamental principles of machine learning on Azure**

- Subdomain 2a: Identify common machine learning techniques

  - 2-1 Identify regression machine learning scenarios

  - 2-2 Identify classification machine learning scenarios

  - 2-3 Identify clustering machine learning scenarios

  - 2-4 Identify features of deep learning techniques

  - 2-5 Identify features of the Transformer architecture

- Subdomain 2b: Describe core machine learning concepts

  - 2-6 Identify features and labels in a dataset for machine learning

  - 2-7 Describe how training and validation datasets are used in machine learning

- Subdomain 2c: Describe Azure Machine Learning capabilities

  - 2-8 Describe capabilities of automated machine learning

  - 2-9 Describe data and compute services for data science and machine learning

  - 2-10 Describe model management and deployment capabilities in Azure Machine Learning

AI models have become the backbone of modern technology. In this chapter, we explore what AI models are and how they serve as the foundation for various applications by learning patterns from data. We break down the steps of training, validating, and testing these models, showing how each phase contributes to building reliable systems. The discussion also covers the types of data required and the challenges that come with managing it, ensuring a clear understanding of the technical aspects behind these models.

We then compare pretrained models with custom ones, highlighting their benefits and tradeoffs in practical scenarios. The chapter also guides you through the process of deploying AI models to Azure, ensuring they run securely and efficiently in the cloud. Finally, we look at continuous learning and model updating, which are essential for keeping models effective as new data emerges. This approach aims to give you a solid, technical foundation in AI model development.

What Are AI Models?

An AI model is a mathematical construct trained to recognize patterns or relationships in data. At its core, it consists of three key components: algorithms, training data, and parameters. Algorithms are the step-by-step procedures that process inputs and generate outputs. Training data serves as the fuel during the development phase, as models learn by analyzing labeled or unlabeled datasets to adjust their internal logic. Parameters are the variables the model "learns" during training, such as weights in a neural network that determine how strongly one neuron influences another. It's important to note that while training data is essential for creating the model, once trained and deployed, the data itself is not deployed alongside the model. Only the learned patterns captured in the parameters remain.

The process of building an AI model involves training, validation, and testing phases. During training, the algorithm iteratively adjusts its parameters to minimize errors and uses techniques like gradient descent. For example, an image recognition model might tweak its weights to distinguish goats from dogs by analyzing thousands of labeled images. Validation ensures the model isn't overfitting (memorizing data instead of learning general patterns) while testing evaluates its performance on unseen data.

Underpinning these components is the model's architecture, which defines its structure. A convolutional neural network (CNN), for instance, uses layers designed to process pixel data hierarchically, making it ideal for visual tasks. Without these elements working in harmony (algorithmic logic, quality data, and optimized parameters), AI models would lack the precision and adaptability needed to tackle real-world problems.

Types of AI Models

There are numerous types of AI models, each of which is appropriate for a certain task. Generally speaking, models can be divided into three categories: supervised, unsupervised, and reinforcement learning models. Supervised models are frequently used in applications like language translation, medical diagnosis, and spam detection. They learn using labeled datasets, where the input data is associated with the proper output. Neural networks, support vector machines (SVMs), and decision trees are examples of popular supervised models.

Unsupervised models, on the other hand, work on unlabeled data and are frequently used to identify hidden patterns or groupings. Applications like customer segmentation, anomaly detection, and data compression are made possible by the prevalence of techniques like clustering (e.g., k-means) and dimensionality reduction (e.g., PCA or t-SNE). When labeled data is difficult to get but insights are still required, these models are important.

A third type of learning is called reinforcement learning, in which models pick up knowledge by interacting with their surroundings and getting feedback in the form of incentives or sanctions. For sequential decision-making tasks, such as teaching a robot to walk or an AI agent to play a video game, this method works well. Large-scale generative models that can produce text, graphics, and audio in response to cues have surfaced more recently, such as GPT and DALL·E. These make use of deep learning architectures based on transformers and are frequently pretrained on large datasets before being adjusted for particular uses.

Evolution and Impact of AI Models

Early rule-based systems and perceptrons laid the foundation for the development of AI models in the 1950s. Machine learning gained popularity in the 1980s as a result of advancements in algorithms and computing capacity. But the emergence of deep learning in the 2010s, driven by huge data and GPUs, signaled a sea change. An AI renaissance was sparked by innovations like AlexNet (2012), which transformed image recognition and showed off the capabilities of layered neural networks.

AI models are changing industries today. Drug discovery is accelerated in the healthcare industry by models such as AlphaFold that predict protein structures. While financial institutions employ predictive models to detect fraud, businesses utilize recommendation systems (like Netflix's algorithms) to customize customer experiences. Even the creative industries are not exempt; programs such as DALL·E challenge conventional ideas about human creativity by producing art in response to text cues.

But there are moral and practical issues with this AI development. As demonstrated by defective facial recognition systems, biased training data can reinforce discrimination.

Debate is also sparked by the "black box" nature of deep learning and the environmental impact of training huge models (such as the energy usage of GPT-3). Notwithstanding these problems, AI models keep innovating and pushing the limits of automation, judgment, and human-AI cooperation. Their future depends on striking a balance between duty and ability, making sure they are instruments for advancement rather than causes of evil.

Training, Validating, and Testing AI Models

The foundation of creating reliable AI systems is training, verifying, and testing. These stages guarantee that models not only pick up trends but also perform well when applied to fresh, untested data, which is essential for dependability in the real world. Models are taught using data during training, refined to prevent overfitting during validation, and tested to assess their ultimate performance in real-world scenarios. This lifecycle, when combined, overcomes issues like bias, scalability, and adaptability and closes the gap between theoretical algorithms and applications that we actually use. This section breaks down the technical processes and procedures that convert unprocessed data into reliable AI solutions.

Training AI Models Using Different Algorithms

Training an AI model is akin to teaching it to recognize patterns by adjusting its internal parameters. This process begins with data preparation, where raw data is cleaned, normalized, and split into training and validation sets. Algorithms like gradient descent then optimize the model's parameters by minimizing a loss function, which quantifies prediction errors. For example, a neural network training on image data iteratively adjusts neuron weights to reduce discrepancies between predicted and actual labels (e.g., "fish" vs. "goat"). The choice of algorithm depends on the task: decision trees split data using entropy-based rules, while support vector machines find hyperplanes to separate classes.

Different algorithms suit different data types and objectives. Supervised learning algorithms require labeled data to map inputs to outputs, ideal for tasks like price prediction. Unsupervised learning methods group unlabeled data into clusters or reduce dimensionality, useful for customer segmentation. Reinforcement learning trains models through reward-based interactions, perfect for game-playing agents or robotics. Hybrid approaches, like semi-supervised learning, combine labeled and unlabeled data to tackle scenarios with sparse annotations, such as medical imaging.

However, training isn't without challenges. Large models (e.g., deep neural networks) demand massive computational resources and time, and they often require GPUs or TPUs (Tensor Processing Units are specialized chips designed specifically for machine learning computations that can process AI workloads faster and more efficiently than traditional CPUs or GPUs). Overfitting, which is where models memorize training data instead of learning general patterns, is mitigated using techniques like dropout or early stopping. For instance, in natural language processing, transformer models like BERT use masked language modeling to learn contextual relationships without overfitting. The training phase's success hinges on balancing model complexity, data quality, and computational efficiency.

Validating Model Accuracy and Performance

Validation is a checkpoint before final testing, ensuring models function effectively on data they haven't seen during training. The dataset is divided into k subsets, and the model is trained k times, each time using a different subset for validation. This is known as k-fold cross-validation. This lessens performance estimate variance and aids in locating stability problems. For instance, a loan default prediction model may perform well in onefold but poorly in another, indicating imbalances in the dataset or a lack of features.

Holdout validation is simpler but riskier: a single portion of data (e.g., 20%) is reserved for validation. While efficient, this method can skew results if the holdout set isn't representative. Metrics like precision, recall, F1 score, and ROC-AUC provide nuanced insights beyond basic accuracy. In medical diagnostics, where false negatives are critical, recall (ability to identify all positive cases) becomes a priority. Hyperparameter tuning, which is adjusting settings like learning rates or tree depths, is often automated using tools like grid search or Bayesian optimization to maximize validation performance.

Validation also addresses bias-variance tradeoffs. High bias (underfitting) occurs when models oversimplify patterns, while high variance (overfitting) reflects excessive sensitivity to training noise. Regularization techniques like L1/L2 penalties or dropout layers help strike a balance. For instance, training a speech recognition model might involve adjusting dropout rates to ensure it generalizes across accents without losing precision. Metrics are only one aspect of validation. Another is increasing trust that the model will act reliably in changing conditions.

Testing for Reliability and Scalability

After training and validating a model, the final stage is to test it on a dataset that the model has never seen before. This step provides a realistic representation of how the model will perform in the real world. Testing is critical for determining the model's resilience, validating that it has not been overfitted to the training data, and ensuring that it can handle edge situations and noise in production scenarios.

Testing for dependability is determining how stable the model is under different input situations. Stress testing, in which the model is subjected to out-of-distribution data or adversarial examples, can assist with identifying latent weaknesses. For example, a sentiment analysis model may be tested with snarky comments or mixed-language inputs to assess its edge-case behavior. To ensure reliability, the model's judgments must also be validated over time, particularly if the business context or data distributions change (a process known as idea drift).

Scalability testing ensures AI models thrive under real-world pressures by simulating production-level demands, like handling thousands of concurrent requests, processing large data volumes, and meeting tight latency thresholds (e.g., real-time fraud detection). But scalability isn't just about raw power, it's about efficiency. For edge devices or mobile apps, testing evaluates CPU usage, memory footprint, and energy limits. A lab-accurate model might fail in production if it's too bulky. Think facial recognition draining a device's battery. Techniques like model quantization (simplifying calculations) or pruning (trimming neural networks) shrink models to fit these constraints without sacrificing accuracy.

The contrast between pristine labs and chaotic real-world conditions emphasizes the importance of scalability testing. A voice assistant trained in a noise-free lab may stumble in the presence of background chatter, but a server-based model may fail due to abrupt traffic spikes. Stress-testing using adversarial conditions, such as network delay or hardware constraints, allows teams to spot mismatches early on and optimize systems in advance. What was the result? AI solutions that are not only clever but also durable, delivering consistent performance under demand while remaining lean enough for real-world hardware.

Data Requirements for AI Models

Data is the lifeblood of AI models. Without it, even the most sophisticated algorithms can't learn, adapt, or make decisions. This section dives into the critical role of data in AI development, covering the types of data needed, how to refine it for usability, and the complexities of handling massive datasets. When developing a chatbot or a self-driving car, knowing the data needs guarantees that the models are scalable, ethical, and accurate. Poor data practices, on the other hand, result in skewed outputs, inefficiency, or complete failure, regardless of how sophisticated the model architecture is. Let's look at how data shapes AI from the ground up.

Essential Data Types for AI Development

AI models rely on a variety of data types, each having a distinct purpose. Structured data, which is arranged in tables or databases (for example, sales records, sensor readings), is good for tasks such as regression or classification because it has apparent patterns. Unstructured data, like text, photos, or audio, necessitates more complex processing; for example, natural language models like GPT-4 learn on large text corpora to grasp context and syntax. Semi-structured data (e.g., JSON files, XML) bridges the gap and is commonly utilized in recommendation systems that combine structured user profiles and unstructured browsing history.

The data type used depends on the problem. Computer vision models require annotated image datasets (e.g., COCO or ImageNet) to recognize objects, whereas time-series data (e.g., market prices, ECG signals) is critical for predicting or anomaly detection. Synthetic data, created with techniques like GANs, is gaining popularity in contexts where real data is limited or privacy-sensitive, such as healthcare simulations. Metadata, or data about data, adds context to model insights by offering things like timestamps or geographical tags.

However, not all data is equal. Models trained on small or unrepresentative datasets suffer from selection bias. For example, a facial recognition system that has been trained primarily on lighter skin tones would underperform for people with darker complexion. Balancing data diversity (e.g., demographics, edge cases) with relevance (e.g., domain-specific attributes) is key. Working with domain specialists ensures that datasets contain the nuances required for reliable performance, whether identifying diseases from X-rays or predicting supply chain problems.

Data Quality, Preprocessing, and Labeling Best Practices

Raw data is rarely AI-ready. It's often noisy, incomplete, or inconsistent. Data quality hinges on accuracy, completeness, and relevance. For instance, a dataset with missing values in patient records could skew a diagnostic model's predictions. Preprocessing steps like cleaning (removing duplicates), normalization (scaling numerical values), and handling outliers (e.g., using z-scores) standardize data for training. Feature engineering, such as converting text to word embeddings or extracting image edges, transforms raw data into formats models can digest.

Labeling, or giving data meaningful tags, is just as important. Supervised learning models require high-quality labeled data, which necessitates careful annotation. Inconsistent labels generate noise, which reduces model reliability. Active learning, in which models prioritize doubtful samples for human review, improves labeling efficiency, lowering costs while preserving accuracy.

Automation cannot replace rigor. For example, when labeling medical pictures for tumor identification, radiologists must ensure that annotations are consistent with clinical standards. Data augmentation, which generates variations through rotation, cropping, or noise injection, expands constrained datasets and improves generalization. However, over-augmentation might distort underlying patterns (for example, changing tumor forms in medical imaging). Balancing automation with subject expertise ensures that data is not only clean but useful, laying the groundwork for models that generalize far beyond training examples.

Managing Large Datasets in AI Projects

Managing large datasets (sometimes terabytes in size) poses logistical and technical challenges. Storage options such as Azure Data Lake Storage enable scalable access to large amounts of data. However, merely storing data is not sufficient; efficient retrieval and processing are required. Frameworks like Azure Databricks parallelize activities by breaking data into chunks that are processed concurrently across clusters, reducing computation time for applications such as training recommendation systems on billions of user interactions.

Data governance adds an additional layer of complication. Version control (e.g., MLflow) keeps track of dataset iterations, assuring model repeatability while retraining. Privacy requirements such as GDPR and HIPAA require anonymization techniques (e.g., differential privacy, k-anonymity) to remove personally identifying information (PII) from datasets. For example, a model evaluating electronic health records may aggregate data to avoid identifying specific patients while maintaining patterns.

Ethical concerns persist. Skewed datasets can introduce bias. Mitigation options include data auditing (finding underrepresented groups) and synthetic oversampling (creating data for unusual classes). Edge computing also addresses scalability difficulties by processing data locally on devices (such as smartphones), minimizing dependency on centralized servers. The goal of handling big datasets is ultimately to build systems that prioritize efficiency, adaptability, and fairness as the data expands and changes, not just infrastructure.

Pretrained and Custom Models

The decision between pretrained and custom AI models is critical for balancing efficiency, specificity, and resource investment. Pretrained models give a shortcut by utilizing prior knowledge, whereas custom models provide personalized solutions to specific issues. This sector explores their definitions, strengths, and tradeoffs, assisting developers and organizations in aligning their AI approach with project objectives such as rapid deployment, niche accuracy, or cost control. Knowing these differences guarantees that teams make well-informed, context-driven judgments rather than forcing solutions or reinventing the wheel.

Pretrained Models and Their Primary Benefits

Pretrained models are AI systems trained on large, general-purpose datasets (e.g., Wikipedia text, ImageNet photos) and made available for reuse. These models, like BERT for language tasks or ResNet for image recognition, capture broad patterns during initial training, which can be fine-tuned for specific applications. The key advantage is transfer learning. Instead of training from scratch, you can adapt the model's existing knowledge to new tasks with smaller, task-specific datasets. For instance, a medical startup could fine-tune a pretrained vision model to detect tumors using a limited set of annotated X-rays.

Beyond speed, utilizing pretrained models can significantly save computing costs. Training a large language model from the ground up requires significant processing power and massive datasets, which might be difficult for smaller teams or individual engineers. Platforms like Azure AI Model Catalog make advanced models more accessible, which allows startups to compete with larger technology corporations. They also simplify deployment for popular use cases. For example, a retailer may use a pretrained sentiment analysis model from the Azure AI Model Catalog to evaluate consumer feedback, which reduces the need for substantial data collection or specialized machine learning knowledge.

What Is the Azure AI Model Catalog?

The Azure AI Model Catalog is a centralized repository where users can discover, evaluate, customize, and deploy a range of AI models. It includes contributions from a variety of vendors, including Microsoft, OpenAI, Meta, and Hugging Face, and addresses tasks such as text production, picture analysis, and time-series forecasting. Users can test model performance using common datasets, fine-tune models using their own data, and seamlessly integrate them into applications. This strategy simplifies the AI development process, allowing firms to focus on innovation rather than the difficulties of model training and deployment.

However, pretrained models are not a universal solution. If their training data is biased, they inherit those biases too; a facial recognition model built on nondiverse datasets may struggle with underrepresented groups. They are also less adaptable to highly specialized tasks. A pretrained model for general object detection may fail to recognize rare bird species unless it is extensively retrained. Despite these limitations, their efficiency and accessibility make them essential for projects with short deadlines or budgets.

Advantages of Custom AI Models

Custom models are created from scratch to solve specific problems involving unique data or requirements. They are tailored to the specific requirements of a project, as opposed to pretrained models, which may include a challenging data format, a specialized field (such as mining equipment diagnostics), or strict privacy regulations. For example, a custom model predicting machinery breakdowns in offshore oil rigs might include sensor data and ambient aspects that generic models do not, resulting in more precision.

When you train a model from scratch, you have complete control over the data it learns from, the architecture you choose, and the hyperparameters you tune. This level of customization allows for more targeted optimization toward the specific problem at hand, frequently resulting in improved efficiency for tasks that are specialized. This is especially important in highly regulated industries such as finance and healthcare, where interpretability and compliance are not optional. A bank developing a fraud detection system may choose a custom model to ensure transparency in decision-making and adherence to auditing standards.

Custom models also perform well in situations when the data is proprietary or domain-specific. A logistics company with decades of shipping route data may train a model to optimize delivery times using variables unique to its operations, and this is something that pretrained models cannot replicate. While resource-intensive, the long-term payoff in accuracy and adaptability frequently compensates the initial investment, particularly for businesses where marginal performance gains translate to significant competitive or financial advantages.

Comparing Pretrained Models to Custom Models

This section will compare pretrained models to custom models in terms of flexibility, performance, and cost.

- **Flexibility:** Because pretrained models are "one-size-fits-most," they are stiff for new issues but perfect for common tasks like face identification or text translation. In contrast, custom models give granular control. A firm developing an AI-powered fashion app might begin with a pretrained vision model for basic garment detection before transitioning to a custom model that includes user-specific style preferences and real-time trend data.

- **Performance:** Pretrained models give good baseline performance quickly but may fail in specific conditions. Custom models, while slower to construct, can outperform them in specific applications. For example, a pretrained speech recognition model may achieve 90% accuracy in general use, whereas a custom model trained on accented speech data from a specific location may achieve 98%, significantly increasing the user experience for that demographic.

- **Cost:** Pretrained models save upfront expenses but may have hidden costs. Fine-tuning and API costs (e.g., GPT-4 per query) accumulate over time. Custom models require larger initial investments in data, technology, and talent (training a bespoke LLM can cost millions), but they eliminate recurring payments and provide scalability. A multinational e-commerce giant may invest in a custom recommendation engine to manage billions of users, while a small blog may rely on a pretrained system for basic recommendations.

Deploying AI Models to Azure

Once an AI model is built and tested, the next step is to make it available for use, whether it's through an app, a web interface, or an internal system. This section focuses on deploying AI models in Azure. However, deploying AI requires careful planning around integration, performance, and ongoing maintenance. This section explores the technical workflows, Azure-specific tools, and best practices for deploying models.

Steps for Deploying AI Models to Azure

Deploying an AI model to Azure involves three important phases, each of which uses Azure services to simplify the process:

1. **Model Preparation and Packaging:** Before deployment, models must be formatted for compatibility. This includes serializing trained models into standardized formats like ONNX (for cross-framework portability) or TensorFlow SavedModel (for TensorFlow-specific deployments). These formats ensure the model can run consistently

across different environments. Next, the model is registered in Azure Machine Learning, a centralized workspace that tracks versions, metadata, and dependencies. Registration acts like a library catalog. It keeps models organized, reproducible, and ready for reuse. For example, a retail company might register multiple versions of a demand forecasting model, each trained on seasonal data.

2. **Compute Target Configuration:** Azure has flexible infrastructure options to host models, known as compute targets. Some are listed below:

   a. Azure Container Instances are ideal for testing or low-traffic applications (such as a prototype chatbot). It is simple to set up but lacks auto-scaling.

   b. Azure Kubernetes Service is intended for production-grade applications (such as a real-time fraud detection API). AKS automatically scales resources to accommodate traffic spikes while ensuring high availability.

   c. Serverless options are best suited for event-driven tasks (such as processing uploaded photographs in Blob Storage).

   Azure Machine Learning eases deployment by abstracting infrastructure management. Developers define the computational goal, and Azure Machine Learning handles the rest, which eliminates the need to manually configure virtual machines or clusters.

3. **Endpoint Creation and Validation:** After configuration, the model is made available as an endpoint, which is a gateway that allows users or programs to submit and receive predictions and data.

   a. Real-time forecasts can be served by managed online endpoints, such as an API for language translation. These APIs automatically log inputs and outputs and connect with Azure Monitor to track performance.

   b. Large datasets can be processed asynchronously using batch endpoints, such as creating weekly sales reports.

After deployment, extensive testing ensures reliability. For example, a healthcare model that predicts patient readmissions may be verified against past data to ensure accuracy. Azure Machine Learning's built-in testing tools imitate real-world traffic and identify problems such as poor response times or integration faults with downstream services (e.g., databases).

Azure Services for Scalable and Secure Deployment

Azure makes it easier to deploy AI models by providing tools that scale with the size of your project and security requirements. Scalability is a key strength. Technologies like Azure Kubernetes Service (AKS) dynamically modify resources to manage traffic spikes, ensuring that models remain responsive even during peak demand. For example, during Christmas sales, a retail recommendation engine may handle thousands of requests per second without crashing. For huge, nonurgent jobs, such as evaluating years of sales data overnight, Azure Batch distributes workloads over numerous servers, accelerating processing. Smaller applications benefit from serverless choices such as Azure Functions, which run code only when called (for example, resizing user-uploaded photographs) and cost nothing when idle. This flexibility enables teams to focus on developing AI solutions rather than managing servers.

Security is built into all layers of Azure. Sensitive data, such as medical records or financial information, is protected via Azure Private Link, which transmits traffic over private, isolated networks rather than the public internet. Azure Key Vault works as a digital lockbox for credentials and API keys, ensuring that only authorized apps or users have access to them. Azure also allows you to manage who may alter or deploy models with Role-Based Access Control (RBAC), such as restricting access to a fraud detection system. These features assist teams in meeting stringent rules (such as GDPR or HIPAA) without the need to design security from scratch.

Azure also ensures that data is secure even when in use. Encryption scrambles data at rest (in databases) and in transit (between services), rendering it unreadable to hackers. Confidential computing gives an added degree of security to highly sensitive processes, such as genetic data analysis. Azure also automates compliance checks to ensure that deployments adhere to industry standards, allowing companies to avoid legal concerns.

Monitoring and Maintaining Models on Azure

Once an AI model is operational, it requires frequent maintenance. Over time, models may begin to "drift"; for instance, a chatbot that was trained on outdated lingo may find it difficult to understand new terms, or a fraud detection system may fail to recognize emerging frauds. Azure tools like Azure Monitor regularly monitor parameters such as response time and error rates. If the model slows down or makes too many errors, Azure delivers notifications so that teams can address problems before users notice. For data drift (when incoming data changes unexpectedly), Azure Machine Learning's Dataset Monitors compare actual data to the original training data, indicating shifts such as rapid changes in customer behavior during a holiday sale.

Maintenance is more than just repairing faults; it is about keeping models fresh. Consider a pizza recommendation algorithm that was trained on last year's toppings; it would be unaware of this year's trendy flavors. Azure allows teams to create automated retraining pipelines that continuously feed new data into the model. To maintain accuracy, a weather prediction model might be retrained weekly with the most recent climate data. If an update goes wrong, version control allows teams to revert to a previous "good" version, similar to erasing a poor software update on your phone. Models remain relevant even as the reality changes around them.

Making AI fair and economical is equally as important as performance. Models can unintentionally favor particular groups, such as a hiring tool that misses people with nontraditional backgrounds. Fairlearn and other tools can assist identify these biases and ensure that decisions are fair to everybody. Azure also helps to manage costs: Azure Cost Management detects unused resources, such as a server running continuously for a model that is only used during business hours.

Continuous Learning and Model Updating

In order for AI models to remain accurate and practical as the world evolves, they require constant maintenance. Continuous learning ensures that models adapt to new data, shifting trends, and changing user needs, keeping them from becoming outdated or biased. This section looks at ways to keep AI systems fresh, relevant, and aligned with real-world expectations, including ideas, techniques, and tactics for maintaining performance over time. For the AI-900 exam, you should focus on understanding why continuous learning is crucial and how Azure enables it.

Continuous Learning and Model Updating

Continuous learning entails continuously upgrading AI models to include new information, similar to how people learn from new experiences. For example, if a model for projecting energy consumption has not witnessed extreme weather patterns, it may perform well today but fail during a heatwave. Data patterns alter over time (known as data drift), as do user behaviors (for example, new lingo in chatbot inputs). Without updates, models lose accuracy and make bad choices. For example, consider a medical tool that fails to detect new illness patterns or a recommendation system that suggests out-of-date products.

Continuous learning is included into Azure's AI lifecycle. Tools such as Azure Machine Learning monitor model performance and alert users when adjustments are required. This approach entails more than just retraining with new data; it also includes ensuring that changes perform as planned and do not cause new mistakes. For example, if lending laws change, a credit scoring model may require revisions to ensure it conforms with requirements while remaining fair.

Remember that continuous learning involves changing models over time when taking the AI-900 exam. Data drift (changes in input data) and model decay (declining performance) are two key words. Azure services such as Azure Monitor help discover these issues automatically, triggering notifications for teams to take action.

Updating Models with New Data

Updating models starts with collecting fresh data, cleaning it, and retraining the model. Azure automates much of this workflow. For example, a retail company might use Azure Pipelines to pull daily sales data, preprocess it (removing duplicates or errors), and retrain a demand forecasting model weekly. Automated pipelines save time and reduce human error, letting teams focus on high-level tasks like validating results.

Retraining isn't always a full overhaul. Techniques like fine-tuning adjust only parts of a model. Imagine a language model trained on general text. Fine-tuning it with legal documents would make it better at understanding contracts without starting from scratch.

Azure Machine Learning supports this with version control, letting teams compare new and old model performances and roll back changes if needed.

However, retraining requires balance. Updating too often wastes resources, while waiting too long risks outdated predictions. Azure tools like Automated ML suggest optimal retraining schedules based on data changes. For instance, a social media sentiment analysis model might retrain monthly unless a viral trend spikes engagement, triggering an urgent update.

Challenges and Strategies for Model Longevity

Keeping models relevant isn't easy. One major challenge is concept drift, where the relationship between inputs and outputs changes. For example, during a recession, traditional economic indicators might no longer predict consumer spending accurately. Detecting drift requires constant monitoring which you can do on Azure Machine Learning.

Another challenge is resource management. Retraining large models (such as deep learning systems) requires a significant amount of computational power and time. Azure's cloud scalability helps with this by spinning up additional servers during retraining and then shutting them down to reduce expenses. For smaller teams, serverless computing (like Azure Functions) automates lightweight updates without infrastructure headaches.

Of course, there are real-world and ethical issues to consider. If you update models too quickly, you may unintentionally introduce biases. For example, a hiring AI trained primarily on polished, standard resumes that overlooks people who pursued unorthodox careers. That's where tools like Fairlearn come in, working as bias detectives to uncover unfair tendencies. Meanwhile, Azure Machine Learning's governance tools preserve a full record of all tweaks and adjustments, ensuring that nothing is overlooked. By combining automation, diligent monitoring, and regular ethics check-ins, teams not only maintain models accurate and cost-effective but also keep them honest long after launch.

Summary

This chapter covered the core concepts of AI models, explaining how they are built, validated, tested, and deployed. It explored different types of models and compared the use of pretrained models with custom ones. The chapter also discussed the critical role of data in model development, highlighting the importance of data quality, labeling, and managing large datasets. The chapter also walked through how to deploy AI models to Azure, covering tools for scalability, security, and performance monitoring, and emphasized the need for continuous learning to keep models accurate and relevant over time.

Exam Essentials

Understand what AI models are and how they work.   Know that AI models are built using algorithms, data, and parameters, and learn how they are trained, validated, and tested to recognize patterns and make predictions.

Identify different types of AI models.   Understand the differences between supervised, unsupervised, and reinforcement learning models, and recognize where each type is used in real-world applications.

Compare pretrained and custom AI models.   Know the benefits and limitations of using pretrained models versus building custom models from scratch, and when each option is most appropriate.

Understand data requirements for AI models.   Learn about the types of data (structured, unstructured, semi-structured), the importance of data quality, preprocessing, labeling, and how to manage large datasets effectively.

Learn how to deploy AI models on Azure.   Understand the steps for packaging, configuring, and exposing AI models as endpoints using Azure Machine Learning, and how Azure services support secure and scalable deployment.

Recognize the importance of continuous learning and model updates.   Know why AI models must be monitored, retrained, and updated regularly to stay accurate and useful, and how Azure tools support this process.

Review Questions

1. A healthcare startup wants to quickly deploy a model to detect tumors in X-rays using limited labeled data. Which approach should they take?

   A. Build a custom model from scratch

   B. Use a pretrained image recognition model and fine-tune it

   C. Use an unsupervised learning model

   D. Use a reinforcement learning model

2. An e-commerce company needs to group customers based on shopping behavior without prior labels. What type of model should they use?

   A. Supervised learning

   B. Reinforcement learning

   C. Unsupervised learning

   D. Transfer learning

3. A bank is developing a fraud detection system and wants full transparency in how the model makes decisions. What kind of model is most appropriate?

   A. Pretrained deep learning model

   B. Custom model with interpretable algorithms

   C. Reinforcement learning model

   D. Pretrained sentiment analysis model

4. What's the best Azure service for deploying a real-time AI model that must handle spikes in user traffic?

   A. Azure Container Instances

   B. Azure Kubernetes Service (AKS)

   C. Azure DevOps

   D. Azure SQL Database

5. A data science team is testing their AI model with adversarial inputs to find hidden flaws. What phase of model development are they in?

   A. Training

   B. Validation

   C. Deployment

   D. Testing

6. Which model type is best for learning through trial and error in an environment like a video game?

   A. Supervised

   B. Unsupervised

C. Reinforcement

D. Pretrained

7. A company wants to monitor its deployed model to detect performance drops. Which Azure tool should they use?

A. Azure Blob Storage

B. Azure Key Vault

C. Azure Monitor

D. Azure Synapse

8. What technique helps avoid overfitting when training deep learning models?

A. Using small datasets

B. Dropout layers

C. Labeling more data

D. Increasing model depth

9. A model performs well during training but poorly on unseen data. What problem does this indicate?

A. Underfitting

B. Overfitting

C. Data drift

D. Model compression

10. What is the main benefit of using a model in ONNX format?

A. Real-time data labeling

B. Automatic data cleaning

C. Cross-platform compatibility

D. Advanced encryption

11. A mobile app needs a lightweight model that won't drain the battery. What technique helps achieve this?

A. k-fold cross-validation

B. Model quantization

C. Data augmentation

D. Batch processing

12. Why might a developer choose a custom model over a pretrained one?

A. They want faster deployment

B. They want general-purpose functionality

C. They need highly specialized performance

D. They have no access to labeled data

13. Which metric is most critical in a medical diagnosis model where missing positive cases is dangerous?

A. Precision

B. Recall

C. Accuracy

D. F1 score

14. A social media platform notices that user language trends have changed. What concept does this illustrate?

A. Model drift

B. Transfer learning

C. Reinforcement decay

D. Hyperparameter tuning

15. What type of data would a computer vision model most likely use?

A. Structured data

B. Semi-structured data

C. Image data

D. Tabular data

16. What challenge is addressed by using synthetic data in model training?

A. High memory consumption

B. Lack of training algorithms

C. Data scarcity or privacy concerns

D. Poor hardware optimization

17. A retail company wants to retrain its demand forecasting model weekly with new sales data. What Azure tool helps automate this?

A. Azure DevTest Labs

B. Azure Pipelines

C. Azure Maps

D. Azure Synapse

18. A team wants to test their model's ability to handle different user accents. What type of testing is this?

A. Accuracy testing

B. Performance testing

C. Edge-case testing

D. Feature engineering

19. What is the main risk of using a pretrained model trained on biased data?

    A. Higher cost

    B. Poor generalization

    C. Longer training time

    D. Inherited bias in outputs

20. A data scientist uses dropout during training. What is the goal?

    A. Increase prediction speed

    B. Prevent overfitting

    C. Improve labeling quality

    D. Adjust learning rate

Chapter

4

Introduction to Machine Learning Concepts

MICROSOFT CERTIFIED: AZURE AI FUNDAMENTALS (AI-900) EXAM OBJECTIVES COVERED IN THIS CHAPTER:

✔ **Domain 2: Describe fundamental principles of machine learning on Azure**

- Subdomain 2a: Identify common machine learning techniques

  - 2-1 Identify regression machine learning scenarios

  - 2-2 Identify classification machine learning scenarios

  - 2-3 Identify clustering machine learning scenarios

  - 2-4 Identify features of deep learning techniques

  - 2-5 Identify features of the Transformer architecture

- Subdomain 2b: Describe core machine learning concepts

  - 2-6 Identify features and labels in a dataset for machine learning

  - 2-7 Describe how training and validation datasets are used in machine learning

In modern AI, machine learning has become a core driver of innovation, enabling computers to learn from data, spot patterns, and make decisions without explicit programming. This shift powers technologies like voice assistants, fraud detection, and self-driving cars. This chapter breaks down the essentials of machine learning, starting with its definition and real-world impact across industries such as healthcare, finance, and retail. You'll then explore the three main types of machine learning: supervised learning, unsupervised learning, and reinforcement learning.

Next, you'll learn how features and labels shape models; how datasets are split into training, validation, and test sets; and why metrics like accuracy and precision matter. We'll cover practical steps like cleaning data, scaling features, and encoding categories to prepare datasets for algorithms. You'll also learn about challenges, along with how to fix those challenges. By the end, you'll have been fully introduced to core machine learning concepts.

Understanding Machine Learning

Machine learning is a subset of AI that enables computers to learn from data and improve their performance over time without being explicitly programmed. At its core, machine learning relies on algorithms that identify patterns in data, make predictions, and optimize decision-making processes. This self-learning capability allows machines to adapt to new information dynamically, mimicking human-like learning behaviors.

The significance of machine learning lies in its transformative impact across industries and daily life. It automates complex tasks, processes vast amounts of data efficiently, and delivers insights at a scale beyond human capability. For example, machine learning powers recommendation systems on platforms like Netflix, enables virtual assistants like the ones we have on our mobile phones, and drives innovations such as autonomous vehicles. As the backbone of modern AI advancements, machine learning has found applications across numerous industries:

- **Healthcare:** Machine learning helps in disease diagnosis through medical image analysis, predicts patient outcomes using predictive models, and personalizes treatment plans. For instance, algorithms can detect early signs of cancer in radiology scans or suggest tailored medication regimens.

- **Finance:** Banks use machine learning to detect fraudulent transactions by analyzing patterns in real time. It also supports algorithmic trading and credit risk assessment by processing vast datasets with precision.

- **Retail:** E-commerce websites use machine learning for personalized recommendations based on user behavior. Retailers use it to optimize inventory management and predict demand trends.

- **Transportation:** Autonomous vehicles rely on machine learning for safe navigation by processing data from sensors and cameras. Ride-sharing apps use it to optimize routes and match drivers with passengers.

- **Marketing:** Businesses use machine learning for targeted advertising by analyzing customer preferences and behaviors. It also enhances customer service through chatbots powered by natural language processing.

Types of Machine Learning

Machine learning is not a one-size-fits-all approach; its methods vary based on the type of data available and the problem being solved. This domain explores the three primary categories of machine learning: supervised learning, unsupervised learning, and reinforcement learning. Each type addresses unique challenges, from predicting outcomes with labelled data to discovering hidden patterns or training systems to make decisions through trial and error. Understanding these distinctions helps you in selecting the right approach for real-world applications.

Supervised Learning

Supervised learning is a machine learning paradigm where algorithms are trained on labeled datasets, consisting of input-output pairs. The goal is to learn a function that maps inputs to correct outputs, allowing the model to make predictions on new, unseen data. This approach is analogous to learning with a teacher, where the algorithm is guided by known correct answers during the training process. In Figure 4.1, you can see the dataflow process for supervised learning.

Key characteristics of supervised learning include the need for labeled data, the ability to handle both classification and regression tasks, and the capacity to generalize from training examples to new situations.

Among the most widely used supervised learning algorithms are Linear Regression and Decision Trees. Linear Regression models the relationship between variables by fitting a linear equation to observed data, making it useful for predicting continuous values. Decision Trees, on the other hand, create a flowchart-like structure of decisions and their possible consequences, excelling in both classification and regression tasks while providing interpretable results. Typical use cases for supervised learning are image recognition, spam filtering, predicting house prices, and medical diagnosis.

FIGURE 4.1   Data flow process for supervised learning.

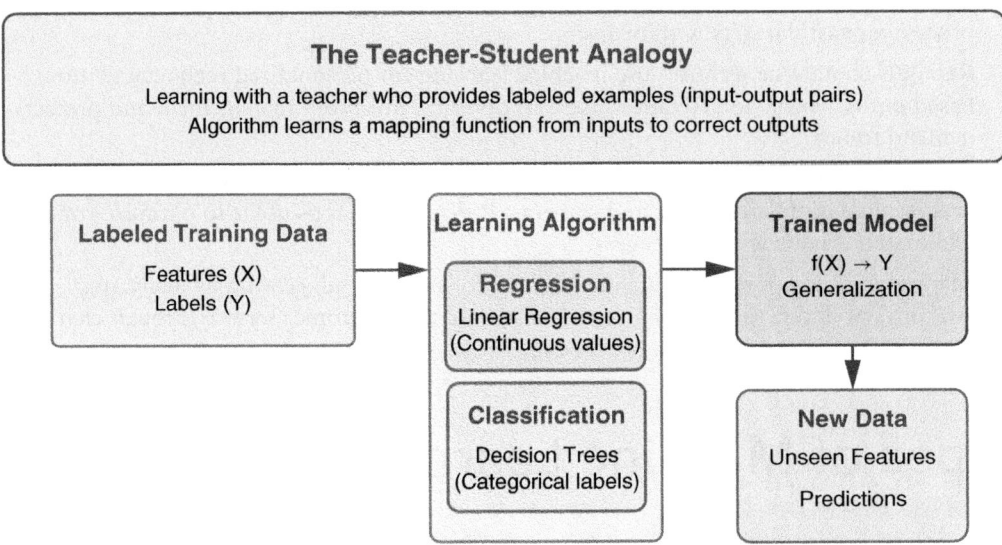

Unsupervised Learning

Unsupervised learning algorithms work with unlabeled data, aiming to discover hidden patterns or structures within the dataset without explicit guidance. This approach is particularly valuable when dealing with large volumes of unstructured data or when the desired outcomes are not known in advance. In Figure 4.2, you can see the dataflow process for unsupervised learning.

The primary characteristics of unsupervised learning include its ability to find patterns and relationships in data, reduce data dimensionality, and group similar data points together. Common applications include market segmentation, anomaly detection, and feature learning for subsequent supervised tasks.

Two prominent unsupervised learning techniques are K-Means Clustering and Principal Component Analysis (PCA). K-Means Clustering partitions data into K distinct, nonoverlapping subgroups or clusters based on similarity, making it useful for customer segmentation or image compression. PCA, a dimensionality reduction technique, transforms high-dimensional data into a lower-dimensional space while preserving as much variance as possible, facilitating data visualization and noise reduction in complex datasets.

Reinforcement Learning

Reinforcement learning is a paradigm where an agent learns to make decisions by interacting with an environment. Unlike supervised or unsupervised learning, reinforcement learning focuses on finding optimal actions to maximize cumulative rewards over time, often in dynamic and uncertain environments.

FIGURE 4.2   Data flow process for unsupervised learning.

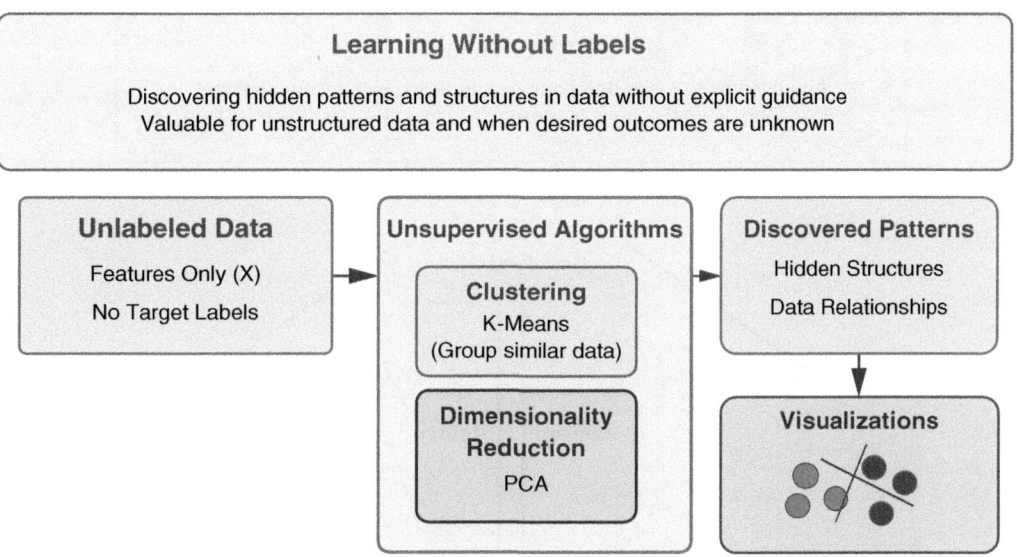

The core concepts in reinforcement learning include agents (decision-makers), actions (choices available to the agent), states (representations of the environment), and rewards (feedback signals). The agent's goal is to learn a policy (a strategy for choosing actions) that maximizes the expected cumulative reward. This learning process involves a balance between exploration (trying new actions) and exploitation (leveraging known good actions). The flow and process is shown in Figure 4.3.

An example of reinforcement learning is teaching a self-driving car to navigate city streets. The car's AI acts like a learning driver, starting with no prior experience. At first, it might brake too abruptly at stop signs, hesitate at intersections, or misjudge gaps in traffic. But every action it takes (steering, accelerating, changing lanes) generates feedback. For instance, staying centered in a lane or smoothly yielding to pedestrians earns positive rewards, while swerving, missing a turn, or getting too close to another car results in penalties. Over countless simulated drives, the AI gradually learns which behaviors lead to the safest, most efficient outcomes.

As training progresses, the car begins to anticipate challenges, like merging onto a busy highway or navigating a construction zone. It learns to balance cautious decision-making (e.g., slowing down in heavy rain) with assertive actions (e.g., seizing a safe gap to change lanes). Companies use this approach because roads are unpredictable: no two scenarios are identical, and rigid programming can't account for every possibility. Reinforcement learning lets the car adapt in real time, refining its strategy through continuous interaction with the environment, much like a human driver gains experience over years behind the wheel. However, the effectiveness of reinforcement learning varies significantly across different driving conditions and cultural contexts. A model trained in Manhattan's aggressive, grid-based traffic patterns may struggle in small-town USA where drivers are more courteous and roads are less structured. Similarly, the transition from right-hand driving in Paris to

FIGURE 4.3 Data flow process for reinforcement learning.

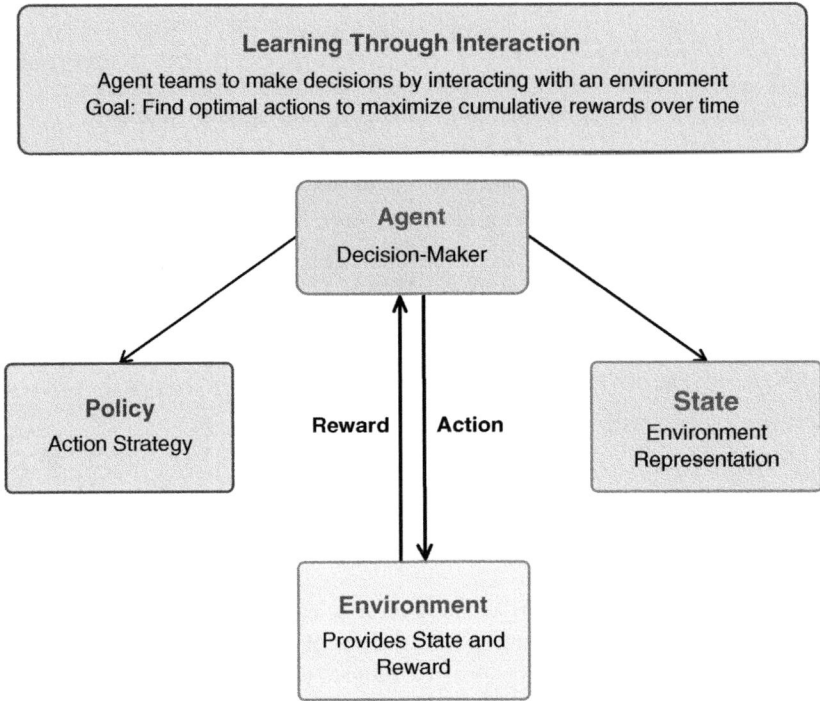

left-hand driving in Sydney, Australia introduces fundamental differences that go beyond simple rule changes. Driver temperament, road layouts, and cultural driving norms all impact how effectively the AI can apply its learned behaviors to new environments.

Core Concepts in Machine Learning

At the heart of every machine learning project lies a set of foundational principles that govern how models learn, generalize, and perform. This domain explores three pillars critical to building effective ML systems: features and labels, which define the structure of data; datasets, which determine how models are trained and validated; and evaluation metrics, which quantify success. In this section, we will cover them in detail.

Features and Labels

Features and labels are critical components of machine learning datasets. Features are the input variables or attributes that describe the data, while labels represent the target outputs or predictions the model aims to generate. They serve as the foundation for supervised learning model training. Depending on the type of dataset, features may be categorical (e.g., gender, product category) or numerical (e.g., age, income). Because redundant or unnecessary features can introduce noise and decrease accuracy, choosing pertinent features is essential for model performance. To improve the quality of preprocessed data, feature engineering techniques including scaling, encoding, and normalization are frequently used.

In supervised learning tasks, where the objective is to forecast results based on input features, labels are usually used. For instance, in a credit scoring system, features might include an individual's income, employment history, and credit utilization. At the same time, the label would indicate whether the person is a "creditworthy" or "non-creditworthy" borrower. Developing predictive models that effectively generalize to new data requires an understanding of the connection between characteristics and labels.

Datasets

Datasets are essential to machine learning workflows because they include the data required to train, validate, and test models. The training set, validation set, and test set are the three subsets that make up a typical dataset. In the process of developing a model, each subset has a specific function. To continue the previous example of self-driving vehicles, specific training datasets would be required for different environments and conditions. A vehicle trained primarily on data from sunny California highways would need additional datasets covering snowy Canadian winters, the narrow cobblestone streets of European cities, or the driving patterns of rural communities where wildlife crossings are common. Similarly, datasets would need to reflect different cultural driving behaviors such as the unique driving styles in Lagos versus the more courteous driving styles found in other Nigerian states. This means that deploying AI systems globally often requires collecting and training on region-specific datasets to ensure the model can handle local conditions, weather patterns, traffic laws, and cultural norms effectively.

The model is trained by exposing it to instances that have both features and labels in the training set. This subset allows the model to discover patterns and relationships in the data. Larger datasets typically result in higher generalization, and model performance is usually influenced by the size of the training set.

The validation set is used during model tuning to assess how well the model performs on unseen data. Simultaneously, they serve as a critical tool for hyperparameter optimization. For instance, parameters like regularization strength and learning rates are adjusted based on validation performance, and this ensures that the model balances complexity with generalizability, sharp enough to capture trends but flexible enough to avoid memorizing noise.

The test set evaluates the model's performance after training is complete. Unlike the validation set, which guides adjustments during development, the test set provides an unbiased assessment of how well the model generalizes to completely new data. Metrics calculated on test sets indicate whether a model is ready for deployment in real-world scenarios.

Model Evaluation Metrics

Solid metrics that measure machine learning models' performance in terms of accuracy, dependability, and task relevance are necessary for evaluation. Precision, recall, accuracy, and the F1 score are common evaluation measures that provide distinct insights into the behavior of the model.

Accuracy refers to the percentage of correct predictions made by a model. Although it gives an overall impression of performance, it might not be the best option for datasets that are unbalanced and dominated by one class; in these situations, accuracy can be deceptive.

The precision of a model is determined by the proportion of its positive predictions that come true. It is especially helpful in situations where false positives have serious repercussions, like when diagnosing illnesses or spotting fraud.

Recall, also known as sensitivity or true positive rate, measures how well a model identifies all actual positive instances in a dataset. It is important in cases where missing positive examples (false negatives) could lead to critical errors, for instance, failing to detect cancer in medical imaging.

The F1 Score computes the harmonic mean of precision and recall to combine them into a single statistic. When both false positives and false negatives must be taken into account, the result is a fair assessment. For unbalanced datasets, where maximizing just one metric might not be enough, this metric is quite useful.

Data Preparation and Feature Engineering

Raw data is rarely ready for machine learning straight out of the box. Before models can learn, data must be cleaned, transformed, and structured into a format algorithms can digest. This section covers the critical steps of data cleaning, feature scaling, and encoding categorical variables, processes that turn messy, real-world data into a refined fuel for powerful models. Skipping these steps risks garbage-in-garbage-out outcomes, no matter how advanced the algorithm.

Data Cleaning Techniques

Data cleaning is the first, and often most time-consuming, step in any machine learning project. One of the biggest headaches is dealing with missing data. You've got a few options here: you can either drop the rows with missing values (if you've got plenty of data to spare), or you can get creative with imputation techniques. Imputation is fancy talk for filling in the blanks, and you can do this using mean values, median values, or even predictive models.

But it's not just about missing data. You've also got to keep an eye out for duplicates. These sneaky doubles can skew your analysis if you're not careful. Most data scientists worth their salt will use tools like pandas in Python to spot and zap these duplicates.

There are also outliers, those data points that are way out in left field. Sometimes they're legit, sometimes they're errors, but you always need to investigate.

Data validation is the final piece when cleaning data. This is where you make sure your data makes sense in the real world. Are there any impossible values, like negative ages or future dates? Have all your categorical variables been entered consistently? It's a tedious process, but it's important for ensuring your model isn't learning from garbage data.

Feature Scaling and Normalization

Feature scaling and normalization are vital techniques used to standardize the range and distribution of your data. Imagine a dataset with "annual income" (ranging from 20k *to* 200k) and "age" (18–80). Algorithms like SVM or K-Nearest Neighbors interpret larger ranges as more significant, unfairly weighting income over age. Scaling fixes this by bringing all features to a common range.

Two key methods to scale features are *standardization* and *min-max scaling*. Standardization adjusts your data so that the average value is 0 and most numbers fall between –1 and 1. This works well for algorithms that assume data is "balanced" around a center (like linear regression). Min-max scaling, on the other hand, squishes all values into a 0–1 range. This is handy for things like image data, where pixel brightness needs to stay within strict limits. Think of it like resizing a photo to fit a frame; it keeps proportions intact but makes everything fit neatly.

Picking a method depends on your data and the algorithm. Standardization handles messy, spread-out data better (like income levels where a few billionaires skew the numbers). Min-max scaling is simpler for bounded data (like ratings from 1 to 5). If you're using algorithms that care about distances between points (like k-nearest neighbors), standardization often works better. For neural networks, min-max scaling keeps inputs predictable. Always try both. Sometimes the difference is small, but it can make or break your model's performance.

Encoding Categorical Variables

Machine learning algorithms thrive on numbers, not text. Categorical variables, like "color" (red/blue/green) or "education level" (secondary school/university), must be converted into numerical formats. The simplest method is *label encoding*, which assigns integers (e.g., red = 1, blue = 2). However, this implies ordinal relationships (blue > red), which can mislead algorithms.

For non-ordinal categories (e.g., cities or product types), *one-hot encoding* is safer. It creates binary columns for each category: a "color red" column (1 if true, 0 otherwise), "color blue," and so on. While effective, this blows up dimensionality in datasets with many categories like ZIP code, leading to sparse matrices. Alternatives like *target encoding* replace categories with the mean of the target variable, but risk overfitting if not regularized.

Choosing the right encoding depends on context. In a fraud detection model, one-hot encoding might capture nuanced patterns in transaction types, while target encoding could leak future information if not carefully implemented. Like scaling, encoding is a balancing act which means that preserving information without introducing noise or computational bloat is very important.

Training and Evaluating ML Models

Beyond picking the correct algorithm, building a machine learning model is also about how you train, validate, and refine it. Some strategies and methods turn raw models into reliable tools, and that's what this section will cover. These methods ensure that models learn meaningful patterns without memorizing noise, validate reliably across diverse scenarios, and reach their full potential through optimization. Let's break down the critical components of this process.

Data Splitting Strategies

Before training begins, data is split into three subsets: training, validation, and test sets. The training set (usually 60–80% of data) is where the model learns patterns, adjusting its parameters to minimize errors. The validation set (10–20%) is used to tweak settings like model complexity or learning speed without peeking at the test data. The test set (10–20%) is reserved to evaluate performance on completely unseen examples.

Why split this way? Without a validation set, you risk overfitting by tuning hyperparameters to the test set, which inflates scores unrealistically. For example, in a spam filter model, if the test set isn't isolated, you might accidentally optimize for specific spam examples, making the model brittle in real-world use. Stratified splitting ensures that each subset reflects the data's class distribution, for example, keeping the same ratio of spam to non-spam emails in all splits.

Cross-Validation Techniques

When data is scarce, cross-validation maximizes its utility. Instead of a single train-validation split, cross-validation rotates subsets of the data. The most common method, k-fold cross-validation, divides the training data into k equal parts (folds). The model trains on k-1 folds and validates on the remaining fold, repeating this k times. Performance is averaged across all runs, giving a more reliable estimate of generalizability. For imbalanced datasets like rare diseases in medical data, stratified k-fold cross-validation maintains class ratios in each fold. This prevents scenarios where a fold might lack critical minority-class examples.

In addition to k-fold cross-validation, other methods like leave-one-out and stratified cross-validation are used depending on the dataset size and class distribution. Cross-validation isn't free. It's computationally heavy, as training repeats multiple times. But for small datasets or models sensitive to randomness, it's worth the cost to avoid skewed results.

Hyperparameter Tuning

Grid search tests every combination of hyperparameters in a predefined range. It's thorough but slow. Imagine testing 10 learning rates and 5 tree depths, requiring 50 training runs.

Random search samples hyperparameters randomly, and it often finds good combinations faster than grid search. For complex models (e.g., deep learning), Bayesian optimization uses past results to guide smarter searches and prioritizes settings likely to improve performance. Tools like AutoML automate this process, but domain knowledge still matters. For example, a high learning rate might overshoot optimal weights in gradient descent, while too low a rate wastes compute time.

Balancing exploration (testing new settings) and exploitation (refining known good ones) is key. Over-tuning can lead to "optimization theater," tiny accuracy gains that don't translate to real-world use. Always validate tuned models on a fresh test set to ensure improvements aren't illusory.

Overfitting and Underfitting

Machine learning models deal with these two challenges: overfitting, where it memorizes noise instead of learning patterns, and underfitting, where it's too simplistic to capture meaningful trends. Striking the right balance is important when trying to build models that perform well on both training data and real-world challenges. This section unpacks the causes, consequences, and fixes for these fundamental issues.

Bias-Variance Tradeoff

The bias-variance tradeoff is the tug-of-war between simplicity and flexibility. Bias refers to errors from overly simplistic assumptions. High-bias models underfit, failing to capture nuances. Variance is sensitivity to noise in the training data. Overly complex models chase every outlier, overfitting. The goal is a middle ground: a model complex enough to learn patterns but simple enough to generalize.

A model that predicts home prices, for instance, may be underfit if it solely takes square footage into account (high bias) but overfit if it also takes into account unimportant factors like the color of the wall paint (high variance). Model complexity must be adjusted to strike a balance: complicated models (neural nets) run the risk of having large variance, whereas simpler models (linear regression) have more bias but lower variance. Methods such as cross-validation (previously discussed) aid in the problem's diagnosis: A big difference between the training and validation errors indicates overfitting, while a high training error indicates underfitting.

Techniques to Prevent Overfitting

Overfitting happens when models "memorize" training data, performing well on paper but poorly in real-world scenarios. Regularization, pruning, and dropout are three methods that practitioners can combine to drastically reduce overfitting and create models that perform better on unknown data.

Regularization, which imposes a penalty for model complexity, is a useful strategy to address this problem. By limiting the model's coefficients, regularization strategies like L1 and L2 penalties lessen the model's propensity to capture noise.

Pruning is an additional strategy that works particularly well with decision trees and neural networks. Pruning is the process of simplifying a model without substantially sacrificing its accuracy by eliminating components that don't add much to its prediction ability. This technique aids in concentrating the model on the most pertinent data patterns and attributes.

A common neural network technique is dropout, which is randomly turning off a portion of the neurons as they are being trained. This encourages a more universal learning process by keeping the model from being unduly reliant on any one component of its network.

Addressing Underfitting

Underfitting is the opposite problem: models are too basic to learn meaningful patterns. Performance on the training and test datasets suffers as a result. Increasing the model's complexity is a popular tactic to deal with underfitting. To enable more complex data representations, this may entail expanding the number of layers in a neural network, selecting a more complex model, or adding more features.

It is important to exercise caution when increasing model complexity since improper management could result in overfitting. To be sure that the added complexity actually enhances learning and does not just capture noise, it is crucial to test and validate the model's performance iteratively. In this iterative process, tools such as cross-validation can be especially helpful in confirming that the improvements result in improved generalization.

Enhancing the caliber and volume of training data is an additional strategy to combat underfitting. The model can learn deeper patterns from more varied and extensive information, which lowers the possibility of oversimplification. Practitioners can successfully overcome underfitting and create models that more accurately reflect the complexities of the problem space by fusing advances in model complexity with improved data quality.

Common Machine Learning Algorithms

Machine learning thrives on its toolbox of algorithms, each designed to tackle specific types of problems, from predicting numbers to grouping similar data points. This section explores three core categories: regression, classification, and clustering. Understanding these algorithms' strengths and quirks helps you match the right tool to the job.

Regression Algorithms

The fundamental instruments for forecasting continuous outcomes are regression algorithms. One of the most basic types, linear regression, simulates the connection between a continuous dependent variable and one or more independent variables. It accomplishes this by fitting observed data to a linear equation, which makes it a helpful place to start for a variety of predicting tasks.

Despite having a similar name, logistic regression is intended for situations involving binary categorization. Logistic regression calculates the likelihood that a given input belongs to a specific class rather than forecasting a continuous value. This method is especially useful for scenarios where outcomes are discrete, like yes/no choices, because it uses a logistic function to convert the result of linear regression.

Because of their ease of use, interpretability, and effectiveness in solving a variety of issues, both logistic and linear regression are highly regarded. They are a typical first step in many machine learning projects because of their simple implementation and underlying assumptions. These algorithms act as a standard for more intricate models in addition to providing rapid insights into data trends.

Classification Algorithms

The purpose of classification algorithms is to categorize inputs into distinct groups. Decision trees offer a straightforward, user-friendly model that divides the data according to feature values, forming a structure resembling a tree with each branch signifying a potential course of action. They are widely used for both exploratory research and final model deployment due to their visual nature and ease of interpretation.

Random forests extend decision trees by generating an ensemble of trees, each trained on a different part of the dataset. This ensemble method boosts model robustness, enhances prediction accuracy, and lowers the chance of overfitting. Random forests are more reliable than a single decision tree at handling complex datasets because they aggregate the predictions of numerous trees.

Support Vector Machines (SVMs) offer another perspective on classification by finding the optimal boundary that separates classes in the feature space. SVMs are particularly effective when there is a distinct margin of separation between classes and in high-dimensional spaces. Their usefulness to a variety of classification problems is further expanded by their capacity to manage nonlinear interactions through kernel functions.

Clustering Algorithms

Clustering algorithms are used to identify natural groupings in data without predefined labels. One of the most often used clustering algorithms, K-Means divides data into a predetermined number of clusters by reducing the variation within each group. Cluster centroids are recalculated and data points are assigned to clusters iteratively until convergence. K-means is computationally efficient but requires specifying the number of clusters in advance.

Using a different strategy, hierarchical clustering creates a structure of nested clusters that resembles a tree. Both top-down (divisive) and bottom-up (agglomerative) approaches can be used for this. The generated dendrogram offers insights into the hierarchical structure of the data and gives freedom in selecting the number of groups.

Hierarchical clustering and K-means each have advantages and disadvantages. While hierarchical clustering can capture more complicated structures and does not require prespecifying the number of clusters, K-means is quicker and more effective for globular clusters. For big datasets, hierarchical clustering can be computationally demanding. The particulars of the data and the analysis's objectives frequently determine which option is best.

Summary

This chapter covered the fundamentals of machine learning by explaining how computers can learn from data without being explicitly programmed. It introduced the main types of machine learning, which are supervised, unsupervised, and reinforcement learning, and explained when each is used. The chapter explored the roles of features and labels; how datasets are divided into training, validation, and test sets; and how metrics like precision and recall help evaluate model performance. It also covered key data preparation steps such as cleaning, scaling, and encoding, along with strategies for training models effectively, tuning hyperparameters, and addressing overfitting or underfitting. Finally, it examined common algorithms used in regression, classification, and clustering, providing a solid foundation for understanding core machine learning systems.

Exam Essentials

Understand what machine learning is. Know how machine learning enables computers to learn from data and improve performance without being explicitly programmed.

Identify the three main types of machine learning. Be able to distinguish between supervised, unsupervised, and reinforcement learning, including how each type works and where it applies.

Recognize core components of machine learning systems. Understand the roles of features, labels, datasets (training, validation, and test sets), and evaluation metrics like accuracy, precision, recall, and F1 score.

Learn essential data preparation techniques. Know how data is cleaned, scaled, and encoded before training a model, and why these steps are critical for building effective systems.

Understand model training and evaluation strategies. Be familiar with data splitting, cross-validation, hyperparameter tuning, and methods for preventing overfitting or underfitting.

Know common machine learning algorithms. Recognize how linear regression, logistic regression, decision trees, random forests, support vector machines, and clustering algorithms like K-means and hierarchical clustering are used in different scenarios.

Review Questions

1. A hospital wants to predict whether a patient will be readmitted within 30 days after discharge using patient records. Which type of machine learning should be used?

   A. Unsupervised learning

   B. Reinforcement learning

   C. Supervised learning

   D. Clustering

2. A marketing team wants to group customers by purchasing behavior to personalize promotions but has no labeled data. Which machine learning technique should they use?

   A. Clustering

   B. Regression

   C. Reinforcement learning

   D. Supervised learning

3. Which dataset split is best used to test final model performance before deployment?

   A. Training set

   B. Cross-validation set

   C. Validation set

   D. Test set

4. An e-commerce company uses a model to recommend products. They observe that it's giving inaccurate recommendations due to duplicate user data. Which preprocessing step would help?

   A. Encoding categorical data

   B. Feature scaling

   C. Data cleaning

   D. Data validation

5. A model correctly identifies 90 out of 100 actual fraud cases, but also flags 50 non-fraud transactions as fraud. What metric would best highlight this problem?

   A. Recall

   B. Accuracy

   C. Precision

   D. F1 Score

6. Which algorithm is best suited to predict house prices based on features like size, location, and age?

    A. Linear Regression

    B. Logistic Regression

    C. K-Means Clustering

    D. Decision Tree (Classification)

7. An autonomous drone learns to fly through a forest by trial and error, improving after each flight. What learning type is this?

    A. Reinforcement learning

    B. Supervised learning

    C. Clustering

    D. Regression

8. Why is standardization useful before using K-Nearest Neighbors (KNN)?

    A. It ensures all features contribute equally

    B. It encodes text

    C. It reduces model complexity

    D. It improves image brightness

9. A team is optimizing a model's learning rate and regularization strength. What process are they using?

    A. Cross-validation

    B. Label encoding

    C. Hyperparameter tuning

    D. Feature engineering

10. In one-hot encoding, what happens to a categorical feature with four unique values?

    A. It is replaced with a number from 1 to 4

    B. It is converted to four binary columns

    C. It is ignored

    D. It is assigned one new column

11. Which evaluation metric is best for a medical diagnosis model where missing a positive case is critical?

    A. Precision

    B. Recall

    C. R-squared

    D. Accuracy

12. A bank wants to assess customer credit risk by predicting default based on past repayment history. What ML type is this?

A. Dimensionality reduction

B. Supervised learning

C. Reinforcement learning

D. Clustering

13. Which process helps ensure that the model does not memorize the training data but generalizes well?

A. Dropout

B. Scaling

C. Encoding

D. Labeling

14. What does high variance in a model usually indicate?

A. Underfitting

B. High accuracy

C. Overfitting

D. Balanced bias

15. Why is stratified splitting useful in classification problems?

A. It removes noisy features

B. It ensures balanced class distribution

C. It increases training speed

D. It reduces dimensionality

16. Which technique reduces the number of features while keeping most of the data's variance?

A. Logistic Regression

B. Principal Component Analysis (PCA)

C. Label encoding

D. One-hot encoding

17. What is the role of the validation set in machine learning?

A. To evaluate final model performance

B. To tune model settings

C. To increase dataset size

D. To perform classification

18. Which evaluation metric is most appropriate when classes are imbalanced and both precision and recall are important?

A. Accuracy

B. Precision

C. Recall

D. F1 Score

19. Which technique randomly disables some neurons during training to avoid over-reliance on specific features?

A. Label smoothing

B. Dropout

C. Pruning

D. Cross-validation

20. Why might a model trained with min-max scaling perform poorly when deployed on data outside the 0–1 range?

A. It encodes incorrectly

B. It overfits

C. It assumes fixed feature range

D. It skips feature selection

Chapter

5

Machine Learning in Azure

MICROSOFT CERTIFIED: AZURE AI FUNDAMENTALS (AI-900) EXAM OBJECTIVES COVERED IN THIS CHAPTER:

✔ **Domain 2: Describe fundamental principles of machine learning on Azure**

- Subdomain 2c: Describe Azure Machine Learning capabilities

    - 2-8 Describe capabilities of automated machine learning

    - 2-9 Describe data and compute services for data science and machine learning

    - 2-10 Describe model management and deployment capabilities in Azure Machine Learning

Machine learning has become a core part of modern application development and data-driven decision-making. In the Azure ecosystem, machine learning capabilities are delivered through a comprehensive, enterprise-grade platform called Azure Machine Learning (Azure ML). This chapter exposes you to Azure's tools, services, and workflows for creating, training, deploying, versioning, and managing machine learning models.

Azure has scalable compute, smooth data integration, and reliable model lifecycle management, regardless of the complexity of the task you're working on, from a simple classification task to the development of a complex deep learning pipeline. You'll discover how to use Azure MLStudio for visual workflows, how AutoML speeds up experimentation, and how Azure's MLOps standards provide stability and governance for machine learning projects. The chapter also discusses how deep learning fits into the larger Azure ML ecosystem.

By the end of this chapter, you'll understand how Azure supports the full machine learning lifecycle from data ingestion to model monitoring in production.

Azure Machine Learning Service

Azure Machine Learning is a cloud-based platform that provides everything you need for creating, training, deploying, and managing machine learning models. Its goal is to make the machine learning process easier and more scalable, particularly in enterprise environments where collaboration, security, and automation are critical. It covers a wide range of use cases, from simple classification tasks to more complicated deep learning scenarios, with an integrated suite of tools that are suitable for both code-first and low-code users.

One of the most significant advantages of adopting Azure Machine Learning is that it removes the need to manage your own infrastructure. You can concentrate on enhancing model performance rather than configuring and managing servers thanks to the service's on-demand compute resources, version control for datasets and models, and simplified deployment choices. Everything from data preparation to model monitoring can be done in one place, which reduces overhead and allows teams to work faster.

Beyond convenience, Azure ML provides enterprise-grade reliability. It has security, compliance, and governance features, which are critical for businesses such as finance, healthcare, and government. It also simplifies tracking model lineage, controlling asset access, and monitoring deployed models over time, bringing machine learning methods in line with larger technology and business standards.

Understanding Azure Fundamentals for Machine Learning

Before creating your Azure ML workspace, it's helpful to understand a few key Azure concepts that form the foundation of how resources are organized and managed in Microsoft's cloud platform:

Azure Subscription serves as your billing and administrative boundary. Think of it as your account with Microsoft Azure. All resources you create will be associated with a subscription, and this is where costs are tracked and managed.

Resource Groups act like folders that help you organize related Azure services together. When you create a Machine Learning workspace, you'll also need supporting services like storage and security components. Grouping these together makes them easier to manage, monitor, and delete as a unit when no longer needed.

Storage Account provides the cloud storage where your datasets, model files, and experiment outputs will be stored. Azure Machine Learning requires this to persist your work and share data between different parts of your ML pipeline.

Key Vault is Azure's secure storage service for sensitive information like passwords, API keys, and certificates. It ensures that credentials needed by your ML models are stored safely and can be accessed securely by authorized applications.

Application Insights monitors your deployed models and applications, providing performance metrics and diagnostic information. This becomes crucial when you have ML models running in production and need to track their health and usage.

These components work together to create a secure, organized environment for your machine learning projects. As shown in Figure 5.1, Azure automatically suggests names for these supporting services when you create a new workspace, but you can customize them based on your organization's naming conventions.

Key Components of Azure ML

To understand how Azure ML works, it's helpful to look at some of its core components.

First is the *workspace.* This acts as a centralized environment for managing everything in your machine learning project. It keeps track of your datasets, models, compute resources, and even your training experiments. Think of it as the main dashboard where your entire ML lifecycle is organized and accessible to your team, with fine-grained access controls that allow you to manage what each team member can do. For example, you might give a data scientist permission to train and experiment with models but restrict their ability to deploy those models into production environments. Similarly, a developer might have

FIGURE 5.1   Creating an Azure Machine Learning workspace.

Home > Azure Machine Learning >

Azure Machine Learning ...
Create a machine learning workspace

| Basics | Inbound Access | Outbound Access | Encryption | Identity | Tags | Review + create |

Resource details

Every workspace must be assigned to an Azure subscription, which is where billing happens. You use resource groups like folders to organize and manage resources, including the workspace you're about to create.
Learn more about Azure resource groups ☐'

Subscription * ⓘ	Azure subscription 1 ⌄
Resource group * ⓘ	(New) adora-test-rg ⌄
	Create new

Workspace details

Configure your basic workspace settings like its storage connection, authentication, container, and more. Learn more ☐'

Name * ⓘ	adora-test-ml-workspace ✓
Region * ⓘ	East US ⌄
Storage account * ⓘ	(new) adoratestmlwor9345300820 ⌄
	Create new
Key vault * ⓘ	(new) adoratestmlwor1514055304 ⌄
	Create new
Application insights * ⓘ	(new) adoratestmlwor4877695860 ⌄
	Create new
Container registry ⓘ	None ⌄
	Create new

| Review + create | | < Previous | Next : Inbound Access |

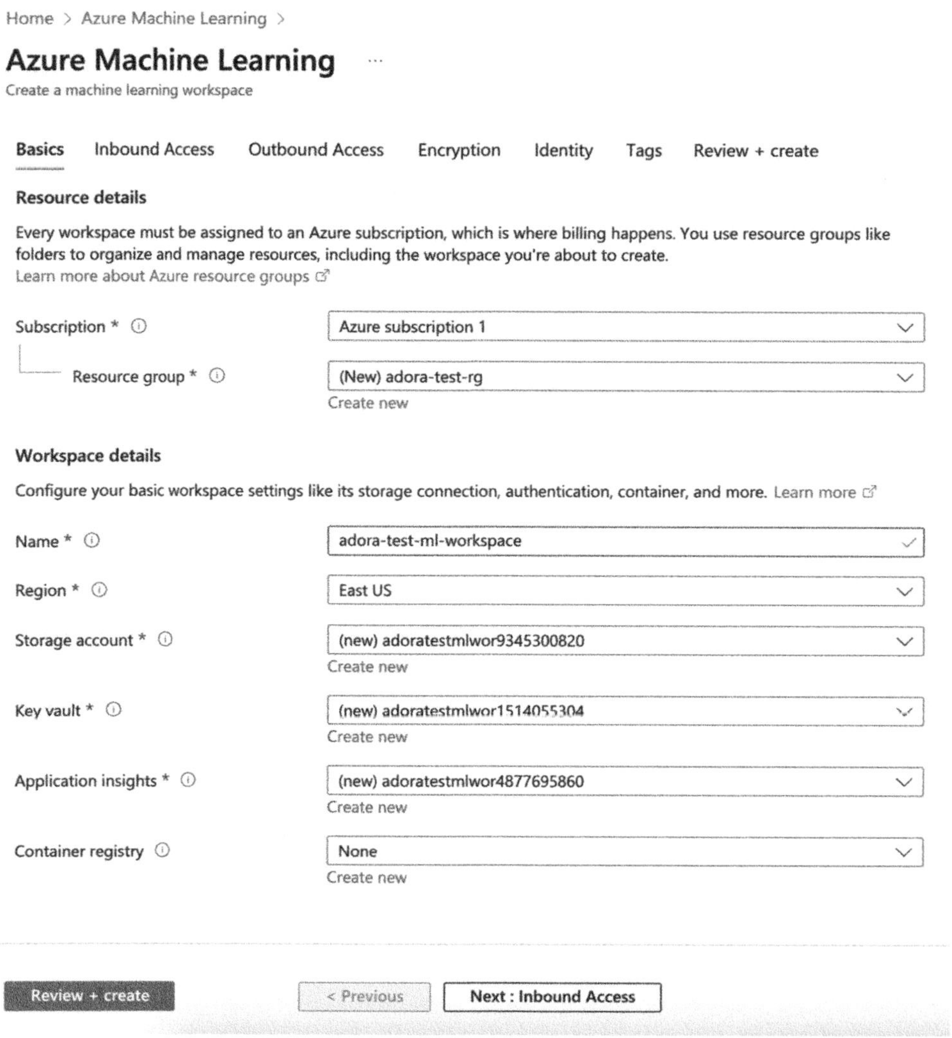

access to view and use existing models but not permission to modify training datasets or delete experiments. Azure Machine Learning integrates with Azure's role-based access control (RBAC) system, allowing administrators to create custom roles that align with their organization's security policies and workflow requirements.

To create an Azure Machine Learning workspace, you can use the Azure portal, as shown in Figure 5.1. The portal guides you through a step-by-step process where you select your subscription, create or choose an existing resource group, and specify a unique workspace name along with the appropriate region and storage settings. Once your workspace is created, you will be able to navigate to Azure MLStudio.

FIGURE 5.2   Managing experiments through the Azure Machine Learning Studio.

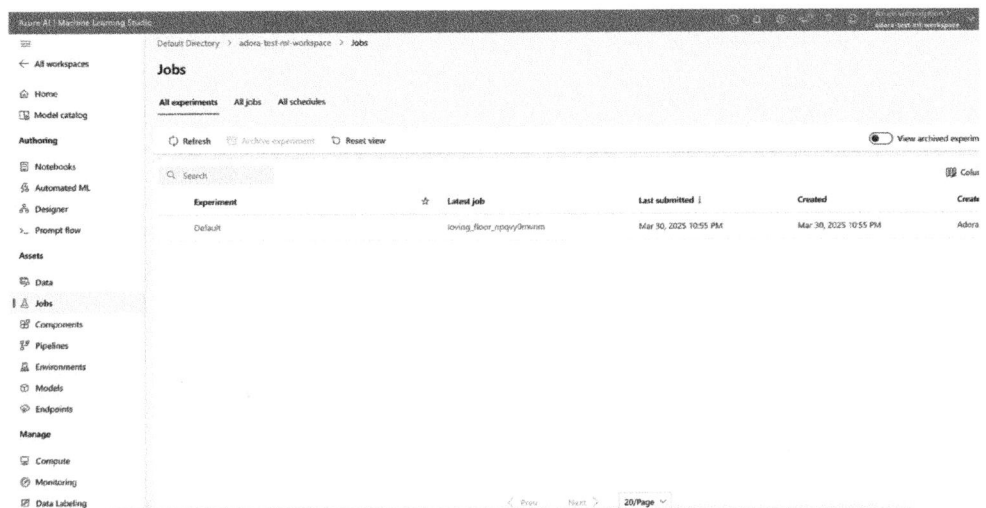

Within a workspace, *experiments* represent individual trials or runs. For instance, if you're testing different algorithms to predict customer churn, each test (e.g., logistic regression vs. random forest) becomes a separate experiment, complete with performance metrics for easy comparison. As shown in Figure 5.2, you can manage all your experiments in the jobs tab of Azure ML Studio.

Pipelines are used to automate and scale the machine learning process. They allow you to break down complex workflows into separate, reusable steps, such as data preprocessing, training, model evaluation, and deployment. Once defined, a pipeline can be run as often as needed, with different inputs or configurations, which is useful for retraining models as new data arrives. Pipelines also support scheduling and integration with version control systems, helping teams build reliable and repeatable ML systems. There are classic prebuilt and custom pipelines as shown in Figure 5.3, offering a range of ready-made templates for tasks like image classification, regression, and recommendation systems. These templates serve as a quick starting point, letting you customize each step (data ingestion, preprocessing, training, and evaluation) without building everything from scratch. Alternatively, you can opt to design a custom pipeline from a blank canvas so that you can tailor each component to match specific project requirements.

Azure ML and the Machine Learning Lifecycle

Azure ML is designed to handle every phase of the machine learning lifecycle, from initial data collection to model deployment and monitoring. The process often starts with data preparation, which can involve cleaning and transforming raw data using Azure tools like Data Factory, Synapse Analytics, or directly within the workspace using Jupyter notebooks and the SDK. Azure supports structured and unstructured data, and you can store and access it through Blob Storage or Data Lake, depending on your scale and performance needs.

FIGURE 5.3   Azure Machine Learning Studio (pipelines view).

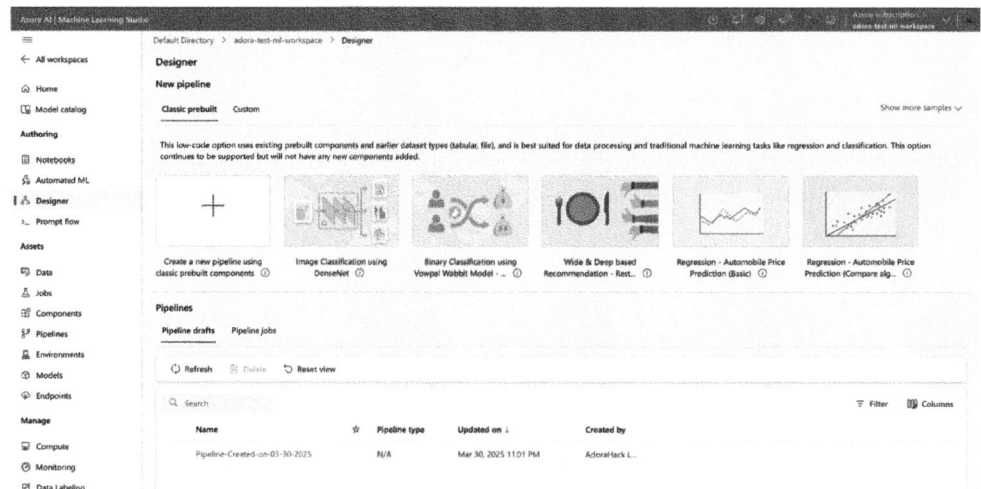

The introduction of Microsoft Fabric has created new opportunities for direct integration with Azure ML. Microsoft Fabric has an analytics platform with OneLake serving as a centralized data lake. Azure ML can directly connect to Fabric's OneLake through the OneLake datastore feature, allowing data scientists to access data stored in Microsoft Fabric lakehouses without requiring data movement or complex workarounds. This native integration means organizations can use Fabric for data engineering and preparation workflows, then use Azure ML's specialized machine learning capabilities for model development, training, and deployment while maintaining a single source of truth for their data.

Once the data is ready, Azure has flexible training options. You can use custom Python scripts, notebooks, or even drag-and-drop tools with the Designer feature. For teams that want quick results, Azure's Automated Machine Learning (AutoML) can test multiple algorithms and hyperparameter settings for you. During training, you can choose from different compute targets (including CPU and GPU clusters) to optimize for speed and cost. Azure also logs metrics like accuracy, loss, and run time, which helps you compare models effectively.

After training, models can be registered, versioned, and deployed using the same workspace. Azure makes it easy to expose models as REST APIs or schedule them for batch scoring. You can deploy models to Azure Kubernetes Service (AKS) for real-time production scenarios or to Azure Container Instances (ACI) for lightweight testing. After deployment, Azure continues to support your model's lifecycle by offering monitoring for drift and performance, along with retraining workflows. These tools are essential for keeping your models accurate and relevant as data evolves over time.

Capabilities of Azure AutoML

AutoML in Azure is essentially a system that automates many of the steps required to build and train a machine learning model. Instead of having to know which algorithm is best for a given problem, how to preprocess the data correctly, or how to tune dozens of parameters, AutoML helps simplify all of this. You provide the data, define the target you're trying to predict or classify, and set a few configuration options, and Azure handles the rest.

The primary purpose of AutoML is to make machine learning more accessible. This is particularly useful for developers, business analysts, and domain specialists who do not have a data science background but wish to build predictive models. It reduces barriers such as the need to grasp the mathematical distinctions between a decision tree and a random forest, as well as manually partitioning the dataset into training and validation sets. AutoML's built-in intelligence helps guide the system toward the most effective model with the least amount of user input.

One of the biggest advantages of AutoML is consistency and repeatability. Since the system follows a structured approach, the results are more standardized and easier to reproduce, especially when working in teams. It also provides full transparency. Even though the process is automated, Azure lets you review every step AutoML takes: the algorithms it tested, the training metrics, and why a particular model performed best. So while it feels automated, it doesn't operate like a black box.

In production environments, AutoML saves time. Instead of spending hours or even days manually experimenting with model setups, AutoML can perform dozens or hundreds of iterations in parallel. This is useful when business teams require quick insights from their data. Even before choosing to enlist a complete data science team, businesses can use AutoML to create proof-of-concept models considerably more quickly and begin providing value sooner.

Using Azure AutoML to Train and Evaluate Models

Using AutoML in Azure begins by deciding how you want to communicate with the service. Azure has two primary interfaces for working with AutoML: the Azure ML Studio UI and the Azure ML SDK, which allows you to work programmatically in a programming environment.

The process begins with selecting a dataset. You can upload data to your Azure Machine Learning workspace or connect to an external source such as Azure Blob Storage or Azure SQL Database. Following that, you specify the target column, which is the value you want your model to predict, and inform AutoML about the type of task you're working on, such as classification, regression, or time-series forecasting. Once this is set, you can configure settings such as the maximum training time and the number of concurrent runs before starting the AutoML experiment.

During training and evaluation, AutoML runs dozens of models simultaneously. It divides the data into training and validation sets and evaluates each algorithm's performance. Models are ranked using metrics such as accuracy, precision, or mean squared error (depending on the problem type). For example, a model for predicting house prices may be assessed based on how well its predictions match actual sale prices.

After this, users review the results in Azure ML Studio. The platform creates visuals such as ROC curves (which plot the true positive rate against the false positive rate to show how well a classification model distinguishes between classes; the closer the curve is to the top-left corner, the better the model performs) for classification and residual plots for regression, making it simple to compare models.

Problem Types and Use Cases for Azure AutoML

Azure AutoML supports three main types of machine learning problems: classification, regression, and time-series forecasting. Classification is used to predict categories or labels, such as if an email is spam or if a transaction is fraudulent. Regression is used to predict continuous values, such as housing prices or revenue. Time-series forecasting is used when your data represents a sequence over time, such as estimating future sales based on historical performance.

Each of these problem types is supported by a diverse set of use cases across industries. In healthcare, for example, categorization models may help in the identification of high-risk patients based on their medical history. In finance, regression models are frequently used to forecast credit risk scores and loan default rates. Retailers typically use time-series models to estimate demand and manage inventory.

The way AutoML adjusts its internal workflow based on the type of problem is what makes it so powerful. If the data for a classification task is unbalanced, it may automatically balance class weights. It uses specific preprocessing techniques for time-series forecasting, such as rolling averages and lagging indicators. It also recognizes which algorithms perform best for specific challenges and adjusts its search accordingly. This intelligence implies that nonexperts can get competitive performance by just selecting the appropriate issue type.

As you prepare for the AI-900 exam, keep in mind that AutoML is not a replacement for in-depth knowledge, but rather a tool for accelerating development and expanding access to machine learning. It's an excellent starting point if you want to prototype rapidly.

Data and Compute Services in Azure for Machine Learning

AI doesn't happen in isolation. Behind every successful machine learning project are two very important things: data and compute resources. This section explores how Azure provides flexible storage, scalable computing power, and smart resource management to handle everything from small experiments to enterprise-scale AI workloads.

Storage and Data Access Options for ML Workloads

When working with machine learning in Azure, one of the first stages is determining where your data will live. Azure has a variety of alternatives for storing and accessing data, and your choice is often determined by the size, type, and structure of the data. *Azure Blob Storage* is a popular option for scalable object storage that works well with both structured and unstructured data. It is often used to store training datasets, pictures, and huge CSV files for machine learning experiments.

Another option is Azure Data Lake Storage, which is intended for big-data analytics. It can store large amounts of data in a hierarchical format, which makes it a good choice for enterprises who currently process data in parallel using technologies such as Apache Spark. For those working with relational data, Azure SQL Database and Azure Synapse Analytics can be useful resources. These services enable you to query structured data using SQL and connect directly to your machine learning experiments via Azure ML Studio or the SDK. In addition to these native Azure services, Azure ML can connect to other data sources. You can import data from public URLs, on-premises storage, or even data shared across multiple Azure subscriptions.

Compute Targets in Azure ML

After data, the next important requirement in machine learning is compute, essentially the raw computing power needed to train and test models. Azure ML has multiple compute options based on your workflow. Compute instances are development environments that include preconfigured tools such as Jupyter notebooks, Python, and the Azure ML SDK. These are personal virtual machines that you can use to write code, test data, or perform lightweight training jobs. They are suitable for individual users.

For more resource-intensive workloads, you can use compute clusters. These are managed pools of virtual machines that can be used to execute large training jobs, parallelize experiments, or handle multiple users at the same time. Clusters may be setup with either CPU or GPU resources, so if you're working on deep learning models that demand a lot of compute, GPU clusters are the way to go.

Managing and Scaling Data and Compute Resources

Azure ML allows you to manage how data is versioned, compute is assigned, and resources are reused across projects. For example, when you generate a dataset in Azure ML, it is saved in your workspace and versioned automatically. That is, if you change your dataset later, you may still refer back to the original version that was used to train a previous model.

On the compute side, Azure allows you to specify resource quotas, configure cluster auto-scaling rules, and track how much each resource is used. Auto-scaling is important because it allows your compute clusters to expand when multiple workloads are submitted and decrease when idle. This helps to decrease costs without losing performance. You can also set compute clusters to shut down after a specific amount of inactivity, which reduces wasted resources on idle VMs. While compute clusters use VMs (an Infrastructure-as-a-Service approach where you manage the underlying virtual machines), Azure ML also offers Platform-as-a-Service alternatives such as ACI for training jobs, Azure Functions for lightweight inference workloads, and fully managed online endpoints that automatically handle scaling and infrastructure. These PaaS options abstract away the VM management entirely. Azure handles the infrastructure automatically, and you only pay for the actual compute time used during model training or inference, without needing to configure or manage any underlying virtual machines.

Another way that Azure helps with resource management is through the reuse of environments and pipelines. Instead of building a new environment for each training task, you can define and register environments including specified Python packages, runtime options, and dependencies. These environments can then be reused for various trials. Pipelines can also be reused and scheduled, allowing recurring tasks such as data preprocessing or model retraining to run automatically without continual supervision.

Managing Datasets in Azure ML

A dataset in Azure ML is a prepackaged version of your data that is ready for machine learning. Rather than treating raw data files as isolated assets, Azure ML allows you to generate datasets that can be reused, versioned, and shared between experiments. These datasets act as smart pointers to your actual data. They don't duplicate the data but provide a reference that can be managed more efficiently inside the workspace.

Azure ML supports two types of datasets called tabular and file-based datasets. Tabular datasets, such as CSVs or SQL tables, are used to store structured data, with rows and columns representing features and records. These are ideal for applications such as regression, classification, and forecasting, where each row can represent a customer, transaction, or time-series entry. When you build a tabular dataset, Azure can automatically infer the structure and conduct basic profiling to help you better understand the data. File datasets, on the other hand, are used to store unstructured data like photographs, audio, and massive collections of files. These datasets are more format-flexible than tabular datasets, but they lack the structured column-and-row view. They are perfect for working on deep learning models that take image folders or binary files as input. With file datasets, you just tell Azure ML, "This is a collection of files I want to work with," and the system handles the tracking.

The value of organizing your data as Azure ML datasets becomes clear when you start building and running multiple experiments. Instead of hardcoding file paths or manually re-uploading files for every model training run, datasets give you a way to work with data repeatedly.

Dataset Versioning, Labeling, and Registration

Imagine working on a team where everyone uses slightly different versions of the same dataset. Chaos will definitely occur over time. Versioning addresses this issue by tracking changes over time. For example, when a dataset of product reviews is updated with new entries, Azure ML saves both the old and new versions. This allows teams to roll back if a model's performance degrades following an update, ensuring reproducibility. Versioning also tracks who made changes and when, which is important for audits in regulated businesses like finance.

Labeling gives meaning to data. Labels are the "answers" from which the model learns in supervised learning (for example, tagging photographs with "cat" or "dog"). Azure ML provides tools for both manual labeling (people annotating data) and semi-automated labeling (using pretrained models to accelerate the process). For example, using a hybrid method makes it possible to label thousands of street scenes for a self-driving car project, AI provides labels like "pedestrian" or "stop sign," while humans refine them.

Registration converts datasets into reusable assets. Once registered in an Azure ML workspace, datasets can be shared between projects without re-uploading files. Consider it a library catalog: instead of browsing through folders, you search for "2023 Sales Data" or "Annotated Chest X-rays" and retrieve the exact version you require. Registration also works with pipelines to provide consistent data inputs for automated training operations.

Data Preparation in Azure ML Studio

Raw data is rarely model-ready; it is often messy, incomplete, or in the wrong format. Azure ML Studio makes data preparation easier with visual tools and automated workflows. The Data Wrangling tool cleans and transforms tabular data with Python code or a drag-and-drop interface. For example, a dataset with missing age values could be improved by filling gaps with averages or removing partial rows.

Transformation workflows turn raw data into features (the variables models use to make predictions). Azure ML Pipelines automates these steps. Imagine preprocessing sales data: a pipeline might remove outliers, standardize currency values, and encode categorical variables (such as converting "Country" to numerical codes) with a single click. These pipelines are reusable, which saves time on future projects.

For file-based data, preparation may include resizing photos, extracting text from PDFs, or converting audio recordings to spectrograms. Azure ML interacts with products such as Azure Cognitive Services for speech-to-text conversion, allowing teams to focus on tasks that are valuable rather than manual preprocessing.

Data drift detection monitors incoming data for changes that might affect model performance. For example, if a model trained on summer sales data begins getting winter sales figures, Azure ML detects the mismatch and prompts retraining.

Model Management and Deployment in Azure

Once a machine learning model has been trained, the next major step is to figure out how to manage and deploy it so that it can be used in the real world. Azure Machine Learning can facilitate the entire workflow, from tracking models during experimentation to deploying them as production-grade endpoints. This section explains how models are registered, deployed, and monitored over time to ensure correctness and value.

Model Registration and Tracking in Azure ML

When a model is trained, it needs a home. Model registration in Azure ML functions similarly to a library system: you "check in" models with metadata (such as training date, algorithm used, and accuracy scores) so that teams may identify and reuse them later. For example, a retail corporation may register numerous versions of a demand forecasting model, each trained on seasonal data, and evaluate their performance over time. Registration helps with storage and traceability. If a model begins to underperform, you can track it back to the specific dataset or code version that was used for training.

Tracking and registration go hand in hand. Every training run in Azure ML generates an experiment tracking log, which includes hyperparameters, metrics, and even visualizations like confusion matrices. Imagine testing five algorithms to forecast customer churn: the logs would reveal which one was the most accurate, how long it took to train, and whether it overfit. This transparency enables teams to interact and prevent repeating mistakes.

Versioning is also very important. As with software upgrades, each registered model is assigned a unique version number. If a new model version reduces performance (for example, a fraud detection model starts flagging too many false positives), teams can easily switch back to a stable version.

Model Deployment Options in Azure

Azure's deployment architecture provides distinct pathways for various inference requirements. Real-time endpoints, which may be deployed using managed services such as AKSAKS, handle low-latency requests and provide automatic scaling capabilities. The deployment process packages models, scoring scripts, and environment specifications into Docker containers, abstracting infrastructure complexity. As seen in SDK examples, deploying MLflow models simplifies this further by automatically inferring dependencies, necessitating just minimal CPU/GPU preparation.

The code snippet below is an example of deploying an MLflow model using the Azure Machine Learning Python SDK. This process demonstrates how Azure ML simplifies deployment by automatically inferring dependencies, requiring minimal configuration for CPU/GPU preparation.

```
from azure.ai.ml.entities import ManagedOnlineDeployment
# Retrieve the latest version of the registered model
model = ml_client.models.get(name="registered_model_name",
version="latest_model_version")
# Define an online deployment configuration
blue_deployment = ManagedOnlineDeployment(
    name="blue",  # Deployment name
    endpoint_name="online_endpoint_name",  # Endpoint name
```

```
    model=model,    # Registered model to deploy
    instance_type="Standard_DS3_v2",  # VM SKU for deployment
    instance_count=1  # Number of instances to deploy
)
# Create the deployment in the workspace
blue_deployment = ml_client.online_deployments.begin_create_or_update(blue_
deployment).result()
# Route all traffic to the "blue" deployment
endpoint.traffic = {"blue": 100}
ml_client.online_endpoints.begin_create_or_update(endpoint).result()
```

Here's an explanation of what's happening.

- **Model Retrieval:** The ml_client.models.get() method fetches the registered MLflow model from Azure Machine Learning's registry.

- **Deployment Configuration:** The ManagedOnlineDeployment class defines the deployment details, including the model, compute instance type (Standard_DS3_v2), and instance count.

- **Deployment Creation:** The ml_client.online_deployments.begin_create_or_update() method initiates the deployment process. Azure ML automatically handles environment setup and scoring script generation for MLflow models (no-code deployment).

- **Traffic Management:** Traffic routing is configured to direct 100% of incoming requests to the "blue" deployment.

Batch endpoints are designed for high-volume asynchronous processing and use parallel compute clusters to evaluate stored datasets. This method works for scenarios such as overnight credit risk assessments or weekly inventory forecasts, in which processing time is less important than throughput efficiency. The batch deployment workflow separates compute resources from storage systems, allowing for cost optimization using spot instances and auto-scaling strategies. Users initiate operations by pointing to cloud-stored data assets, and outputs are automatically archived to specific blob stores.

The controlled rollout feature introduces deployment sophistication through traffic splitting. Teams can A/B test model versions by progressively shifting user percentages between endpoints to reduce rollout risks. Blue/green deployment techniques become executable via SDK commands that change traffic weights between deployments. This functionality is useful when upgrading fraud detection models or recommendation systems, as it allows for performance comparison under real-world conditions.

Specialized deployment types address niche requirements. Container instances are ideal for rapid development, whereas IoT edge deployments enable on-premise inference such as a manufacturing plant using computer vision models to detect defective products on an assembly line in real time, where sending images to the cloud would introduce unacceptable latency and require reliable internet connectivity. The management console provides visibility across all endpoint types, displaying metrics for latency and error rates. Importantly, all installations interact with Azure's monitoring package, which leads to consistent operational management regardless of inference strategy.

Post-Deployment Monitoring and Version Control

Deployed models aren't "set and forget." Over time, data patterns shift (data drift), user behavior changes, and models decay. This phenomenon can reduce a model's accuracy and reliability, which makes regular monitoring and repair necessary. Azure ML has tools to discover these issues early on, such as tracking how incoming data varies from data utilized during training. For example, if a retail model trained on physical store sales begins to get data on internet transactions as part of a new marketing effort, its forecasts may become less accurate. Azure ML helps identify these changes and alerts teams to take corrective actions, ensuring the model continues to deliver reliable results.

Versioning is another critical feature that makes managing deployed models easier. Every update or change to a model is saved as a new version, along with details like the dataset used for training and performance metrics. This allows teams to roll back to an earlier version if a new update performs poorly. For instance, if a fraud detection model's latest version misses more fraudulent transactions than before, Azure ML lets you quickly revert to the previous version without disrupting operations.

To keep models performing well over time, Azure ML supports automated retraining pipelines. When monitoring detects severe declines in accuracy (for example, a recommendation system failing to react to new client preferences), the system can retrain the model with new data. Once retrained, the modified model is stored as a new version and tested prior to deployment. This seamless integration of monitoring, versioning, and retraining ensures that models stay adaptable and dependable in dynamic situations.

Managing the Full Lifecycle of ML Models

Training a machine learning model is only half of the process. In real-world projects, particularly within businesses, it is necessary to manage the model's full lifecycle, from development to deployment and even after it has gone live. This is what MLOps is all about. MLOps (short for Machine Learning Operations) is a set of practices that provide the same structure and stability to machine learning as DevOps does to software engineering. MLOps is a primary priority in Azure because it enables teams to build, deploy, and manage models at scale, while being safe and efficient.

Understanding MLOps helps beginners see that machine learning isn't just about writing code or picking the best algorithm. In the real world, models must be tested, versioned, deployed, monitored, and sometimes replaced. They interact with live systems and users, and they need to stay up-to-date as data changes. MLOps offers the tools and processes to manage all of that, ensuring that machine learning stays useful and reliable over time.

What Is MLOps, and Why Does It Matter?

MLOps combines DevOps with machine learning to manage the whole AI model lifespan, from training to retirement. Consider building a car: MLOps involves not just designing the engine (the model) but also maintaining it, refueling it with new data, and ensuring it responds to new road conditions (real-world data shifts). For businesses, this is important since models can "rust" over time. For example, a fraud detection algorithm trained on 2020 transaction patterns may fail in 2025 when criminals develop new strategies. MLOps addresses this by establishing repeatable procedures for updating models, tracking changes, and ensuring alignment with business objectives.

MLOps are important because they can transform AI from a one-time effort into a long-term asset. Without it, teams face "model chaos": innumerable untracked versions, incompatible data pipelines, and silent failures. MLOps tools, such as Azure Machine Learning, provide safeguards to ensure models are reproducible (any team member can rerun workflows), scalable (works for 10 users or 10 million), and compliant (meets GDPR rules).

CI/CD for Machine Learning in Azure

Continuous Integration/Continuous Delivery (CI/CD) in machine learning automates the journey from code to production. Azure ML makes this easier by providing pipelines for operations such as verifying model accuracy, packaging code into containers, and delivering updates. A retail corporation, for example, may create a pipeline that uses new customer data to retrain its sales forecasting model on a weekly basis. If the updated model outperforms the old one, Azure will replace them during off-peak hours, no manual action required.

Azure's CI/CD tools also promote collaboration. Data scientists can work in isolated "sandboxes" to experiment, while DevOps engineers manage deployment rules. This integrates with Azure Monitor and Application Insights to provide end-to-end observability. Teams can track not just code changes through Git but also monitor model performance metrics, API response times, and error rates in production. OpenTelemetry integration allows for standardized telemetry collection across the entire ML pipeline, giving teams visibility into everything from training job performance to real-time inference latency. Git integration lets teams track code changes, and prebuilt templates standardize environments (like specific Python library versions) to avoid "it works on my laptop" issues. For beginners, think of CI/CD as a factory assembly line: raw materials (data and code) go in, and polished models come out, ready for action.

Monitoring, Governance, and Retraining

Even after a model is deployed, it still needs attention. Monitoring is the practice of watching how the model behaves in the real world, checking for things like unusual predictions, long response times, or changes in data patterns. Azure ML provides tools to help track these signals. If something looks off, you can investigate and take action, like retraining the model or rolling back to a previous version. This makes monitoring a safety net that keeps machine learning systems healthy and trustworthy.

In MLOps, governance and retraining are equally important. Governance refers to having clear policies in place for who can access, deploy, or update models, which is critical in areas with strict regulations like healthcare and banking. Retraining is about keeping models fresh. Over time, fresh data is collected, and the model may need to learn from it. Azure allows you to automate the retraining process as part of your pipeline, so your model continues to learn and improve even after deployment.

Creating and Deploying a Simple ML Model

Creating and deploying a simple machine learning model in Azure ML Studio is a good way to understand the basics of building and operationalizing AI solutions. Here, we'd cover three key steps: creating, training, and evaluating a model; deploying it as a web service; and testing the deployed model using REST endpoints. For beginners, Azure ML Studio's drag-and-drop interface simplifies the process, making it accessible even without extensive coding experience.

Creating, Training, and Evaluating a Model in Azure ML Studio

Before building the model in Azure ML Studio, it's important to understand the structure of the dataset being used. The dataset, titled **student_performance_data**, contains sample records representing students, their academic behaviors, and whether they ultimately passed. Each row represents a student, and each column captures a feature that may influence their performance. Table 5.1 shows a sample of the dataset used for model training and evaluation.

Now that we have sample data, it's time to experiment in Azure ML Studio. To build your first machine learning model in Azure ML Studio, you'll use a tool called the Designer. It's a drag-and-drop interface where you build workflows visually, no coding required. In this example, we'll build a classification model that predicts whether a student passed based on study habits and academic performance (shown in Table 5.1). Azure provides all the components you need; you just need to find them and connect them correctly.

After opening Azure ML Studio, go to the left-hand menu and click Designer under the "Authoring" section. From here, select "Classic prebuilt" and click the plus icon to create a new pipeline. On the canvas, you'll see a blank workspace. This is where your pipeline will come together. The components you'll need (such as Split Data, Train Model, and

TABLE 5.1   Sample of `student_performance_data` Used for Model Training

Hours_studied	Past_failures	Attendance_rate	Sleep_hours	Internet_access	Final_grade	Passed
4	2	85	6	yes	60	no
8	0	95	7	yes	88	yes
2	3	70	5	no	45	no
6	1	90	8	yes	78	yes
1	4	60	4	no	38	no
7	0	92	7	yes	85	yes

Score Model) are in the left pane under the Component tab. If you don't see them, click the Component tab or use the search bar to find them by name. This step is important. Some users accidentally stay in the "Graph validation" view and think the modules are missing.

Start by dragging your uploaded dataset (**`student_performance_data`**) onto the canvas. Then use the search bar to find *Select Columns in Dataset* and drag it in. Connect the dataset output to this module. Double-click it to open the settings, and select the columns you want: the inputs (**`hours_studied, past_failures, attendance_rate, sleep_hours, internet_access`**) and the target (**`passed`**). This ensures the model will only train on relevant information.

Next, search for *Split Data*, drag it in, and connect it to the output of "Select Columns in Dataset." This module splits your data into training and testing sets. Set the split ratio to 0.7 so 70% of the data is used for training and 30% for testing. Then search for *Two-Class Logistic Regression* (under Machine Learning Algorithms) and drag that in, followed by *Train Model*. Connect the left output of Split Data to Train Model, and connect the logistic regression module to Train Model as well. In Train Model's settings, set the label column to **`passed`**.

To finish the pipeline, search for *Score Model* and connect it to both the trained model (Train Model output) and the right output of Split Data (this is your test set). Finally, drag in *Evaluate Model* and connect it to *Score Model*. Your finished pipeline should look like the one shown in Figure 5.4, where the data flows through preparation, training, scoring, and evaluation steps. Once everything is connected, click *Validate*, then *Submit*, choose a compute target, and run the pipeline.

After the run finishes, right-click Evaluate Model and select Visualize to see performance metrics like accuracy and AUC. This tells you how well the model predicts student outcomes using the features provided in Table 5.1. These results help determine whether the model is good enough to be deployed or if it needs improvement. Figure 5.5 shows what the visualized results look like.

FIGURE 5.4   Completed pipeline in Azure Machine Learning Studio with dataset input, feature selection, data splitting, model training, scoring, and evaluation steps.

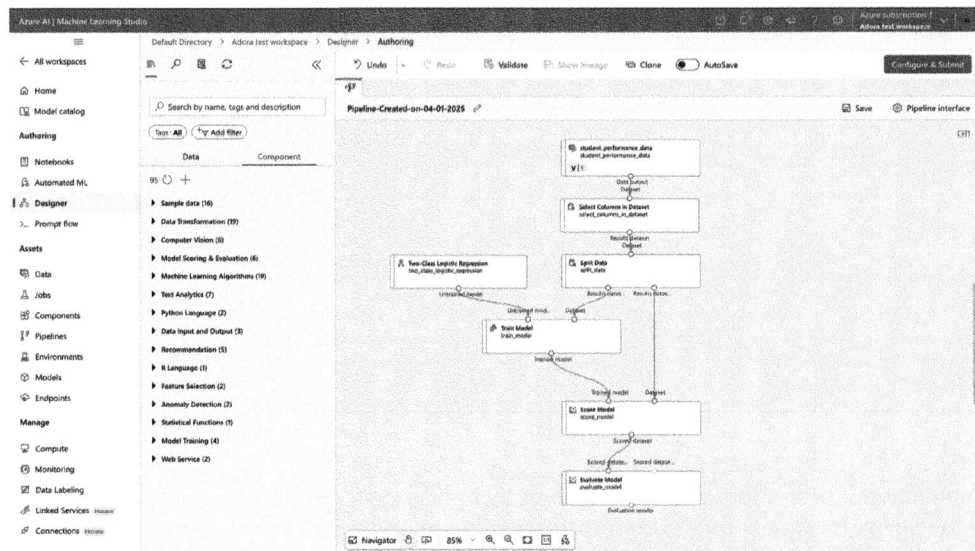

It demonstrates Azure ML Studio's comprehensive model evaluation dashboard, which provides multiple visualizations to assess classification model performance from different perspectives. The **ROC curve** (top left) plots the true positive rate against the false positive rate, showing how well the model distinguishes between classes. The closer the curve hugs the top-left corner, the better the performance. The **Precision-Recall curve** (top center) is particularly valuable for imbalanced datasets, displaying the tradeoff between precision (accuracy of positive predictions) and recall (ability to find all positive cases). The **Lift curve** (top right) shows how much better the model performs compared to random selection, with steeper curves indicating greater predictive power.

Below these charts, the **confusion matrix** provides a detailed breakdown of correct and incorrect predictions, allowing you to see exactly where the model makes mistakes. The threshold slider lets you adjust the decision boundary and immediately see how it affects key metrics like accuracy, precision, recall, and F1 score, which are displayed in real time. The detailed metrics table at the bottom provides precise numerical values for various performance measures, enabling you to compare different models quantitatively. This comprehensive view allows data scientists to understand not just whether their model is performing well but specifically how and where it succeeds or fails, making it easier to identify areas for improvement and communicate results to stakeholders.

Deploying the Model as a Web Service

After building and running your machine learning pipeline in Azure ML Studio, the next step is to make the model available as a web service so it can be used in real-world applications.

FIGURE 5.5   Visualized pipeline results in Azure Machine Learning Studio.

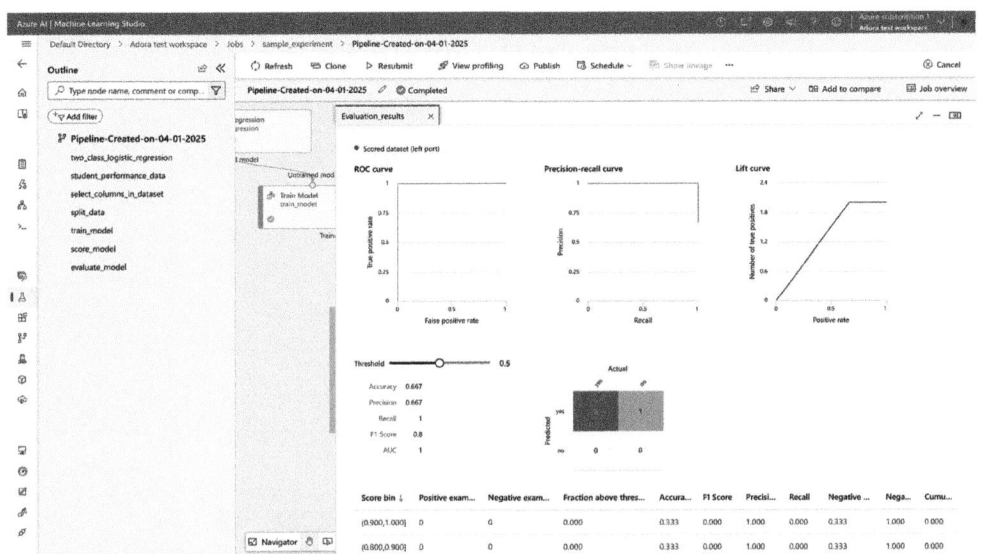

In Azure, this is done by publishing a pipeline as an endpoint, which exposes your model behind a REST API. This allows external tools, apps, or users to send data to your model and receive predictions in real time.

Once your real-time inference pipeline is complete and successfully run (as described in the previous section), go to the **Designer** view or the **Jobs** tab and open the pipeline run. From here, click the **"Publish"** button at the top. Azure will open a dialog to publish the pipeline as a **PipelineEndpoint**. In the form that appears (shown in Figure 5.6), choose "Create new" and give your endpoint a clear name. Leave the checkboxes checked for "Set as default pipeline" and "Continue on failure step." Then click **Publish**.

Once the pipeline is published, Azure will display the **Published pipeline overview** screen (shown in Figure 5.7). This view confirms that your endpoint is active and provides the essential details you'll need for testing and integration. Under the **Properties** section, you'll see the **REST endpoint URL**, which is the address your client applications will use to send requests to the model. You'll also see metadata like who published the pipeline, when it was last updated, and its current status. At this point, your model is no longer just a local experiment, it's officially a production-ready prediction service.

Unlike model-centric deployment using AutoML or the Models registry, the approach you've followed here uses a **pipeline-based deployment,** where the trained model and scoring logic are part of a reusable pipeline flow. This method is especially useful when the inference logic involves more than just a model, such as when data transformations or post-processing steps are included. Azure handles the hosting and scaling for you using **ACI** by default, making it easy for beginners to deploy without worrying about infrastructure setup.

FIGURE 5.6 Publishing the real-time inference pipeline as a new versioned endpoint.

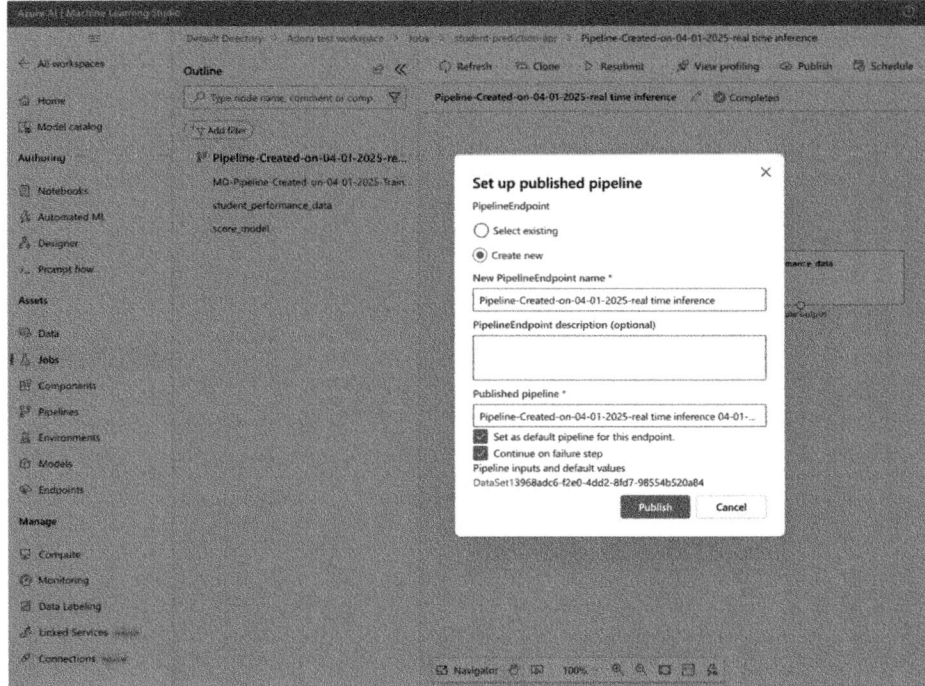

FIGURE 5.7 Overview of the published pipeline, including the REST endpoint URL and status details.

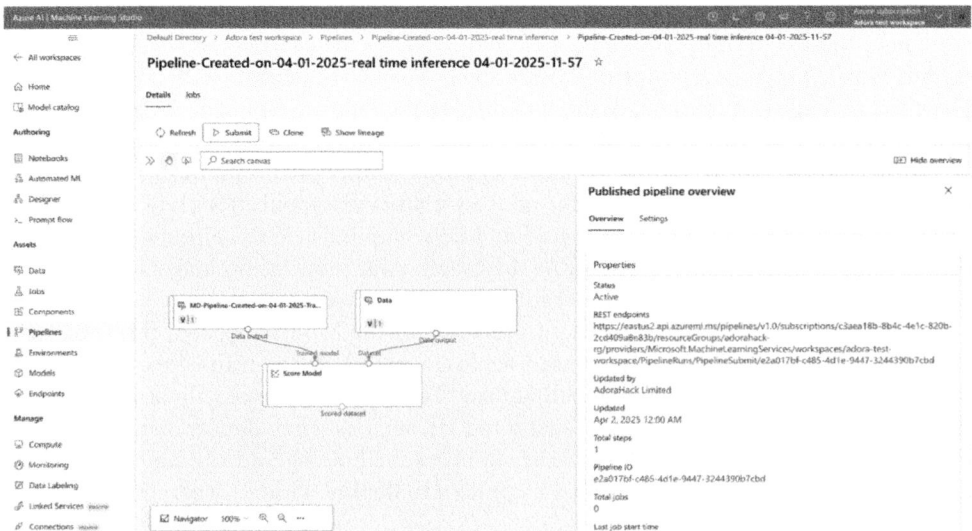

Testing the Deployed Model

After publishing your model as a pipeline endpoint, the final step is to test that it works properly. You do this by sending sample data to the endpoint and checking the prediction output. Azure provides a REST API for this purpose, and you can test it using tools like Postman, curl, or a simple Python script.

Step 1: Send a Test Request

Use tools like Postman or a Python script to send data to the scoring URI. For example, to predict whether a student will pass, send a JSON payload that includes values for features such as hours studied, attendance rate, and internet access.

Sample Python Code:

```python
import requests
data = {
    "input_data": {
        "columns": ["hours_studied", "past_failures", "attendance_rate",
"sleep_hours", "internet_access"],
        "data": [[6, 1, 90, 7, "yes"]]
    }
}
headers = {
    "Content-Type": "application/json",
    "Authorization": "Bearer YOUR_API_KEY"
}
response = requests.post("YOUR_SCORING_URI", json=data, headers=headers)
print(response.json())
```

Step 2: Validate the Response

Check if the model's prediction makes sense. If it returns errors, troubleshoot and try again.

Step 3: Integrate with Apps

Once you've confirmed the endpoint is working, developers can integrate the API into websites, mobile apps, or internal tools. For example, an education dashboard could automatically show predictions for student outcomes based on new data input.

Deep Learning in Azure

Deep learning is a type of artificial intelligence that mimics how the human brain works, using layers of artificial neurons to learn patterns from data. Unlike simpler AI methods, it thrives on large amounts of unstructured data like images, audio, or text, making it ideal for tasks like recognizing faces in photos or translating languages. In Azure, deep learning tools are designed to be accessible, even for beginners, by handling complex setup and letting users focus on solving problems. This section breaks down what deep learning is, the tools Azure offers, and how to put models into action.

Deep Learning vs. Traditional Machine Learning

Deep learning and traditional machine learning both aim to teach computers to make decisions, but they do it differently. Traditional machine learning often relies on structured data (like spreadsheets) and requires humans to manually identify important features. For example, predicting house prices might involve selecting features like square footage or neighborhood. Deep learning, however, works with unstructured data (like photos or speech) and automatically finds patterns through layers of neural networks. Imagine training a model to recognize cats: instead of telling it to look for whiskers or tails, you show it thousands of cat pictures, and it figures out the features itself.

The biggest difference is scalability. Deep learning shines with massive datasets and complex tasks, like transcribing speech or generating art, but it demands more power, often requiring clusters of GPUs instead of basic computers. Traditional ML is faster and cheaper for smaller, simpler tasks, like sorting emails into folders.

For the AI-900 exam, remember:

deep learning = unstructured data + neural networks, while traditional ML = structured data + human-guided features.

Another key distinction is adaptability. A deep learning model can improve as it gets more data, while traditional models might plateau. However, deep learning's "black box" nature makes it harder to interpret *why* a decision was made. Azure bridges this gap with tools that simplify training and provide transparency, like automated experiment tracking.

Deep Learning Frameworks in Azure

Azure supports popular frameworks like **PyTorch** and **TensorFlow**, which are like toolkits for building neural networks. PyTorch is flexible and favored by researchers, while TensorFlow is powerful for large-scale projects. Both work smoothly with Azure Machine Learning, allowing you to create Python code and run it on cloud GPUs without worrying about hardware configuration.

In addition to TensorFlow and PyTorch, Azure also supports Keras, ONNX, and MXNet, as well as interoperability between them. For example, a PyTorch model can be exported to the ONNX format and deployed using Azure services that are optimized for ONNX. This is helpful when you want to use different tools for training and deployment, or when optimizing for specific hardware like edge devices. What's important to remember is that Azure isn't limited to one way of doing deep learning. It has support for a variety of frameworks and helps you scale them up using cloud infrastructure.

Training and Deploying Deep Learning Models

Training deep learning models on Azure typically requires larger datasets, more complicated model architectures, and longer training times than classical machine learning. As a result, one of the most critical concerns is selecting the appropriate compute resources. Azure gives access to GPU-powered servers, which can significantly shorten the time required to train a deep learning model. This is especially beneficial when working with data sources such as photos, videos, or long text sequences that require the model to process hundreds, if not millions, of parameters.

Unlike typical ML workflows, which can be designed using simple interfaces such as the Azure ML Designer, deep learning models are frequently trained using more customized settings that take use of distributed training, parallel processing, and memory optimization. Azure makes this possible by providing not only GPU compute but also multi-node clusters, low-priority VMs for cost savings, and managed environments that scale up and down dynamically based on workload. These features are useful when working on time-sensitive or computationally intensive projects such as real-time object identification or speech recognition.

Once the model has been trained, the Azure deployment process is similar to that of other ML models: register the model, create an inference configuration, and select a deployment destination. The difference is in the infrastructure required to support deep learning inference. These models are typically larger in size and require more memory to load and execute, so they should be deployed to AKS for production or ACI for lightweight testing. Azure also has model optimization approaches such as converting models to ONNX format, which reduces inference time and improves deployment efficiency across diverse hardware settings.

After deployment, deep learning models can be monitored and updated using the same tools provided by Azure ML. You can monitor performance indicators, detect concept drift, and create automated retraining pipelines as needed. However, because deep learning models are more sensitive to changes in data and more difficult to interpret, post-deployment monitoring and governance are very important. Azure assists with this by providing model versioning, rollback options, and connections with monitoring tools.

Summary

This chapter covered how Azure supports the end-to-end machine learning process using a range of integrated tools and services. It explained the role of Azure ML Studio, Automated ML, and MLOps in simplifying tasks such as model training, deployment, and monitoring. The chapter described how datasets are versioned and reused, how compute and storage resources are managed, and how pipelines automate repeated workflows. It also explored deployment strategies, post-deployment monitoring, and continuous retraining. Finally, the chapter introduced deep learning in Azure, highlighting the use of GPUs, supported frameworks, and scalable infrastructure for building complex AI models.

Exam Essentials

Understand how Azure supports machine learning workloads.   Learn how Azure Machine Learning enables end-to-end workflows for various problem types such as classification, regression, and time-series forecasting, using a cloud-based environment.

Recognize the role of AutoML in simplifying model development.   Understand how Azure AutoML automates model selection, training, and evaluation, making machine learning accessible to users without deep technical backgrounds.

Understand how Azure manages data and compute resources.   Learn how Azure handles dataset versioning, storage integration, compute clusters, and environment reuse to support scalable and efficient ML projects.

Learn how models are deployed, monitored, and retrained in Azure.   Understand the different deployment options for real-time and batch scoring, how Azure tracks performance, and how retraining pipelines keep models accurate over time.

Understand the role of MLOps in Azure Machine Learning.   Know how MLOps brings structure to machine learning projects through version control, automated workflows, CI/CD pipelines, and governance practices.

Recognize how Azure supports deep learning workloads.   Learn how Azure provides GPU-enabled infrastructure, supports frameworks like PyTorch and TensorFlow, and handles the complexity of training and deploying deep learning models.

Review Questions

1. A data analyst wants to create a model that predicts housing prices but has little experience with machine learning. Which Azure feature should they use to simplify this process?

   A. Azure Synapse Analytics

   B. Azure Data Lake

   C. Azure AutoML

   D. Azure Blob Storage

2. A team has trained multiple versions of a fraud detection model. They want to compare results and switch back to a previous version if needed. Which Azure ML feature supports this?

   A. Dataset registration

   B. Model versioning

   C. Labeling tool

   D. Compute instance

3. A company wants to automatically retrain their recommendation model weekly using new customer data. Which Azure ML capability makes this possible?

   A. AutoML

   B. Manual re-deployment

   C. MLOps pipelines

   D. Compute instances

4. An education platform wants to predict whether students will pass based on their academic habits. What kind of machine learning problem is this?

   A. Time-series forecasting

   B. Classification

   C. Regression

   D. Clustering

5. Which compute option in Azure ML is best for training deep learning models on image data?

   A. Compute instance with CPU

   B. Azure SQL Database

   C. GPU-based compute cluster

   D. Azure Logic Apps

6. A business analyst is using Azure AutoML. What must they define before running an experiment?

   A. The scoring script

   B. The compute instance's OS

   C. The target column

   D. The model architecture

7. What is the purpose of registering a model in Azure ML?

   A. To automate feature engineering

   B. To deploy pipelines

   C. To store and track models with metadata

   D. To manage compute scaling

8. Which Azure ML feature helps detect when a model is no longer performing well due to changes in input data?

   A. Dataset registration

   B. Data drift detection

   C. Container Instances

   D. AutoML

9. Which deployment option should be used for a model that needs to process predictions in real time with low latency?

   A. Azure Container Registry

   B. Azure Batch Endpoints

   C. Azure Kubernetes Service (AKS)

   D. Azure Data Factory

10. A retail company wants to automate sales forecasting weekly. What kind of ML problem are they trying to solve?

    A. Clustering

    B. Regression

    C. Time-series forecasting

    D. Classification

11. Which Azure ML feature allows teams to automate steps such as training, evaluation, and deployment in a repeatable workflow?

    A. Pipelines

    B. Model tracking

    C. AutoML

    D. SQL Queries

12. An ML team wants to reduce idle resource costs when their cluster is not in use. What Azure ML feature should they configure?

A. Data labeling

B. Cluster shutdown policy

C. Compute quotas

D. Model scoring

13. What does Azure ML use to store unstructured data like images and audio?

A. Tabular datasets

B. Azure SQL Database

C. File datasets

D. AutoML experiments

14. Which framework can be used in Azure ML for deep learning tasks?

A. Hadoop

B. SparkSQL

C. PyTorch

D. Power BI

15. A team wants to version their training data to ensure reproducibility. What Azure ML capability supports this?

A. Labeling tool

B. Dataset versioning

C. Batch deployment

D. REST endpoints

16. Which service allows training models in Azure without managing infrastructure manually?

A. Azure Virtual Machines

B. Azure Container Registry

C. Azure Machine Learning

D. Azure Key Vault

17. What kind of machine learning is best suited for analyzing large amounts of unstructured data such as images and speech?

A. Reinforcement learning

B. Time-series forecasting

C. Deep learning

D. Regression

18. Which Azure tool can help non-coders build a model using a visual interface?

A. Azure CLI

B. Azure Monitor

C. Azure ML Designer

D. Azure DevOps

19. Why is MLOps important in enterprise machine learning?

A. It improves GPU usage

B. It supports marketing strategies

C. It ensures models are reliable, scalable, and governable

D. It helps design model features

20. Which Azure ML option is best for a quick test of a deployed model's REST endpoint?

A. Azure Synapse

B. Python script with requests library

C. AutoML run history

D. Blob storage

Chapter

6

Introduction to Computer Vision

Computer vision is another important part of artificial intelligence. It gives machines the ability to "see" and understand the world through images, videos, and live feeds, just like humans do, but at an advanced scale and speed. Computer vision quietly powers countless innovations we rely on today. It could be a self-driving car recognizing a stop sign, a phone unlocking with your face, or a doctor analyzing medical scans.

In this chapter, we'll start by breaking down what computer vision really means and how it turns pixels into useful information. You'll learn about core tasks like spotting objects in photos, reading text from documents, and even detecting emotions in faces.

Fundamentals of Computer Vision

Computer vision is the technology that enables machines to extract useful information from visual data such as images, movies, and live camera feeds. Unlike humans, who recognize patterns, colors, and things immediately, computers process pixels (the small dots that comprise an image) using algorithms and mathematical models. Computer vision is fundamentally about bridging the gap between raw visual data and usable information. A security camera can do more than record footage; by running real-time computer vision algorithms, it can detect unfamiliar faces or flag suspicious movements and immediately send an alert.

In the broader context of AI, computer vision acts as a sensory input system. AI systems assess their environment using computer vision, same as humans do with their eyesight. This capacity is critical for applications like robotics, where machines must avoid obstacles, and agriculture, where drones monitor crop health. Combining computer vision with other AI approaches, such as machine learning, allows computers to learn from visual data over time, which can improve accuracy in tasks such as disease diagnosis from medical scans and image-based product recommendations.

How Computer Vision Extracts Information from Visual Data

To understand how computer vision works, consider teaching young children to identify a cat in an image. You would show them examples, point out distinguishing features such as whiskers or ears, and correct their mistakes. Similarly, computers learn to recognize patterns after reviewing thousands of annotated photos. They convert visual data into numerical representations, using techniques like edge detection (identifying object boundaries) and color analysis to isolate important features.

Modern computer vision systems rely significantly on deep learning, a type of machine learning in which artificial neural networks mimic the structure of the human brain. These networks, especially convolutional neural networks (CNNs), process images in layers. The first layer may detect simple edges, whereas deeper layers recognize complex shapes such as wheels or faces. For example, when you post a photo to social media, the CNN may scan it and propose tags based on faces or landmarks.

But how is raw visual data transformed into valuable information? Let's break it down: A camera captures an image as a grid of pixels, each with a color value represented as a combination of individual values for red, green, and blue, often with an additional opacity value. Algorithms preprocess this data by altering brightness, cropping, or decreasing noise to make it easier to interpret. Next, the system extracts features (such as textures and forms) and compares them to patterns learned during training. If it is analyzing a street scene, it may divide the image into sections like roads, pedestrians, and vehicles to better understand the context.

Core Tasks in Computer Vision

There are several tasks encompassing computer vision, and each of them solve unique problems. Let's start with image classification, the simplest yet foundational task. Here, the goal is to assign a label to an entire image, like "cat" or "sunset." Think of it as sorting photos into folders based on their content. Training a model for this involves feeding it labeled images until it learns to distinguish features, for example, recognizing that sunsets often have warm colors and horizon lines.

A step beyond classification is object detection, which locates and labels multiple objects within an image. Instead of just saying "this is a street scene," object detection draws bounding boxes around cars, pedestrians, and traffic lights. This is important for applications like self-driving cars, where identifying the position of nearby vehicles is as important as recognizing them. Advanced models like YOLO (You Only Look Once) or Faster R-CNN (Region-Based Convolutional Neural Network) do this in real time, balancing speed and accuracy.

Optical Character Recognition (OCR) extracts text from photographs and converts it into machine-readable letters. When you scan a document or take a picture of a sign, OCR converts the visual text into editable and searchable data. Tools like Azure AI Vision's Read API use this technology to digitize text from a variety of sources, including corporate papers, posters, and street signs. The OCR process involves detecting text regions within an image, segmenting individual characters or words, and recognizing them using advanced machine learning models. This allows applications to process and use text from images effectively, and it supports functionalities like automatic data entry, content indexing, and accessibility enhancements.

There's also facial analysis and it extends beyond recognizing faces to interpreting information such as age, emotion, and even identity. Your phone's Face ID uses this to unlock safely, while social networking platforms use it to tag friends or apply funny filters. Facial analysis includes several techniques, including recognizing faces in a frame, aligning facial characteristics (such as the eyes or nose), and assessing patterns (for example, smile intensity). Ethical considerations, like privacy and bias, are crucial in this context because these technologies can impact real lives.

Image Classification

This section will cover image classification, what it is, how it works, and why it's such a big deal in the world of AI. You'll get a feel for how machines learn to recognize what's in an image and label it, kind of like how we look at a photo and instantly know if it's a cat, a pizza, or a traffic sign. We'll also look at real-life examples, from spotting spam images to helping doctors read medical scans. If you're preparing for the AI-900 exam, understanding image classification is important, and by the end of this section, it'll all make a lot more sense.

Understanding Image Classification

Image classification assigns a single label to an entire image based on its content. For instance, if you show a picture of a beach, the system might label it "coastline" or "vacation." Unlike object detection, which identifies multiple items within an image, classification focuses on the bigger picture. This approach works well when the goal is to understand the overall context rather than specific details. For example, a social media website might use classification to automatically tag uploaded photos as "landscape," "food," or "selfie" to improve search and recommendations.

The process starts with labeled training data, which is thousands of pictures already categorized by humans. These labels act as "answers" for the AI model during training. If you're building a model to differentiate bananas from potatoes, you'd feed it images labeled "potato" or "banana" until it learns patterns like ear shape or texture. It's also important to note that classification isn't foolproof. Ambiguous images, such as a banana and a potato placed side by side, can confuse the model, highlighting the need for high-quality, diverse training data.

Labeling entire images also has limitations. If a photo contains both a cat and a dog, the model must choose one dominant label unless it's designed for multi-class classification. This all-or-nothing approach simplifies analysis but sacrifices granularity. Despite this, classification remains widely used because it's fast, efficient, and sufficient for many applications, such as sorting photo libraries or flagging inappropriate content.

How Classification Models Learn Patterns and Categories

Training an image classification model is like teaching a child to recognize animals using flashcards. You show the child a picture, say "banana," and repeat until they can identify bananas on their own. Similarly, AI models learn by processing vast amounts of labeled images. Each image is converted into numerical data (pixels), and the model looks for patterns like edges, colors, and textures that correlate with specific labels.

FIGURE 6.1   Chihuahua or muffin.

Modern classification models often use CNNs, which mimic how the human brain processes visual information. These networks have layers that detect simple features first (like lines or curves) and gradually combine them into complex shapes (like ears or wheels). During training, the model makes guesses, compares them to the correct labels, and adjusts its internal parameters to reduce errors. Over time, it becomes adept at recognizing subtle differences, for example, distinguishing a muffin from a Chihuahua, a famously tricky task even for humans (see Figure 6.1).

Training requires balancing two factors: accuracy (making correct predictions) and generalization (working well on new, unseen images). A model that memorizes training data but fails on real-world examples is overfit. To avoid this, developers use techniques like splitting data into training and testing sets or augmenting images with rotations and flips to simulate variations. For instance, a model trained to classify X-rays should work reliably across different lighting conditions or patient positions.

Real-World Applications

Image classification quietly shapes many aspects of our daily life. Email providers like Outlook use it to detect spam images containing phishing links or misleading ads. The system flags risky emails before they reach your inbox by analyzing visual features like suspicious logos or crowded text. Similarly, some social media apps automatically filter inappropriate content, such as graphic violence or nudity, using classification models trained to recognize policy violations.

Another example is organizing personal photo libraries. These photo library apps can classify images into categories like "birthdays," "pets," or "sunsets," which make it easier to search thousands of photos. This demonstrates how classification turns chaos into order. Even retail has benefits, for example, online marketplaces use it to tag product images, so searching "blue dress" returns relevant results without manual input.

However, these systems aren't perfect. Misclassifications can occur, like labeling a harmless meme as "inappropriate" or missing subtle spam. This is why many platforms combine AI with human moderation. For instance, a social media site might use classification to flag 90% of problematic content automatically, then have moderators review the remaining 10% for edge cases.

Object Detection in Images and Videos

Object detection goes a step further than image classification by locating and labelling multiple objects within a single image or video frame. While classification answers the question, "What is the main subject of this image?" detection asks, "What objects are here, and where are they?" For example, a photo of a kitchen might be classified as "kitchen," but object detection would identify the refrigerator, oven, and pots within it. This granularity is critical for tasks like autonomous driving, where knowing the exact position of a stop sign or another car is as important as recognizing it.

The difference lies in complexity. Classification treats an image as a whole, while detection breaks it into regions and analyzes each for potential objects. This requires models to handle both recognition (identifying objects) and localization (marking their positions). Modern object detection systems use advanced algorithms like YOLO (You Only Look Once) or Faster R-CNN, which balance speed and accuracy. For instance, YOLO processes images in one pass, making it fast enough for real-time video analysis, while Faster R-CNN offers higher precision for static images.

Bounding Boxes and Multi-Object Identification

At the heart of object detection are bounding boxes, which are digital rectangles drawn around detected objects to highlight their location. If you take a photo of a park and draw boxes around every person, dog, and bench you see, that would be a real-world version. Bounding boxes provide coordinates (like top-left and bottom-right corners) to define each object's position. This spatial data allows systems to track movements, count items, or avoid collisions. For instance, a drone navigating a forest uses bounding boxes to identify trees and adjust its flight path.

The process of identifying multiple objects involves scanning the image for potential regions of interest. Early methods used sliding windows, where the model examines small sections of the image sequentially. Modern approaches, like anchor boxes in YOLO, predict multiple bounding boxes and class probabilities simultaneously. These predictions are refined to eliminate overlaps and inaccuracies.

Accuracy depends on balancing two metrics, precision (avoiding false detections) and recall (finding all true objects). A security camera system with low recall might miss intruders, while low precision could trigger false alarms from rustling leaves. Techniques like non-maximum suppression help by filtering redundant boxes, and this ensures that only the most confident detections remain. Training data quality also plays a role because models struggle with rare objects or unusual angles if not exposed to diverse examples during training.

Real-World Applications: From Everyday Tasks to Industry Transformations

Object detection is already embedded in technologies we interact with daily. Take pedestrian detection systems in cars, which use cameras to spot people crossing roads and trigger automatic braking. This same technology powers traffic management systems that track vehicles in real time, reducing congestion by adjusting traffic lights based on traffic flow. Stores also use object detection to automate inventory counting, with cameras scanning shelves to flag out-of-stock items.

The impact extends to public safety and security. Surveillance systems analyze live video feeds to detect unattended bags in airports or overcrowding at events, alerting staff to potential risks. Drones equipped with object detection assist search-and-rescue teams by identifying human shapes in disaster zones, speeding up response times. For example, during wildfires, drones can locate stranded individuals by detecting movement or body heat signatures in smoke-filled areas where human visibility is severely limited. These applications save lives while reducing reliance on manual monitoring.

In robotics and automation, object detection enables machines to interact intelligently with their surroundings. Warehouse robots use it to locate and pick items from shelves, navigating around obstacles in real time. Fulfillment centers for retail companies can deploy robots that detect and transport packages, and this can slash delivery times. In healthcare, surgical robots assist doctors by identifying organs or tools in endoscopic videos, improving precision during operations. Even agriculture benefits from this because farmers use drones to detect pests or diseased crops, enabling targeted treatment and reducing pesticide use.

A groundbreaking application is autonomous vehicles. Self-driving cars rely on object detection to interpret their environment, identifying lanes, traffic signs, pedestrians, and other vehicles. Autonomous vehicles can process feeds from multiple cameras to create a real-time map, adjusting speed and direction based on detected objects. This technology highlights the delicate balance between innovation and safety; misdetections could lead to accidents, underscoring the need for rigorously tested models. Beyond cars, autonomous delivery robots use detection to navigate sidewalks, avoiding pedestrians and obstacles to drop off packages.

OCR and Document Scanning

A big part of how AI helps us in the real world is by working with the kinds of information we use every day, especially written text. But machines can't read printed or handwritten words the way we do unless that text is turned into a digital format they can understand. Optical Character Recognition, or OCR, helps with this. OCR is a computer vision technique that extracts text from images or scanned documents and converts it into machine-readable data. It's used everywhere, from scanning receipts to reading road signs to automating entire document workflows.

In this section, we'll break down what OCR is and how it works, then explore where it's being used. As you prepare for the AI-900, understanding OCR is important because it's one of the most practical and widely used applications of AI-powered computer vision.

What OCR Does and How It Works

At its core, OCR is the process of teaching machines to recognize characters like letters, numbers, and symbols, from images or handwritten notes and turn them into actual text that a computer can process. When you take a photo of a receipt or scan a form, that image is really just a bunch of pixels. OCR analyzes those pixels, detects patterns that look like text, and matches them to known characters so it can reconstruct what's written.

This might sound simple, but there's a lot going on under the hood. OCR systems need to handle different fonts, handwriting styles, background noise, lighting conditions, and distortions like wrinkles or shadows on the paper. More advanced OCR systems even go beyond recognizing individual letters; they understand the structure of documents, like where a paragraph starts or which parts are headers or tables.

Once the text is extracted, it can be saved, searched, edited, or used by other software systems. For example, if you scan a printed form using OCR, you can store the name, address, or ID as structured data in a spreadsheet or database. The machine doesn't just see the paper, it reads and understands the content in a way that's useful.

Everyday Uses of OCR

You've probably used OCR without even thinking about it. One common example is scanning receipts. Many budgeting apps let you snap a picture of your receipt, and they'll automatically extract the date, store name, and total amount. This helps you track spending without manually typing everything in. OCR does all the behind-the-scenes work to pull that text from the image.

Another place you'll see OCR in action is with signs and printed text in the real world. Apps like Azure Cognitive Services' Computer Vision use OCR to recognize foreign text on signs or menus, then translate it instantly. If you're traveling and don't know the language, OCR makes it possible to read and understand what's around you using just your phone's camera.

OCR is also used to digitize paper documents. Schools and libraries often scan old books or records and use OCR to make them searchable. Instead of flipping through hundreds of pages, you can just search for a word or phrase and go straight to the right part. This has made archives more accessible and has helped preserve valuable information in a digital format.

Industry Examples: Banking, Logistics, and Healthcare

In banking, OCR is used to scan checks, process forms, and verify documents like passports or licenses. When you deposit a check using your phone, the app uses OCR to read the handwritten amount and account number. Banks also use it to extract information from identity documents for fast onboarding of new customers.

In logistics and shipping, OCR helps track and manage packages. Labels with barcodes, tracking numbers, or handwritten addresses are scanned, and the text is extracted to keep everything organized and searchable. This is useful when dealing with high volumes of packages or when labels get smudged or damaged during delivery.

Healthcare is another major area where OCR is making a difference. Medical facilities use it to digitize handwritten notes, scan lab results, or pull data from forms that patients fill out. This helps reduce paperwork, improves accuracy, and makes patient records easier to access. When combined with natural language processing, OCR can even help systems understand medical terminology and structure the data for analysis.

Beyond just reading words, OCR is speeding up workflows, reducing human error, and helping organizations handle data more efficiently in different industries. The AI-900 exam may not ask you to build these systems, but knowing how OCR supports industries like finance, logistics, and healthcare will help you identify use cases quickly and accurately.

Why OCR Matters for Automation and Accessibility

Beyond saving time, OCR is also about making information more accessible and usable. One major benefit is automating data entry. Instead of having someone manually type in names, numbers, or details from paper forms, OCR systems can do that instantly. This reduces the chances of human error and speeds up tasks that used to take hours. Businesses can process applications, invoices, or customer records much faster thanks to OCR-powered tools.

It also plays a huge role in accessibility. People who are blind or visually impaired can use screen readers and OCR together to understand printed materials. OCR makes it possible for assistive technologies to read out loud from books, menus, signs, and more because it turns printed text into digital format. This kind of inclusive design helps make technology usable by more people, regardless of ability.

Facial Detection and Analysis

Faces are one of the most recognizable forms of visual information, both for humans and AI. In computer vision, being able to detect and understand faces opens up many possibilities. It makes it possible for the facial phone unlock feature to exist, and it can also help with improving customer experiences in apps and stores. This section explores how facial detection and facial analysis work, where they are used, and what kinds of challenges and ethical concerns come with them. It also explains the difference between analyzing faces for general insights and actually identifying who someone is.

Facial Detection vs. Analysis

In interpreting human faces, facial detection is the first step. It's about locating human faces in an image or video frame. This technology answers the question, "Where are the faces?" but doesn't go deep into who they are or what they're feeling. Applications range from basic photo tagging to ensuring drivers stay attentive by detecting if their face is turned away from the road.

Facial analysis goes deeper by interpreting attributes of the detected faces. It can estimate age, gender, emotional expressions, or even detect accessories like glasses. For example, a virtual makeup app might use analysis to suggest lipstick shades based on your facial features. However, these systems don't inherently know who you are; they focus on what your face reveals in the moment.

The distinction is important. Detection is purely about presence, while analysis extracts information from that presence. Both rely on machine learning models trained on diverse datasets to handle variations in lighting, angles, or skin tones. However, limitations exist. A face obscured by shadows or tilted sideways might confuse detection, while analysis of emotions can be subjective, for example, the system can misread concentration as anger.

Practical Applications for Facial Detection and Analysis

Facial analysis powers access control systems that verify identity without passwords. For example, some workplaces use facial features to grant entry to secure areas, comparing live camera feeds to approved employee profiles. Similarly, smartphones use Face ID to unlock devices, and this blends detection (finding a face) with recognition (matching it to stored data).

In emotion tracking, brands use facial analysis to gauge customer reactions. A retail store might deploy cameras to analyze shoppers' expressions as they view products, and this can help them identify which displays spark joy or confusion. Streaming platforms could also (hypothetically) use this to recommend shows based on your real-time reactions, though privacy concerns make this controversial.

In entertainment and gaming, facial analysis is used to enhance user interaction. Some games use your facial expressions to control characters or adjust the game environment. Virtual reality systems can also track your reactions to make digital experiences feel more immersive and responsive.

Ethical Challenges

As powerful as facial analysis can be, it also comes with serious concerns. One of the biggest is bias. AI models trained on limited or unbalanced data may perform better on certain faces than others, often recognizing lighter-skinned faces more accurately than darker-skinned ones, or making incorrect guesses about age, gender, or emotion based on cultural assumptions. This can lead to unfair treatment, especially if the technology is used in sensitive areas like law enforcement or hiring.

Privacy is another major concern. Even if a system is only analyzing expressions and not identifying people, it's still working with highly personal data. People may not always know they're being analyzed, and they may not have consented to it. This can create a sense of being watched, even in situations where nothing harmful is intended. Responsible AI design means being transparent about when and how facial analysis is being used. Then there's the issue of surveillance. In some places, facial detection and analysis are used by government or security agencies to monitor public spaces. While this can help with things like crowd safety, it can also lead to overreach if not carefully managed. Constant monitoring, especially without consent, can threaten individual freedoms and create mistrust in public institutions.

These concerns are part of a broader conversation about ethical AI. For AI-900, it's important to understand that facial analysis isn't just a technical task, it's also a social one. Microsoft and other companies emphasize the need to use this technology responsibly, and this makes fairness, transparency, and privacy top priorities.

Facial Analysis vs. Facial Recognition

It's easy to confuse facial analysis with facial recognition, but they are not the same thing. Facial analysis is all about understanding the features of a face, like whether someone is smiling or wearing glasses. It focuses on general traits and doesn't try to figure out who the person is. It's useful in systems that want to personalize content or check for human presence without needing to identify individuals.

Facial recognition, on the other hand, is about identity. It compares a detected face against a database of known faces to find a match. For example, a security system might use facial recognition to confirm whether someone is allowed into a building by checking their face against a list of employees. This process requires much stricter controls because it deals with uniquely identifying people.

The difference matters, especially when we're thinking about ethical and legal implications. Facial analysis is generally considered less invasive because it doesn't involve identity tracking, but it still carries risks if used improperly. Facial recognition raises even more questions, especially around consent and accuracy, because a mistake in identity could have serious consequences. As you get ready for the AI-900 exam, you should be able to tell the difference between analyzing a face for characteristics and recognizing a face for identity. Both involve computer vision, but they serve very different purposes and come with different responsibilities. Knowing where that line is drawn will help you make better decisions about when and how this technology should be applied.

Challenges and Limitations of Computer Vision

Computer vision has transformed industries, but like any technology, it's not perfect. There are still a number of real-world limitations and challenges that can affect how well these systems perform. Understanding these limitations helps us build more realistic expectations of what computer vision can and cannot do and why it might not work the same in every situation. In this section, we'll go over some of the most common challenges.

When Vision Systems Can't See Clearly

One of the most basic challenges in computer vision is dealing with poor-quality input. Just like a human might struggle to recognize a face in a blurry photo or in dim lighting, AI models also have a harder time interpreting images that aren't clear. Poor lighting can wash out details or cast heavy shadows that confuse the system. Low-resolution images can make it difficult for the model to detect fine details, like the edges of a letter or the outline of a small object.

Occlusion is another problem. This happens when part of the object is blocked by something else. For example, if someone is standing behind a tree, the model might only see part of their body and fail to recognize them. Similarly, if a product on a shelf is partially covered by another item, the system might mislabel or miss it entirely. These issues are especially common in real-world environments where the camera doesn't have perfect conditions.

AI models try to compensate for these challenges by being trained on a variety of images with different lighting and angles, but there are limits to how much they can handle. If the system has only seen perfect images during training, it might struggle in more unpredictable conditions. That's why real-world testing and feedback loops are so important in computer vision projects.

Why Biased Data Leads to Biased Results

Bias in training data is one of the most serious issues in all of artificial intelligence, and computer vision is no exception. When models are trained on datasets that don't fairly represent the diversity of the real world, they often struggle to perform equally well across different groups of people or types of content. This can result in systems that work well for some users but poorly for others, especially when it comes to recognizing faces or interpreting human expressions. For example, if a face detection model is trained mostly on lighter-skinned individuals, it might not recognize darker-skinned faces as accurately. Or if a clothing detection model is trained mostly on Western-style clothing, it might mislabel traditional garments from other cultures. These problems aren't always obvious during development, especially if the training dataset doesn't include much diversity.

The consequences of bias can be serious, especially when AI systems are used in hiring, law enforcement, or healthcare. A misclassified image or an unfair prediction can lead to real harm. That's why fairness and inclusivity are big priorities when building and deploying vision models. It's very important to test systems against a wide range of data and to continuously monitor performance for signs of bias.

Real-Time vs. Batch Processing

Another challenge in computer vision has to do with how the model is used, specifically, whether it needs to respond in real time or if it's processing data after the fact. Real-time applications, like self-driving cars or security cameras, require fast, on-the-spot decisions. The system has to analyze video frames quickly and reliably, often within milliseconds. In these cases, speed is just as important as accuracy.

The problem is that faster models sometimes sacrifice accuracy to deliver results more quickly. In contrast, batch processing, where data is collected first and analyzed later, can afford to be more thorough. For example, analyzing thousands of medical images overnight doesn't require split-second responses. The model can take its time and run more complex computations to get the most accurate results.

Choosing between real-time and batch processing depends on the use case. A video game that tracks your face for expressions needs to work instantly, even if it occasionally makes a mistake. But a medical tool reviewing X-rays can take more time to ensure the diagnosis is correct. These tradeoffs have to be carefully balanced during development. For the AI-900 exam, it's helpful to understand that not all computer vision systems are built the same. Some are optimized for speed, some for accuracy, and some try to balance both. The key idea is that how the system performs often depends on how, and where, it's being used.

Why Good Data Matters More Than You Think

Even though models can be incredibly powerful, they're only as good as the data they're trained on. High-quality datasets make all the difference. These datasets should be large enough to capture different scenarios and diverse enough to represent the real world. If the training data is too narrow or full of errors, the model won't be able to generalize, that means it won't perform well on new or unfamiliar images.

Generalization is the ability of a model to apply what it has learned to situations it hasn't seen before. A well-generalized model can recognize cats whether they're sitting, jumping, or hiding under a blanket. It can spot a stop sign whether it's clean, dirty, slightly covered, or lit by a streetlamp. This flexibility is what makes computer vision models useful in the real world.

Creating these kinds of datasets isn't easy. It requires careful collection, labeling, and often the help of humans to check the quality. In some cases, synthetic data or data augmentation techniques are used to fill in gaps and add variety. These steps improve generalization and reduce the risk of overfitting, which is when a model performs well on training data but poorly on anything new.

Summary

This chapter covered the fundamentals of computer vision, explaining how machines use algorithms and deep learning models to extract useful information from images and videos. It explored key tasks like image classification, where entire images are labeled based on content, and object detection, which locates and identifies multiple items within a single frame. The chapter also introduced optical character recognition, a technique used to convert text in images into machine-readable data, and facial analysis, which interprets features and expressions from faces. Real-world applications across healthcare, retail, security, and entertainment were discussed, along with challenges like data bias, poor image quality, and the tradeoffs between real-time and batch processing. These concepts are essential for understanding how computer vision systems are developed and used in practical scenarios.

Exam Essentials

Understand what computer vision is.   Learn how computer vision enables machines to interpret images and videos by extracting useful information from pixels using algorithms and AI models.

Identify core computer vision tasks.   Know the difference between image classification, object detection, OCR (optical character recognition), and facial analysis, and when each is used.

Explain how image classification works.   Understand how models assign labels to entire images using training data and how CNNs detect patterns and features.

Describe the purpose of object detection.   Learn how object detection locates and labels multiple items in an image using bounding boxes and why this is important for applications like self-driving cars.

Understand OCR and its applications.   Know how OCR turns text in images into machine-readable data and how it's used in industries like banking, healthcare, and logistics.

Recognize the importance of responsible AI in facial analysis.   Understand ethical concerns around bias, privacy, and fairness when using facial detection and analysis technologies.

Review Questions

1. A company wants to build an app that categorizes user-uploaded photos as either "outdoor" or "indoor." What type of computer vision task is most suitable?

   A. Object detection

   B. Image classification

   C. Optical character recognition (OCR)

   D. Semantic segmentation

2. A retail store uses cameras to track when shelves are empty by identifying missing products. What computer vision technique is being used?

   A. Image classification

   B. OCR

   C. Object detection

   D. Anomaly detection

3. A logistics company wants to automatically extract handwritten tracking numbers from delivery forms. Which Azure service should they use?

   A. Azure Form Recognizer

   B. Azure Custom Vision

   C. Azure Face API

   D. Azure Bot Services

4. An app detects whether people in a photo are smiling or not. What computer vision feature is being used?

   A. Face recognition

   B. Face detection

   C. Facial analysis

   D. Semantic segmentation

5. Which of the following best describes the function of bounding boxes in object detection?

   A. Assigns a label to the entire image

   B. Identifies whether the image contains a face

   C. Draws a region around detected objects

   D. Highlights emotional expressions on a face

6. What is the main difference between facial analysis and facial recognition?

   A. Facial analysis detects faces; facial recognition creates new ones

   B. Facial recognition focuses on general traits; facial analysis identifies people

   C. Facial analysis reads expressions; facial recognition identifies individuals

   D. They are the same technology

7. A healthcare provider scans handwritten doctor notes to store them digitally. Which technology is used here?

   A. Computer vision

   B. Image classification

   C. Facial analysis

   D. Reinforcement learning

8. Which AI task would be most appropriate for detecting multiple types of vehicles in traffic camera footage?

   A. OCR

   B. Image classification

   C. Object detection

   D. Knowledge mining

9. A customer uses an app that recommends makeup by analyzing their facial features. Which computer vision capability does this rely on?

   A. Face detection

   B. Facial analysis

   C. Image classification

   D. OCR

10. A drone scans a farm and identifies dry areas in the soil. Which describes this AI task best?

    A. Facial analysis

    B. Object detection

    C. Image classification

    D. Reinforcement learning

11. Which of the following best helps a computer vision model generalize to new, unseen images?

    A. Increasing training time

    B. Using high-resolution cameras

    C. Using diverse training datasets

    D. Reducing the number of labels

12. A face detection system works poorly in low lighting. What is the likely reason?

    A. Overfitting

    B. Poor feature extraction

    C. Weak model architecture

    D. Poor input quality

13. Which technique helps reduce overlapping boxes in object detection outputs?

   A. Gradient descent

   B. Data augmentation

   C. Non-maximum suppression

   D. Transfer learning

14. A camera identifies a customer in a store by comparing their face to a database. What technique is this?

   A. Facial analysis

   B. Face detection

   C. Facial recognition

   D. OCR

15. An AI system misclassifies cultural clothing due to limited training examples. What issue is this?

   A. Underfitting

   B. Label noise

   C. Data bias

   D. Feature leakage

16. Which of the following is NOT a typical use case for OCR?

   A. Scanning medical forms

   B. Detecting pedestrian positions

   C. Reading road signs

   D. Extracting text from receipts

17. Why is image classification not ideal for scenes with multiple different objects?

   A. It requires high-resolution images

   B. It assigns only one label per image

   C. It has slower inference speed

   D. It uses facial recognition

18. A car's onboard system identifies traffic lights, other cars, and pedestrians. What is this an example of?

   A. Image classification

   B. Object detection

   C. OCR

   D. Reinforcement learning

19. What role do CNNs play in computer vision?

A. Convert text to audio

B. Translate spoken language

C. Detect patterns in images

D. Simulate facial expressions

20. A banking app uses OCR to extract handwritten amounts from checks. What happens after OCR detects the characters?

A. The app deletes the image

B. It labels the check with a category

C. It converts characters into digital text

D. It locks the account for review

Chapter

7

Azure Tools for Computer Vision

MICROSOFT CERTIFIED: AZURE AI FUNDAMENTALS (AI-900) EXAM OBJECTIVES COVERED IN THIS CHAPTER:

✔ **Domain 3: Describe features of computer vision workloads on Azure**

- Subdomain 3a: Identify common types of computer vision solution

  - 3-1 Identify features of image classification solutions

  - 3-2 Identify features of object detection solutions

  - 3-3 Identify features of optical character recognition solutions

  - 3-4 Identify features of facial detection and facial analysis solutions

- Subdomain 3b: Identify Azure tools and services for computer vision tasks

  - 3-5 Describe capabilities of the Azure AI Vision service

  - 3-6 Describe capabilities of the Azure AI Face detection service

Azure has the tools to help machines "see" and understand the world like humans do, but at scale. This chapter breaks down how these technologies work, from prebuilt AI models that recognize objects, text, and emotions to custom solutions you train yourself for specialized tasks.

You'll learn how services like Computer Vision API, Face Service, and Video Indexer fit into real-world scenarios. You'd see how they help with automating workflows and enhancing apps with smart features. We'll cover the basics: pricing tiers, regional availability, and how to call APIs securely. But we'll also dive deeper, exploring how to fine-tune models, handle privacy responsibly, and integrate vision AI into apps using code or no-code tools like Power Platform.

By the end, you'll know not just what Azure's vision services can do but how to choose the right tools.

Introduction to Azure Computer Vision

Azure Computer Vision is like giving superpowers to computers and teaching them to "see" images, videos, and text the way humans do but faster and at massive scales. This section introduces you to the basics: what these tools are, how they're priced and deployed, and which services you'll use most often.

Azure AI Vision in Context

Azure AI Vision is part of Azure Cognitive Services, a collection of prebuilt APIs that enable developers to add features like image recognition, text extraction, and facial analysis to applications. You don't need deep expertise in computer vision algorithms to start. With a few lines of code or clicks in the Azure portal, you can transform a raw image into structured information like labels for objects, transcribed text, identified faces, and more.

Within Microsoft's AI portfolio, Azure AI Vision is housed under Cognitive Services, which comprises turnkey, domain-specific APIs that you can consume directly. This contrasts with Azure ML, which is the broader platform for building, training, and deploying your own custom models. While Cognitive Services delivers ready-to-use capabilities, Azure ML gives you the freedom to experiment with data, customize pipelines, and fine-tune models. Sometimes you'll use Cognitive Vision APIs out of the box; other times you might export data from Cognitive Services into Azure ML for advanced customization or retraining.

Service Tiers, Regions, and Costs

Azure's vision services aren't one-size-fits-all. They come in different tiers (free and paid) and aren't available in every region. The free tier is perfect for experimenting, like analyzing a few images per month to test ideas. But if you're running a business app that processes thousands of images daily, you'll need a paid tier with higher limits and advanced features, such as priority support or detailed analytics.

Regional availability is critical too. If your users are in Europe, deploying your service in the "North Europe" Azure region reduces latency and ensures compliance with data residency laws like GDPR. Pricing varies by region and tier. Some charge per image analyzed, others per hour of video processed. For example, the Computer Vision API might cost $1 per 1,000 transactions, while Video Indexer could bill based on minutes of video indexed.

Core Azure Vision Services

Azure's vision tools address diverse scenarios:

- **Computer Vision API:** Extracts text (OCR), detects objects, and generates image descriptions. For instance, a tourism app could use it to auto-caption landmark photos.

- **Custom Vision:** Trains models to recognize domain-specific visuals, like identifying defects in manufacturing parts using labeled images.

- **Face Service:** Analyzes facial attributes (age, emotion) and supports recognition for authentication systems.

- **Video Indexer:** Extracts metadata from videos, such as spoken words or scene changes, useful for media archives.

- **Content Moderator:** Filters inappropriate images or text, critical for social platforms managing user-generated content.

These services share Azure's security and compliance standards, ensuring data privacy. Before committing to a plan, you can explore them through Azure's free tier.

Azure Computer Vision API

The Azure Computer Vision API is your gateway to turning images into information for customers/businesses. It can extract everything from high-level descriptions to fine-grained object data. This section dives into how the API works, from basic image analysis to advanced features, and teaches you how to integrate it securely into apps.

Rich Image Analysis Features

Azure's Computer Vision API can turn a simple image into a wealth of metadata in a single request. At its core, the API can generate tags, which are single words that describe the content of an image. These tags are helpful for quick search indexing or basic categorization. It can also assign images to more structured categories like "outdoor," "indoor," "food," or "transport," giving you a higher-level understanding of what the photo contains.

Beyond tagging and categorization, the API can detect and locate individual objects within an image. You might point it at a photo of a living room and have it draw bounding boxes around the sofa, coffee table, and television. This object detection capability is powered by deep learning models trained on millions of examples, so you get reliable, real-time data without managing your own compute cluster. For a beginner, it's as simple as sending a POST request with the image URL or binary data and parsing the JSON response.

The service also supports more advanced analyses, such as detecting brands in images (logos on billboards or labels on products), as well as recognizing celebrities or landmarks from a growing catalog of thousands of entities. These domain-specific models fall under the same image analysis endpoint but require you to specify which features you want. That way, you only incur costs for the operations you need, and your code remains clean and focused.

Evolving Text Recognition: Read API vs. Legacy OCR

Text extraction in Azure Computer Vision has matured considerably over the years. The legacy OCR (optical character recognition) and handwriting recognition endpoints could read printed or cursive text from images, but they worked best on clear, high-contrast scans and struggled with complex layouts. As a beginner, you might find them adequate for basic scenarios like reading street signs or business cards but less reliable on handwritten notes or text embedded in noisy backgrounds.

Then, the Read API came. It's a modern and powerful service built on neural networks that can handle multi-column layouts, irregular fonts, and even cursive handwriting with far greater accuracy. Instead of a single synchronous call, the Read API uses an asynchronous pattern: you submit your image, receive an operation-location URL, and then poll that URL until the service returns the extracted text. This workflow lets Azure use more compute behind the scenes without blocking your application.

One of the major benefits of the Read API is its support for multiple languages and scripts, making it ideal for global applications. If you need to transcribe a Japanese newspaper clipping or a French receipt, the Read API can automatically detect the language and apply the appropriate model. It also returns coordinates for each line of text, so you can overlay the results on the original image or feed them into a layout-aware workflow.

Domain-Specific Recognition Models

Beyond general-purpose analysis, Azure Computer Vision has specialized models finely tuned for particular scenarios. If you're working with travel or geography apps, for instance, the landmark-recognition model can identify famous monuments, like the Eiffel Tower or the Colosseum, and return their names along with confidence scores. This opens up possibilities for interactive tours or travel-logging applications that automatically tag photos with location info.

Similarly, the celebrity-recognition model draws on a database of thousands of public figures. Upload a red-carpet snapshot, and the API will let you know which actors, musicians, or athletes appear in the frame. Brand detection is another domain-specific feature, which spots logos from a global database. A marketing team could use this to track brand visibility in social media posts. These models simplify tasks that would otherwise require custom training, though they're limited to predefined categories.

For other unique needs, developers can train custom models using Custom Vision, but AI-900 candidates should focus on understanding when to leverage Azure's prebuilt models versus building from scratch.

API Access and Security

Interacting with Computer Vision is straightforward whether you prefer REST or a language SDK. A REST call involves sending an HTTP POST to the Azure endpoint URL you provisioned, including your subscription key in the header and the image data in the body. The JSON response you get back includes all the details you requested, for example, tags, text lines, object bounding boxes, and they are ready for your app to consume.

If you'd rather work in code, Microsoft has the Azure Cognitive Services Computer Vision SDK. In Python, you install it with:

```
pip install azure-cognitiveservices-vision-computervision
```

For .NET developers, you can install the NuGet package:

```
Install-Package Microsoft.Azure.CognitiveServices.Vision.ComputerVision
```

SDKs are also available for Java, JavaScript/Node.js, and Go. For other programming languages or the most current SDK availability, check the official Azure documentation at https://learn.microsoft.com/en-us/azure/ai-services/computer-vision/.

Once the library is installed, you create a client and call the analysis method in just a few lines. The following code snippet shows how you would do this in Python:

```
from azure.cognitiveservices.vision.computervision import ComputerVisionClient
from msrest.authentication import CognitiveServicesCredentials
endpoint = "https://<your-resource-name>.cognitiveservices.azure.com/"
key      = "<your-key>"
client = ComputerVisionClient(endpoint, CognitiveServicesCredentials(key))
result = client.analyze_image("https://example.com/image.jpg", ["Tags",
"Categories"])
for tag in result.tags:
    print(f"{tag.name} ({tag.confidence:.2f})")
```

Early on, you'll typically secure requests with an API key you manage in the Azure portal. For production scenarios, swap that out for a managed identity by replacing the

`CognitiveServicesCredentials(key)` with `DefaultAzureCredential()` from the `azure-identity` package. This way your application retrieves tokens automatically, you keep secrets out of code, and Azure handles credential rotation behind the scenes.

Azure Face Service

Azure Face Service brings human-centric vision capabilities to your applications, letting you detect faces, understand facial attributes, and verify or identify people at scale. Regardless of the solution you're building, the Face API gives you a suite of prebuilt models that handle everything from locating a face in an image to matching it against a gallery of known individuals. This section explores how Face Service detects and describes faces, how it organizes and recognizes people, the choices between real-time and batch processing, and the important privacy and compliance considerations you need to follow.

Detecting Faces and Extracting Attributes

At its simplest, the Face Service can scan an image and tell you precisely where any human faces appear. When you call the detect endpoint, you get back rectangles marking each face and a unique face ID for subsequent operations. This is the first step in any face-centric workflow, knowing exactly where to look in the image so you can focus further analysis on those regions.

Beyond just spotting faces, the API can peek under the hood and pull out a variety of attributes. Emotion detection surfaces feelings like happiness, sadness, or surprise; the head-pose feature tells you the angle of someone's gaze; and you can even detect facial hair, eyewear, and smile intensity. These attributes come with confidence scores, so you can decide how much to trust each prediction in your application logic.

All of this runs in milliseconds on Microsoft's managed cloud, so you don't need to curate your own face-analysis models or manage GPU clusters. The service handles the complexity of computer vision training and inference, exposing a simple JSON schema that you can plug into dashboards, databases, or event-driven workflows. For a beginner, it feels like magic: one request and suddenly your app "sees" people.

Identity Verification and Group Management

Once you've detected faces, you'll often want to know who they belong to. Face Service supports two related patterns: verification (one-to-one) and identification (one-to-many). Verification answers the question "are these two faces the same person?" useful for unlocking a device or confirming a user. Identification takes an unknown face and searches it against a "person group," returning the most likely matches.

Person groups are simply collections of labeled face data. You create a group, add "person" entries with their own face images, and then train the model. Training is a quick operation in the cloud that updates the group's recognition model with your data. After that, you call the identify endpoint with a new face ID, and the service returns the person ID plus a confidence score.

This workflow is powerful for applications like employee check-in systems or photo-tagging services. You can keep your person group up-to-date by adding or removing faces, retraining as needed. And because Face Service handles the underlying feature extraction and matching, you don't need deep ML expertise to build robust recognition systems.

Real-Time and Batch Processing

In some scenarios you'll need instant feedback. For example, a security camera that watches a door and unlocks it when a known face appears. For those real-time workflows, you call the detect and identify endpoints on each frame or every few seconds, keeping latency low so your application can respond immediately. You'll need to consider API quotas and manage the flow of frames so you don't overwhelm the service.

Other situations call for batch processing, like indexing a library of archived photographs or processing thousands of hours of recorded video. Here, you might write a script that submits images or video clips in batches, then aggregates the results into a database. Azure's asynchronous patterns where you submit work and poll for results fit nicely into batch pipelines, letting you scale analysis across large datasets without real-time constraints.

Choosing between real-time and batch isn't just about speed. Real-time pipelines often run on edge devices or in event-driven microservices, whereas batch jobs can use parallel compute resources in Azure Batch or Data Factory. Your architecture will reflect those needs.

For the AI-900 exam, remember that real-time systems need robust infrastructure (like GPUs for fast processing), while batch systems focus on cost efficiency.

Privacy, Compliance, and Responsible AI

Working with facial data comes with serious ethical and legal responsibilities. Azure Face Service gives you controls to manage how long you retain face images and metadata. You can delete face IDs and person groups when they're no longer needed, and you should build your application to purge data on a regular schedule or based on user requests.

Under GDPR and other privacy regulations, you must obtain clear consent before capturing or storing biometric data. That means informing users how their facial information will be used, giving them options to opt out, and responding promptly to deletion requests. Azure's compliance documentation and Data Processing Addendum help you understand which data protection obligations Microsoft covers as the cloud provider and which responsibilities remain yours.

Responsible AI is also very important here. You should monitor your face-recognition models for fairness across demographic groups, be transparent about error rates, and provide human-in-the-loop review for high-stakes decisions. Face recognition is powerful but controversial, so you should prioritize compliance as you build out your solution.

Azure Custom Vision

Azure Custom Vision lets you build tailored image classification and object detection models without writing low-level machine learning code. Instead of relying solely on Microsoft's prebuilt vision APIs, you supply your own labeled images, train a bespoke model in the cloud, and then deploy it wherever you need: the edge, an IoT device, or as a real-time endpoint. In this section, you'll learn how to kick off a Custom Vision project, train and measure your model's performance, deploy it for inference, and manage its lifecycle so it stays accurate over time.

Getting Started with Classification and Object Detection Projects

When you first enter the Custom Vision portal, you choose between classification, where each image gets a single tag or multiple tags, or object detection, which draws bounding boxes around items of interest. Deciding which project type to start depends on your scenario. Use classification to sort photos by scene or mood, and object detection to locate products on a shelf or defects on a production line. Either way, you'll upload your images and then add labels yourself, drawing boxes for objects or simply selecting tags for whole images.

As you label, it's important to be consistent: use the same tag names and draw boxes with the same precision so your model learns clear distinctions. The portal even offers an annotation tool that highlights images needing labels, helping you focus your effort where it matters most. From a beginner's perspective, this process feels like teaching: you show the system examples of "this is a teddy bear" or "this is a cracked bolt," and it gradually figures out the patterns that separate one class or object from another.

Behind the scenes, Custom Vision handles data splitting for you, reserving a percentage of images for testing the model after each training run. This ensures that the evaluation metrics you see reflect how the model will perform on new, unseen data. You don't have to write any ETL pipelines: just upload, label, and click "Train," and the service orchestrates the data preparation, model fitting, and validation steps.

By the end of this stage, you'll have a trained model iteration you can explore in the portal. You'll see visual confusion matrices, sample predictions, and raw metrics that reveal how well your tags are separated or how precisely your bounding boxes align. These learnings will guide your next steps as you refine the model for production use.

Training, Evaluating, and Tuning Your Model

Once your images are labeled, hitting *Train* kicks off an iteration; an automated process where Custom Vision uses transfer learning to teach a neural network on your data. This usually takes only a few minutes, depending on how many images you have. When training completes, you receive metrics like precision (how often your positive predictions are correct) and recall (how many true positives you found), which together paint a picture of accuracy.

A key evaluation metric for object detection projects is mean Average Precision, or mAP, which balances precision and recall across all your object classes. Custom Vision shows you the mAP score for each iteration, so you can compare different training runs objectively. If you see that one label consistently underperforms, you might add more images or adjust your labeling strategy to give the model clearer examples.

Custom Vision also has domain-specific tuning presets: choosing between general, food, or retail presets, for example, tweaks the underlying training algorithm to better suit your scenario. This is especially helpful for beginners, as you get optimized defaults without diving into hyperparameter configurations. You can iteratively refine by adding images or switching presets until your evaluation metrics meet your quality bar.

Throughout this process, the portal provides graphs and tables that break down performance by tag or object class. Use these visuals to spot weaknesses (maybe your "animal" images vary too much in lighting, causing low recall) or to verify that your "defect" bounding boxes are tightly aligned. When you iterate on data and monitor metrics, you'll learn how small changes in labeling or preset choices can boost your model's effectiveness.

Did You Know?

For a reasonable baseline model in Custom Vision, aim for at least 50–100 labeled images per class, and try to capture a variety of angles, lighting conditions, and backgrounds. A balanced, diverse dataset helps your first few training runs deliver meaningful information, so you'll spend less time chasing random errors and more time iterating on real weaknesses.

Exporting and Deploying Anywhere

After you've trained a satisfactory model, the next step is deployment. Custom Vision gives you two main options: a real-time prediction endpoint in the cloud or container exports for edge and IoT scenarios. With the real-time endpoint, you simply call a REST URL or use the SDK in Python, C#, or JavaScript to send images and receive predictions instantly. This model-as-a-service approach is perfect for apps that need up-to-the-second results.

If you need to run offline or close to the hardware, you can export your trained model as a Docker container. Custom Vision generates a self-contained image that you can pull to an edge device, enabling low-latency inference without calling the cloud. This is ideal for factory floors with intermittent connectivity or privacy-sensitive applications where data must stay on-premises. You choose from CPU or GPU variants to match your device's capabilities.

For bulk processing scenarios, you can also run batch jobs using the container or the hosted endpoint, feeding dozens or hundreds of images at once. This option can be helpful for validating performance at scale or processing historical datasets. The same model powers both real-time and batch workloads, which gives you a consistent prediction interface across use cases.

In both cloud and container cases, Custom Vision has usage statistics and logs, which show data like how many predictions you've made, average response time, and any errors encountered. Monitoring these metrics helps you plan capacity and cost, and ensure that your deployed model remains reliable as usage grows.

Versioning, Tagging, and Automated Retraining

Models aren't static. As your needs change (e.g., new products or environments), you'll retrain them. Each time you retrain, whether it's because you've added new images or you are simply rerunning the training, it creates a new iteration. You can tag iterations with friendly names like "v1-prototype" or "v2-with-night-images," making it easy to roll back if a change degrades performance. The portal maintains a history of all iterations, so you never lose track of your model's progression.

To operationalize continuous improvement, you can hook Custom Vision into Azure pipelines or Logic Apps. For instance, you might set up a scheduled job that pulls newly labeled images from storage, triggers retraining, evaluates the new iteration's metrics, and, if it meets your thresholds, automatically deploys it to production. This automated retraining pipeline ensures your model adapts as your data shifts.

Under the hood, Custom Vision stores each iteration's model artifacts in the model registry, which you can query via REST or SDK. This registry becomes the source of truth for your deployments, letting you manage rollout strategies, A/B test new versions, and audit which model powered specific predictions. For beginners, the notion of a model registry might feel advanced, but it's simply a structured way to track and retrieve the models you've trained.

Model Registry Deep Dive

Think of a model registry as a library for your trained models. Every time you hit "Train," Custom Vision engineers spin up a new model iteration, complete with its weights, summary of the data it saw, and key performance metrics like precision, recall, or mAP. The registry keeps all of those iterations organized and searchable by name, tag, or metric, so you can compare versions side by side, roll back to a proven "golden" model if a new iteration underperforms, and drive automated pipelines that promote only models meeting your quality gates.

In short, a model registry is your central, trusted record of every model you've built. It's complete with the "what," "when," and "how well" for each one, so you never lose track of the work you've done.

Azure AI Video Indexer

Azure AI Video Indexer is a cloud and edge service that transforms video and audio files into searchable information using over 30 AI models. It is designed for media analysis and automates tasks like transcription, object detection, and sentiment analysis, which makes it very valuable for content creators, marketers, and other professionals that deal with media.

Workflow Fundamentals: Upload, Encode, Index

The process begins when you bring your video into the AI Video Indexer. You can drag and drop a file in the portal, call a REST API, or connect a storage account so that new videos automatically flow in. Behind the scenes, Video Indexer ingests your file and stages it for processing, giving you an immediate job ID to track progress.

Next comes the encoding phase, where Video Indexer transcodes your content into adaptive bitrate formats and prepares it for smooth streaming and analysis. This step ensures that the same video can serve mobile viewers on slow networks and desktop users on high-speed connections, and it lays the groundwork for extracting frame-level information. You don't see these details in your code, but you can monitor encoding health and performance metrics in the portal.

Once encoding finishes, the real magic happens: Video Indexer launches its AI pipelines to index your media. It splits the footage into scenes based on visual and temporal cues, extracts audio tracks for speech-to-text transcription, and runs computer vision models on each segment. All of this work happens automatically and in parallel, so even long videos finish indexing in a matter of minutes rather than hours.

At the end of the process, you receive a rich index that you can explore in the portal or query via API. Every scene, spoken phrase, on-screen text snippet, and detected face is cataloged with timestamps and confidence scores. This structured metadata transforms passive video into a live resource you can search, filter, and act upon.

Uncovering Insights from Video Content

After indexing, Video Indexer lets you dive into the granular details of your footage. Scene-change detection segments your video into logical chapters, and it's ideal for building navigable players or generating highlights automatically. Each scene marker comes with a thumbnail and a timestamp so you can jump straight to the action that matters.

Optical character recognition in video goes beyond static images: Video Indexer reads any text that appears on screen (subtitles, brand logos, even car license plates) and then makes it searchable. Imagine indexing hours of surveillance footage to find a particular logo or scanning webinar slides for specific keywords. The portal shows you the text overlayed on frames, and the API returns each occurrence with its exact time window.

Speech-to-text transcription transforms spoken words into searchable transcripts, complete with speaker diarization so you know who said what. Whether you're analyzing interviews, customer support calls, or board presentations, having a timestamped transcript speeds review and unlocks sentiment or keyword-based alerts. Video Indexer even supports multiple languages and accents, making it a versatile tool for global content.

Face and speaker recognition tie everything together by identifying recurring individuals. As you index more videos, you can build speaker profiles or face models that auto-tag known people, whether they appear on camera or just speak off-screen. Coupling voice and visual identification gives you a comprehensive view of participants, which is invaluable for compliance logging or personalized content delivery.

Integrating Video Indexer into Your Solutions

Video Indexer isn't a standalone tool; it integrates with services you already use. Once you have indexed metadata, you'll want to surface it in your own apps. Video Indexer has embed widgets and REST endpoints so you can build custom web or mobile players that let users search inside videos, skip to relevant scenes, or download transcripts. A few lines of JavaScript or an SDK call is all it takes to put AI-powered navigation controls into your portal.

For large-scale media workflows, Video Indexer can plug into Azure Media Services. You might orchestrate an end-to-end pipeline that ingests raw camera feeds, indexes with Video Indexer, then streams with Media Services and distributes via a CDN. This kind of integration ensures your video library is both intelligent and highly available to viewers around the globe.

If you prefer low-code automation, you can connect Video Indexer to Power Platform or Logic Apps. For example, you could create a Power Automate flow that watches a SharePoint folder, triggers Video Indexer when new videos arrive, then sends a Teams notification with key highlights once indexing completes. Bringing Video Indexer into your architecture shows you how AI services interoperate across Azure's ecosystem.

Summary

This chapter covered the main Azure tools for computer vision, starting with an introduction to Azure Computer Vision and its place within Cognitive Services, then exploring service tiers, regional availability, and cost considerations. We examined the Computer Vision API's rich image analysis features, including tagging, object detection, and advanced text recognition with the Read API, as well as specialized models for landmarks, celebrities, and brands. You learned how to secure and call these APIs, before diving into the Face Service for detecting faces, extracting attributes, verifying identity, and balancing real-time versus batch processing under privacy and compliance guidelines. We then walked through Custom Vision's workflow for classification and object detection projects, model training, tuning, deployment, and versioning, and finished with Video Indexer's end-to-end pipeline for ingesting, encoding, indexing, and integrating video insights.

Exam Essentials

Understand core Azure Vision services.   Learn the key offerings (Computer Vision API, Custom Vision, Face Service, Video Indexer, Content Moderator) and their primary use cases.

Master image analysis features.   Know how to generate tags and categories, perform object detection, and extract text using both legacy OCR and the Read API, plus apply domain-specific models for landmarks, celebrities, and brands.

Describe Face Service workflows.   Understand face detection and attribute extraction (emotion, head-pose, facial features), plus verification (one-to-one) and identification (one-to-many) with person groups.

Differentiate service tiers and pricing models.   Compare free versus paid tiers, regional availability for latency and compliance, and billing methods (per transaction, per video minute).

Execute Custom Vision projects.   Follow the end-to-end process for classification and object detection: uploading and labeling images, training and evaluating models (precision/recall/ mAP), tuning presets, exporting for cloud or edge, and managing versioned iterations.

Implement Video Indexer pipelines.   Grasp how to ingest, encode, and index video content, then extract and integrate insights such as transcripts, scene markers, OCR on frames, and face/speaker recognition via APIs or low-code tools.

Review Questions

1. You need to automatically generate descriptive captions for user-uploaded photos in your tourism app. Which Azure service should you use?

   A. Custom Vision

   B. Computer Vision API

   C. Video Indexer

   D. Content Moderator

2. Your app must read printed and handwritten notes from images with high accuracy. Which feature of the Computer Vision API is best?

   A. Legacy OCR

   B. Read API

   C. Tagging endpoint

   D. Object detection

3. You need to detect a sofa and a television in living room photos. Which API feature should you call?

   A. Tagging

   B. Domain-specific models

   C. Object detection

   D. Text extraction

4. A multinational client wants to process images in Europe with GDPR compliance and low latency. What should they consider when provisioning their Azure vision service?

   A. Use the free tier in any region

   B. Deploy in North Europe paid tier

   C. Deploy in global endpoint

   D. Deploy in West US for cost savings

5. You want to recognize the Eiffel Tower in travel photos without custom training. Which feature do you use?

   A. Custom Vision

   B. Landmark-recognition model

   C. Celebrity-recognition model

   D. Face Service

6. Your security app must verify a user's identity by comparing a live selfie to a stored face. Which Face Service operation applies?

A. Detect

B. Identify

C. List Person Groups

D. Verify

7. To build an employee check-in system that matches faces against a directory of staff, which Face Service workflow should you implement?

A. Detection → Verify

B. Detection → Identify using a person group

C. Identification → Detection

D. Classification → Person group

8. You need to enforce data deletion policies on facial data under GDPR. Which practice aligns with responsible AI?

A. Never delete face IDs

B. Store face data indefinitely for audit

C. Purge person groups regularly based on policy

D. Use unmanaged storage for facial data

9. A developer wants to train a model to detect defects on their factory line using labeled images. Which service should they choose?

A. Computer Vision API

B. Face Service

C. Custom Vision

D. Video Indexer

10. After training a Custom Vision model, you need to run it on an offline IoT device. What is the best deployment option?

A. Cloud prediction endpoint

B. Export as Docker container

C. Use Computer Vision API

D. Use Face Service container

11. You run multiple Custom Vision training iterations and see mAP scores for each. What does mAP measure?

A. Mean accuracy of precision only

B. Mean average precision across classes balancing precision and recall

C. Maximum accuracy possible

D. Memory allocation policy

12. Your video-processing pipeline must index spoken words, scene changes, and on-screen text. Which Azure service fits?

A. Computer Vision API

B. Custom Vision

C. Video Indexer

D. Face Service

13. You need to embed a searchable video player in your app that jumps to key scenes. Which feature of Video Indexer helps?

A. REST analysis endpoint

B. Embed widget with scene markers

C. Custom Vision export

D. Face Service identify

14. A marketing team wants to track brand logos in social media images. Which Computer Vision feature should they call?

A. Tagging

B. Domain-specific brand detection

C. Text extraction

D. Custom Vision

15. To secure production calls to Computer Vision in a deployed app, which authentication method is recommended?

A. Hard-coded API key

B. Managed identity with DefaultAzureCredential

C. Publicly exposed key in JavaScript

D. Username/password auth

16. You must process thousands of stored images asynchronously and write results to a database. Which pattern should you use?

A. Real-time detection per image

B. Embed widget

C. Live stream API

D. Batch processing with polling

17. Which metric combination gives you a balanced view of a Custom Vision detection model's accuracy?

A. Precision and recall

B. Tags and categories

C. Emotion and head-pose

D. Pricing and latency

18. After exporting a Custom Vision container, you run low-throughput inference on a GPU-enabled edge device. Which container variant do you choose?

A. CPU

B. GPU

C. Serverless

D. Free tier

19. A multi-language news aggregator needs to extract text from images in French and Japanese. Which Computer Vision feature should be used?

A. Legacy OCR

B. Read API automatic language detection

C. Tagging

D. Face Service

20. Your application processes frames from a live camera to unlock a door when an authorized face appears. Which design choice is most important?

A. Batch processing every hour

B. Use Read API

C. Real-time detection at low latency

D. Export Custom Vision model

Chapter

8

Introduction to Natural Language Processing (NLP)

MICROSOFT CERTIFIED: AZURE AI FUNDAMENTALS (AI-900) EXAM OBJECTIVES COVERED IN THIS CHAPTER:

✔ **Domain 4: Describe features of Natural Language Processing (NLP) workloads on Azure**

- Subdomain 4a: Identify features of common NLP Workload Scenarios

  - 4-1 Identify features and uses for key-phrase extraction

  - 4-2 Identify features and uses for entity recognition

  - 4-3 Identify features and uses for sentiment analysis

  - 4-4 Identify features and uses for language modeling

  - 4-5 Identify features and uses for speech recognition and synthesis

  - 4-6 Identify features and uses for translation

Most of the digital communication, search, and decisions you make every day, whether scrolling through social media, using voice commands, or even relying on autocorrect, are powered by Natural Language Processing (NLP). This field is what lets machines "understand" human language. But how does it actually work? How does a computer turn messy, ambiguous sentences into structured data it can use? That's what we're here to unpack.

This chapter will begin by exploring the scope and evolution of NLP, tracing its journey from rule-based systems to today's neural architectures. You'll learn the linguistic foundations that help machines untangle sentences like "I saw her duck" (bird or action?) or resolve pronouns in a paragraph.

Next, you'll see how raw text is preprocessed (tokenization, lemmatization) and converted into numerical formats so algorithms can analyze it. We'll break down language models, the engines behind autocomplete and generative AI, from simple n-gram statistics to neural architectures like BERT and GPT. You'll learn how these models predict the next word in a sentence, classify sentiment in reviews, or flag fake news.

We'll also explore named entity recognition, machine translation, and speech recognition. You'll see how chatbots use sequence-to-sequence models to simulate dialogue and why prompt design is critical for steering AI outputs.

By the end, you'll understand the engineering behind the tech you interact with daily. But we'll also tackle tougher questions: How do we evaluate if an NLP system works well? What happens when models inherit biases from training data? How do we build systems that are both powerful and ethical? This chapter is the foundation you need to properly understand how NLP works.

Introduction to NLP

Natural Language Processing, often shortened to NLP, is the branch of artificial intelligence that focuses on enabling computers to understand, interpret, and generate human language. As part of the AI-900 curriculum, this section lays the groundwork for appreciating how machines bridge the gap between raw data and meaningful communication. At its core, NLP explores the interaction between people and computers through language whether that language is spoken, written, or even gestured in some advanced systems.

In your journey through AI-900, you'll see that NLP draws on linguistics, computer science, and statistics. It uses algorithms to process text or voice data, and turns unstructured input into information that machines can work with. This transformation involves breaking down language into components (words, sentences, meanings) and then applying mathematical models to extract patterns. Here, you'd understand what NLP is, how it evolved, and why it's reshaping industries today.

Understanding NLP and Its Boundaries

NLP is the branch of artificial intelligence that focuses on teaching machines to understand, analyze, and generate human language. Think of it as the bridge between how humans communicate (with all our slang, typos, and sarcasm) and how computers process data (structured, logical, and numerical). NLP solves problems like: How do you make sense of a sentence? How do you translate text between languages? How do you filter spam emails?

The scope of NLP stretches far beyond simple tasks. It includes everything from grammar rules (syntax) to meaning (semantics) to context (pragmatics). For example, when you type "weather today" into a search bar, NLP systems parse the keywords, infer you want a forecast, and fetch location-based results. But it also tackles tougher challenges, like detecting emotions in text or resolving ambiguous phrases (e.g., "He saw the man with the telescope," who has the telescope?).

NLP isn't limited to English or tech giants. It's used in healthcare to analyze patient notes, in finance to monitor market sentiment, and in education to grade essays. However, its scope has limits. Language is messy, and machines still struggle with nuance, like sarcasm ("Great, another meeting!") or cultural references. Understanding these boundaries helps set realistic expectations for what NLP can and can't do today.

A Brief History of NLP

NLP didn't start with ChatGPT or voice assistants. Its roots go back to the 1950s, when early researchers tried to program machines with rigid grammatical rules. For example, the Georgetown-IBM experiment in 1954 automatically translated Russian sentences into English using a tiny vocabulary and hand-coded rules. These rule-based systems worked for narrow tasks but failed with real-world language's complexity.

The 1980s and 1990s brought statistical methods. Instead of relying on predefined rules, computers learned patterns from data. For instance, probabilistic models could guess that "bank" in "river bank" refers to geography, not finance, by analyzing word frequencies in large text corpora. This shift made systems more flexible but still limited by computational power and data scarcity.

The 2010s revolutionized NLP with deep learning and neural networks. Models like Word2Vec (2013) turned words into numerical vectors, capturing meanings mathematically (e.g., "king" – "man" + "woman" ≈ "queen"). Then came transformers in 2017, which introduced attention mechanisms to process entire sentences at once. This led to breakthroughs like BERT and GPT-3, which generate human-like text.

Real-World NLP Applications

You interact with NLP daily, even if you don't realize it. When Outlook suggests a sentence to finish your email, that's autocomplete powered by language models. When Teams transcribes a meeting in real time, that's speech-to-text conversion. And when you use Bing to search for "best budget laptops," NLP parses your query, ignores stop words like "best," and retrieves relevant results.

Beyond everyday tools, NLP drives enterprise solutions. Sentiment analysis scans social media to gauge public opinion about a product. Named Entity Recognition (NER) extracts dates, names, and locations from legal documents. Translation services like Microsoft Translator break language barriers in global teams. But NLP also tackles specialized problems. In healthcare, it mines patient records to predict disease outbreaks. In customer service, chatbots handle routine queries, freeing humans for complex issues. Even creative fields use NLP: tools like GitHub Copilot suggest code snippets by "reading" your comments. The key takeaway is that NLP is a versatile tool across industries.

Core Concepts in Linguistic Analysis

At the heart of every NLP system lies a simple question: How do computers make sense of words? Human language is full of ambiguity, slang, and hidden meanings, yet machines somehow parse it. This section explores the three pillars of linguistic analysis: syntax (structure), semantics (meaning), and pragmatics (context). These layers let algorithms break down sentences, infer intent, and even mimic human-like understanding.

Syntax and Sentence Structure

Syntax is the study of how words are arranged to form grammatically correct phrases and sentences. For example, in "The boy cooked for the girl," syntax tells us "boy" is the subject (the doer) and "girl" is the object (the receiver). In NLP, part-of-speech (POS) tagging assigns labels like noun, verb, or adjective to each word. This helps machines identify relationships: "cooked" is an action, so it connects the boy and girl.

But syntax isn't just labeling. Parsing builds sentence diagrams (like you might've hated in school) to show hierarchy. Take the sentence "She saw the man with glasses." A parser determines if "with glasses" describes the man (he's wearing them) or the act of seeing (she used glasses to see). This ambiguity matters for tasks like search engines or voice assistants. Misinterpreting syntax leads to wrong answers.

Modern tools automate this. Libraries like spaCy or Microsoft's Text Analytics API use pretrained models to tag and parse text at scale. For example, when you tell an AI assistant, "Remind me to call Mom tomorrow," POS tagging identifies "remind" as a verb, triggering an action, and "tomorrow" as a date entity. Syntax turns chaotic words into structured commands.

Semantics and What We Really Say

Semantics answers the question: What does this actually mean? Consider the word "bank." In "I deposited money at the bank," it's a financial institution. In "We sat by the river bank," it's land. Word sense disambiguation (WSD) resolves this using context. Machines analyze surrounding words ("deposited" vs. "river") to pick the right meaning, and this is a critical step for accurate translation or search. But semantics goes deeper. Semantic roles identify who did what to whom. In "Ngozichukwu emailed the report to the team," "Ngozichukwu" is the agent (doer), "report" is the theme (object acted upon), and "team" is the recipient. This helps extract actionable data: In customer feedback like "The app crashes on startup," the verb "crashes" points to a problem, and "app" is the subject, which is key for prioritizing bug fixes.

Modern NLP systems use knowledge graphs and contextual embeddings to model meaning. For example, Microsoft's Azure Cognitive Search leverages semantics to improve search relevance. If you query "AI courses for beginners," it understands "courses" as educational programs (not golf courses) and "beginners" as novices, filtering results accordingly.

Pragmatics and How Language Connects

Pragmatics examines how context shapes meaning, such as interpreting "Can you pass the salt?" as a request to pass salt rather than a yes/no question. Machines need pragmatics to grasp implied intent. Discourse analysis examines how sentences connect in a conversation or paragraph. If someone says, "I'm starving. There's a suya place nearby," pragmatics links the two statements to infer a suggestion to eat.

A major challenge is coreference resolution, tracking pronouns and references. In "Emeka said he'll submit the report. It's due tomorrow," "he" refers to Emeka, and "it" refers to the report. Errors here cascade: Misassigning "it" to "tomorrow" would break task-tracking systems. Tools like Microsoft's Language Service API handle this by analyzing entire documents, not just isolated sentences.

Pragmatics also deals with cultural nuance. For instance, "Let's circle back later" in a US meeting means "discuss this again," but literal translations in other languages might confuse. Voice assistants like Azure Bot Service use pragmatics to maintain conversation history, allowing follow-up questions like "What about tomorrow?" without re-stating context.

Text Preprocessing and Representation

Before a computer can analyze language, raw text like emails, social media posts, or documents, need to be cleaned, organized, and converted into a format algorithms can digest. This section covers the essential steps to transform messy, unstructured text into structured data. We'll explore splitting text into pieces, standardizing words, and turning words into numbers, as this is the foundation of every NLP pipeline.

Tokenization and Sentence Segmentation

Tokenization is the process of slicing a stream of text into discrete units, typically words, phrases, or symbols, that serve as the basic building blocks for analysis. Imagine reading a sentence aloud and pausing between words; tokenization automates those pauses. Depending on the language and application, tokens might include punctuation marks or special symbols, but the ultimate goal is to define consistent elements that algorithms can count, compare, and manipulate.

Sentence segmentation complements tokenization by determining where one sentence ends and another begins. This isn't always as simple as splitting on periods; consider abbreviations like "Dr." or ellipses in casual writing. Sophisticated segmentation tools use language-specific rules and statistical cues to handle such quirks, ensuring that analyses like sentiment scoring or entity extraction respect sentence boundaries and don't mix contexts.

In Azure's Text Analytics and Language Understanding (LUIS) services, tokenization and segmentation happen under the hood, freeing you from manual implementation. However, awareness of these processes empowers you to troubleshoot issues such as a model misidentifying "U.S.A." as three separate tokens or failing to split sentences in news headlines. It's important to know how segmentation and tokenization work, so that you can interpret service outputs and adjust pre- and post-processing steps better.

Normalization Techniques

Once text is tokenized, normalization cleans and standardizes those tokens to reduce noise and variability. Lowercasing is the simplest example: by converting "Apple" and "apple" to the same form, you prevent redundant entries in your vocabulary. However, normalization goes beyond this and tackles inconsistencies that could skew analyses, such as multiple spellings of the same word or common stop words that add little semantic value.

Stop-word removal strips out frequent but uninformative words (like "and," "the," or "is") that appear so often they cloud the meaningful signals. While stop-word lists vary by language and application, removing these filler tokens can shrink vocabulary size and speed up processing without sacrificing critical information.

Stemming and lemmatization both aim to reduce words to their root forms but differ in approach. Stemming applies heuristic rules to chop off suffixes, which turns "running," "runs," and "runner" into "run," often producing non-dictionary stems. Lemmatization, by contrast, uses vocabulary and part-of-speech information to return proper base forms, handling irregularities like "ran" back to "run." Choosing between stemming and lemmatization balances speed against linguistic accuracy, especially when building generalized models in Azure.

Effective normalization can dramatically improve model performance by consolidating variants of the same word and removing distracting tokens. Microsoft's Azure Cognitive Services often uses lemmatization for tasks like document summarization, where precision matters.

Text Representations

Computers don't understand words, they understand numbers. Bag-of-Words (BoW) is the simplest representation because it counts how often each word appears in a text. For example, "The cat chased the mouse" becomes {"the":2, "cat":1, "chased":1, "mouse":1}. BoW ignores word order but works well for spam detection or topic classification.

Term Frequency-Inverse Document Frequency (TF-IDF) improves BoW by weighting words based on importance. Frequent words in a document (high TF) but rare across all documents (high IDF) get higher scores. For instance, in a corpus about pets, "cat" might have a lower IDF (common) versus "gerbil" (rare). This helps search engines rank relevant results or recommend articles.

Word embeddings (e.g., Word2Vec, GloVe) capture semantic meaning by mapping words to dense vectors. Similar words cluster in vector space: "king" and "queen" are closer than "king" and "car." Modern models like BERT generate contextual embeddings, where "bank" has different vectors in "river bank" versus "bank account." Microsoft's Azure OpenAI Service uses these embeddings to power semantic search and chatbots that grasp nuanced queries.

Language Modeling

Language modeling is the art (and science) of predicting what comes next in a sequence of words. It's why your phone suggests "you" after you type "I love" or why chatbots can hold conversations. This section explores how machines learn patterns in language, starting with simple statistics, advancing to neural networks, and culminating in models that understand context.

Statistical N-gram Models

N-gram models are one of the earliest approaches to language modeling. They work by predicting the next word based on the previous n words. For example, a bigram model (n = 2) looks at pairs: In "I want to __," if "to" is often followed by "play" in training data, it guesses "play." These models rely on probability tables built from massive text corpora. They're fast and lightweight, making them useful for early spell-checkers or basic autocomplete.

But n-grams have limits. They struggle with long-range dependencies. Take the sentence: "The book I borrowed from the library, which was about ancient Igboland, is __." A 3-gram model only sees "Igboland, is __" and might guess "interesting" instead of "overdue." They also fail with rare phrases. If a specific 4-gram isn't in the training data, the model returns zero probability, and this is a problem called sparsity.

Despite these flaws, n-grams are still used in hybrid systems. For instance, they power quick suggestions in search bars or simple grammar checks. They're a stepping stone to understanding why modern models evolved.

Neural Language Models

Neural language models marked a turning point in NLP by using artificial neural networks to learn rich representations of words and contexts. Early incarnations used recurrent neural networks (RNNs), which process sequences one token at a time and maintain a hidden state that captures information about previous tokens. In theory, RNNs can learn dependencies across long text spans, but in practice they often struggle with vanishing gradients, making it hard to remember distant context.

Long Short-Term Memory networks, or LSTMs, addressed these challenges by introducing specialized gating mechanisms that regulate the flow of information. LSTMs can capture longer dependencies when they selectively remember or forget inputs at each step. This makes them ideal for tasks like speech recognition or machine translation. In the Azure ecosystem, custom model deployments may still use LSTM-based architectures when moderate complexity and strong sequence modeling are required without the full overhead of transformers.

More recently, transformer models have reshaped neural language modeling by dispensing with recurrence altogether. Transformers use self-attention mechanisms to weigh the importance of every token in the input sequence relative to every other token. Unlike RNNs, transformers process all words in a sentence at once using attention mechanisms, like highlighting relevant words as you read. For example, in "Ada gave Obiageli the ice cream because Obiageli was sad," the transformer focuses on "Ada" and "Obiageli" to link "sad" to the reason for giving ice cream. This parallel processing made models faster and more accurate, and enabled breakthroughs like real-time translation in models.

Contextual Embeddings

Traditional word embeddings gave each word a fixed vector, ignoring context. But "bank" in "blood bank" versus "bank account" should have different meanings. Contextual embeddings are very helpful here. Models like BERT and GPT generate dynamic vectors based on surrounding text. For example, BERT reads entire sentences bidirectionally, so "He deposited cash in the bank" versus "They picnicked by the bank" produces distinct embeddings for "bank."

BERT (Bidirectional Encoder Representations from Transformers) excels at understanding context for tasks like answering questions or sentiment analysis. When you ask an AI assistant, "What's the weather in Enugu next week?" BERT-style models parse the intent (weather forecast) and entities (Enugu, next week). GPT (Generative Pretrained Transformer), on the other hand, specializes in generating text. It's why Azure OpenAI Service can draft emails or write code snippets by predicting sequences word by word. These models are pretrained on large collections of digital text data, then fine-tuned for specific tasks.

Text Classification and Sentiment Analysis

Text classification and sentiment analysis investigate patterns in words to categorize documents or detect opinions. This section covers how machines learn to label text, the battle between rule-based and AI-driven sentiment tools, and how to measure if they're doing a good job.

Feature Engineering for Classification

Feature engineering is the process of turning text into signals that algorithms can learn from. If you're teaching a child to sort fruits: You might say, "Apples are red and round; bananas are yellow and curved." For text classification, features could be word frequencies (how often "discount" appears in spam emails), sentence length, or even punctuation marks like exclamation points.

In the early days, engineers handcrafted these features. For example, a spam detector might flag emails with words like "free" or "urgent." But this approach misses subtle patterns. Modern methods like TF-IDF automatically highlight important words. If "password" appears often in security alerts but rarely in general emails, TF-IDF gives it a high weight, helping the model prioritize it.

However, raw features can be noisy. Emojis, typos, or slang ("gr8" for "great") require cleaning and normalization. Tools like Azure Machine Learning automate much of this, and convert text into numerical matrices while handling edge cases. For instance, a customer support classifier might use features like product mentions ("Surface Pro," "Xbox") and urgency keywords ("broken," "refund") to route tickets to the right team.

Sentiment Analysis Approaches

Sentiment analysis helps evaluate if the text is positive, negative, or neutral. The approaches generally fall into two categories called lexicon based and machine learning based. Lexicon-based approaches use predefined dictionaries where words have sentiment scores. For example, "happy" = +1, "terrible" = –2. The model sums these scores: "The service was quick but overpriced" might net to –1 (negative). This method is transparent and works without training data, so it's great for quick prototypes or domain-specific jargon (e.g., "sick" meaning "cool" in slang).

But lexicons struggle with context. Sarcasm like "What a great idea!" negations like "not bad," or phrases like "kill it" (which could mean "succeed" or literal violence) trip them up. Machine learning–based models solve this by learning from labeled examples. A classifier trained on thousands of product reviews learns that "battery life is a joke" is negative, even if "joke" isn't in the lexicon. Given enough annotated data (for example, tweets tagged as positive or negative, for instance) these models learn patterns that correlate with sentiment. They can pick up on subtle cues and combinations of words that lexicons miss. In Azure, you might use the Text Analytics service's built-in sentiment API for a quick solution or train a custom model with Azure Machine Learning when you need finer control or specialized domains, such as financial news or product reviews.

Hybrid solutions blend both worlds, starting with a lexicon-based assessment and then refining scores using learned adjustments from a machine learning model. This strategy can yield strong performance even with limited data, as the lexicon provides a solid baseline and the model corrects its weaknesses. Ultimately, the choice of method depends on your data volume, domain specificity, and performance requirements. Azure's flexible tooling means you can begin with a prebuilt API to validate your use case, then graduate to custom training when you need to squeeze out extra accuracy or address specific challenges.

Evaluation Metrics

Once you've built a classifier or sentiment model, you need ways to measure how well it performs. Evaluation metrics tell you if your classifier is a genius or a guesser. Accuracy seems simple, but it's misleading for imbalanced data. If 95% of emails are not spam, a model that labels everything "not spam" scores 95% accuracy but misses all spam.

Precision and recall give you a clearer picture. Precision tells you, of all the items your model labeled as positive (or spam), how many truly were. High precision means few false alarms, which is critical when a mistake carries a real cost, like misclassifying a genuine customer complaint. Recall, by contrast, measures coverage: of all true positive instances in the data, what fraction did the model catch? A high recall rate ensures you miss few actual positives, and this is important in safety-critical contexts, for example, flagging toxic content. Since precision and recall often tradeoff against each other, the F1 score is a single measure that balances both. It's the harmonic mean of precision and recall, rewarding models that perform well on both fronts rather than optimizing one at the expense of the other.

In practice, tradeoffs depend on the use case. A sentiment model for product reviews might prioritize recall (catching all negative feedback) over precision, while a spam filter needs high precision to avoid trashing important emails.

Deep Dive into Precision, Recall, and F1 Score

When evaluating a classification model (whether it's flagging spam emails or detecting sentiment), you often start with a confusion matrix, which breaks down predictions versus actual labels. For a binary problem (positive vs. negative), it looks like Table 8.1.

This table is the foundation for all three metrics. Each element tells a story: TP is when the model correctly identifies positives, FP is when it cries wolf, and FN is when it misses a real positive.

Precision asks, "When my model predicts positive, how often is it right?" Mathematically:

Precision = TP / (TP + FP)

TABLE 8.1   The Confusion Matrix

	Predicted positive	**Predicted negative**
Actual positive	True Positives (TP)	False Negative (FN)
Actual negative	False Positives (FP)	True Negatives (TN)

A precision of 0.80 means that 80% of the items your model flagged as positive truly were positive. High precision is critical when false alarms carry high cost. For instance, if an email firewall wrongly quarantines important business mail.

Recall (also called sensitivity) flips the question: "Of all the actual positives, how many did my model catch?"

Mathematically:

Recall = TP / (TP + FN)

A recall of 0.75 implies your model finds 75% of the real positives but misses the other 25%. Recall is vital in scenarios like medical diagnostics, where missing a true condition can have serious consequences. In these high-stakes environments, explainable AI is equally critical. Medical professionals need to understand not just the prediction but also the reasoning behind it, allowing them to validate the model's logic against their clinical knowledge.

Because there's often a tradeoff, raising precision can lower recall and vice versa, we use the F1 score to balance them. The F1 score is the harmonic mean of precision and recall:

F1 = 2 × ((Precision × Recall) / (Precision + Recall))

Unlike a simple average, the harmonic mean punishes extreme imbalances. If precision is 1.0 but recall is 0.0, the F1 score is 0.0, highlighting that you can't ignore one metric in favor of the other. An F1 of 0.85 tells you your model has struck a good balance, correctly flagging most positives while keeping false alarms reasonably low.

Information Extraction

Information extraction turns unstructured text into structured knowledge. Imagine reading a news article and instantly highlighting names, dates, and key events or scanning a research paper to pull out main topics and their connections. This section covers the tools that automate this process.

Named Entity Recognition

Named Entity Recognition (NER) identifies and classifies specific "things" in text—like people, organizations, dates, or locations. For example, in "Adora Nwodo became an Engineering Manager in 2023," NER tags "Adora Nwodo" as a person, "Engineering Manager" as a job/role, and "2023" as a date. This helps machines answer questions like "What does Adora Nwodo do?" or "When did Adora Nwodo become an Engineering Manager?"

Under the hood, NER models often combine linguistic rules with machine learning approaches. Rule-based components might flag capitalized words at the start of sentences, while statistical or neural network models learn from annotated examples to recognize entities in more complex contexts. Azure's Text Analytics service has a prebuilt NER API that handles dozens of entity types out of the box, but you can also train custom models to detect domain-specific entities like medical terms or legal clauses.

But NER isn't foolproof. Ambiguity is a major hurdle. In the example below, is "Apple" a fruit or a tech giant? Context matters. In "Apple released a new iPhone," the model uses surrounding words ("released," "iPhone") to infer it's the company. Another challenge is handling variations: "Dr. Orah" versus "Elizabeth Orah, PhD" both refer to a person with a doctorate degree.

Key-Phrase Extraction

Key-phrase extraction identifies the most informative words and multi-word expressions within a document, those snippets that capture its essence. Unlike NER, which focuses on predefined categories, key-phrase extraction is domain-agnostic: it surfaces terms like "machine learning pipeline," "customer churn," or "annual revenue" based purely on their importance to the text.

Techniques for extracting key phrases range from statistical methods, such as scoring phrases by frequency and position, to graph-based algorithms that model words as nodes and connections as edges. Simple methods like TF-IDF score phrases based on how often they appear in a document versus a larger corpus. Words like "innovation" might score high in a tech blog but lower in a cooking blog. Machine learning models, such as BERT, take this further by understanding context. For instance, in "Python is a versatile language," BERT recognizes "Python" as a programming language, not a snake, making it a relevant key phrase.

Relation Extraction Basics

Relation extraction identifies how entities are connected. For example, in "Adora Nwodo authored the AI-900 study guide in 2025," the model detects an "authoring" relationship between "Adora" (person) and "AI-900 study guide" (book), with "2025" as the date. This turns isolated facts into knowledge graphs, enabling queries like "Which books has Adora Nwodo authored?"

Early approaches used pattern-based rules, like looking for verbs such as "authored" or "wrote." Modern systems employ machine learning to recognize diverse relationships, even implicit ones. In "Adora Nwodo authored the AI-900 study guide and Beginning Azure DevOps," a model infers two "author" relationships without explicit verbs like "created."

Challenges include ambiguity and context. The sentence "Apple grows in California" could mean the company's expansion or literal fruit farming. Pretrained models like BERT use attention mechanisms to weigh context clues, such as "grows" (business growth) versus "grown" (agriculture).

Language Generation and Conversational NLP

Language generation and conversational systems are where NLP meets creativity. Imagine asking a chatbot for cooking tips, drafting an email with AI assistance, or having a virtual assistant book a meeting. These tasks require machines not just to understand language but to generate it coherently and contextually. This section explores the architectures and techniques that let AI systems chat, create, and collaborate like humans.

Sequence-to-Sequence Architectures

Sequence-to-sequence (seq2seq) architectures changed language generation by introducing an encoder-decoder framework capable of handling variable-length inputs and outputs. The encoder converts the input into a compact numerical representation (a context vector), and the decoder uses this to generate the output word by word. This flexible design paved the way for neural machine translation and beyond.

Early seq2seq models used RNNs, but they struggled with long sentences like translating a complex paragraph, where the encoder might forget key details by the time it reached the end. The introduction of attention mechanisms changed the game. Attention mechanisms solved this by giving the decoder a way to *look back* at different encoder outputs at each generation step, assigning weights that highlight the most relevant tokens. As a result, the model learns not just a single summary vector but a dynamic view of the entire input, greatly improving translation quality and enabling new tasks like summarization.

Modern systems like transformers (used in models such as GPT and BERT) replaced RNNs with self-attention, processing entire sentences in parallel. This massively improved speed and accuracy, enabling real-time applications like live captioning or instant translation in tools like Microsoft Translator.

When working with seq2seq systems, it's important to consider decoding strategies (greedy decoding, beam search, or sampling techniques) to balance speed, diversity, and coherence. Beam search explores multiple candidate outputs to find high-probability sequences, while sampling adds randomness that can produce more varied or creative text.

Building Chatbots

Chatbots are pipelines of interconnected components that process user utterances, decide on actions, and craft responses. First, the system processes the user's input using natural language understanding (NLU) to identify intent (e.g., "book a flight") and extract entities (e.g., "Enugu," "tomorrow"). Next, dialogue management tracks context across turns. If a user says, "What about hotels?" after booking a flight, the system infers they want lodging in the same location and dates.

Modern chatbots often use hybrid approaches, combining rule-based logic for reliability (e.g., handling "Reset my password") with machine learning for flexibility (e.g., parsing vague requests like "Find me something fun to do"). Platforms like Microsoft Bot Framework has tools to design these workflows, integrating with databases and APIs to fetch real-time data.

A key challenge is maintaining coherent, multi-turn conversations. If a user asks, "What's the weather today?" followed by "Will it rain tomorrow?" the bot must remember the location and adjust the timeframe. Techniques like state tracking and context windows (storing recent dialogue history) help models stay on topic.

But chatbots aren't perfect. They can falter with ambiguous queries or cultural nuances. Powerful systems include fallback mechanisms, like escalating to a human agent or asking clarifying questions. This blend of autonomy and guardrails makes chatbots useful in customer service and education.

Fundamentals of Prompt Design

Prompts are instructions that guide AI-generated text. It is a critical skill for driving large pretrained models toward desired outputs without explicit retraining. A well-constructed prompt sets context, conveys the task, and provides any necessary formatting cues to shape the model's response.

Effective prompt design balances specificity and flexibility. A vague prompt like "Explain quantum computing" might produce a textbook definition, but adding "Explain it like I'm 10" simplifies the language. Advanced techniques include few-shot learning, where examples are embedded in the prompt (e.g., "Translate 'Hello' to French: Bonjour. Translate 'Goodbye' to French: __").

However, prompts can also expose model limitations. Asking "When did Adora write her first book?" might yield a wrong date if the model's training data is outdated. Similarly, biased prompts ("Why is X the best company?") can lead to skewed answers. Designing ethical, clear prompts requires understanding both the model's capabilities and its blind spots.

Tools like Azure OpenAI Service let developers experiment with prompts, tuning parameters like response length and creativity. Mastery of prompt design is critical for applications ranging from content generation (drafting blogs) to code completion (suggesting Python functions). It transforms raw AI potential into practical, user-friendly solutions.

Speech Processing Basics

Every time you ask a virtual assistant for the weather, listen to an audiobook narrated by AI, or use live captioning in a meeting, you're interacting with systems that convert speech to text and vice versa. This section explores the pipelines that make voice interfaces possible.

Automatic Speech Recognition Pipeline

Automatic Speech Recognition (ASR) turns spoken language into written text. Imagine shouting "Set a timer for 10 minutes!" to your smart speaker: The ASR pipeline starts by capturing your voice as an audio waveform. This raw sound is split into tiny frames (milliseconds long) to analyze pitch, volume, and frequency patterns. Noise reduction algorithms then clean up background sounds, like filtering out a barking dog or traffic hum.

Next, the system converts these acoustic features into phonemes, the smallest units of sound (e.g., the "k" in "cat" or "sh" in "shoe"). Machine learning models, often trained on thousands of hours of labeled speech, map these phonemes to words. A language model (like those used in text prediction) refines the output by guessing the most probable word sequences. For example, "Let's eat, Obiora!" versus "Let's eat Obiora!" The model uses context to avoid accidental cannibalism.

But ASR isn't flawless. Accents, mumbling, or overlapping speech can challenge accuracy. They also need to meet performance targets. Some applications demand instant feedback, while others can process recordings more leisurely. Balancing these needs influences architectural choices and service configurations, making it crucial to grasp both the theory and practical tradeoffs in speech processing.

Text-to-Speech Synthesis Pipeline

Text-to-Speech (TTS) synthesis does the reverse: It turns written words into spoken audio. Think of GPS navigation saying, "Turn left in 500 meters." The first step is text analysis, where the input string is normalized: numbers become words ("123" to "one hundred twenty-three"), abbreviations are expanded, and punctuation is interpreted for prosody cues. This ensures the text is in a form that the synthesis model can handle predictably.

Next, the system breaks text into prosodic units (phrases and sentences) to predict rhythm, stress, and intonation. Should "Really?" sound skeptical or curious? Modern TTS uses neural networks to model these nuances. Waveform generation then produces the actual sound. Early systems spliced recordings of human voices, which resulted in robotic monotony, but today's neural TTS generates fluid, expressive speech by mimicking human vocal patterns.

Machine Translation Fundamentals

Machine translation empowers computers to convert text or speech from one language into another, breaking down communication barriers across the globe. But how do algorithms turn "Ụtụtụ ọma" or "Bonjour" into "Hello" while preserving meaning, tone, and nuance? We'll explore the evolution from rigid rulebooks to AI-driven systems and how we measure if they're doing it right.

Rule-Based and Statistical Methods

Early machine translation systems relied on rule-based approaches, where linguists manually wrote dictionaries and grammar rules. For example, to translate French to English, rules might swap adjective-noun order ("chat noir" → "black cat") and map vocabulary ("bonjour" → "hello"). These systems worked for simple, predictable sentences but stumbled over idioms, slang, or complex grammar. Translating "It's raining cats and dogs" into French using rules alone might yield literal gibberish about falling animals.

In the 1990s, statistical machine translation took over. Instead of handcrafted rules, SMT analyzed massive bilingual text corpora to calculate probabilities. For instance, it learned that "maison" most often translates to "house" by observing millions of aligned French-English sentences. Phrase-based translation broke sentences into chunks (phrases) and recombined them statistically, improving fluency.

Despite their advantages, SMT systems had limitations. They struggled with long-distance dependencies, often confusing word order and generating awkward phrasing when the statistical evidence was sparse. Models required careful smoothing techniques and large corpora to handle rare words or idiomatic expressions. Because SMT operated on fixed-length phrases, it sometimes failed to capture nuanced meanings that crossed phrase boundaries, leading to mistranslations in complex sentences.

The statistical foundation also taught valuable lessons about translation probabilities, alignment models, and the importance of diverse training data. It set the stage for neural approaches by demonstrating that machine learning could outperform rigid, rule-based pipelines. As you explore modern translation services, you'll see that SMT's influence remains in concepts like phrase alignment and evaluation strategies, even as neural methods have largely taken center stage.

Attention-Driven Machine Translation

Neural machine translation (NMT) upended the statistical paradigm by using end-to-end neural networks to learn translation directly from data. Early NMT models employed an encoder-decoder architecture: the encoder read the entire source sentence and compressed it into a fixed-size vector, while the decoder generated the target sentence token by token. This design produced more fluent translations but struggled when dealing with long or complex sentences, as a single vector could not capture all the necessary information.

The introduction of attention mechanisms was a breakthrough in NMT. Instead of relying on a single summary vector, attention allowed the decoder to peek back at the encoder's hidden states for every target word it produced. By computing dynamic weights like attention scores over the source tokens, the model learned to focus on the most relevant parts of the input at each generation step. This ability to align and attend improved translation quality dramatically, especially for longer sentences and subtle language phenomena.

Building on attention, transformer architectures removed recurrence altogether, relying solely on stacked self-attention layers. Transformers process all tokens in parallel, modeling relationships between every pair of words in a sentence simultaneously. This parallelism speeds up training and better captures global context. Most modern translation services now use transformer-based NMT, benefiting from faster convergence, superior fluency, and strong handling of long-range dependencies.

Yet NMT isn't perfect. It can hallucinate translations for unknown words or cultural concepts (e.g., local idioms). Training also requires massive computational power and clean data. Still, NMT's ability to capture context and produce natural-sounding text makes it the gold standard today.

Measuring Translation Quality

How do we measure if a translation is good? Human evaluation is ideal but slow and expensive. Automated metrics like BLEU (Bilingual Evaluation Understudy) and METEOR fill the gap. BLEU compares machine-translated text to human reference translations by counting matching n-grams (word sequences). For example, if the output shares 3-grams like "the black cat" with the reference, it scores higher. However, BLEU ignores synonyms and grammar, a translation could have perfect n-grams but sound robotic.

METEOR addresses some BLEU flaws by incorporating synonyms, stemming (matching "running" with "ran"), and sentence structure. It also penalizes fragmentation, rewarding fluent, coherent sentences. For instance, "fast feline" might partially match "quick cat" in METEOR but not in BLEU. While more nuanced, METEOR still can't capture creativity or cultural appropriateness.

Another valuable approach involves comparing outputs from multiple translation models on the same source text. When models produce different translations for the same sentence, examining these variations reveals strengths and weaknesses. For instance, one model might excel at preserving technical terminology while another captures conversational tone better. Areas where models consistently disagree often signal challenging linguistic phenomena that warrant human review.

Both automated metrics and model comparison have blind spots. A translation might score poorly on BLEU but be perfectly valid (e.g., rephrasing "How are you?" as "How do you do?"). Conversely, a high-scoring translation could miss nuances like formality or humor. Human-in-the-loop evaluation remains critical for high-stakes domains like legal or medical translation. Despite limitations, BLEU and METEOR drive progress. Researchers use them to benchmark models, and companies rely on them to iterate on systems.

Evaluation, Challenges, and Ethics

When we build language systems, it's vital to ask not just "Does this model work?" but "In what ways does it work, and at what cost?" Evaluation, challenges, and ethics form the final frontier in natural language processing, guiding us from raw performance metrics to responsible deployment.

Evaluating NLP systems involves intrinsic and extrinsic methods. Intrinsic evaluation measures standalone performance on specific tasks. For example, testing a sentiment analyzer's accuracy by comparing its outputs to human-labeled data. Metrics like precision, recall, or BLEU scores (for translation) fall here because they're precise but narrow.

Extrinsic evaluation, on the other hand, tests how well a system performs in real-world scenarios. If a chatbot's goal is to reduce customer service calls, extrinsic metrics might track call volume before and after deployment. This approach measures practical impact but is harder to control. External factors (e.g., a product recall) could skew results.

Both methods have tradeoffs. Intrinsic metrics are reproducible and isolate model performance but risk overfitting to benchmarks. Extrinsic metrics reflect real-world value but are noisy and context-dependent. Modern NLP combines both. A translation tool might ace BLEU scores (intrinsic) but fail in user surveys because it sounds robotic (extrinsic). Choosing the right evaluation depends on the goal. A spell-checker needs high intrinsic accuracy (catching errors), while a medical chatbot requires extrinsic validation (do doctors trust it?). Balancing both ensures systems are both technically sound and practically useful.

It's also important to note that NLP models are only as good as the data they're trained on. Data annotation transforms raw text into labeled examples like tagging entities in news articles, marking sentiment in tweets, or aligning sentences in parallel corpora. For instance, labeling movie reviews as "positive" or "negative" trains sentiment models. But annotation is labor-intensive and subjective. Two annotators might disagree on whether "This movie is something" is sarcastic or sincere, introducing noise.

Benchmarks (standard datasets and tasks) drive progress. Examples include GLUE (General Language Understanding Evaluation), a collection of tasks designed to evaluate a model's ability to understand language, and SQuAD (Stanford Question Answering Dataset), a reading comprehension benchmark that tests whether models can answer questions based on a given passage for question answering. These let researchers compare models objectively. However, benchmarks have blind spots. If a dataset mostly contains formal English text, models trained on it might fail with slang or dialects.

Corpora (large text collections) also shape what models learn. A corpus of news articles will teach different language patterns than Reddit comments. Biases in corpora, like overrepresentation for certain demographics, leak into models. For example, a resume-screening tool trained on male-dominated tech industry data might undervalue female applicants. A hiring tool might favor resumes with "executive" titles (historically male-dominated) or a chatbot might associate "nurse" with "she." These biases stem from skewed training data, cultural stereotypes, or flawed annotations. The consequences are enforced discrimination, eroded trust, and legal risks.

Fixing bias isn't just technical. Fairness involves defining what "fair" means in a context. Is it equal error rates across groups? Equal access to outcomes? For example, a speech recognition system that mishears non-native accents more than native ones is unfair in customer service but acceptable in a local call center. Tools like Fairlearn or Azure's Responsible AI Dashboard help quantify and mitigate disparities, but they require human judgment to set fairness goals

Ethical NLP goes beyond bias. It asks: Should we build this? A deepfake text generator could help authors brainstorm or spread misinformation. Also transparency is key. Can users tell if they're talking to a bot? Does a model explain its decisions in healthcare? Regulations like GDPR (requiring explicability) push developers to prioritize accountability.

Ultimately, ethical NLP is a moving target. It demands collaboration with engineers, ethicists, and impacted communities to audit systems, iterate on guidelines, and prioritize harm reduction. The goal isn't perfect neutrality (this is impossible in a biased world) but conscious responsibility.

Summary

The chapter covered the evolution of NLP from rule-based methods to transformer-based models and the importance of tokenization, lemmatization, and normalization for preparing raw text. It described how text is represented numerically through bag-of-words, TF-IDF, and contextual embeddings, and how language models predict word sequences. The chapter explained building and evaluating text classifiers and sentiment analyzers using precision, recall, and F1 score, as well as extracting structured data with named entity recognition, key-phrase extraction, and relation detection. It examined sequence-to-sequence and prompt-design approaches for generating text and chatbots, detailed speech processing pipelines for automatic speech recognition and text-to-speech synthesis, and traced the shift in machine translation from statistical to attention-driven neural systems measured by BLEU and METEOR. Finally, it addressed intrinsic and extrinsic evaluation methods, the challenges of bias and ambiguity, and the ethical considerations essential for responsible NLP deployment.

Exam Essentials

Define natural language processing and its main applications. Understand how NLP enables classification, sentiment analysis, named entity recognition, language generation, and speech interfaces.

Describe text preprocessing and representation. Know tokenization, sentence segmentation, normalization (stemming and lemmatization), and numerical encoding techniques like bag-of-words, TF-IDF, and word embeddings.

Compare language modeling approaches. Contrast statistical n-gram models, neural networks (RNNs and LSTMs), and transformer architectures for predicting word sequences.

Outline information extraction and generation workflows. Recognize how named entity recognition (NER), key-phrase and relation extraction structure text, and sequence-to-sequence models and prompt design power chatbots.

Explain speech processing and machine translation pipelines. Learn the stages of automatic speech recognition and text-to-speech synthesis, and the evolution from rule-based and statistical translation to attention-driven neural systems evaluated by BLEU and METEOR.

Apply evaluation metrics and ethical principles. Use precision, recall, F1 score, BLEU, and METEOR for intrinsic evaluation, understand extrinsic assessment, and consider bias, fairness, and responsible deployment.

Review Questions

1. A retail company wants to automatically flag negative product reviews in near real time using Azure. Which service and approach should they choose for the highest out-of-the-box accuracy with minimal configuration?

   A. Azure Text Analytics sentiment API (machine learning based)

   B. Azure Machine Learning with a custom lexicon-based model

   C. Azure Cognitive Search with TF-IDF scoring

   D. Azure Bot Service with rule-based sentiment rules

2. An engineer needs to split a batch of customer support emails into sentences before further analysis. Which preprocessing step in Azure's Text Analytics pipeline handles this?

   A. Sentence segmentation

   B. Tokenization

   C. Lemmatization

   D. Word embedding

3. A healthcare startup must extract patient names, dates, and medication dosages from clinical notes. Which Azure feature best accomplishes this with minimal custom training?

   A. Custom model in Azure Machine Learning

   B. Translation API with metadata extraction

   C. Cognitive Search with key-phrase extraction

   D. Prebuilt named entity recognition in Text Analytics

4. During feature engineering for a text classifier, an analyst chooses TF-IDF over bag-of-words. What advantage does TF-IDF provide in this scenario?

   A. Captures word order

   B. Reduces vocabulary size

   C. Provides contextual embeddings

   D. Weighs rare but important words higher

5. A fraud detection team trains a model on highly imbalanced transaction descriptions. Which metric should they monitor to ensure they catch as many fraudulent cases as possible?

   A. Accuracy

   B. Precision

   C. Recall

   D. BLEU score

6. An AI-900 student implements a lexicon-based sentiment analyzer and notices it fails on "I can't say this service is bad." What is the likely cause?

   A. Missing entity recognition

   B. Inability to handle negation

   C. Poor tokenization

   D. Overfitting on training data

7. A global enterprise needs to translate user feedback from French to English in a chatbot. They require the most fluent output for long sentences. Which Azure service and model type fit best?

   A. Translator Text with neural (transformer) translation

   B. Translator Text with rule-based pipeline

   C. Custom neural model in Azure Machine Learning

   D. Statistical machine translation in Cognitive Search

8. A developer is building a chatbot that books flights. After recognizing intent and entities, which component ensures the bot remembers user choices across turns?

   A. Language model

   B. Relation extraction

   C. Dialogue management/state tracking

   D. Key-phrase extraction

9. An ASR pipeline on Azure receives audio from a noisy factory floor. Which stage specifically reduces background noise before phoneme recognition?

   A. Noise reduction

   B. Frame splitting

   C. Language modeling

   D. Prosody prediction

10. Which embedding type would allow contextual distinction between "bank" in "river bank" and "bank account" when using Azure OpenAI?

    A. Bag-of-words embeddings

    B. Contextual embeddings (BERT/GPT)

    C. TF-IDF vectors

    D. Static Word2Vec embeddings

11. A data scientist tests two sentiment models: Model A has precision 0.90 and recall 0.60; Model B has precision 0.70 and recall 0.85. For a scenario where false negatives are costly, which model is preferred?

    A. Model A

    B. Model B

    C. The one with higher precision

    D. Neither

12. During machine translation evaluation, a team relies solely on BLEU scores but receives user feedback complaining about awkward phrasing. What additional evaluation should they incorporate?

    A. F1 score

    B. Precision and recall

    C. N-gram perplexity

    D. METEOR or human evaluation (extrinsic)

13. Which Azure service simplifies building a custom voice assistant that converts text responses into human-like speech?

    A. Speech Service (Text-to-Speech)

    B. Text Analytics API

    C. Azure Bot Service

    D. Cognitive Search

14. A marketing team needs to identify recurring multi-word terms in product feedback dashboards without predefined categories. Which Azure feature should they use?

    A. Named entity recognition

    B. TF-IDF normalization service

    C. Key-phrase extraction in Text Analytics

    D. Relation extraction

15. An e-commerce search feature uses semantic search powered by embeddings. Which representation underlies this capability?

    A. One-hot encoding

    B. Bag-of-words counts

    C. Contextual embeddings from Azure OpenAI

    D. TF-IDF weights

16. When designing prompts for an Azure OpenAI text generation task, which practice helps ensure consistent formatting in the output?

    A. Using a single vague instruction

    B. Providing few-shot examples in the prompt

    C. Omitting any examples to avoid bias

    D. Relying on default temperature without guidance

17. A legal firm deploys an NLP pipeline that tags "Plaintiff," "Defendant," and "Court Dates." They notice tag confusion for "Court of Appeals." How can they improve accuracy?

    A. Increase LSTM layers

    B. Switch to TF-IDF feature extraction

    C. Lower the model's threshold

    D. Use a custom NER model with domain-specific training data

18. A podcast platform wants to provide real-time captions. Which combination of Azure services and pipelines should they integrate?

A. Speech Service ASR for transcription and display in UI

B. Text Analytics for sentiment and Cognitive Search for indexing

C. Azure Bot Service for dialogue and Translator Text for captions

D. Speech Service ASR for transcription and Text-to-Speech for playback

19. In a customer service scenario, an NLP classifier flags too many false positives. Which metric adjustment could reduce false positives?

A. Increase recall threshold

B. Decrease precision threshold

C. Increase decision threshold to favor precision

D. Use BLEU instead of F1

20. An ASR implementation on Azure mishears accented speech frequently. Which action could improve recognition accuracy?

A. Use a transformer-based language model only

B. Train a custom acoustic model with accented speech samples

C. Increase audio frame length indefinitely

D. Disable noise reduction

Chapter

9

Azure Tools for NLP Workloads

MICROSOFT CERTIFIED: AZURE AI FUNDAMENTALS (AI-900) EXAM OBJECTIVES COVERED IN THIS CHAPTER:

✔ **Domain 4: Describe features of Natural Language Processing (NLP) workloads on Azure**

    ▪ Subdomain 4a: Identify features of common NLP Workload Scenarios

        ▪ 4-1 Identify features and uses for key phrase extraction

        ▪ 4-2 Identify features and uses for entity recognition

        ▪ 4-3 Identify features and uses for sentiment analysis

        ▪ 4-4 Identify features and uses for language modeling

        ▪ 4-5 Identify features and uses for speech recognition and synthesis

        ▪ 4-6 Identify features and uses for translation

    ▪ Subdomain 4b: Identify Azure tools and services for NLP workloads

        ▪ 4-7 Describe capabilities of the Azure AI Language Service

        ▪ 4-8 Describe capabilities of the Azure AI Speech Service

The previous chapter covered NLP fundamentals. Now that you know how natural language processing works and why it matters, we'll see how Azure brings all these pieces together. In this chapter, you'll meet the core Azure services for NLP: the AI Language Service for text analysis and custom models, the Speech Service for turning words into text and back again, and the Translator Service for fast, accurate language conversion. You'll also learn how Cognitive Search can enrich and index your text, and how to connect these services into your own apps using REST calls, SDKs, serverless functions, or containers.

By the end of this chapter, you'll know how to choose the right Azure service for your needs and combine them into real solutions. Whether you're building a chatbot, translating documents, or extracting data from forms, you'll have the groundwork to get started. Let's dive in.

Azure AI Language Service

Azure AI Language Services is a collection of cloud-based tools designed to help developers analyze, interpret, and process human language. It can simplify language tasks like understanding customer feedback, extracting insights from documents, or building chatbots. Azure uses machine learning models (both prebuilt and customizable) to add language intelligence to applications without needing to build algorithms from scratch. This section explores the core capabilities of the service and the steps to set up and secure these tools.

Core Text Analysis Capabilities

At the heart of Azure AI Language Service are the prebuilt text analytics features that let you extract meaning from any block of text with minimal setup. Some of these features are Sentiment analysis, Key phrase extraction, and Entity recognition.

Sentiment analysis evaluates whether a piece of writing is positive, negative, or neutral, and it gives you an immediate gauge of customer mood or public opinion. Key phrase extraction pulls out the most important words and phrases, so that you can summarize long documents or identify topics at a glance. Both features require only a few lines of code or a quick call through the Azure portal, making them ideal for rapid prototyping.

Entity recognition helps to improve text analysis by identifying and classifying named items like people, organizations, locations, and more, so that you can index documents or

FIGURE 9.1   Azure AI language service features.

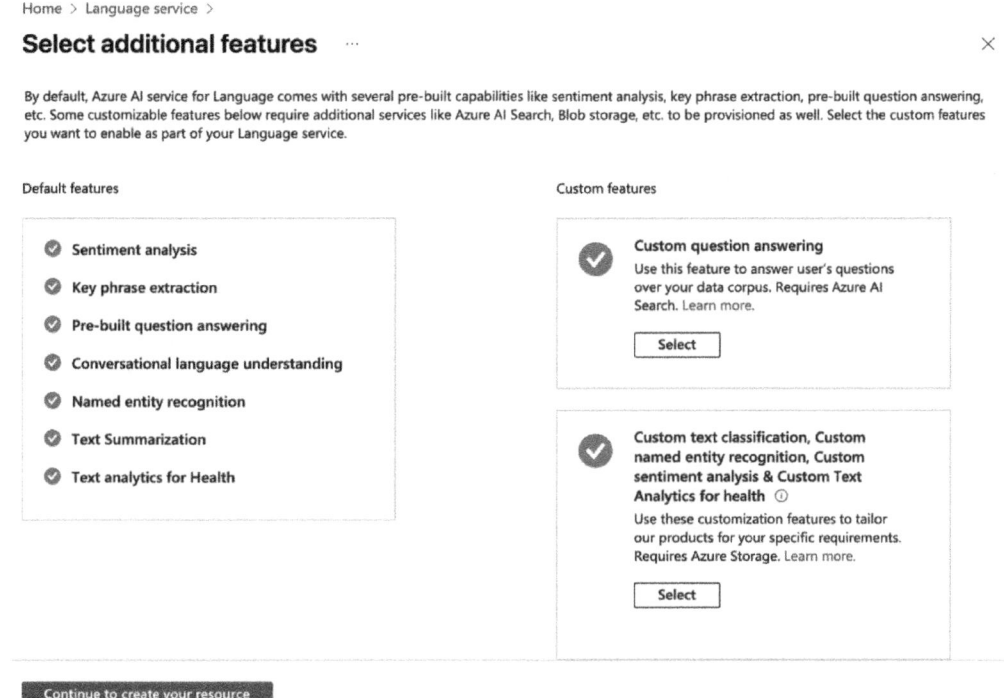

enrich user experiences. If you're processing financial reports, for example, the service can automatically highlight company names, dates, and monetary amounts. Figure 9.1 shows a screenshot of the different features in Azure AI Language Service.

For scenarios where data privacy is important, Personally Identifiable Information (PII) detection locates sensitive details like Social Security numbers, credit card data, or email addresses and redacts them automatically. This helps you meet compliance requirements under regulations like GDPR or HIPAA without manual review. You might chain PII detection with sentiment analysis in a single process to ensure that while you learn what customers feel, you never expose their private information.

Building Custom Models with Language Studio

While prebuilt tools cover many scenarios, sometimes you need a solution that can be specific to what you're building. Azure's Language Studio lets users train custom models without writing code. For example, custom text classification allows businesses to categorize support tickets into unique labels like "Billing" or "Technical Issues" based on their specific needs. Custom Named Entity Recognition (NER) goes further, by letting you define domain-specific entities—such as product codes, internal project names, or even specialized terminology like medical conditions and drug names in healthcare scenarios—that standard models might miss.

Conversational Language Understanding (CLU) is also another key feature. It trains models to interpret user intents in chatbots or voice assistants. Suppose you're designing a marketplace for apartments like Shortlet or Airbnb, CLU could recognize phrases like "Book an apartment with a view of the ocean" as a reservation intent or a specific kind of apartment.

Automating Document Processing with Document Intelligence

Document Intelligence, formerly known as Form Recognizer, specializes in extracting structured data from images, PDFs, and scanned documents. Its OCR engine converts printed or handwritten text into machine-readable form, while layout extraction identifies tables, headers, and footers. This helps in transforming unstructured documents into organized data you can query or store. For beginners, it's a concrete example of applying AI to everyday tasks like digitizing invoices or processing receipts.

The "layout" feature goes beyond simple text extraction by preserving spatial relationships on the page. Imagine you have a complex financial report: Document Intelligence can distinguish a balance sheet's rows and columns, capturing the hierarchy of headers and sub-tables. This structured output integrates seamlessly into downstream analysis workflows—including tools like Microsoft Fabric—where the cleaned data can feed into data lakes, semantic models, or custom dashboards without manual cleanup.

Invoice and receipt processing are specialized templates that recognize common fields such as vendor name, invoice date, total amount, and line-item details. You simply point the service to a folder of example invoices, and it learns the layout variations automatically. The trained model then generalizes to new invoices, saving hours of manual data entry and allowing you to integrate real-time processing into your applications.

Provisioning and Securing Language Resources

Before you can call any of these AI Language endpoints, you need to provision a Language resource in Azure. Using the Azure portal, CLI, or ARM templates, you specify the resource name, pricing tier, and region where your data will reside. Figure 9.2 shows how to create a language resource on the Azure portal. Choosing the right tier matters so that you don't get charged for things you don't need. The free tier gives you access to Sentiment analysis, Key phrase extraction, Language detection, Custom question answering, Prebuilt question answering, Named entity recognition, PII detection, Conversational language understanding, Orchestration workflow, Custom text classification, and Custom named entity recognition for the first 5,000 text records every month. The standard tier gives you these and some more features, but at a cost.

Authentication is equally important. Microsoft Entra ID gives you OAuth-based tokens that you can use to secure every call to the language endpoint. When you register your application or service principal in Entra ID, you avoid embedding keys directly in code and can enforce fine-grained access controls using role-based access control (RBAC). You'll also

FIGURE 9.2   Creating an Azure AI language resource.

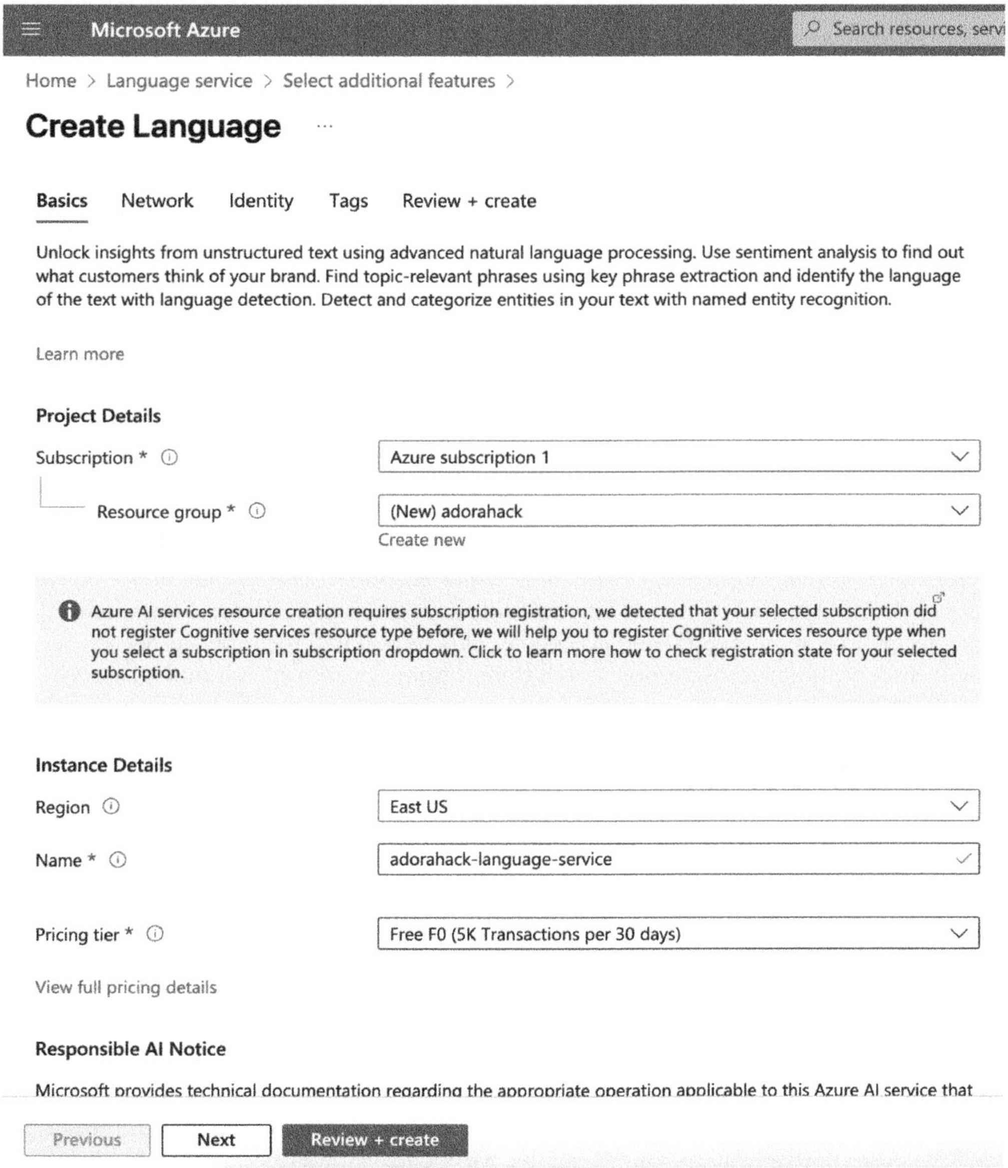

be able to grant roles like "Cognitive Services Contributor" so that only authorized users or services can manage your language resource.

For scenarios where you want to simplify identity management, managed identities are a simple way to authenticate code running in Azure. Your application could live in an Azure Function, App Service, or Virtual Machine. With managed identities, you can enable a system-assigned identity and grant it access to your language resource so that you won't need secrets or certificates. This approach illustrates best practices in secure development, which are often tested as part of exam objectives around governance and security.

Azure AI Speech Service

The main difference between Azure AI Speech Services and Azure AI Language Services is their focus. While Language Services analyze and process written text, Speech Services specialize in understanding and generating spoken language through cloud-based models. These services act as a bridge between voice and text, enabling applications to transcribe audio, synthesize speech, translate conversations in real time, and even assess pronunciation. Compared to on-device solutions like Apple's SpeechAnalyzer, Azure's cloud-based approach offers greater scalability, broader language support, and more advanced customization options, making it suitable for enterprise scenarios and large-scale deployments. While on-device models are optimized for offline use and responsiveness, cloud services provide richer capabilities for real-time translation and integration with other Azure tools. If Language Services help chatbots read customer messages, Speech Services let those chatbots respond aloud or understand voice commands. When they are used together, they empower developers to build applications that interact with users through both text and speech, making technology more natural and accessible. This section will focus on the Speech Service and will cover real-time transcription, batch transcription, custom speech tuning, speech translation workflows, text-to-speech, and pronunciation assessment on Azure.

Real-Time vs. Batch Transcription

When you need to convert spoken words into text, Azure has both real-time streaming transcription and batch transcription for pre-recorded audio. Real-time transcription is ideal for live scenarios like call centers or interactive voice assistants, where you need instant text output as people speak. The service handles audio streams, processes them continuously, and returns partial results to give your application an ongoing transcript, improving user engagement and responsiveness.

Batch transcription, on the other hand, is designed for offline processing of large audio files. If you have hours of recorded interviews, lectures, or podcasts, you can submit them in bulk and let the service process them asynchronously. This mode optimizes for throughput rather than latency and allows you to queue multiple files and retrieve completed transcripts later. It's a cost-effective way to handle massive workloads without needing to maintain live audio connections.

Within real-time transcription, conversation transcription adds another layer by automatically separating out speakers and labeling who said what, a feature known as diarization. This is very important when you have to analyze multi-participant meetings or interviews, as it preserves the conversational context and lets you attribute each sentence to the correct speaker.

Custom Speech Tuning

While prebuilt speech-to-text models work well for general purposes, custom tuning improves accuracy for unique scenarios. Acoustic model adaptation adjusts how the system handles background noise, accents, or specialized vocabulary, and these are critical for industries like healthcare, where medical terms might confuse standard models. Language model adaptation refines predictions based on context, such as prioritizing product names in a retail app.

Another customization tool is the phrase list, which boosts recognition of specific words or phrases. Imagine a voice-controlled factory tool: Adding terms like "emergency shutdown" or "machine ID" to a phrase list ensures the system detects them reliably. Azure's Custom Speech portal has a no-code interface for uploading audio samples, testing adjustments, and deploying improved models. This flexibility makes speech technology accessible even to teams without deep AI expertise.

Speech Translation Workflows

Azure Speech Service goes beyond transcription by providing real-time speech translation, turning spoken words in one language into text or audio in another. A typical translation flow, as shown in Figure 9.3, captures input audio in the source language, processes it through the speech-to-text engine, and then feeds the transcript into a text-to-speech system in the target language. End users experience near-instant translations, making multilingual meetings or global support calls far smoother.

In practice, you might embed translation into a web app or mobile client, where a user speaks into a microphone and hears back a translated response through headphones. Alternatively, batch translation can convert large audio or video files, generating subtitle tracks or translated transcripts for global distribution. Both real-time and batch modes share the same underlying translation engine and ensure that there is consistent quality across scenarios.

Text-to-Speech and Voice Styles

Turning text into spoken words is a key part of many applications. For example, we use text-to-speech features in audiobook generation, accessibility features, or interactive agents. Azure's text-to-speech capabilities rely on neural voices, which use deep learning to produce highly natural intonation and pacing.

Speech Synthesis Markup Language (SSML) lets you fine-tune the output: you can adjust pitch, rate, emphasis, and pauses, or insert audio cues and phoneme hints. SSML tags give you control over every aspect of the spoken delivery, so you can craft a presentation or announcement that matches your brand's tone. For example, you might slow down for clarity when narrating instructions or speed up for dynamic alerts.

Azure also has voice fonts and speaking styles that go beyond plain narration. Styles like "cheerful" or "empathetic" modify prosody to convey emotion, and this can help chatbots or virtual assistants respond in ways that resonate with users. You select a voice, a style, and

FIGURE 9.3   Azure speech service translation workflow.

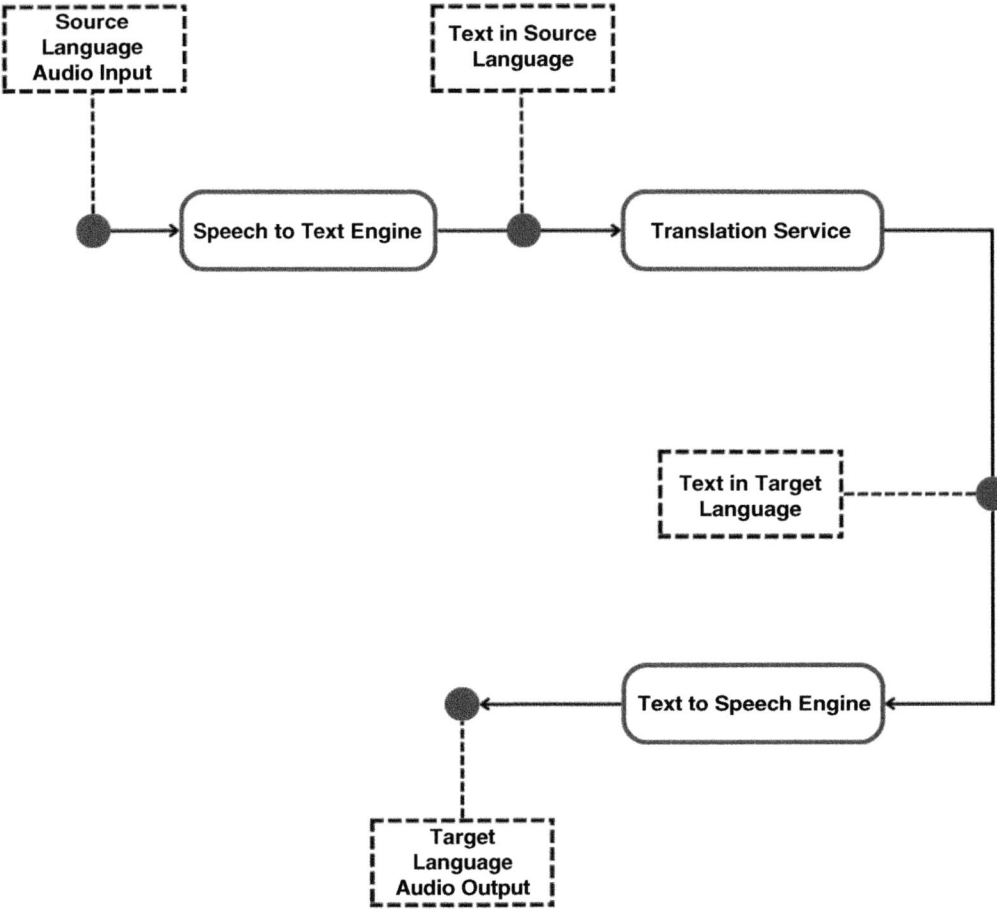

optionally an SSML script, and the service returns an audio stream you can play back in your application or store as an audio file.

Improving Communication with Speech Analytics

Beyond basic transcription, Azure Speech Services includes tools to analyze speech quality and content. Pronunciation assessment evaluates language learners' accuracy, fluency, and intonation, and provides feedback similar to a human tutor. This is very important for apps teaching foreign languages or helping professionals refine public speaking skills.

Speech analytics digs deeper into audio data. For example, a call center could analyze customer interactions to detect frustration in a caller's tone or track how often agents mention promotional offers. Combined with sentiment analysis, these learnings help businesses improve training programs and customer experiences. For beginners, experimenting with Azure's Speech Studio demos is a great way to see how these tools can solve real-world problems.

Azure Translator Service

Azure Translator Service is used to translate text and documents between over 100 languages, enabling applications to communicate globally. Unlike Language Services, which focus on analyzing text, or Speech Services, which handle spoken language, Translator Service specializes in converting content from one language to another.

How Neural Machine Translation Works

Neural machine translation (NMT) uses deep learning models to learn patterns across entire sentences rather than individual words. Instead of translating piece by piece, the model encodes the full context of an input sentence into a numerical representation, then decodes it into the target language.

To train an NMT model, you'd need to feed it with a lot of aligned text pairs, sentences in one language mapped to their translations in another. The model gradually learns to predict the most probable translation given a new input. Because it's data-driven, the quality of output improves with the diversity and volume of training examples. Azure's prebuilt Translator service benefits from large, continually updated corpora, so you get industry-leading accuracy without managing your own training pipeline.

One of the strengths of NMT is its ability to generalize across domains. A well-trained model can handle casual conversation, technical documentation, and everything in between. However, for highly specialized content, legal contracts, medical reports, or marketing slogans, you might still encounter mistranslations or unnatural phrasing. Recognizing these limitations is the first step toward deciding whether to use custom terminology or glossaries to fine-tune results.

Real-Time and Document Translation APIs

Azure Translator has real-time text translation and document translation. The real-time API is ideal for dynamic applications, like translating chat messages in a multilingual social platform or providing instant subtitles for a live video stream. It processes text in milliseconds, ensuring seamless user interactions. For example, a traveler using a language learning app could type a sentence in English and see it translated to Japanese immediately.

The document translation API, on the other hand, handles bulk processing. It supports formats like PDF, Word, and PowerPoint, making it perfect for translating entire manuals, contracts, or marketing materials. A global company could use this to localize product documentation for different regions automatically. Both APIs support custom glossaries (more on that later), ensuring brand-specific terms like "cloud compute" stay consistent across languages. Azure also has language detection, so you don't need to specify the source language. This is useful for apps with diverse user bases.

In practice, you might chain calls to the translation API with other Azure services. For example, you could translate incoming customer emails via Logic Apps, store the results in Cosmos DB, and trigger analytics workflows in Microsoft Fabric or Power BI.

Custom Translator and Terminology Management

While prebuilt models work well for general use, Custom Translator lets you fine-tune translations for niche scenarios. Suppose you're a medical device company needing precise translations for terms like "MRI scanner" or "biopsy report." By uploading parallel texts (matching documents in source and target languages), you train a custom model to prioritize industry-specific vocabulary.

Glossaries and terminology management add another layer of control. A glossary is a list of terms (e.g., product names, legal phrases) that must be translated in a specific way. For instance, "Azure AI Services" might stay untranslated in some languages to maintain brand consistency. Custom Translator integrates these glossaries during training, ensuring the model adheres to your guidelines. This is important for industries like legal, finance, or healthcare, where mistranslations could have serious consequences.

Embedding Translation into Your Architecture

Integrating translation into an application can follow multiple patterns depending on your needs. In-app translation calls the API directly from the client side, such as a web browser or mobile app, and provides immediate feedback to users. This pattern shines for chat apps or real-time collaboration tools, but requires careful handling of keys or tokens in the client and attention to latency.

A middleware approach inserts translation services into your backend layer. For instance, you might expose a translation microservice that other components call, centralizing authentication and caching. This design simplifies key management, lets you apply common policies (like rate-limiting or logging), and offloads translation compute to controlled, scalable infrastructure. It's especially useful in large organizations where multiple applications require translation.

Hybrid models also exist. You can pre-translate static content through batch jobs and cache translated pages on a CDN, while using real-time translation for dynamic user input. This ensures fast load times for most users and still supports ad hoc translation needs. Designing such a solution demonstrates thoughtful consideration of performance, cost, and user experience.

The pattern you choose ultimately depends on factors like volume, latency tolerance, security requirements, and cost constraints. When you compare these integration styles and their tradeoffs before you make a decision, you'll be well-prepared to architect translation into diverse application scenarios.

Azure Cognitive Search for NLP Scenarios

Azure Cognitive Search goes beyond traditional keyword-based search by integrating natural language processing (NLP) to understand context, relationships, and user intent. Think of it as a smart search engine that can analyze documents, extract information, and even recognize patterns in unstructured data like emails or PDFs. While services like Translator focus on language conversion and Speech Services handle voice interactions, Cognitive Search organizes and enriches data to make it easily discoverable. This section explores how AI-powered search pipelines work, how to optimize them for speed and accuracy, and how to fix common issues when building intelligent search solutions.

Building AI Enrichment Pipelines

An AI enrichment pipeline is a workflow that processes raw data (like text, images, videos, etc.) to make it searchable and meaningful. For example, imagine a legal firm uploading thousands of contracts to a database. The pipeline uses skill sets, which are collections of prebuilt or custom AI models, to extract key details like client names, dates, or clauses. Built-in skills include text analytics for sentiment analysis, entity recognition (detecting organizations or locations), or language detection.

Custom skills let you add specialized logic. Suppose the legal firm wants to classify contracts by type (e.g., "NDA" or "Employment Agreement"). A custom skill could use a machine learning model trained on their own document templates. The pipeline processes data in stages: extracting text, enriching it with insights, and storing results in a search index. This transforms messy, unstructured data into a structured format that users can query intuitively.

Leveraging Semantic and Vector Search

Beyond simple keyword matching, Azure Cognitive Search has semantic search, which uses deep learning to understand the intent and context behind queries. Semantic ranking reorders results based on relevance signals derived from language models, ensuring that documents closely aligned with a user's meaning rise to the top. Features like query expansion and answer extraction let you not only find documents but pinpoint the exact passages that best answer a user's question.

Vector search takes this further by representing text as numerical vectors (arrays of numbers) that capture semantic relationships. Similar vectors indicate similar meanings. Imagine a recipe app: Searching "quick vegetarian dinners" could return dishes tagged as "fast" and "meat-free," even if those exact words aren't used. Vector search excels at finding conceptually related content, like recommending articles on "budget travel" when a user reads about "affordable vacations." These features work together to deliver results that feel almost human-curated.

Configuring and Optimizing Search Indexers

An indexer is the component that connects your data source (like Azure Blob Storage or a SQL database) to the search pipeline. Configuring it involves setting parameters such as how often to check for updates (e.g., hourly or daily) and which fields to include in the index. For example, a news website might index article titles, authors, and publication dates but exclude draft posts.

Performance tuning ensures the indexer runs efficiently. Large datasets can slow down processing, so strategies like batch processing (handling documents in groups) or parallel execution (using multiple workers) help speed things up. You might also prioritize critical fields, like product names in an e-commerce catalog, to improve query response times.

Troubleshooting Cognitive Search Pipelines

Even the most carefully designed pipelines can run into issues: skill failures, document parsing errors, or runaway indexer loops. When something goes wrong, you'll rely on indexer execution logs and enriched field previews to pinpoint where data transformation broke down. Clear understanding of diagnostic settings in Azure Monitor and the search service's built-in logging will guide your investigation.

One common problem is data format errors. For example, a PDF with scanned images (no text) might fail to process. The solution will be to use OCR (Optical Character Recognition) skills to extract text from images first. Another issue is skill execution failures, where a custom skill crashes due to unexpected input. Testing skills with diverse data samples during development helps catch these edge cases.

Authentication errors often arise when the indexer can't access the data source. Double-checking credentials or firewall settings usually resolves this. For slow queries, check if the index is properly optimized; adding filters or reducing the number of searchable fields can boost speed.

Integrating NLP Services into Applications

Modern language capabilities are only valuable when they can be folded smoothly into the software people use every day. This section shows you how to wire Azure's natural language APIs into code, secure those calls, and automate end-to-end flows.

Choosing Between REST APIs and Language-Specific SDKs

The most direct path to an Azure language service is the REST API. You craft an HTTPS request, add a JSON body, attach an authentication header, and parse the response. This low-level approach works in any environment that can open a web connection, from microcontrollers to legacy systems, and it exposes every parameter the service offers as soon as it is released.

Language-specific SDKs wrap those same calls in native objects and idioms. In Python you work with classes like `TextAnalyticsClient`; in .NET you might call `AnalyzeSentimentAsync`; Java and JavaScript follow similar patterns. The SDKs handle retries, pagination, and response deserialization, freeing you to focus on business logic rather than HTTP minutiae.

Performance differences are usually negligible because both routes hit the same Azure endpoint, yet SDKs do add a small dependency footprint. In highly constrained environments, or when you need a feature that the SDK team has not yet surfaced, the raw REST call still shines. Conversely, when developer productivity and readability matter, SDKs reduce boilerplate and make unit testing easier.

In real projects you will often mix the two. Rapid prototypes start with the SDK; production code may stick with it or switch to REST to shave dependencies. Understanding both methods ensures you can read samples in documentation, troubleshoot network traces, and optimize throughput or cost when milliseconds and kilobytes count.

Securing Access with Authentication Methods

Every application using Azure NLP services needs secure authentication. Service principals act as "user accounts" for your app, providing credentials (like a client ID and secret) to access Azure resources. For example, a CI/CD pipeline deploying an NLP model might use a service principal to authenticate during automated builds. This method has fine-grained control over permissions but requires managing secrets securely (e.g., using Azure Key Vault).

Managed identities eliminate secret management by letting Azure handle authentication internally. If your app runs on an Azure VM or App Service, you can enable a system-assigned identity, and Azure automatically provides credentials. This is safer for scenarios like a hospital app processing patient notes, where leaking secrets could risk data privacy. However, managed identities only work within Azure, so hybrid or on-premises apps might still need service principals.

Orchestrating Workflows with Serverless Tools

Once a single call works, the next step is stringing calls together. Serverless platforms like Azure Functions and Logic Apps let you orchestrate NLP tasks without managing servers. Azure Functions are code snippets triggered by events like processing a newly uploaded document in Blob Storage with the Form Recognizer API. For instance, a function could automatically extract invoice data and save it to a database. Bindings (prebuilt connectors) simplify integrating with other Azure services, reducing boilerplate code.

Logic Apps are also event-driven, but they take a visual approach. With Logic Apps, you can design workflows with drag-and-drop blocks. Imagine a content moderation system where Logic Apps route user comments to the Language Service for sentiment analysis, flag negative posts, and notify moderators via email, all without writing code. These tools are perfect for gluing together NLP services with minimal development effort, though complex logic might still require custom code in Functions.

Packaging Cognitive Services in Containers

Sometimes cloud connectivity is unreliable, data must stay on-premises, or latency targets are measured in single-digit milliseconds. For those cases Azure releases many language services as Docker images that you can run in any Kubernetes cluster or even on a developer's laptop. The container exposes the same REST surface as the hosted service, so client code remains unchanged.

Deploying models to Azure Container Instances (ACI) or Azure Kubernetes Service (AKS) lets you process data locally, bypassing cloud latency. A retail store analyzing in-store customer feedback in real time, for example, could use ACI to run sentiment analysis on-premises without internet dependency.

AKS scales better for high-demand applications. A news aggregator processing millions of articles daily might deploy containers to AKS, automatically adding resources during traffic spikes. Containers also support hybrid cloud setups like a banking app using cloud-based training but on-premises inference for sensitive data. While many Cognitive Services are also available in Azure Government and classified Azure regions, containers offer the flexibility to run completely offline—ideal for air-gapped, regulated, or disconnected environments. However, managing containers requires Docker and Kubernetes knowledge, which might be a hurdle for beginners.

Summary

This chapter covered the main Azure services for Natural Language Processing (NLP) workloads. It explored Azure AI Language Service with its text analysis capabilities like sentiment analysis, entity recognition, and PII detection, as well as custom model building through Language Studio. The chapter examined Azure AI Speech Service, which bridges spoken language and text through real-time and batch transcription, custom speech tuning, translation workflows, and text-to-speech capabilities. It detailed Azure Translator Service for translating content between languages using neural machine translation. The chapter also introduced Azure Cognitive Search with AI enrichment pipelines, semantic and vector search for understanding context beyond keywords. It also covered integration methods including REST APIs versus SDKs, authentication options, serverless orchestration with Azure Functions and Logic Apps, and container deployment for on-premises scenarios. These services provide a comprehensive toolkit for developers building intelligent language applications.

Exam Essentials

Understand Azure AI Language Service capabilities.   Know the difference between prebuilt text features (sentiment analysis, key phrase extraction, entity recognition, PII detection) and custom models built with Language Studio.

Recognize speech-to-text options in Azure.   Understand the differences between real-time transcription, batch transcription, and how custom speech tuning improves accuracy for specialized vocabulary and environments.

Know how neural machine translation works.   Understand how Azure Translator Service processes entire sentences rather than individual words and the difference between real-time API and document translation.

Master document processing workflows.   Know how Document Intelligence (formerly Form Recognizer) extracts structured data from images and PDFs, including its layout detection and specialized templates.

Understand AI enrichment pipelines.   Learn how Azure Cognitive Search uses skill sets to transform unstructured data into searchable content, and know the differences between semantic search and vector search.

Know integration methods for NLP services.   Understand when to use REST APIs versus SDKs, how to secure access using Microsoft Entra ID or managed identities, and when container deployment makes sense versus serverless options.

Recognize authentication and security patterns.   Understand how to provision language resources, set appropriate access controls, and implement secure identity management for AI services.

Review Questions

1. A company wants to automatically categorize customer support tickets into "Billing," "Technical," or "General" categories based on the ticket description. Which Azure service should they use?

   A. Azure AI Document Intelligence

   B. Azure AI Speech Service

   C. Azure AI Language Service with custom text classification

   D. Azure Cognitive Search

2. An insurance company is processing thousands of scanned claim forms daily. They need to extract specific fields like claim number, policy holder name, and incident date. Which Azure service is most appropriate?

   A. Azure AI Speech Service

   B. Azure AI Document Intelligence

   C. Azure Translator Service

   D. Azure AI Language Service sentiment analysis

3. A healthcare company wants to analyze patient feedback to determine whether comments are positive, negative, or neutral. Which Azure AI Language Service feature should they implement?

   A. Entity recognition

   B. Key phrase extraction

   C. Sentiment analysis

   D. PII detection

4. A global retail company needs to process customer service calls in multiple languages for quality assurance. Which Azure service combination would be most effective?

   A. Azure AI Speech Service for transcription followed by Azure Translator Service

   B. Azure Cognitive Search with custom skills

   C. Azure AI Language Service with custom entity recognition

   D. Azure AI Document Intelligence with layout analysis

5. A developer needs to extract the most important phrases from large product review documents. Which Azure AI Language Service feature should they use?

   A. PII detection

   B. Sentiment analysis

   C. Entity recognition

   D. Key phrase extraction

6. A multinational company wants to deploy an Azure AI service for language translation but needs to ensure data privacy by keeping all processing within their own infrastructure. Which deployment option should they choose?

    A. Deploy using Azure Functions

    B. Use containerized Cognitive Services

    C. Implement with Azure Logic Apps

    D. Access via REST API only

7. A language learning application needs to evaluate how well users pronounce words and phrases in a foreign language. Which Azure AI service feature should they implement?

    A. Azure AI Speech Service's pronunciation assessment

    B. Azure Translator Service's custom dictionary

    C. Azure AI Language Service's named entity recognition

    D. Azure Cognitive Search's semantic ranking

8. A financial services company wants to automatically identify and redact sensitive information like credit card numbers and Social Security numbers from customer support transcripts. Which Azure AI Language Service feature should they use?

    A. Sentiment analysis

    B. PII detection

    C. Key phrase extraction

    D. Entity recognition

9. A publishing company needs to convert their extensive audio interview archive into searchable text. They don't need real-time processing but require high accuracy on large files. Which Azure AI Speech Service option is most appropriate?

    A. Real-time transcription

    B. Batch transcription

    C. Conversation transcription

    D. Custom speech models

10. A company wants to enrich their search system to understand the intent behind user queries rather than just matching keywords. Which Azure Cognitive Search feature should they implement?

    A. AI enrichment pipeline

    B. Vector search

    C. Semantic search

    D. Custom analyzers

11. A medical research company has thousands of scientific papers they need to categorize by specific medical conditions mentioned in the text. Which Azure AI Language Service capability would be most helpful?

A. Custom named entity recognition

B. Sentiment analysis

C. PII detection

D. Text summarization

12. A customer service department wants to implement a system that can transcribe ongoing phone conversations and identify who is speaking. Which Azure AI Speech Service feature should they use?

A. Batch transcription

B. Real-time transcription

C. Conversation transcription

D. Custom speech model

13. A company wants to make their voice assistant respond to specific industry terms with high accuracy. Which Azure AI Speech Service feature would be most helpful?

A. Neural voices

B. Speech translation

C. Phrase lists

D. Conversation transcription

14. A mobile app developer wants to add a feature that translates user reviews automatically while preserving brand-specific terms exactly as they appear in the original language. Which Azure Translator Service feature should they implement?

A. Neural machine translation

B. Document translation API

C. Custom translator

D. Custom glossary

15. A developer is building an application that needs to authenticate to Azure AI Language Service in the most secure way without managing secrets. The application runs on Azure App Service. What authentication method should they use?

A. API keys

B. Microsoft Entra ID with service principal

C. Managed identities

D. Shared Access Signatures (SAS)

16. A company wants to implement a solution that can take audio in English, translate it to Spanish, and output Spanish audio. Which combination of Azure services should they use?

   A. Azure AI Speech Service (speech-to-text) → Azure Translator Service → Azure AI Speech Service (text-to-speech)

   B. Azure AI Language Service → Azure Translator Service → Azure AI Speech Service

   C. Azure Translator Service → Azure AI Speech Service

   D. Azure AI Speech Service → Azure AI Language Service

17. A retail company wants to analyze customer reviews to extract key topics and evaluate sentiment. Which Azure AI Language Service features should they use together?

   A. Entity recognition and PII detection

   B. Key phrase extraction and sentiment analysis

   C. Document translation and key phrase extraction

   D. Conversational language understanding and entity recognition

18. A text-heavy application needs to process files locally due to unreliable internet connectivity. Which deployment option for Azure AI services would be most appropriate?

   A. Using Azure Functions

   B. Containerized deployment

   C. Using REST API with caching

   D. Azure Logic Apps integration

19. A company is building an application that converts PDF documents to searchable content with AI-enhanced metadata. Which Azure service should form the foundation of this solution?

   A. Azure AI Language Service

   B. Azure AI Speech Service

   C. Azure Cognitive Search with AI enrichment pipeline

   D. Azure Translator Service

20. A language learning platform needs to evaluate how accurately users pronounce words in Igbo language. Which Azure AI service should they use?

   A. Azure AI Speech Service with pronunciation assessment

   B. Azure Translator Service

   C. Azure AI Language Service with sentiment analysis

   D. Azure Cognitive Search with semantic ranking

Chapter

10

Introduction to Generative AI

MICROSOFT CERTIFIED: AZURE AI FUNDAMENTALS (AI-900) EXAM OBJECTIVES COVERED IN THIS CHAPTER:

✔ **Domain 5: Describe features of generative AI workloads on Azure**

- Subdomain 5a: Identify features of generative AI solutions

  - 5-1 Identify features of generative AI models

  - 5-2 Identify common scenarios for generative AI

  - 5-3 Identify responsible AI considerations for generative AI

- Subdomain 5b: Identify generative AI services and capabilities in Microsoft Azure

  - 5-4 Describe features and capabilities of Azure AI Foundry

  - 5-5 Describe features and capabilities of Azure OpenAI service

  - 5-6 Describe features and capabilities of Azure AI Foundry model catalog

In the current state of the industry, generative AI is literally everywhere from chatbots that write emails to tools that turn text into images, code, or even music. But how does it actually work? This chapter breaks down the gears under the hood. We'll start by clarifying what makes generative AI unique. Then, we'll walk through the key ideas, models, and techniques that power these systems, from the basic math to the clever tricks engineers use to make them reliable.

You'll learn how generative AI models generate human-like text, why image generators need "diffusion," and what makes training these systems both powerful and tricky. We'll also cover real-world tradeoffs: Why do some models spit out nonsense? How do companies balance creativity with control? By the end of this chapter, you'll see how generative AI isn't magic, just a mix of smart algorithms, mountains of data, and careful tuning.

Foundations of Generative AI

Generative AI represents one of the most transformative technological developments of our time. At its core, generative AI encompasses a family of artificial intelligence systems designed to create new content whether that's text, images, audio, code, or other data types. Unlike traditional AI approaches that primarily categorize or predict outcomes based on existing data, generative AI can produce entirely new content that didn't exist before. This capability has reshaped our understanding of machine creativity, with applications spanning creative industries, healthcare, business, and beyond. The foundations of generative AI involve understanding its core concepts, various techniques, and the remarkable historical journey that has led to today's powerful systems.

What Makes Generative AI "Generative"?

Generative AI fundamentally differs from traditional discriminative approaches in how it processes and works with data. While discriminative models focus on drawing boundaries between categories, essentially answering "which category does this belong to?," generative models learn the underlying distribution of data to create new samples similar to what they've been trained on.

While generative AI creates new content, discriminative AI, which you've already encountered in earlier chapters, focuses on classifying or categorizing data. The supervised learning methods from Chapter 4, image classification in Chapters 6 and 7, and text analysis in Chapters 8 and 9 all rely on discriminative approaches that learn boundaries between categories. Think of discriminative AI as the "judge" that decides which category something belongs to (Is this email spam? Is this image a cat?), whereas generative AI is the "creator" that produces new content based on what it has learned.

When working with generative models, the system learns the probability distribution of the training data, enabling it to generate new instances that resemble that data. For example, a generative text model trained on books learns language patterns, grammar, facts, and narrative structures, allowing it to produce new text that feels authentic. Meanwhile, discriminative models would focus on tasks like determining whether a text was written by a particular author or categorizing text by genre. Generative models typically need more training data and computational resources because creating new content requires a more comprehensive understanding than simply distinguishing between existing categories.

The evaluation criteria also differ significantly between these approaches. Discriminative models are typically evaluated on metrics like accuracy, precision, and recall, how often they correctly classify instances. Generative models require more nuanced evaluation, often involving human judgment about quality, creativity, coherence, and authenticity of the generated content. This subjective evaluation component makes benchmarking generative models particularly challenging, though researchers continue developing more sophisticated metrics to assess generative outputs. Understanding this distinction is crucial for anyone looking to work with or implement AI systems, as it fundamentally shapes how we approach problem-solving with artificial intelligence.

The Building Blocks of Generative Techniques

Generative AI encompasses a diverse array of techniques and architectures, each with unique strengths and applications. At the broadest level, we can organize generative models into several families based on their underlying mathematical approaches and architectures. These include autoregressive models that generate content sequentially (like GPT), variational models that learn compressed representations (like VAEs), adversarial models that use competing networks (like GANs), diffusion models that gradually transform noise into data, and energy-based models that learn probability distributions through energy functions. Each approach represents a different conceptual way of teaching machines to create content.

These generative techniques exist within the broader AI landscape alongside other major branches like reinforcement learning, supervised learning, and unsupervised learning. Generative AI frequently overlaps with these areas, borrowing concepts and combining approaches. For instance, many modern generative systems use reinforcement learning with human feedback to refine their outputs based on human preferences. While traditional supervised learning focuses on mapping inputs to predefined outputs and unsupervised learning discovers patterns without labeled data, generative AI focuses specifically on creating new content based on learned patterns. This specialized focus has led to breakthrough applications in creative domains previously considered uniquely human.

The application landscape for generative techniques continues to rapidly expand. Text-to-image models like DALL·E, Midjourney, and Stable Diffusion have democratized visual creation. Large language models power conversational assistants, content creation tools, and code generation systems. Audio generation models can create music, clone voices, and generate realistic sound effects. Scientific applications include designing new molecules for drug discovery, generating protein structures, and simulating physical systems. Each application area leverages different generative approaches based on the specific requirements of the domain, demonstrating the versatility of generative techniques across disparate fields.

Understanding where generative AI fits within the broader technology ecosystem helps contextualize its capabilities and limitations. While generative AI excels at creating content based on patterns in training data, it works best when complemented by other AI approaches like discriminative models for verification, reinforcement learning for refinement, and knowledge graphs for factual grounding. The most powerful AI systems often combine multiple approaches, using generative components alongside other techniques to create comprehensive solutions. As generative AI continues evolving, its integration with other AI branches and technologies will likely deepen, and this will create increasingly sophisticated systems that blend generation, discrimination, reasoning, and learning in novel ways.

The Evolution of Generative AI

The journey of generative AI begins in the early days of neural networks with autoencoders, which emerged in the 1980s but gained significant traction in the 2010s. These networks learn to compress data into a compact representation and then reconstruct it, effectively learning the essence of the data. The breakthrough came with variational autoencoders (VAEs) in 2013, which added a probabilistic twist to this approach, allowing for more controlled generation of new content. VAEs represented one of the first practical approaches to teaching machines to create new data that resembled training examples but wasn't simply copying them. These early models demonstrated that neural networks could not just classify but also create, and this opened the door to a new paradigm in artificial intelligence.

The generative landscape transformed dramatically in 2014 with the introduction of Generative Adversarial Networks (GANs) by Ian Goodfellow and colleagues. GANs introduced an adversarial training process where two networks, a generator creating content and a discriminator evaluating it, compete in a miniature game. This competition drives both networks to improve: the generator becomes increasingly skilled at creating realistic content while the discriminator becomes better at detecting fakes. This approach led to remarkable improvements in image generation quality, with subsequent GAN variants like StyleGAN producing stunningly realistic faces and scenes. The GAN revolution demonstrated that adversarial training could push generative capabilities far beyond what previous approaches had achieved.

While GANs dominated visual generation, the text generation world was revolutionized by the transformer architecture introduced in the 2017 "Attention Is All You Need" paper. Transformers enabled efficient processing of sequences through the self-attention mechanism, allowing models to capture long-range dependencies in text. This architecture formed the foundation for models like GPT (Generative Pretrained Transformer) and BERT, triggering an explosion in natural language processing capabilities. The scaling of these models, from millions to billions and eventually trillions of parameters, revealed that remarkable capabilities emerged as models grew, including few-shot learning, reasoning, and creative text generation that closely mimics human writing.

The most recent chapter in generative AI has been marked by diffusion models and multimodal approaches. Diffusion models, which generate data by gradually denoising random noise, have surpassed GANs in image quality while offering more stable training. This technique powers models like Stable Diffusion and DALL·E, enabling unprecedented control over image generation. Simultaneously, multimodal models that bridge text, images, audio, and even video have emerged, allowing systems to understand and generate across different types of content. Looking at this historical progression reveals a pattern of increasingly sophisticated approaches that capture deeper aspects of data structure, leading to today's generative models that can write essays, create artwork, compose music, and even assist in scientific discovery, and these are capabilities that seemed like science fiction just a decade ago.

Generative Model Families and Architectures

When people say that generative AI has exploded in the last few years, they are really talking about specific architectural breakthroughs that suddenly made it practical to synthesize text, pictures, sound, and even 3D scenes. Each family of models, transformers, diffusion systems, adversarial networks, and more, has its own strengths, weaknesses, and data types. Understanding the high-level ideas behind these families is important when you want to spot which tool is right for a given project and why certain techniques have become the defaults in industry. In this section you will meet the most influential architectures, look at how they work under the hood, and learn the tradeoffs that drive real-world design choices.

Transformers

Transformer-based Large Language Models have revolutionized text generation through their unique architectural design centered around the attention mechanism. Unlike earlier recurrent neural networks that processed text sequentially, transformers can analyze relationships between all words in a text simultaneously. This parallel processing allows them to capture long-range dependencies and contextual relationships between words regardless of how far apart they appear in the text. The self-attention mechanism essentially lets each word in a sequence "pay attention" to every other word, weighting their importance for predicting the next word, which results in a much richer understanding of language context.

The dominance of transformer-based LLMs in text generation stems from their remarkable scaling properties. Researchers discovered that simply increasing the size of these models (adding more parameters and training on more data) leads to emergent capabilities that weren't explicitly programmed. As these models scale from millions to billions of parameters, they don't just get incrementally better at existing tasks, they suddenly demonstrate new abilities like few-shot learning, reasoning, and creative writing. This phenomenon has driven the development of increasingly larger models like GPT-4, Claude, and Gemini, each pushing the boundaries of what's possible in natural language generation and understanding.

Transformer architectures have proven extraordinarily versatile, adapting to handle various languages, technical domains, and creative writing tasks. Their pretraining and fine-tuning approach allows them to first develop general language understanding on massive text datasets before specializing for particular applications. Modern LLMs can now write everything from poetry and essays to technical documentation and programming code, often matching or approaching human-level quality in many domains. Their ability to maintain coherence over long outputs, follow complex instructions, and adapt their tone and style to different contexts makes them powerful tools for content creation, communication, and problem-solving across countless applications.

Diffusion Models

Diffusion models are a revolutionary approach to content generation, and they work by gradually transforming random noise into structured data. The process mirrors how particles naturally spread from areas of high concentration to low concentration, a physical phenomenon called diffusion. These models work in two phases: first, during training, they learn how to gradually add noise to real data until it becomes pure noise (the forward diffusion process); then, they learn to reverse this process, starting with random noise and progressively removing it to create structured content (the reverse diffusion process). This approach has proven remarkably effective for generating high-quality images, audio, and 3D content with unprecedented levels of detail and realism.

The success of diffusion models across multiple content types stems from their stable training dynamics and fine-grained control capabilities. Unlike some earlier approaches that suffered from training instability or mode collapse, diffusion models provide consistent, high-quality results with fewer training complications. They excel at conditional generation (creating content based on specific inputs like text prompts), which has enabled powerful text-to-image systems like DALL·E, Midjourney, and Stable Diffusion. By conditioning the diffusion process on text embeddings, these models can generate images that match detailed descriptions, opening new possibilities for creative expression and design.

Diffusion technology has expanded beyond images to revolutionize audio and 3D content creation. In the audio domain, diffusion models can generate realistic speech, music, and sound effects by treating audio spectrograms or waveforms as the target data structure. For 3D generation, diffusion approaches create detailed models by either directly generating 3D point clouds or mesh structures, or by creating consistent multi-view images that can be converted to 3D representations. This versatility makes diffusion models increasingly central to creative workflows in visual arts, game development, product design, and entertainment. As computational resources continue improving, these models are becoming more accessible, enabling creators without technical expertise to bring imaginative concepts to life across multiple media formats.

Comparing Generative Approaches: GANs, VAEs, and RAG

Generative Adversarial Networks (GANs) pit two neural networks against each other: a generator that creates fake data and a discriminator that tries to detect flaws. This rivalry pushes the generator to produce increasingly realistic outputs. GANs excel at creating high-resolution images, deepfakes, or even synthetic faces for video games. However, they're notoriously hard to train. If one network overpowers the other, the system fails.

Variational Autoencoders (VAEs) take a gentler approach. They compress input data into a simplified format (like a summary) and then reconstruct it. VAEs are great for tasks requiring smooth interpolation, such as morphing one face into another in a video. But their outputs often lack the sharpness of GANs, appearing slightly blurry.

Retrieval-Augmented Generation (RAG) combines generative models with external knowledge sources. Instead of relying solely on training data, RAG systems "look up" relevant information (e.g., articles or databases) to enhance their outputs. For example, a chatbot using RAG could pull recent news to answer questions about current events. This hybrid approach improves accuracy but requires efficient retrieval systems to avoid delays.

Each architecture has its niche: GANs for realism, VAEs for controlled generation, and RAG for fact-aware tasks. Choosing the right one depends on the project's goals, whether it's artistic expression, data augmentation, or accurate information synthesis.

Training Generative Models

Training generative AI models is like teaching a machine to become an artist, writer, or composer. It involves feeding the system lots of data and guiding it to recognize patterns, make predictions, and eventually create original content. This section explores the nuts and bolts of how models learn, from initial "pretraining" on general tasks to specialized "fine-tuning" for specific jobs. Whether you're curious about how ChatGPT writes essays or how DALL·E generates images, understanding training workflows is key. Let's dive into the methods that turn raw data into creative AI.

The Building Blocks of Pretraining

Pretraining is the foundational phase where models learn general skills by digesting massive datasets. One common objective is next-token prediction, where the model guesses the next word in a sentence (like autocomplete on steroids). For example, given "The sky is … ," it might predict "blue." This teaches the model grammar, context, and common phrases. Another approach is masked-token prediction, where random words in a sentence are hidden (masked), and the model fills in the blanks. Imagine covering parts of a crossword puzzle. The model learns to infer missing pieces based on surrounding clues. This method, popularized by models like BERT, helps systems understand bidirectional context, improving tasks like translation or sentiment analysis.

Denoising objectives train models to recover clean data from corrupted inputs. For instance, adding static to an image and asking the model to remove it. This technique, central to diffusion models, teaches robustness and attention to detail. These objectives equip models with a broad skill set, preparing them for more specialized tasks later.

Tailoring Models with Fine-Tuning and Beyond

Once pretrained, models often undergo fine-tuning to specialize in specific tasks. During this process, a model that has already learned general knowledge during pretraining is further trained on a smaller, more focused dataset representing the target application. For example, a language model pretrained on general text might be fine-tuned on medical literature to better handle healthcare topics or on programming repositories to enhance code generation abilities. Fine-tuning adjusts the model's existing knowledge toward specific patterns, terminology, and conventions of the target domain without requiring the computational expense of full pretraining. This approach allows organizations to customize powerful foundation models for their specific needs with relatively modest resources.

Instruction tuning represents a specialized form of fine-tuning that teaches models to follow human instructions and respond appropriately to prompts. Rather than optimizing for a single task, instruction tuning uses datasets of instruction–response pairs that demonstrate how to interpret and fulfill diverse user requests. This training helps models become more helpful, honest, and harmless by teaching them to understand user intent and generate appropriate responses across countless scenarios. Modern techniques often incorporate human feedback through processes like RLHF (Reinforcement Learning from Human Feedback), where human evaluators rate model outputs, and these ratings train a reward model that guides the AI toward more preferred responses. This combination of instruction tuning and human feedback alignment has been crucial in developing today's most useful conversational AI systems.

Continual learning addresses a fundamental challenge in AI: how to update models with new information without forgetting what they've already learned. Unlike traditional approaches where models remain static after training, continual learning workflows allow systems to acquire new knowledge, adapt to changing circumstances, and refine their capabilities over time. Techniques like parameter-efficient fine-tuning (which updates only small portions of the model), knowledge distillation (transferring knowledge from one model to another), and rehearsal methods (reviewing previous examples while learning new ones) help maintain performance on original tasks while accommodating new information. As the world changes and new information emerges, continual learning becomes increasingly important for keeping AI systems relevant, accurate, and useful across their deployment lifetime.

Data Processing and Scaling Considerations

Data curation stands as perhaps the most critical yet often overlooked aspect of training high-quality generative models. The careful selection, cleaning, and organization of training data directly determines what the model learns, including both its capabilities and its biases or limitations. Effective curation involves assembling diverse, representative data sources; filtering out low-quality, harmful, or inappropriate content; deduplicating redundant information; and balancing different topics, styles, and perspectives. Modern curation pipelines often combine automated filtering with human review processes to ensure training data meets quality standards while representing the breadth of knowledge the model should acquire. As models have grown more powerful, the focus has increasingly shifted from simply gathering more data to ensuring that training data is high-quality, ethically sourced, and aligned with human values.

Tokenization transforms raw text, images, or audio into the discrete units that models actually process during training and generation. For language models, tokenizers split text into vocabulary units that might be characters, words, subwords, or byte pairs, converting human-readable content into numerical sequences the model can work with. The choice of tokenization strategy significantly impacts model performance, affecting how efficiently it represents different languages, how it handles rare words or technical terms, and even its ability to work with code or mathematical notation. Vision and audio models similarly convert pixels or waveforms into manageable tokens through various encoding techniques. Well-designed tokenization helps models make efficient use of their context windows and computational resources while accurately representing the full diversity of content they might encounter.

Scaling laws have revolutionized our understanding of how generative models improve as they grow in size and training data. Research has revealed remarkably consistent mathematical relationships showing that model performance improves predictably with increases in model size (number of parameters), dataset size, and computational resources dedicated to training. These scaling laws guide critical resource allocation decisions, helping researchers determine optimal model architectures, training dataset sizes, and compute budgets to achieve desired performance levels. They've shown that many capabilities emerge naturally as models scale up without requiring architectural changes. However, scaling isn't just about making everything bigger; it requires careful balancing of model size, data quality, and training efficiency. Understanding these relationships has fueled the rapid advancement of generative AI by providing clear roadmaps for how to build increasingly capable systems in cost-effective ways.

Inference and Generation Mechanics

Once a generative AI model is trained, the real magic happens during inference, which is the process where it creates outputs based on inputs. This generation phase is where users actually interact with the model, providing prompts and receiving AI-created content in return. While training determines what a model can potentially do, the inference mechanisms control how it applies that knowledge in practice. These generation mechanics include how we communicate with models through prompts, which strategies the model uses to select its next words or pixels, and how we can extend models with external tools and capabilities. Understanding these inference processes is essential for anyone looking to effectively use generative AI systems, as they directly impact the quality, creativity, reliability, and efficiency of the content these models produce. That's what we cover in this section.

Prompts and Context Windows

A prompt is more than the first thing you type; it is the entire conversational frame that guides the model's reply. Good prompts set clear intent, provide any special instructions or style constraints, and offer relevant context so the model does not have to invent missing details. Adding examples, sometimes called "few-shot" prompting, can nudge the model toward the format or reasoning pattern you want, much like showing a student solved homework problems before giving them new questions.

Every generative model has a fixed context window, the maximum number of tokens it can consider at once. If your conversation, reference text, or code snippet is too long, older tokens must be trimmed or summarized, which risks losing crucial information. Techniques such as "chunk-and-summarize," hierarchical prompts, or sliding-window retrieval keep the most relevant pieces in view. Planning what to keep, what to shorten, and what to drop is a quiet but vital part of prompt engineering, especially for tasks like legal reasoning or code refactoring where details matter.

Decoding Strategies and Their Personalities

Once the model has predicted a probability for every possible next token, a decoding strategy turns those probabilities into an actual word. The simplest choice is greedy decoding (always pick the top-scoring token) yielding fast but sometimes repetitive text. Beam search explores several high-probability paths in parallel, balancing quality and speed yet still leaning toward safe, common phrasing.

Sampling-based decoding strategies introduce controlled randomness to generate more diverse and creative outputs. Temperature sampling adjusts how much the model favors high-probability tokens, higher temperatures produce more surprising and creative results, while lower temperatures yield more focused, conservative outputs. Top-k sampling narrows the selection to only the k most likely next tokens, while nucleus (or top-p) sampling dynamically selects from the smallest set of tokens whose cumulative probability exceeds threshold p. More advanced approaches like contrastive search balance quality and diversity by considering both token probability and output repetition. Understanding these strategies helps users select the right approach for different applications, using deterministic methods for factual or technical content and sampling-based approaches for creative writing or brainstorming.

Advanced Inference Capabilities

Tool use and function calling capabilities dramatically extend what generative AI systems can accomplish by allowing them to interact with external systems and data sources. Rather than being limited to generating text based solely on their training data, models equipped with tool use can perform calculations, retrieve up-to-date information, execute code, interact with APIs, and use specialized reasoning frameworks. This process typically involves the model recognizing when a task requires external functionality, generating a properly formatted function call with appropriate parameters, and then incorporating the returned results into its continued generation. Function calling enables sophisticated applications like AI agents that can research topics, analyze data, make reservations, or control other software, greatly expanding the practical utility of generative models beyond simple content creation.

Generation mode decisions like choosing between streaming and batch inference involve important tradeoffs between responsiveness, efficiency, and resource utilization. Streaming inference presents generated tokens to users as they're produced, creating a more interactive experience where users see results emerging in real time, similar to watching someone type. This approach reduces perceived latency and allows users to interrupt generation if it's heading in an unwanted direction but may require maintaining dedicated resources for each active session. Batch inference, on the other hand, processes multiple prompts simultaneously and returns complete responses, maximizing throughput and computational efficiency but potentially increasing wait times for individual users. The right approach depends on the specific application needs: streaming works best for interactive conversations and creative applications where the generation process itself provides value, while batch processing excels in high-volume scenarios where efficiency is paramount.

Evaluation and Alignment

Creating powerful generative AI systems isn't enough. We must also ensure they perform well and align with human values. This section focuses on how we measure the quality of AI outputs and ensure systems behave responsibly. From automated scoring to human oversight, these processes act as a "quality control" pipeline, catching errors, biases, or harmful outputs before they reach users. Regardless of what you're building, understanding evaluation and alignment is critical to making AI trustworthy and effective.

Measuring Quality with Automatic Metrics

Automatic metrics give a quick, repeatable snapshot of how a model is doing without waiting for human judges. In text generation, BLEU and ROUGE compare the model's output to one or more reference sentences by counting shared n-grams. BLEU is stricter, rewarding exact word sequences; ROUGE is looser, focusing on recall of key phrases. It is handy for summarization tasks where covering main points matters more than wording.

Perplexity takes another angle: it looks at how "surprised" a language model is by a known test set. Lower perplexity means the model assigns high probability to correct continuations, hinting at stronger fluency and grammar.

Image and multimodal outputs need different yardsticks. The Fréchet Inception Distance, or FID, measures how close the statistics of generated images are to real ones in the space of a pretrained vision network; lower scores signal more realistic pictures. CLIP score leverages a joint image-text model: it checks whether a generated image matches its caption in semantic space, making it useful for text-to-image systems. None of these metrics fully capture human taste, but they are fast and objective, letting teams iterate quickly before moving on to deeper checks.

Why Humans Still Matter

Human evaluation remains the gold standard for assessing generative AI quality, bringing judgment and contextual understanding that automated metrics can't replicate. Typical human evaluation processes involve presenting evaluators with model outputs alongside clear criteria for assessment, such as accuracy, helpfulness, coherence, or safety. Preference modeling extends this approach by having evaluators compare outputs from different models or variations, creating ranked preferences that help identify which approaches perform better for particular tasks. These human judgments can then train reward models that predict human preferences, guiding further model improvements. As evaluations become more sophisticated, they often incorporate diverse evaluator pools to surface blind spots and reduce cultural or demographic bias, especially since models may reflect norms from overrepresented regions or groups in their training data. While generative AI doesn't inherently know a user's gender or location, the content it produces can unintentionally favor certain perspectives unless human oversight catches and corrects it.

Beyond passive rating, teams run red-teaming exercises. These are intentional stress tests where experts try to coax bad behavior. They craft adversarial prompts, search for policy violations, and probe edge cases like ambiguous requests or harmful content. The findings feed back into safety filters, prompt defenses, or additional fine-tuning. Preference modeling can even turn these human likes and dislikes into a reward signal so that the model gradually steers toward responses most people favor.

Aligning AI with Human Values

Reinforcement Learning from Human Feedback (RLHF) formalizes the idea of learning from preferences. After a base model generates multiple answers to the same prompt, humans rank them. A separate reward model learns to predict those rankings, and the generator is fine-tuned with policy-gradient methods to maximize that reward. The process nudges the model toward helpful, harmless, and honest behavior without hard coding every rule.

Reinforcement Learning from AI Feedback (RLAIF) extends the idea by letting a strong but slower reference model, or an ensemble of earlier checkpoints, provide the comparisons instead of humans. This synthetic feedback is cheaper and can scale to billions of examples, though it must be curated to avoid amplifying existing biases. Both RLHF and RLAIF are often combined with supervised instruction tuning and safety layers, forming a multi-stage pipeline where alignment is tightened at each step. The result is a model that not only sounds smart but also reflects the values and constraints set by its developers and users.

Representative Use Cases for Generative AI

Generative AI has rapidly transformed from a research curiosity to a practical technology with applications across virtually every industry and domain. These powerful systems are changing how we work, create, and solve problems by automating content creation, assisting with complex tasks, and generating novel outputs that would be difficult or impossible to produce manually. Understanding the major use cases for generative AI helps illuminate both its current impact and future potential. While the underlying technology (large language models, diffusion models, and other generative architectures) remains similar across applications, the way these systems are adapted, fine-tuned, and deployed creates remarkably different experiences for end users. From conversational systems that help us navigate information to creative tools that expand human artistic capabilities, generative AI is finding its way into countless workflows and processes. The most successful applications typically combine the creative and analytical strengths of AI with human judgment, expertise, and oversight, creating partnerships that leverage the unique capabilities of both.

The most familiar face of generative AI is the conversational assistant or "copilot." Unlike the scripted chatbots of a few years ago, modern assistants draw on large language models that can reason across long conversations, reference documentation, and even call external tools. Customer service teams deploy them to triage tickets before a human steps in; software companies bake them into development environments so developers can ask for code snippets or explanations right where they work; health systems experiment with "ambient scribing," letting a model turn the free-flow dialogue of a clinic visit into structured notes. The pattern is the same across industries: the model acts as a first-pass expert that handles routine dialogue, escalates edge cases, and frees up professionals for higher-value tasks.

Beyond full conversations, generative models excel at focused language tasks such as drafting, summarizing, translating, or writing code. A journalist might paste raw interview transcripts into a summarizer that condenses hours of talk into tight bullet points; business analysts translate market reports in seconds and pivot to drafting slide decks; programmers lean on autocomplete systems that finish function bodies, suggest tests, or translate legacy code to a new language while citing relevant docs. The common thread is that the model absorbs context, whether that is a paragraph, a whole repository, or an entire corporate knowledge base, and then produces a first draft that a human can accept, tweak, or discard, shrinking ideation cycles from days to minutes.

The creative power of generative AI extends to pixels, sound waves, and three-dimensional scenes. Designers iterate mood boards by typing natural-language prompts that yield photorealistic images; film studios pre-visualize complex shots with AI-generated storyboards; musicians feed a few bars into a model that riffs new melodies; game developers build synthetic 3D assets that match the art style of their worlds. In more specialist domains, the same capability shows up as synthetic data generation, hospital systems create de-identified patient records to test billing software, banks simulate transaction logs to calibrate fraud detectors, and researchers render rare wildlife sounds to train conservation models. These image, audio, and domain-specific workflows all share a core benefit: they remove the bottleneck of scarce or sensitive data, letting teams explore ideas safely and at pace.

Summary

This chapter covered the foundations of generative AI, explaining how it differs from discriminative approaches by creating new content rather than just classifying existing data. We explored major model architectures including transformers that power large language models, diffusion models for image generation, and alternatives like GANs and VAEs, each with their distinct strengths and applications. The chapter detailed training workflows from pretraining on massive datasets to fine-tuning for specific tasks, along with important considerations in data processing and scaling laws. We examined inference mechanisms including prompting techniques, decoding strategies, and tool integration that determine how models generate outputs. Finally, we discussed evaluation methods and alignment techniques like RLHF that ensure models produce high-quality content aligned with human values, before reviewing real-world applications across industries from conversational assistants to creative content generation, showing how generative AI is transforming workflows across diverse sectors.

Exam Essentials

Understand the distinction between generative and discriminative AI.   Know that generative AI creates new content while discriminative AI classifies or categorizes existing data, and recognize the different evaluation criteria for each approach.

Recognize major generative model architectures.   Understand why transformers dominate text generation, how diffusion models work for image creation, and the tradeoffs between approaches like GANs, VAEs, and RAG systems.

Know the training workflow for generative models.   Differentiate between pretraining objectives (next-token prediction, masked-token prediction, denoising), fine-tuning approaches, and alignment techniques like RLHF and RLAIF.

Understand inference and generation mechanics.   Learn how prompts and context windows affect model outputs, how different decoding strategies balance creativity with coherence, and how tool use extends model capabilities.

Recognize evaluation approaches for generative AI.   Know the automatic metrics used for different content types, understand why human evaluation remains essential, and learn how alignment techniques ensure models reflect human values.

Identify key generative AI applications.   Understand how conversational assistants and copilots work across industries, recognize language-focused workflows like summarization and code generation, and know how generative AI enables creative tasks in visual and audio domains.

Review Questions

1. Your team is developing an AI solution to generate product descriptions based on specifications. Which type of AI approach would be most appropriate for this task?

   A. Discriminative AI

   B. Generative AI

   C. Supervised learning

   D. Unsupervised clustering

2. A retail company wants to implement a chatbot that can assist customers with complex product inquiries and help with troubleshooting steps. Which generative AI architecture would be most appropriate?

   A. GAN (Generative Adversarial Network)

   B. Transformer-based LLM

   C. Diffusion model

   D. VAE (Variational Autoencoder)

3. Your team needs to create photorealistic images of furniture products based on text descriptions. Which generative model family would be most appropriate?

   A. Transformer models

   B. Diffusion models

   C. Recurrent Neural Networks

   D. Decision Trees

4. A healthcare company is developing an AI system that needs to answer medical questions with factual information. Which approach would help ensure the model provides accurate information rather than hallucinations?

   A. Increasing model size

   B. Using GANs for text generation

   C. Implementing Retrieval-Augmented Generation (RAG)

   D. Using higher temperature settings during generation

5. What is the primary advantage of transformer architectures over earlier recurrent neural networks for text generation?

   A. They require less training data

   B. They can process all words in a sequence simultaneously

   C. They always generate shorter outputs

   D. They use less computational resources

6. Your organization needs to implement a model that can generate synthetic customer data for testing. Which generative AI training approach would help ensure the synthetic data maintains the statistical properties of real customer data?

    A. RLHF (Reinforcement Learning from Human Feedback)

    B. Token-level classification

    C. Distribution learning via techniques like VAEs or diffusion models

    D. Instruction tuning

7. A company wants to use generative AI to summarize customer support tickets. Which evaluation metric would be most appropriate for automatically assessing the quality of the summaries?

    A. BLEU score

    B. Perplexity

    C. FID (Fréchet Inception Distance)

    D. ROUGE score

8. Your team wants to ensure that your generative AI assistant provides responses aligned with company values and avoids harmful outputs. Which technique would be most effective for this purpose?

    A. Increasing model size

    B. Using greedy decoding

    C. Using lower learning rates during pretraining

    D. Implementing RLHF (Reinforcement Learning from Human Feedback)

9. In which scenario would using a higher temperature setting during text generation be most appropriate?

    A. Generating factual responses about medical treatments

    B. Creative brainstorming for marketing campaign ideas

    C. Producing technical documentation for a software product

    D. Creating structured data entries for a database

10. A financial services company is implementing a generative AI assistant that needs to answer questions based on the latest regulations and policies. Which approach would best help the model stay current with changing information?

    A. Implementing continual learning workflows

    B. Using beam search decoding

    C. Fine-tuning on a larger dataset

    D. Increasing the model's parameter count

11. Your company is developing an AI system to create realistic 3D models for architectural visualization. Which generative model family would be most suitable for this task?

A. Transformer-based models

B. Diffusion models

C. Recurrent Neural Networks

D. Decision Trees

12. What does the context window refer to in large language models?

A. The maximum number of tokens the model can consider at once

B. The graphical user interface where users interact with the model

C. The library of predefined responses the model can select from

D. The time period during which the model was trained

13. A software development team wants to implement an AI assistant that can help generate code based on natural language descriptions. Which generative AI implementation would be most appropriate?

A. Diffusion model

B. GAN (Generative Adversarial Network)

C. VAE (Variational Autoencoder)

D. Transformer-based LLM with programming data fine-tuning

14. Your team is implementing a generative AI solution that needs to process large documents to extract information and generate summaries. What technique would help overcome context window limitations?

A. Increasing the temperature parameter

B. Using greedy decoding instead of sampling

C. Switching to a GAN architecture

D. Implementing chunk-and-summarize approaches

15. A marketing team wants to use generative AI to create product descriptions that match their brand voice. Which training approach would be most appropriate for customizing a general-purpose language model to their specific style?

A. Pretraining from scratch

B. Fine-tuning on brand-specific content

C. Implementing RLHF

D. Using different tokenization strategies

16. In generative AI evaluation, why is human evaluation still considered the gold standard despite the availability of automated metrics?

A. Human evaluation is less expensive than automated metrics

B. Automated metrics cannot be computed for most generative outputs

C. Human evaluators can assess subjective qualities like creativity and appropriateness

D. Human evaluation is always perfectly consistent across evaluators

17. Your organization is implementing a generative AI system for creating educational content. Which technique would help ensure the generated content is factually accurate?

A. Using higher temperature settings

B. Implementing Retrieval-Augmented Generation (RAG)

C. Using top-k sampling with a small k value

D. Increasing model size without external knowledge sources

18. Which pretraining objective involves gradually adding noise to data and then learning to reverse the process?

A. Next-token prediction

B. Masked language modeling

C. Denoising

D. Adversarial training

19. A research team needs to generate synthetic medical images for training diagnostic algorithms. Which approach would be most important to ensure the synthetic images maintain critical diagnostic features?

A. Using the highest resolution possible

B. Implementing human-in-the-loop evaluation and feedback

C. Using only GANs for generation

D. Maximizing batch size during training

20. Your company is implementing an AI assistant to help with customer inquiries. Which technique helps the assistant provide more accurate responses about company-specific information?

A. Increasing model parameter count

B. Using higher temperature settings

C. Implementing tool use and function calling capabilities

D. Switching to a GAN architecture

Chapter

11

Azure OpenAI Service

Now that you understand the basics of Generative AI, it's time to explore how Microsoft has integrated these powerful capabilities directly into the Azure platform. The Azure OpenAI Service brings the innovative models developed by OpenAI into Microsoft's cloud ecosystem, giving organizations access to cutting-edge AI tools. This chapter will introduce you to the core concepts of Azure OpenAI Service, covering what these AI models can do, how they fit into the Azure environment, and the kinds of problems they can solve for businesses.

We'll focus on understanding what these AI capabilities do. You'll learn about the different models available, their typical use cases, and how Azure provides a layer of enterprise features around them. By the end of this chapter, you'll grasp how Azure OpenAI Service differs from standalone AI offerings and why organizations might choose this path for implementing AI solutions.

Introduction to Azure OpenAI Service

Before diving into the details, picture the Azure OpenAI Service as Microsoft's managed front door to the same large-language-model technology that powers ChatGPT, Copilot, and many other modern AI apps. Instead of standing up GPUs, setting up container images, or worrying about scaling, as a developer, you will be able to call a familiar Azure resource and instantly tap into models that understand and generate natural language, code, images, and even speech. What follows unpacks four foundational ideas you should be comfortable with as you start working with the service.

Understanding Azure OpenAI Service

The Azure OpenAI Service is a fully managed platform that gives you OpenAI's generative models behind an Azure ARM resource. When you create the resource, Azure hosts a copy of the model in the region you choose, exposes the familiar **/chat/completions**, **/embeddings**, or **/images/generations** endpoints, and lets you call them through REST or the Python, JavaScript, C#, Java, and Go SDKs that follow the same schema OpenAI publishes. Because it is an Azure service, all traffic, data at rest, and model weights sit inside Microsoft-owned infrastructure.

Behind that convenience sits Microsoft's compliance envelope. Your prompts, outputs, embeddings, and fine-tuning data never leave Microsoft-controlled infrastructure, are not shared with other customers, and are not used to retrain the foundation models. The service is operated under the same Microsoft Product Terms as other Azure resources, and access is gated by a Limited-Access program to help Microsoft enforce its Responsible AI Code of Conduct. Organizations subject to GDPR, HIPAA, FedRAMP, or similar regulations can therefore treat Azure OpenAI like any other regulated cloud workload, while still tapping the very latest model releases.

The service forms an important component in Microsoft's broader AI ecosystem, acting as a bridge between cutting-edge AI research and business applications. It integrates seamlessly with other Azure services and enables developers to build comprehensive AI solutions that can address complex business challenges. For instance, while Azure Cognitive Services might handle speech recognition or image analysis, Azure OpenAI tackles more complex challenges like writing essays, translating code, or generating art.

This integration means developers can mix and match services. Imagine building an app that uses Cognitive Services to analyze user sentiment from voice recordings and then uses Azure OpenAI to draft personalized email responses. This reduces barriers to adoption and allows organizations to focus on solving problems rather than setting up infrastructure.

The Evolution of OpenAI in Azure

OpenAI's first API hit the public internet in mid-2020, but accessing it from Azure required custom networking or Functions work-arounds. In late 2021 Microsoft opened a private preview that let selected customers deploy GPT-3 inside their own subscriptions, with the promise of enterprise-grade security. That preview eventually became the Azure OpenAI Service, publicly announced at Microsoft Build 2022 and moved to general availability in January 2023.

Integration has tightened ever since. Azure AI Studio (formerly simply "OpenAI Studio") has a low-code interface for prompting, evaluation, and fine-tuning, while Azure AI Foundry consolidates model catalogs, data labeling, and deployment patterns across Microsoft's AI lineup. At the same time, traditional Azure controls like Key Vault, Private Link, and Managed Identities were wired in so that generative AI follows the same governance story as storage accounts or app services.

2024 and 2025 have also brought multimodal and reasoning models. GPT-4 Turbo with Vision, GPT-4o, and GPT-4.1 introduced native image input, faster tokens, and extended context windows; the o-series emphasized chain-of-thought-style reasoning. Each release immediately appeared in Azure regions such as East US, West Europe, and Japan East. Availability in Azure Government and classified regions typically follows later, based on compliance and regulatory requirements. The result is a service that now spans text, code, vision, audio, embeddings, and tool-calling workflows, all accessible through the same REST pattern first published for GPT-3.

Available Models and Their Capabilities

Azure hosts most of OpenAI's flagship models. At the premium end, GPT-4o and GPT-4.1 accept both text and images, return structured JSON when asked, and can call user-defined functions. This is ideal for conversational agents that need to trigger downstream APIs. GPT-4 Turbo with Vision offers similar multimodality but is tuned for lower latency and cost, while classic GPT-4 remains for workloads that were validated on its earlier snapshots.

Mid-tier options include GPT-4o mini and GPT-3.5-Turbo. They trade some reasoning depth for speed and price, and they are popular for chatbots, summarization, or high-volume code completion. Specialized families sit alongside them: embedding models such as text-embedding-3 convert text into numeric vectors for semantic search, while the DALL·E 3 image models generate original artwork from prompts, and Whisper-based speech models handle transcription and text-to-speech.

There's also a newer branch called the o-series and it consists of models like the o4-mini, o3, o1, and more. These models focus on multi-step reasoning. They spend extra compute cycles "thinking," making them strong at mathematics, scientific explanations, and planning tasks. They can process up to 200 k tokens of context, allowing applications to feed entire code repositories or long policy documents without chunking. What's good about this catalog is that you can match model to use-case rather than force every workload through one giant network.

Azure OpenAI vs. OpenAI: Why Choose One Over the Other?

When comparing Azure OpenAI Service with standalone OpenAI, several key differences emerge that can influence an organization's choice between the two. Azure OpenAI prioritizes enterprise features like enhanced security, compliance certifications, and integration with Azure's identity and access management systems. These features make it attractive for organizations with strict governance requirements or those already heavily invested in the Microsoft ecosystem. The service also offers predictable billing and service level agreements that can be crucial for business planning.

OpenAI's direct offerings, on the other hand, often provide earlier access to the latest models and features. This earlier access comes with the tradeoff of potentially less stability and fewer enterprise controls. For organizations prioritizing new AI capabilities or innovation over governance features, or for individual developers and smaller teams, the direct OpenAI services might be a more flexible and possibly more cost-effective option depending on usage patterns.

Another significant distinction lies in the data handling policies. Azure OpenAI Service has clearer commitments regarding data privacy and retention, with options to ensure that data isn't used for model training without explicit permission. This addresses concerns about intellectual property and confidentiality that many enterprises have when considering AI services. Additionally, Azure has regional deployment options that can help organizations meet data residency requirements, a feature that may be limited or unavailable with standalone OpenAI services.

Core Capabilities of Azure OpenAI

Generative AI only becomes valuable when it solves real problems, and Azure OpenAI ships a set of baseline skills that let you move from "just a cool demo" to a dependable solution. Here, we'd look at what the service can actually do with text, images, and speech; how you steer those abilities with carefully worded prompts; the guardrails that keep content safe and policy-compliant; and finally the places where businesses are already turning these features into day-to-day productivity gains.

Everyday Language Skills at Scale

Large language models inside Azure OpenAI approach human-like fluency in reading and writing. They can summarize an earnings call transcript into a concise press note, translate a German support ticket into English while keeping any domain-specific jargon intact, or rephrase a legal clause so that a non-lawyer can understand it. Under the hood these feats rely on transformer networks that have internalized patterns from trillions of tokens, allowing them to infer meaning and generate context-aware completions instead of merely copying text they have seen before.

Beyond plain text, today's GPT-4o family can interpret images and short audio clips, which means a single model can read a photograph of a menu, identify allergens, and then speak the answer back to the user in natural speech. The same multimodal backbone also powers code completion tasks: feed it a partially written Python function and it predicts the remaining lines while following project-level style conventions. Those experiences run through the same **/chat/completions** and **/audio/completions** endpoints, so upgrading from text-only GPT-3.5 to a multimodal GPT-4o deployment is largely a configuration change rather than a rewrite.

Another everyday capability is *embeddings* generation. When you send a sentence or paragraph to the text-embedding-3 model, the service returns a numeric vector that captures semantic meaning. Applications feed those vectors into Azure AI Search or a vector database so that end users can look up "red running trainers" and still find "scarlet athletic shoes." Because embeddings reduce language to mathematics, they work across languages and can even cluster product descriptions, incident reports, or research abstracts that have no overlapping keywords.

Crafting Good AI Prompts

If the model is the engine, the prompt is the steering wheel. Good prompts establish the model's persona, delimit its scope, and spell out the desired output format so that the response arrives structured and on-topic. A proven habit is to start with a system message that sets the rules ("You are a helpful assistant who always answers with a JSON payload containing 'summary' and 'riskLevel' fields"). By explicitly naming the fields you want, you prevent the model from wandering into chatty prose or unexpected table formats.

Specificity is your friend. Instead of asking "Summarize this article," you can say "Write a 100-word abstract, include one bullet on ethical concerns, and end with a question that invites reader feedback." Repetition also helps: restating the instruction at the end of the prompt nudges the model to keep the requirement in short-term memory during generation. Developers often embed variables (like the user's query or a document excerpt) between clear delimiters so that the model can unambiguously tell the difference between user input and instructions.

Iterative refinement closes the loop. After you inspect the first few responses, adjust settings to balance creativity with determinism, tweak wording that the model may be interpreting too broadly, and save successful prompt variants in your codebase or Azure AI Studio playground. Over time, you will build a library of "prompt templates" and they could be very useful. One could be for product descriptions, another for code reviews, a third for customer-friendly policy summaries. Treat these templates/reusable prompts the way you would reusable functions, tested, version-controlled, and documented for teammates.

Building Great Prompts

Don't make the mistake of thinking that a prompt is just a question, it's not. It's the entire set of instructions the AI model will lean on to decide who it should be, what it should do, and how it should shape the result. A high-quality prompt usually has four clear ingredients:

1. **Role framing**: A short line that casts the model in a specific persona ("You are a bilingual tech-support agent …"). This primes the network's internal attention toward the right tone and domain.

2. **Task description**: An explicit statement of the action you want ("… translate and simplify the error message below"). Ambiguity is the fastest way to get hallucinations.

3. **Context or data**: Everything the model needs to complete the task, wrapped in obvious delimiters so it can tell instruction from input (for example, <<<BEGIN>>> and <<<END>>>).

4. **Output constraints**: The required structure, length, or format ("Return a JSON object with summary and riskLevel properties"). These guard against rambling and make the answer machine-readable.

A good mental check is this: *Could a colleague who has never seen the project read the prompt and still guess the exact shape of the expected answer?* If the prompt leaves room for interpretation, tighten the wording, add an example, or break the task into smaller chained calls.

Three Sample Prompts

1. **Executive-Style Summary**

   You are an executive briefing assistant. Summarize the following earnings call transcript in 150 words, use neutral language, end with one bullet on future risks, and cite the time stamps you pulled quotes from.

   ```
   <<<BEGIN TRANSCRIPT>>>
   ... (paste transcript) ...
   <<<END TRANSCRIPT>>>
   ```

   Return the output as plain text, no markdown.

2. **Code Reviewer for Security Issues**

   You are a senior security engineer. Review the JavaScript snippet below for vulnerabilities related to user-supplied input. List findings as an array of objects with fields: "issue," "severity" (Low/Medium/High), and "patchSuggestion."

   ```
   <<<CODE>>>
   ... (paste code) ...
   <<<END CODE>>>
   ```

   If no issues are found, return an empty array.

3. **Customer Support Reply Generator**

   You are a polite, empathetic customer support agent for an online shoe retailer. Craft a response to the customer message below. Address the client by first name, apologize if needed, and provide a return-label link that uses {ReturnLink}. Keep the tone cheerful, under 120 words, and end with a single follow-up question.

   ```
   <<<CUSTOMER MESSAGE>>>
   ... (paste message) ...
   <<<END MESSAGE>>>
   ```

   Notice how each prompt nails the four ingredients: persona, task, context, and constraints. Follow that template and you'll spend less time debugging model behavior and more time delivering features.

Implementing Content Safety Measures

Every request and response in Azure OpenAI is scanned by a content filtering system that looks for violence, self-harm, sexual imagery, hate speech, and other disallowed material. If the classifier detects a violation in either the user prompt or the model's draft answer, it can block the call outright or apply a "safe completion" that removes the problematic portion while still returning a helpful reply. This process happens within milliseconds and requires no extra code from the developer.

Administrators can customize thresholds and allowed categories through the Azure portal or management APIs. For instance, a healthcare chatbot might permit medical descriptions of human anatomy that would normally be filtered as sexual, while a gaming community tool might enforce a stricter stance on profanity. Although Azure's content filters don't automatically adjust based on user identity, developers can implement additional logic to fine-tune moderation by user context—for example, applying stricter settings for a 14-year-old user than for a 34-year-old. These controls integrate with familiar Azure governance features such as role-based access control and diagnostic logs, making safety configurations auditable just like firewall rules or storage policies.

For more granular scenarios, organizations can layer Azure AI Content Safety, which is a separate but complementary service that scores text and images, returns confidence metrics, and even highlights the exact spans that triggered a flag. Combining these signals with the model's own moderation endpoint lets developers build multi-stage pipelines: first reject unacceptable content, then rewrite borderline cases into a neutral style before handing them to the main model for further processing.

Business Applications of Language Models

Language models have transformed how businesses approach communication, content creation, information processing, and many other tasks across numerous departments and functions. Customer support is one of the earliest successes. Retailers plug chat completions into their help portals so that shoppers can ask, "Where's my package?" or "Does this coat shrink in the wash?" and receive instant answers sourced from order systems and product manuals. Contact-center agents get AI-generated suggested replies, cutting average handling time without sacrificing accuracy because the human still signs off before the message goes out.

Content creation and management are another significant business application for language models. Marketing teams use these models to draft blog posts, social media content, product descriptions, and email campaigns, which often reduces content creation time from days to minutes. Legal departments leverage language models to summarize lengthy contracts and legal documents, highlighting key terms and potential issues that require attorney review. In human resources, these models assist with writing job descriptions, screening resumes for relevant qualifications, and generating personalized communications to candidates. The efficiency gains across these departments can substantially impact an organization's productivity and output quality.

Knowledge management comes next. Consultants or lawyers feed thousands of documents into an embeddings-backed vector store and let staff ask natural language questions over the entire repository. The model retrieves the top-ranked passages, stitches them into a concise answer, and cites sources so that professionals can verify every claim.

This "retrieve-augment-generate" pattern now appears in industries from pharmaceutical research to supply chain auditing.

Innovation labs are using generative AI to dream up new products. Beauty brands test marketing slogans and personalized skincare advice, while manufacturers analyze sensor data and maintenance logs to predict downtime and recommend process tweaks. In each case the language model acts as a reasoning layer that converts raw text, images, or numbers into actionable insights a human can act on whether that means launching a new lipstick shade or rescheduling a factory line for preventive repair.

Image Generation in Azure OpenAI

Image generation is one of the most fascinating and rapidly evolving capabilities in Azure OpenAI. This technology allows users to create completely original images simply by describing what they want in natural language. Rather than requiring design skills or specialized software, users can generate visuals by typing text prompts like "a serene mountain landscape at sunset with a cabin by a lake" and watching as the AI transforms those words into a detailed image. This capability opens up creative possibilities for individuals and organizations who may lack traditional design resources or expertise.

The integration of image generation within Azure OpenAI marks a significant step forward in making visual AI accessible to businesses and developers. It represents the convergence of natural language processing and computer vision, two previously separate domains of artificial intelligence. By bringing these capabilities together in a managed cloud service, Microsoft has made it possible for organizations to experiment with and deploy visual AI without needing to build the underlying infrastructure or develop the complex models themselves.

As we explore the various aspects of image generation in Azure OpenAI, you'll gain an understanding of how this technology works, what it can create, and how businesses are using it today.

DALL·E in the Azure Environment

The DALL·E models live in Azure as deployable resources. When you create a new deployment in Azure AI Studio or the portal, DALL·E 3 now appears in the model picker; once provisioned, it answers POST requests sent to the same OpenAI-style **/images/ generations** endpoint that consumer users know, but with traffic and data confined to Microsoft data centers.

Provisioning follows a familiar workflow: choose a region, decide on pay-as-you-go or Provisioned Throughput Units, and then grab the endpoint URL and key. Under the hood Azure hosts a copy of the model weights on GPU clusters, handles autoscaling, and logs metrics to Azure Monitor. That means the same observability stack you use for virtual machines or databases also covers image generation, letting operations teams track latency, error rates, and token (or in this case pixel) consumption.

Because DALL·E sits inside the broader Azure ecosystem, it easily links with other services. Logic Apps can trigger image creation when a new row hits a spreadsheet, Functions can resize or watermark results, and Blob Storage can archive every rendition for compliance. The integration extends to Power Platform and Dynamics, so low-code builders can drop generative visuals straight into customer apps without knowing a single GPU spec.

Creating and Customizing AI-Generated Images

Text-to-image prompts remain the heart of the experience, but Azure exposes extra dials so teams can balance speed, fidelity, and cost. The quality parameter offers **standard** and **hd**; the high-definition path draws more compute for sharper edges and richer textures, while standard returns faster for iterative workflows. DALL·E 3 in Azure currently limits n (the number of images per call) to one, encouraging parallel calls when a campaign needs dozens of variants.

Beyond generation, the same endpoint supports in-context edits. Supply an existing PNG and a transparent mask, and the model will "inpaint" only the masked region. This is useful for swapping shirt colors, localizing packaging text, or adding seasonal motifs without redrawing the entire scene. Conversely, by sending a larger canvas with blank borders you can "outpaint," extending artwork horizontally or vertically to fit new aspect ratios. These manipulations let designers recycle a single hero image across banners, billboards, and social posts with minimal editing time.

Developers drive all this through the OpenAI SDKs. A single Python snippet sets the prompt, uploads the source image if needed, tweaks quality, and streams the resulting binary directly into Azure Storage. Sample notebooks on GitHub show how to batch prompts, retry transient errors, and pipeline outputs into Vision AI models for automated tagging. The result is a workflow where code, not click-work, owns the creative iteration loop.

Built-In Safeguards for Responsible Imagery

Every prompt and every pixel generated by DALL·E passes through Azure's content filtering system before it reaches your application. A cascade of classifiers scores material for violence, sexual content, hate symbols, and other restricted themes; if scores cross predefined thresholds, the call is either blocked or returned with a blurred placeholder. This enforcement happens on Microsoft-controlled hardware and adds only milliseconds to the round trip, keeping user-facing latency predictable.

Teams that need tighter or looser thresholds can create custom filter profiles in Azure AI Foundry. These profiles let administrators raise tolerance for medical imagery, clamp down on profane text embedded inside memes, or flag any depiction of minors for manual review. The same portal also surfaces metrics so compliance officers can audit how many prompts were filtered each week and which policy category they hit most often.

For industries under strict regulation, Azure AI Content Safety extends the pipeline. It provides granular scores, bounding boxes for problematic regions, and integration hooks so a downstream function can automatically redact, decline, or route the image for human moderation. All events flow into Azure Monitor and can be exported to SIEM tools, ensuring that generative visuals adhere to the same governance playbook as customer PII or payment data.

Real-World Applications Across the Enterprise

Product design studios were among the earliest adopters. Mattel's Hot Wheels team feeds DALL·E sketches like "Bonneville salt-flats racer merged with a 1970s muscle car" and instantly sees multiple stylistic takes, sparking ideas that would have taken days of manual concept art. These AI-generated drafts are not final blueprints, but they accelerate brainstorming and free human designers to refine only the most promising options.

Marketing departments quickly followed. Coca-Cola used Azure OpenAI to build an interactive holiday campaign where users chatted with a digital Santa, who in turn produced personalized snow-globe artworks on demand. By combining text, image, and speech models behind a single Azure backend, the brand reached millions with customized visuals while keeping latency low enough for real-time engagement.

Across retail, e-commerce, and media, companies now rely on generative imagery for tasks ranging from rapid A/B testing of ad creatives to automated product photo localization in dozens of languages. Industry analysts note that the same platform also surfaces legal and ethical questions (copyright, misinformation, brand consistency) but Azure's blend of policy controls and private data boundaries lets enterprises experiment while enforcing their own comfort level with risk.

Azure OpenAI Integration with Azure Services

Large-language-model magic rarely lives in isolation. In production the model must talk to microphones, cameras, databases, and dashboards already running in the cloud. Microsoft has spent the last two years weaving Azure OpenAI into the fabric of Azure so that developers can chain capabilities together rather than juggling separate APIs. The sections that follow explore four of the most common integration touchpoints and show how they unlock practical end-to-end solutions.

Blending Foundation Models with Cognitive Services

Azure's classic Cognitive Services suite (Speech, Vision, Language, and Search) acts as a set of sensors that collect raw signals while GPT-class models do the higher-level reasoning.

A popular pattern captures an audio stream with Azure AI Speech, converts it to text through real-time transcription or the Whisper model, then sends the transcript to GPT-4o for summarization or sentiment analysis. Everything flows through Azure's network so no data ever leaves the Microsoft boundary, keeping compliance simple for industries such as finance and healthcare.

Vision scenarios work the same way. Azure AI Vision extracts text from a product label or identifies objects in a warehouse photo; the textual description is then appended to a prompt so GPT-4o can generate an inspection report or a plain-language explanation. Search joins in through the Retrieval-Augmented Generation architecture, where Azure AI Search retrieves the top passages for a question and the language model stitches those passages into a fluent answer, adding citations so users can verify the source.

Implementation sits on familiar SDKs and orchestrators. The Azure OpenAI, Speech and Vision client libraries share the same authentication schemes and retry logic, while open-source frameworks like Semantic Kernel and LangChain wire the calls together in just a few lines of code. Microsoft's reference project "azure-search-openai-demo" shows the whole pipeline (ingestion, vector search, grounding, and chat) in under 300 lines of Python, making it a solid starting point for prototypes.

Building Advanced Solutions with Azure Machine Learning

Azure Machine Learning helps with developing, training, and deploying custom machine learning models, which can be combined with Azure OpenAI to create highly specialized AI solutions. While Azure OpenAI has powerful pretrained models, some business problems require additional models trained on domain-specific data or focused on particular tasks. Azure Machine Learning enables organizations to develop these custom models and integrate them alongside OpenAI models in unified solution architectures. This combination allows businesses to leverage the best of both worlds: the broad capabilities of foundation models and the targeted precision of custom-trained models.

The integration between these services typically follows several patterns. In a sequential pattern, an Azure Machine Learning model might process data before it's sent to Azure OpenAI, perhaps classifying documents to determine which ones should be summarized by the OpenAI model. Alternatively, Azure OpenAI might generate initial content that's then refined or classified by a custom model. In a parallel pattern, both services might analyze the same input independently, with their outputs combined to provide a more comprehensive response. For instance, an Azure Machine Learning model might extract specific data points from a document while Azure OpenAI generates a narrative description, with both results presented to the user as complementary insights.

Azure Machine Learning also provides tools for fine-tuning and customizing OpenAI models to better suit specific domains or tasks. Through transfer learning techniques, organizations can start with the powerful foundation of a pretrained OpenAI model and adapt it to their particular needs using their own data. This process typically requires less data and computing resources than training a model from scratch while still achieving strong performance on specialized tasks. Azure Machine Learning's experiment tracking, model registry, and deployment capabilities help manage this customization process, ensuring that the refined models are properly versioned, evaluated, and deployed alongside other components of the solution. This approach to model development promotes reproducibility and facilitates collaboration across data science teams.

Development in Azure AI Studio

Azure AI Studio is a unified platform that brings together Azure OpenAI, Cognitive Services, and Machine Learning into a single workspace. Think of it as a digital workshop where developers can experiment, build, and deploy AI solutions without switching between tools. For example, you could design a chatbot in AI Studio that uses OpenAI for conversations, Cognitive Services to analyze user sentiment, and Machine Learning to personalize recommendations.

The studio has drag-and-drop interfaces and prebuilt templates, making AI accessible to beginners. A marketing team might use a template to create a campaign analyzer: upload customer feedback (stored in Azure Data Lake) and use Cognitive Services to detect key themes and Azure OpenAI to draft improvement strategies. Everything happens in one place, reducing complexity and speeding up development.

Collaboration is another key feature. Teams can share projects, track versions, and monitor performance metrics within AI Studio. For instance, a healthcare startup could collaborate on a patient triage tool where data scientists refine models in Machine Learning, developers integrate OpenAI for symptom analysis, and designers test the user interface—all within the same environment. This seamless workflow turns ideas into production-ready apps faster.

Powering AI with Azure Data Services

Out of the box, GPT models know nothing about last quarter's sales or a company's internal policy memos. Azure's "On Your Data" and Retrieval-Augmented Generation capabilities bridge that gap by fusing AI Search indexes with OpenAI completions. You can ingest documents and structured data from sources like Azure Data Lake or Microsoft Fabric, generate vector embeddings with text-embedding-3, and store them alongside keywords. At query time, the search index returns the most relevant chunks, which are appended to the prompt so the model can answer with up-to-date, source-grounded facts.

Scale often lives in Synapse Analytics or Microsoft Fabric, and those platforms now include first-class OpenAI hooks. SynapseML lets Spark jobs broadcast prompts across executor nodes so you can label millions of rows or generate synthetic data in parallel, while notebooks in Fabric call the same REST endpoints to enrich lakehouse tables. Because both engines run inside the Microsoft backbone, data residency and network isolation match the rest of the analytics stack.

Traditional data stores plug in as well. Stored procedures in Azure SQL can invoke a Logic App that sends a row to GPT-4o and writes back a classification label, Cosmos DB change-feed triggers can summarize IoT messages in real time, and Synapse pipelines can schedule nightly sentiment passes over customer feedback. In each case OpenAI operates as just another REST target inside the orchestrator, benefiting from existing retry, logging and alerting frameworks that data engineers already know.

Summary

This chapter covered Azure OpenAI Service, Microsoft's enterprise-grade implementation of OpenAI's powerful generative AI models within the Azure ecosystem. We explored the core capabilities of this service, including how it provides access to models like GPT-4o, GPT-4.1, and DALL·E 3 while maintaining Microsoft's compliance framework and security controls. The chapter examined the fundamentals of prompt engineering, explaining how to craft effective prompts with role framing, task descriptions, context provision, and output constraints. We also discussed Azure's implementation of DALL·E for image generation, including how it integrates with other Azure services and includes built-in safeguards for responsible use. Finally, the chapter explored how Azure OpenAI connects with other Azure services like Cognitive Services, Azure Machine Learning, and data services to create comprehensive AI solutions that can address complex business challenges across various industries.

Exam Essentials

Understand Azure OpenAI Service fundamentals.   Know how Microsoft has integrated OpenAI's models into the Azure ecosystem with enterprise-grade security, compliance, and governance features that distinguish it from standalone OpenAI offerings.

Identify available models and their capabilities.   Recognize the different model families in Azure OpenAI (GPT-4o, GPT-3.5-Turbo, embedding models, DALL·E) and understand their specific strengths, use cases, and performance characteristics.

Master prompt engineering concepts.   Understand the four key components of effective prompts: role framing, task description, context provision, and output constraints. Know how to craft specific, unambiguous instructions that produce consistent, high-quality outputs.

Understand content safety implementation.   Learn how Azure OpenAI implements content filtering systems that scan both prompts and responses for prohibited content, and how administrators can customize these safety thresholds.

Comprehend DALL·E integration in Azure.   Know how DALL·E models are deployed as Azure resources and how they connect to the broader Azure ecosystem, and understand the different parameters available for image generation and customization.

Recognize Azure OpenAI integrations.   Understand how Azure OpenAI works with other Azure services including Cognitive Services, Azure Machine Learning, Azure AI Studio, and Azure Data Services to create comprehensive AI solutions.

Identify real-world business applications.   Know how organizations are applying language models and image generation capabilities across customer support, content creation, knowledge management, and product design to solve business problems.

Review Questions

1. Your company wants to implement an AI solution that can generate text while ensuring compliance with industry regulations like GDPR and HIPAA. Which of the following statements about Azure OpenAI Service is most accurate?

   A. Azure OpenAI models are identical to OpenAI's models but cost more

   B. Azure OpenAI provides standard generative AI models with no additional governance features

   C. Azure OpenAI ensures all data remains within Microsoft-controlled infrastructure and provides compliance controls

   D. Azure OpenAI is faster than regular OpenAI but offers fewer model options

2. A healthcare organization is deploying Azure OpenAI for analyzing medical data but is concerned about content safety. Which Azure OpenAI capability should they configure?

   A. Provisioned Throughput Units

   B. Multimodal token limits

   C. Function calling features

   D. Content filtering system with custom thresholds

3. A developer is looking to improve the consistency of responses from an Azure OpenAI model. Which key component of prompt engineering should they focus on?

   A. Token counting

   B. Key Vault integration

   C. Output constraints

   D. Model temperature settings

4. Which Azure OpenAI model family would be most appropriate for converting text into numeric vectors for semantic search?

   A. GPT-4o

   B. text-embedding-3

   C. GPT-3.5-Turbo

   D. DALL·E 3

5. A marketing team wants to generate multiple creative concepts for a new product campaign. Which Azure OpenAI integration pattern would be most efficient?

   A. Azure OpenAI with DALL·E integration for visual concepts

   B. Azure OpenAI with Content Safety for content moderation

   C. Azure OpenAI connected to Azure AI Search for Retrieval-Augmented Generation

   D. Azure OpenAI with Speech Services for audio transcription

6. What is the primary advantage of using Azure OpenAI Service over standalone OpenAI for enterprise applications?

   A. Exclusive access to models not available elsewhere

   B. Lower cost per token for high-volume applications

   C. Ability to train custom models from scratch

   D. Enhanced security, compliance certifications, and integration with Azure's ecosystem

7. A developer is creating a system that needs to combine Azure OpenAI with custom machine learning models for domain-specific tasks. Which service should they use?

   A. Azure Machine Learning

   B. Azure Logic Apps

   C. Azure Functions

   D. Azure App Service

8. Which component is essential in a well-crafted prompt for Azure OpenAI to ensure the model understands its purpose?

   A. Token counting

   B. Temperature setting

   C. Role framing

   D. Model version number

9. A customer service team wants to implement an AI solution that can answer customer queries by referring to company documentation. Which Azure OpenAI pattern should they implement?

   A. Fine-tuning

   B. Retrieval-Augmented Generation (RAG)

   C. Multimodal processing

   D. Function calling

10. What is the primary purpose of the Azure AI Studio in relation to Azure OpenAI?

    A. A tool for creating custom language models from scratch

    B. A development environment exclusive to GPT-4 models

    C. A monitoring tool for tracking OpenAI model usage

    D. A unified platform for experimenting, building, and deploying AI solutions

11. A retail company wants to implement a chatbot that can handle customer queries about products while adhering to brand guidelines. Which Azure OpenAI prompt engineering technique is most important?

    A. Task description with specific output constraints

    B. Increasing the temperature parameter

    C. Reducing the token limit

    D. Using multiple system messages

12. Which Azure OpenAI model family would be most appropriate for a high-volume, cost-sensitive chatbot application that doesn't require complex reasoning?

A. GPT-4.1

B. GPT-4o

C. GPT-3.5-Turbo

D. o3

13. A design agency needs to generate multiple variations of product packaging based on a base design. Which Azure OpenAI DALL·E capability should they use?

A. High-definition generation

B. In-context edits with masks

C. Multimodal prompting

D. Outpainting for aspect ratio changes

14. Which data type can GPT-4o process that earlier GPT models cannot?

A. Images and short audio clips

B. JSON documents

C. Markdown tables

D. Video streams

15. A government agency is implementing Azure OpenAI but needs to ensure data residency requirements are met. Which Azure OpenAI feature addresses this concern?

A. Multimodal processing

B. Token-based pricing

C. Regional deployment options

D. Function calling capabilities

16. What is the correct endpoint format for generating images using DALL·E in Azure OpenAI?

A. /completions

B. /images/generations

C. /embeddings

D. /chat/completions

17. A financial institution wants to use Azure OpenAI to summarize earnings call transcripts. Which prompt component is most important to include?

A. High temperature setting for creative responses

B. Multiple examples of previously summarized calls

C. Character limits for each section

D. Output constraints specifying a structured format with risk assessment

18. A company wants to connect their internal knowledge base to Azure OpenAI for employee queries. Which Azure service should they integrate with?

A. Azure AI Search

B. Azure Logic Apps

C. Azure Container Instances

D. Azure API Management

19. Which feature of Azure OpenAI is designed to help prevent the model from generating harmful content?

A. Embedding generation

B. Content filtering system

C. Token counting

D. Provisioned Throughput Units

20. A software development team wants to use Azure OpenAI for code completion tasks. Which model capability is most important?

A. Audio transcription

B. Fast token processing

C. Understanding context and following project-level style conventions

D. Multimodal inputs

Chapter

12

AI Agents in Azure

MICROSOFT CERTIFIED: AZURE AI FUNDAMENTALS (AI-900) EXAM OBJECTIVES COVERED IN THIS CHAPTER:

✔ **Domain 1: Describe Artificial Intelligence workloads and considerations**

    ▪ Subdomain 1a: Identify features of common AI workloads

        ▪ 1-2 Identify natural language processing workloads

✔ **Domain 5: Describe features of generative AI workloads on Azure**

    ▪ Subdomain 5a: Identify features of generative AI solutions

        ▪ 5-2 Identify common scenarios for generative AI

    ▪ Subdomain 5b: Identify generative AI services and capabilities in Microsoft Azure

        ▪ 5-4 Describe features and capabilities of Azure AI Foundry

        ▪ 5-5 Describe features and capabilities of Azure OpenAI service

Agentic AI has emerged as one of the most transformative developments in artificial intelligence. These AI agents go beyond simple question-answering systems by combining powerful language models with the ability to plan, reason, and take actions on your behalf. Microsoft has positioned itself at the forefront of this revolution through its Copilot ecosystem and Azure AI agent capabilities, creating systems that can understand complex instructions, maintain ongoing conversations, and interact with various tools and data sources to accomplish tasks that previously required human intervention.

What makes these agents particularly valuable is their capacity to bridge the gap between powerful AI models and practical business applications. Unlike traditional AI systems that operate within narrow boundaries, agents can navigate across different contexts, remember previous interactions, and adapt their responses based on changing circumstances. Throughout this chapter, we'll explore how Microsoft has implemented agentic AI across its ecosystem, from the foundational components that power these systems to the practical applications that are transforming how people work. You'll learn how these technologies operate, the responsible AI principles guiding their development, and the real-world scenarios where they're creating the most impact.

Introduction to AI Agents

AI agents are software programs designed to perform tasks autonomously by perceiving their environment, making decisions, and acting to achieve specific goals. These agents are the backbone of modern intelligent systems, enabling machines to mimic human-like reasoning, adapt to new information, and solve complex problems. Understanding AI agents is essential for grasping how technologies like virtual assistants, recommendation systems, and automated customer service tools work. This section explores their definition, evolution, relationship with advanced AI models, and how they differ from traditional software.

What Exactly Is an AI Agent?

An AI agent is a piece of software that perceives its environment, applies some form of reasoning to decide what to do, and then takes an action toward a goal. In practice, that "environment" might be as small as the text in a chat window or as large as a company's order-processing system. The essential point is that the agent does not wait for a human to spell out every instruction; instead, it owns the loop of observe → decide → act.

Where older automation scripts tend to be brittle (for example, failing the moment the input varies), agents rely on machine-learning models to interpret ambiguous inputs. A language model lets a customer support agent understand a free-form complaint email, while a vision model might help a warehouse robot locate a damaged box. By turning raw sensory data into structured meaning, the model frees the agent to focus on goals and policies rather than low-level parsing.

In a larger intelligent system, agents often serve as the "brains" that coordinate specialized components. For instance, one agent might break a complex request into subtasks, delegate each task to smaller agents (a coding agent, a search agent, and a scheduling agent), then assemble the final answer for the user. This orchestration role explains why modern AI architectures talk about "agent teams" rather than a single monolithic bot.

You already interact with simple agents today: email triage tools that draft replies, navigation apps that reroute you around traffic, or a conversational assistant that can set a reminder. Each relies on the same core idea, which basically translates a goal into a chain of tool calls.

The Microsoft AI Agent Journey

Microsoft's earliest foray into agent-like software was the 1990s Office Assistant, better known as Clippy, a rule-driven character that watched for patterns in Word documents. Although limited, it foreshadowed the idea that software could proactively assist rather than merely respond. A more sophisticated step arrived with Cortana in Windows 10, which blended speech recognition, search, and a personal assistant persona but remained bounded by preset skills.

The cloud era unlocked richer possibilities. In 2016 Microsoft introduced Azure Bot Service and Language Understanding (LUIS) so developers could host conversational logic at scale. Those services then merged into Azure Cognitive Services, giving bots access to vision, speech, and decision APIs. Parallel work in GitHub Copilot and Microsoft 365 Copilot showed how generative models could drive contextual, task-focused helpers directly inside coding and productivity tools.

By late 2024 the company began to formalize full-fledged agent patterns. Azure AI Agent Service was unveiled at Ignite 2024 to provide managed memory, tool orchestration, and enterprise-grade security for stateful, autonomous agents. Around the same time, Microsoft Research released AutoGen, an open-source framework that lets developers wire up multiple collaborating agents with observability and debugging built-in.

The trajectory accelerated in 2025: Azure AI Foundry added a Semantic Kernel–based agent framework that drastically reduces boilerplate for coordinating multi-agent systems, and the Agent Service entered public preview with playground tooling inside Azure AI Studio. Taken together, these offerings signal Microsoft's shift from isolated bots to composable, production-ready agent platforms.

The Power Behind AI Agents

Foundation models, such as OpenAI's GPT or DALL·E, are large-scale AI systems trained on massive datasets to perform a wide range of tasks. These models serve as the "brains" behind many AI agents, providing the knowledge and adaptability needed to handle diverse scenarios. For instance, a customer service agent powered by GPT can understand nuanced questions, generate human-like responses, and even detect emotions in text.

The relationship between agents and foundation models is symbiotic. Agents rely on foundation models for core intelligence, while foundation models depend on agents to apply their capabilities in real-world contexts. For example, a healthcare agent might use a medical-focused foundation model to analyze patient data and suggest treatments, combining domain-specific knowledge with the agent's decision-making logic.

However, foundation models alone aren't enough. Agents add layers of customization and purpose. A retail agent might fine-tune a foundation model to prioritize product recommendations based on a user's purchase history, location, or browsing behavior. This tailoring ensures agents meet specific business needs while leveraging the broad knowledge of foundation models.

Challenges remain, such as ensuring foundation models are unbiased and energy-efficient. But their integration with AI agents represents a leap forward in creating systems that learn, reason, and adapt, transforming industries from education to finance.

What Makes AI Agents Unique

The distinction between AI agents and traditional applications shows a fundamental shift in how software interacts with the world. Traditional applications function within tightly defined parameters, executing specific instructions without genuine understanding of context or purpose. They follow predetermined paths and require explicit programming for every function they perform. In contrast, AI agents possess awareness of their environment, can interpret ambiguous instructions, and adapt their responses based on changing circumstances.

The autonomy exhibited by AI agents marks another crucial difference from conventional software. Where traditional applications wait for specific user commands before taking action, agents can proactively identify opportunities to assist, anticipate needs, and take initiative when appropriate. This self-directed behavior allows them to discover solutions that might not be immediately obvious to human users. The agent's ability to operate independently makes them valuable partners rather than passive tools, especially in complex or rapidly changing situations.

Learning capability sets AI agents apart in profound ways from their traditional counterparts.

Conventional applications remain static until manually updated by developers, performing exactly the same way regardless of how frequently they're used. AI agents, however, continuously improve through experience, refining their understanding and approaches based on successes and failures. This means the agent working for you today may be noticeably more effective than the same agent last month, having learned from countless interactions in between.

Perhaps most significantly, AI agents exhibit a form of reasoning that traditional applications simply cannot match. Where conventional software follows linear logic paths, agents can engage in sophisticated problem-solving that considers multiple factors simultaneously. They can manage uncertainty, weigh competing priorities, and even understand the intent behind ambiguous requests. This reasoning capability enables them to handle nuanced situations that would confound traditional applications, making them particularly valuable for complex tasks that resist simple algorithmic solutions.

Core Components of AI Agents

When people talk about the "next generation" of intelligent software, they often point to spectacular demos: chatbots that draft policies, voice assistants that plan vacations, or warehouse robots that sort packages on the fly. Yet behind every impressive outcome sits a set of core components that turn an AI agent from a clever idea into a working system. This section breaks those components down so you can see how they fit together, why they matter, and where you will encounter them when you build or evaluate real solutions.

Building Blocks of AI Agents

Every AI agent has a *blueprint* that defines how it operates. At its core, these agents contain sensors (or perceptual inputs) that gather information from the environment, it could be text from a user, images from a camera, or data from connected systems. These inputs provide the raw material that the agent must make sense of before it can respond effectively. Think of these sensors as the agent's eyes and ears, constantly collecting information about the world around it.

Once information is gathered, it flows into the agent's processing engine, which is the computational brain that makes sense of incoming data. This component typically consists of various algorithms and models working together to understand context, identify patterns, and formulate responses. In modern AI agents, this processing engine often incorporates machine learning models that have been trained on vast amounts of data, allowing them to recognize complex patterns and make increasingly sophisticated decisions. The quality and capabilities of this processing component largely determine how intelligent and effective the agent appears to users.

After processing information, the agent must decide what actions to take through its decision-making component. This element evaluates possible responses against the agent's goals and selects the most appropriate course of action. In simple agents, this might involve following predetermined rules, while advanced agents might use complex reasoning strategies that weigh multiple factors before choosing how to respond. The decision-making process represents the bridge between understanding and action, transforming the agent's comprehension into tangible results.

Finally, AI agents include actuators or output mechanisms that carry out the chosen actions in the environment. These might generate text responses, control physical devices, update databases, or trigger other systems. The effectiveness of these actuators determines

FIGURE 12.1   Building blocks of AI agents.

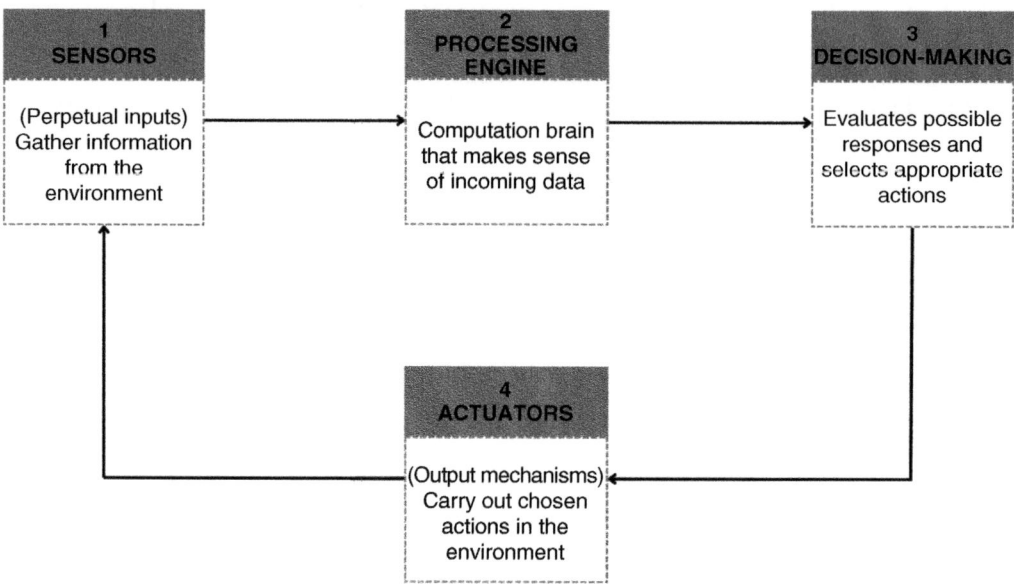

whether the agent can successfully translate its decisions into real-world impact. Figure 12.1 shows how these four components (sensors, processing engine, decision-making system, and actuators) create a continuous cycle of perception, cognition, and action that enables AI agents to interact meaningfully with their environment and the humans who use them.

Types of AI Agents

AI agents come in various forms, and each agent helps to solve specific problems. The five primary types, which are simple reflex agents, model-based reflex agents, goal-based agents, utility-based agents, and learning agents, differ in how they perceive, reason, and act. Understanding these categories helps explain why some agents excel at quick reactions (like turning on a light) while others handle complex planning (like managing a supply chain).

Simple reflex agents are the most basic type. They act based on predefined rules tied directly to current inputs, like a thermostat turning on the AC when the temperature crosses a threshold. These agents don't "remember" past events or plan for the future—they simply react. For example, a spam filter that blocks emails containing certain keywords works this way. While fast and efficient, these agents struggle in dynamic environments where rules can't cover every possible situation. Consider a self-driving car that encounters a police vehicle blocking a road during an active crime scene: without broader context, it might attempt to drive around the obstruction based solely on immediate sensor input. In one real incident, a full self-driving system tried to creep past a police car while officers were responding to an unfolding hostage situation, forcing the human driver to take control. Such scenarios underscore the need for more advanced agent types capable of reasoning, learning, and ethical judgment—far beyond what reflex-based logic can support.

Model-based reflex agents add an internal "model" of the world to handle incomplete information. Unlike simple reflex agents, they track changes over time. Imagine a smart home system that notices you usually turn lights off at 10 p.m. Even if you forget, the agent uses its model of your habits to automate the task. These agents combine real-time data with historical patterns, making them better at handling uncertainty. However, they still focus on immediate reactions rather than long-term goals.

Goal-based agents take a step further by working toward specific objectives. They evaluate possible actions to achieve a desired outcome, like a delivery drone calculating the fastest route while avoiding obstacles. These agents use search algorithms or decision trees to plan ahead. For instance, a chess-playing AI analyzes moves to checkmate the opponent. While more flexible than reflex agents, they can get bogged down in complex scenarios with too many variables, requiring careful balancing of speed and accuracy.

Utility-based agents introduce the concept of "quality" to decision-making. Instead of just achieving a goal, they aim for the best outcome based on a utility function (a mathematical measure of success). For example, a stock-trading agent might prioritize maximizing profit while minimizing risk. Utility-based agents are ideal for tasks where tradeoffs matter, like healthcare systems allocating limited resources. However, designing accurate utility functions is challenging, because what's "best" can be subjective or context-dependent.

Learning agents, which are currently the most advanced category, improve their performance over time through experience. They use machine learning algorithms to adapt to new data, like a Netflix recommendation system refining suggestions based on your viewing history. These agents often include components for experimenting (trying new strategies), receiving feedback (e.g., user ratings), and updating their models. While powerful, they require large datasets and can make unpredictable errors during the learning phase.

In practice, many modern agents blend these types. A self-driving car, for instance, might use reflexes for emergency braking, a model to track road conditions, goals to reach a destination, utility to prioritize passenger safety, and learning to adapt to new traffic patterns. Choosing the right type or combination depends on the problem's complexity, the need for adaptability, and the cost of mistakes.

Managing Agent Memory and Context

Humans rely on memory to have coherent conversations or solve multi-step problems, and AI agents need this too. Agent memory stores past interactions, preferences, and environmental data. For example, a shopping assistant remembers your size and style to suggest clothes, while a travel agent recalls your past trips to recommend destinations. But memory isn't just about storage, it's about context management. Agents must understand how past events relate to current tasks. Imagine a chatbot that forgets your name halfway through a conversation, it would feel frustratingly disconnected. Advanced agents use techniques like short-term memory (for active tasks) and long-term memory (for user history) to maintain context.

Memory can be stored in many ways. For conversational agents, vector databases hold embeddings that support semantic search, retrieving "send me the Q4 pipeline" even if the user types "quarter-four opportunities." For task-oriented bots, a simple key-value cache might track progress: stage = "awaiting approval," id = 42. The architecture often layers these stores so the agent can jump between ephemerals and long-term data without confusion.

The quality of an agent's memory directly impacts its ability to provide personalized experiences and build meaningful relationships with users. When memory functions effectively, agents can recall user preferences without repeated instruction, reference previous conversations to provide continuity, and learn from past interactions to improve future responses. This persistence of identity and knowledge creates the impression of an agent that genuinely knows and understands the user, rather than starting from scratch with each interaction. For many users, this sense of being remembered and understood represents one of the most compelling aspects of interaction with advanced AI agents, making memory management a critical factor in user satisfaction and adoption.

Understanding Human Language

For AI agents to work with humans, they need to understand our language. Natural Language Understanding (NLU) lets agents interpret text or speech, grasp intent, and respond appropriately. When you ask Microsoft Copilot, "What's the weather today?" NLU breaks down the sentence into components: the subject ("weather"), time ("today"), and intent ("get information").

At its essence, this capability allows agents to interpret the meaning behind words, phrases, and sentences rather than simply recognizing patterns of text. The process begins with parsing incoming language into its component parts, identifying nouns, verbs, adjectives, and their relationships within sentences. This structural analysis provides the foundation for deeper semantic understanding, where the agent extracts the actual meaning and intent behind the words.

The complexity of human language presents numerous challenges for AI agents, including ambiguity, idioms, cultural references, and contextual meanings. Consider the phrase "I'm feeling blue," a simple expression that could indicate sadness, reference a color preference, or have entirely different meanings depending on cultural context. Advanced natural language understanding systems employ sophisticated techniques to navigate these complexities, analyzing not just the words themselves but also their relationship to previous statements, common usage patterns, and even emotional cues in the text. These systems continuously improve their understanding through exposure to diverse language samples, gradually building more nuanced interpretations of human communication.

Intent recognition represents a particularly important aspect of language understanding for AI agents. Beyond comprehending the literal meaning of words, agents must identify what the user actually wants to accomplish. When someone asks, "What's the weather like?" they typically want current conditions rather than a philosophical discussion about meteorology. Effective agents recognize these underlying intentions and respond accordingly, even when requests contain implied rather than explicit instructions. This capability requires mapping language patterns to potential user goals, often through machine learning models trained on thousands of example conversations.

Natural language understanding enables AI agents to engage in conversational interactions that feel intuitive and human-like. Rather than forcing users to learn specialized commands or navigate complex interfaces, well-designed agents allow people to communicate in their preferred style using everyday language. This accessibility dramatically reduces the learning curve for new users and makes AI assistance available to people with varying levels of technical expertise. As natural language understanding capabilities continue to advance, the conversation between humans and AI agents becomes increasingly fluid and nuanced, enabling more complex tasks and deeper collaboration between people and the intelligent systems that support them.

Interaction with Tools and External Systems

AI agents rarely work alone. They rely on external tools and systems to complete tasks. For example, a travel booking agent connects to airline databases, payment gateways, and weather APIs to plan your trip. These connections let agents access real-time data and perform actions beyond their internal capabilities.

APIs (Application Programming Interfaces) are the bridges agents use to interact with external services. When you ask your AI agent to send a message, it uses the Messages app's API to execute the task. Similarly, a warehouse management agent might use robotics APIs to control forklifts. Developers often integrate prebuilt tools (like calendar apps or mapping services) to save time and ensure reliability.

Agents also interact with databases to retrieve or update information. A healthcare agent might pull patient records from a hospital's database, analyze them, and then save new notes. In industrial settings, agents monitor IoT sensors (e.g., temperature gauges) to predict equipment failures. This requires secure, fast communication channels to avoid delays or data breaches.

Effective tool use by AI agents demands contextual intelligence about when and how to use different resources. Sophisticated agents can identify which tools are relevant to particular tasks, determine the appropriate sequence for using multiple tools, and translate between the user's natural language requests and the structured inputs required by external systems. This orchestration capability allows agents to solve complex problems by combining specialized tools in innovative ways, much as human experts might integrate multiple approaches when tackling challenging situations. The most advanced agents can even learn from experience which tools work best in different scenarios, gradually optimizing their tool selection and usage patterns.

The ability to interact with external systems transforms AI agents from isolated information processors into powerful mediators between users and the digital ecosystem. This integration creates significant value by simplifying access to complex capabilities, reducing the cognitive load associated with using multiple separate systems, and enabling interactions that span traditional application boundaries. Rather than requiring users to navigate different interfaces for each task, an agent with robust tool integration can serve as a consistent point of contact across diverse activities. As integration capabilities continue to evolve, AI agents increasingly function as personal digital assistants that can leverage the full power of connected systems while presenting a seamless, intuitive experience to the humans they serve.

Microsoft Copilot Agents

Microsoft Copilot is a leap forward in how artificial intelligence assists people across work and daily life. This family of AI-powered assistants works alongside users to enhance productivity, creativity, and problem-solving capabilities. Unlike traditional software tools that simply respond to commands, Copilot agents actively collaborate with users, understanding context and offering relevant suggestions. These intelligent assistants have been designed to integrate seamlessly into the workflows and applications people already use, making advanced AI capabilities accessible without requiring specialized technical knowledge. As organizations and individuals increasingly adopt these tools, understanding how Copilot agents function and the various ways they can be deployed becomes essential knowledge for anyone interested in modern computing environments.

The Copilot Assistant Ecosystem

Microsoft Copilot is a network of AI assistants designed to work together within Microsoft's apps and services. At its core, Copilot uses advanced language models, like GPT-4, to understand context, generate text, and automate workflows. Think of it as a smart collaborator that's always available: it can summarize a lengthy email thread in Outlook, suggest agenda items for a Teams meeting, or create a PowerPoint presentation from a rough outline.

What sets Copilot apart is its deep integration with Microsoft's cloud infrastructure, including Azure AI and Microsoft Graph. This allows Copilot to access organizational data securely (like calendars, documents, and chat history) while respecting privacy controls. For example, if you ask Copilot in Teams, "What did we decide in last week's project meeting?" it can pull notes from OneDrive, highlight action items, and even remind you of pending tasks, all without leaving the app.

Copilot also learns from user interactions. If you frequently ask it to format reports in a specific style, it adapts to prioritize those preferences. However, it doesn't operate in a vacuum. Microsoft has built safeguards to prevent errors or biases, such as requiring human review for sensitive tasks like contract drafting. This balance of automation and accountability makes Copilot a reliable partner rather than a replacement for human judgment.

Key Copilot Variants Across Microsoft Products

The flagship is Microsoft 365 Copilot, an assistant embedded in Word, Excel, PowerPoint, Outlook, and Teams. It taps both web data and Microsoft Graph to draft documents, analyze spreadsheets, build slide decks, and summarize meetings. Although branded like a suite, it is technically one Copilot that adapts its toolset to each host application.

GitHub Copilot serves developers. Available in Visual Studio, VS Code, Xcode 26, JetBrains IDEs, and even the command line, it suggests code, explains diffs, and answers repository-specific questions. The enterprise tier adds context from private code bases and integrates Bing search so the assistant can cite external knowledge alongside local files.

Dynamics 365 Copilot appears inside Sales, Service, Finance, and other business apps. It accelerates CRM updates, auto-drafts responses to customers, reconciles financial data in Excel, and offers AI-infused routing for contact-center cases. By living in the transaction system of record, it reduces tab-switching and keeps all actions auditable.

Security Copilot targets defenders. Announced in March 2025, it now ships a set of autonomous agents that triage phishing alerts, optimize conditional-access policies, and curate daily threat-intelligence briefings, all while integrating with Defender, Entra, and Purview dashboards.

Enhancing Productivity with Microsoft 365

Copilot's integration with Microsoft 365 applications transforms how people interact with familiar productivity tools by adding an intelligent layer that understands both content and context. In Word, Copilot can help draft documents, suggest revisions, summarize lengthy text, and even reformat content for different audiences. This assistance goes beyond simple spelling and grammar checks by understanding the purpose of the document and offering substantive improvements to structure and clarity. Users can provide high-level instructions like "draft a project proposal based on these notes" or "make this technical document more accessible to nonexperts," and Copilot will generate appropriate content while preserving the user's voice and intent.

Excel gains powerful analytical capabilities through Copilot integration, allowing users to interact with data using natural language rather than complex formulas or programming. Users can ask questions about their data, request specific analyses, or get help creating visualizations that highlight key insights. For example, someone might ask, "What were our top-performing products in the Southeast region last quarter?" and receive both the answer and supporting visualizations without needing to construct formulas or create charts manually. This natural language interface makes data analysis more accessible to people without specialized technical skills while helping experienced users work more efficiently by automating routine analytical tasks.

PowerPoint presentations benefit from Copilot's ability to generate content suggestions, design improvements, and speaking notes based on topic guidance. Users can start with a basic outline or even just a title, and Copilot will suggest slide content, appropriate imagery, and logical structure to create compelling presentations. For existing presentations, it can recommend design enhancements, alternative visual approaches, or additional content to strengthen key messages. During presentation delivery, Copilot can provide real-time speaking suggestions and help address audience questions by drawing on information from connected organizational resources, making presenters more effective and confident.

Teams and Outlook round out the story. Copilot in Teams writes meeting agendas, captures action items, and produces recap messages that link back to the recording and chat. Outlook's integration with Copilot helps manage the ever-increasing volume of email and calendar commitments by prioritizing messages, suggesting responses, and automating scheduling tasks. It can summarize email threads to quickly bring users up to speed on lengthy discussions, draft contextually appropriate responses based on previous communications, and even suggest when certain messages might need immediate attention. For meeting scheduling, Copilot can understand natural language requests like "find a time next week when everyone's available for a project review" and handle the coordination details automatically. These capabilities significantly reduce the time spent on email management and administrative tasks, allowing users to focus on more valuable work.

Business Transformation Through Copilot

Beyond saving time, Copilot also unlocks new ways to solve problems. Take meeting management: Copilot in Teams can record discussions, assign action items, and send summaries to absent colleagues. Sales teams use it to analyze call recordings, identifying customer pain points or training opportunities.

In customer service, Copilot in Dynamics 365 reviews support tickets to suggest solutions, draft empathetic responses, or escalate urgent cases. It can also predict customer churn by analyzing interaction history, helping businesses retain clients. For data-driven decision-making, Copilot in Excel transforms spreadsheets into dashboards, explains anomalies, or generates "what-if" scenarios to guide strategy.

Content creation is another key area. Marketing teams use Copilot to brainstorm campaign ideas, write blog posts, or adapt messaging for different audiences. HR departments automate onboarding by generating training materials, FAQs, and personalized welcome emails. Even compliance benefits: Copilot scans documents for regulatory risks, flags outdated policies, or generates audit reports.

Small businesses, meanwhile, leverage Copilot to compete with larger teams. A solo entrepreneur can use it to design a website in Power Apps, manage invoices in Excel, and handle customer inquiries via a Copilot-powered chatbot, all without hiring specialists. These scenarios highlight Copilot's versatility: it's not just a tool but a multiplier for innovation across industries.

Building Blocks of Azure AI Agents

Before an AI agent can plan tasks or draft emails, it needs a sturdy foundation of services that manage prompts, retrieve knowledge, call functions, and keep everything secure. Microsoft gathers those ingredients inside Azure AI Studio, a web workspace that blends model playgrounds, prompt-flow editors, and a fully managed Agent Service. As you explore the four building blocks below (framework, orchestration, grounding, and tool-calling), you will see how raw language-model power is shaped into production-ready assistants that respect enterprise rules.

The Azure AI Studio Framework

Azure AI Studio provides an end-to-end canvas where you design, test, and deploy agents without wiring up your own infrastructure. Inside a single project you can choose a large language model, attach memory and policy modules, and spin up a sandbox chat to watch each reasoning step unfold. The studio persists prompts, connections, and secrets so collaboration across a team feels like sharing a workbook rather than passing code snippets.

At the heart of the framework sits Azure AI Agent Service, a managed runtime in public preview when this book was written. It wraps every agent in secure endpoints, scales compute automatically, and offers telemetry on token spend, latency, and success rate. Because the runtime hides the underlying containers, you focus on improving prompts or swapping models instead of patching VMs.

A typical agent project in the studio has three layers. The conversational layer formats user input and model output, the orchestration layer decides which tool or sub-flow to call next, and the grounding layer injects authoritative data. Each layer is configurable through either a UI panel or YAML, which means beginners can click their way to a prototype while advanced users script CI/CD pipelines.

Governance features round out the framework. Role-based access control limits who can view logs or change prompts, while built-in content safety checks warnings or blocks before text returns to the user. Those guardrails mirror the enterprise boundary used by Microsoft 365 Copilot, making it easier to pass security reviews when your agent graduates from lab to line-of-business workflow.

Orchestrating Agent Intelligence

Prompt flow is Azure AI Studio's visual orchestrator that lets you drag LLM calls, Python scripts, and data connectors onto a canvas and link them with arrows that show execution order. Each node runs in its own container, giving you the freedom to mix stateless functions with long-running retrieval steps in the same graph.

Flows are iterative by design. You can clone a branch, tweak a system prompt, then run both versions side by side to see which produces fewer hallucinations or lower cost. The studio records metrics for every run (tokens, latency, custom scores) so evidence replaces guesswork when you decide which version to ship.

When a flow is ready, one click publishes it as an endpoint that the Agent Service can call like any other tool. Because both flow and agent live under the same resource group, authentication, logging, and cost attribution stay centralized, making DevOps hand-offs smoother than juggling separate clouds or repos.

The real power of prompt flow emerges when developers connect specialized components to handle specific aspects of agent intelligence. These components might include tools for extracting entities from user messages, modules for retrieving information from knowledge bases, or utilities for formatting responses in user-friendly ways. When these components are connected through well-defined interfaces, prompt flow creates a modular architecture where individual pieces can be improved or replaced without disrupting the entire system.

This modularity supports continuous improvement over time, allowing organizations to enhance specific capabilities as needs evolve or new technologies become available.

Grounding Agents in Knowledge

AI agents need accurate information to be useful. A medical advice agent can't just "guess" diagnoses. Knowledge bases act as the agent's reference library, storing facts, FAQs, or company policies. For example, an IT helpdesk agent might pull troubleshooting guides from a knowledge base to resolve user issues. Azure AI allows agents to connect to databases, SharePoint, or even proprietary documents, ensuring answers are fact-checked and up-to-date.

Grounding ensures agents stay tethered to reality. Without it, agents might hallucinate (make up facts) or provide generic answers. Imagine asking a retail agent, "What's the return policy for electronics?" Grounding pulls the latest policy PDF from the company's knowledge base, letting the agent cite exact terms. Azure's AI tools can automatically update these sources, so agents adapt as information changes.

However, managing knowledge bases requires care. Outdated or conflicting data can mislead agents. Developers use techniques like semantic search (finding relevant info based on meaning, not just keywords) and data validation (flagging inconsistencies). Privacy is also critical because agents must access only data users are permitted to see. For example, an HR agent should restrict salary information to authorized employees.

When done right, grounding transforms agents from chatbots into trustworthy experts. They combine the speed of AI with the precision of curated knowledge, making them invaluable for industries like law, healthcare, and finance.

Extending Agent Capabilities

AI agents aren't limited to chatting, they can *do* things. Function calling lets agents trigger actions, like checking the weather, processing a payment, or updating a spreadsheet. For instance, when you ask a voice assistant, "Add milk to my shopping list," it calls a function to edit your list in a connected app. Azure AI agents use predefined functions that developers integrate, ensuring tasks are executed securely and accurately. With function calling, a language model can return a JSON stub that matches a schema you define, for example, `{"name": "bookFlight", "arguments": {"date": "2025-06-01", "from":"LHR"}}`. The Agent Service reads that stub, invokes your API, and feeds the response back into the next model prompt, closing the loop between intent and execution.

Plugins wrap that pattern in reusable packages. A plugin bundles the schema, endpoint URL, authentication settings, and even a logo, so any agent in your tenant can add "SendInvoice" or "CreateSupportTicket" without re-authoring JSON examples. Under the hood it still uses function calling, but the packaging means business users can enable capabilities from a catalog rather than editing code.

You can expose existing workflows as plugins through Azure Logic Apps or REST services. A video tutorial from Microsoft shows how a Logic App that posts to Teams becomes a plugin callable by GPT-4 with a single registration step, illustrating how low-code assets gain new life inside AI agents. Security travels with each function. The Agent Service enforces per-plugin scopes, rate limits, and budget ceilings, and because it shares Azure AD with the rest of your cloud resources, role assignments and audit logs integrate seamlessly. That consistency means you can move fast without opening unmonitored backdoors tomorrow.

Enterprise AI Agent Capabilities

Within organizations, AI agents need specialized capabilities to deliver genuine business value while addressing corporate requirements around security, accuracy, and domain-specific knowledge. This section looks at the capabilities that make that possible. First we explore the plumbing that lets an agent tap internal documents without exposing them. Next we'd go through retrieval-augmented generation, the pattern that fuses search with synthesis so answers stay accurate. We finish by showing how enterprises mold general-purpose models into industry-savvy problem-solvers that feel at home in finance, healthcare, retail, or any other line of business.

Secure Organizational Data Access

Enterprise data rarely lives in one place, and much of it is confidential. To keep control, agents authenticate through the same identity provider (Microsoft Entra ID) that employees already use. Single-sign-on tokens flow to downstream services such as SharePoint, Fabric, or SQL, letting the agent inherit a user's existing permissions instead of storing new credentials. That "run-as-user" model enforces least privilege automatically, so an agent can reference a marketing slide deck yet remain blind to the HR payroll folder.

Fine-grained controls come from Microsoft Purview, which labels sensitive files, applies encryption, and audits every access. When an agent requests a chunk of text, Purview's Data Security Posture Management layer checks policy first; if the label requires encryption at rest or prevents export, the agent receives only the allowed view. All reads and writes land in a unified log, simplifying compliance reviews and incident investigations.

Network boundaries reinforce these checks. Agents that run inside Azure AI Studio stay within the tenant's private link endpoints, so data never crosses the public internet. Service tags restrict outbound calls to approved SaaS endpoints, and Azure Private DNS prevents accidental leaks to look-alike domains. Combined with role-based access on the agent project itself, the system forms a zero-trust chain from the user to the model to the storage layer.

Finally, content filters operate in both directions. Before user prompts reach the model, they pass through classifiers that strip credentials or personally identifiable information. When the model generates a response, outbound filters scrub any secrets that may have slipped through and flag offensive language for review. These layers mean developers focus on business logic while the platform shoulders the heavy lift of data hygiene and compliance.

Enhancing Responses with Retrieval

Even the smartest AI models can't know everything, especially fast-changing details like product prices or policy updates. Retrieval Augmented Generation (RAG) solves this by letting agents fetch real-time data from trusted sources before answering questions. This approach addresses one of the fundamental limitations of traditional AI models, which is their reliance on information included in their training data, which may be outdated or incomplete. When using retrieval augmentation, agents don't simply generate responses based on general patterns learned during training; instead, they actively search for relevant information in company documents, databases, and knowledge bases before formulating their answers. This dynamic information gathering allows agents to provide responses that reflect the organization's current reality rather than generic or potentially outdated knowledge.

For instance, a customer support agent using RAG might pull the latest return policy from a company's database to resolve a complaint. Without RAG, it might rely on outdated training data, leading to incorrect answers. In finance, a stock analysis agent could retrieve real-time market data to explain a sudden price drop, grounding its response in facts rather than speculation.

The process of RAG typically follows a multi-step workflow that begins with analyzing the user's query to understand the information needed. Once the agent identifies the key concepts and requirements, it searches across connected data sources to find relevant content, often using sophisticated semantic search technologies that look beyond simple keyword matching to understand the meaning behind the query. After retrieving potentially useful information, the agent evaluates these search results to identify the most relevant content for addressing the specific question. Finally, it generates a response that incorporates this retrieved information while maintaining a natural conversational flow. This structured approach ensures that responses are both relevant to the user's needs and grounded in accurate organizational information. Azure AI uses vector search tools to find semantically relevant information, even if the user's wording doesn't match the database exactly. For example, a user asking, "How do I reset my password?" triggers the agent to search for terms like "account recovery" or "login issues" in the knowledge base.

This approach reduces "hallucinations" (made-up facts) and keeps agents adaptable. When a retail chain updates its holiday return window, the agent doesn't need retraining, it just retrieves the new policy. RAG turns agents into dynamic problem-solvers, bridging the gap between static AI models and ever-changing business realities.

Business-Specific Agent Customization

A one-size-fits-all AI agent won't work for a hospital, a bank, or a manufacturing plant. Customization ensures agents speak the language of the industry and follow its rules. For example, a legal agent might be trained on case law and contract templates, while a retail agent focuses on inventory codes and customer loyalty programs.

Customization starts with domain-specific training data. A healthcare agent ingests medical journals, patient interaction transcripts, and FDA guidelines to handle terms like "hypertension" or "MRI contraindications." In contrast, a logistics agent learns shipping manifests, weather patterns, and delivery routes. Fine-tuning models on this data helps agents understand context, like distinguishing between "monitor" (a screen) and "monitor" (to track patient vitals) in a hospital setting.

Integration with domain-specific tools and systems further enhances an agent's ability to deliver value in specialized business contexts. When connected to industry-specific software, databases, and reference materials, agents gain access to the information and capabilities needed to address domain-specific challenges. A legal assistant might integrate with case management systems, legal research databases, and document management tools, while a retail-focused agent might connect to inventory systems, customer relationship platforms, and product catalogs. These integrations allow the agent to perform actions relevant to the domain without requiring users to navigate multiple systems manually. This specialized connectivity transforms the agent from a general information provider into a valuable assistant that helps professionals accomplish domain-specific tasks more efficiently.

Compliance and regulatory considerations play particularly important roles in domain customization, especially for industries with strict governance requirements. Agents serving regulated industries like healthcare, financial services, or legal must incorporate understanding of relevant regulations and maintain appropriate controls around information handling. This regulatory awareness might include recognizing when certain questions touch on compliance-sensitive areas, applying appropriate data handling procedures for protected information, or providing appropriate disclaimers when addressing topics with legal implications.

Responsible AI in Agent Systems

We laid the groundwork for responsible AI back in Chapter 2, where we talked about fairness, accountability, transparency, and privacy. Those principles become even more critical once an AI agent can not only talk but also act because every action carries the possibility of real-world harm. Responsible design therefore starts by mapping the users the agent will serve, the power it will wield, and the contexts in which it might be misunderstood. From the outset, teams ask whether an agent could amplify bias, reveal confidential information, or make decisions that should stay in human hands, then build safeguards directly into the architecture rather than bolting them on afterward.

Safety and ethical considerations revolve around two complementary layers. The technical layer screens both prompts and model outputs for hate, violence, sexual content, and self-harm, automatically throttling or blocking material that crosses predefined thresholds. The human layer adds judgment where rules run out of clarity: cross-functional review boards test edge-case scenarios, red-teamers probe the system with adversarial inputs, and domain experts verify that recommendations line up with professional standards. Together these layers aim to prevent obvious misuse (like generating discriminatory language) but also subtler failures, such as an agent confidently recommending an off-label medical treatment it found in a forum.

Governance turns ideals into enforceable practice. Enterprises set up role-based access so only approved personnel can change prompts or connect new data sources, and every change flows through version control and peer review just like traditional code. Before an agent goes live, it must pass a Responsible AI Impact Assessment that documents data flows, intended users, and potential harms, and those findings become a living record that auditors can revisit after each major release. Continuous telemetry tracks things like content safety triggers, rates of hallucination, latency, and cost, giving leadership the feedback loop needed to halt or roll back a deployment if the metrics drift outside agreed limits.

Even with governance in place, specific risks still remain. Hallucinations can spread misinformation, tool access can let an agent spend excessive cloud credits or spam customers, and unsecured prompts can leak personal or proprietary data. Mitigations line up with each threat: retrieval-augmented generation grounds responses in verifiable documents and attaches citations, rate-limited function calls cap financial or reputational exposure, and sensitivity-label filters mask or redact confidential fields before they reach the model. No single control is foolproof, but stacking them together minimizes the odds that a single weakness escalates into a major incident.

AI Agent Use Cases and Applications

As previous sections of this chapter have emphasized, AI agents aren't just futuristic concepts; they're already transforming how businesses and individuals work. This section explores practical examples of AI agents in customer service, data analysis, document management, and personal productivity. The diversity of these applications highlights the versatility of agent technologies, showing how the same fundamental capabilities can be adapted to address different challenges across varied contexts. As we explore these use cases, you'll understand how organizations are currently benefiting from AI agents and where future opportunities might emerge.

Transforming Customer Interactions

AI-powered customer service agents are changing how businesses handle support requests, and you've probably already interacted with them. Remember the last time you visited a company website and a chat window popped up asking if you needed help? That was likely an AI agent ready to answer your questions. These digital assistants can understand when you ask "Where's my order?" or "How do I reset my password?" and provide immediate answers without making you wait on hold. They work around the clock, so whether you're shopping at midnight or checking your account status during breakfast, they're ready to help. For businesses, this means they can support customers at any time while ensuring everyone gets the same accurate information.

These customer service agents aren't just limited to answering simple questions. The more advanced ones can walk you through solving complex problems step by step. Imagine your internet stops working, and instead of waiting for a technician, an AI agent guides you through troubleshooting: "Let's check if your router is connected properly. See the blinking lights? Great, now let's try resetting it ..." The agent remembers everything you've already tried and adjusts its suggestions based on your specific situation. It's like having a patient tech expert available instantly, guiding you through the solution without technical jargon or frustration. This kind of interactive support helps customers solve problems faster while feeling empowered rather than confused.

The best customer service agents remember who you are and tailor their help to your specific situation. If you've contacted a company before, the agent might say something like, "I see you purchased our Premium Plan last month. Based on your subscription, you have access to these additional features ..." This personalized approach means you don't have to explain your situation repeatedly or wade through irrelevant information. The interaction feels more natural and efficient. For businesses, this personalization helps build stronger customer relationships while resolving issues more quickly.

Many companies now use a tag-team approach where AI agents handle routine questions but seamlessly bring in human agents for complex situations. Think about calling your bank. An AI might help you check your balance or review recent transactions, but when you mention refinancing your mortgage, it connects you to a human financial advisor. The transition feels smooth because the AI provides your information to the human agent, so you don't need to repeat yourself. After the human resolves your complex question, the interaction helps the AI learn and improve. This collaborative approach gives you the best of both worlds, quick answers for simple questions and human expertise when you need it, while making the overall experience feel connected and thoughtful.

Revealing Insights from Business Data

Data analysis agents are making complex data accessible to everyone, not just the technical experts. Imagine being in a marketing meeting and wondering how your recent campaign performed. Instead of waiting for the analytics team to create a report, you could simply ask an AI agent, "How did our social media promotion affect website traffic last month?" The agent translates your question into the necessary technical queries, pulls the relevant data, and creates a clear visualization showing the relationship. It's like having a data analyst on standby who never gets annoyed by your questions. This accessibility means everyone from sales representatives to department managers can make data-informed decisions without needing specialized technical training.

The most advanced data agents don't just answer your questions, they also proactively spot important patterns you might have missed. Think of them as attentive business partners who tap you on the shoulder to say, "Hey, I noticed something interesting." For example, an AI might alert a retail manager with a message like: "Customer returns for the new summer collection are 40% higher than normal, primarily due to sizing issues with the beach wear line." This early warning allows the team to address the problem before it becomes more serious. It's similar to how your credit card company might alert you to unusual spending. The AI constantly watches for meaningful patterns that need your attention, helping you stay ahead of problems instead of just reacting to them.

Data agents can also serve as collaborative partners when you're trying to understand complex business questions. Imagine you're trying to figure out why sales are declining in a particular region. The agent might suggest: "Have you considered looking at competitor activity in those areas? I can show you how our market share has changed over the last three quarters." As you explore different angles, the agent keeps track of what you've already investigated and suggests new approaches based on what's working.

Many organizations connect these conversational agents to their existing dashboards and reporting systems, making those tools much easier to use. Instead of clicking through multiple screens to find the right report, you can simply ask, "Show me our quarterly sales dashboard," or even better, "What's driving the growth in our enterprise segment this quarter?" The agent helps you navigate directly to the relevant information and can explain confusing metrics or acronyms when needed.

Enhancing Information Management

Document processing agents can read through mountains of paperwork in seconds, pulling out exactly what you need. Imagine having to review 500 supplier contracts to find all the payment terms. Ideally, this is a task that might take a human team weeks. An AI agent can process these documents overnight, creating a summary table showing each supplier's payment timeline, discount terms, and late payment penalties. The agent doesn't just search for keywords; it actually understands what constitutes a payment term even when it's phrased in different ways across contracts. This capability is transforming how legal teams review documents, how finance departments manage agreements, and how research teams synthesize findings from multiple sources.

Knowledge retrieval agents help you find answers buried deep in your company's information without having to know where to look. Think about being a new employee wondering about the company's parental leave policy. Instead of digging through the employee handbook or searching the intranet, you simply ask, "What's our parental leave policy for adoptive parents?" and the agent finds the specific information, highlighting the relevant passage and explaining any related benefits. It's like having a colleague who has read every company document and can instantly recall any detail. These agents are particularly valuable for companies with large, distributed workforces where important information often gets scattered across multiple systems and repositories.

AI agents are also becoming valuable partners in creating and improving documents. Imagine you need to write a project proposal but aren't sure where to start. You might tell an agent, "I need a proposal for implementing a new inventory system at our warehouse locations," and it would generate a structured draft following your company's template, including sections for background, objectives, timeline, and budget considerations. Once you have a draft, the agent can help refine it by suggesting clearer phrasing for technical concepts or identifying places where additional supporting data would strengthen your argument. It's like having an experienced editor and writing coach available whenever you need them, helping you produce better documents in less time.

Knowledge management agents help capture and organize the valuable insights that often get lost in day-to-day work. For example, an agent might notice an important troubleshooting technique shared in a team chat and suggest, "This solution for the database connectivity issue would be valuable to add to the support knowledge base. Would you like me to create an entry?" The agent can also help connect related public information across the organization. For example, when you're researching a topic, it might mention, "The marketing team created a research report on this same customer segment last quarter that might be helpful for your analysis." This approach helps break down information silos and ensures valuable knowledge isn't lost when employees change roles or leave the company, creating a more connected and informed organization.

Simplifying Individual Productivity

Personal assistant agents help tackle the small tasks that fill your workday, giving you more time for meaningful work. Imagine starting your morning and having an AI assistant greet you with, "Good morning! You have three urgent emails from yesterday that need responses, a budget proposal due by noon, and a team meeting at 2 p.m. I've gathered the documents you'll need for each task." Throughout the day, the assistant might draft responses to routine emails ("Would you like me to send a standard appointment confirmation to Dr. Nwodo?"), remind you of upcoming deadlines, or organize information you'll need for your next meeting. It's like having a personal secretary who knows exactly what you need before you ask, helping you stay organized and focused on your priorities instead of getting lost in administrative details.

Workflow automation agents smooth out the complicated processes that often get stuck as they move between different people and systems. Think about the last time you submitted an expense report, it probably moved from you to your manager to the finance department, with potential delays at each step. An AI workflow agent keeps this process moving by automatically routing the report to the right approver, sending gentle reminders when someone needs to take action, and updating the status so you can see where things stand. When unusual situations arise (maybe you're submitting an expense that exceeds the usual limit), the agent knows to route it to a senior manager with a note explaining the exception. This intelligent coordination eliminates those frustrating situations where work gets stuck in someone's inbox or falls through the cracks entirely.

Meeting enhancement agents are changing how teams collaborate, making your time together more productive. Before your project kickoff meeting, an agent might send everyone a personalized brief: "Here's a 2-minute summary of the project background and the three decisions we need to make today." During the meeting, it captures the conversation, highlighting key points: "The team decided to delay the international launch until Q3, with Ngozi responsible for revising the timeline." Afterward, it distributes a summary with action items automatically assigned in your project management system. It's like having a team coordinator who ensures everyone arrives prepared, captures what matters, and transforms discussions into clear next steps. This support is especially valuable for remote and hybrid teams who need to make the most of their limited synchronous time together.

Learning support agents help you continuously build your skills right when you need them. Imagine struggling with creating a complex spreadsheet formula, and an AI coach offers, "I notice you're trying to calculate conditional averages. Would you like me to explain how AVERAGEIF works with a simple example?" Or perhaps you're preparing for a new role, and the agent suggests: "Based on your upcoming project management responsibilities, these three short courses on budget tracking would be most relevant to start with." The agent adapts to your learning style and schedule, breaking complex topics into manageable chunks that fit into your workday. It's like having a patient tutor who's always available exactly when you get stuck, making learning feel less like a separate activity and more like a natural part of getting your work done. This ongoing skill development helps both you and your organization adapt to changing requirements without disrupting productivity.

Summary

This chapter covered the fundamental concepts and applications of AI agents in Azure. It started by defining AI agents as software programs that perceive their environment, make decisions, and take actions to achieve specific goals. The text explored the evolution of Microsoft's AI agent journey, from early implementations like Clippy to sophisticated systems like Azure AI Agent Service. It detailed the core components of AI agents, including sensors, processing engines, decision-making components, and actuators, while explaining different types of agents from simple reflex agents to advanced learning agents. The chapter also described Microsoft's Copilot ecosystem, showing how these AI assistants enhance productivity across Microsoft 365 applications. It examined the building blocks of Azure AI agents, including the Azure AI Studio framework, orchestration capabilities, knowledge grounding, and function calling. Finally, it explored practical applications of AI agents in customer service, data analysis, document management, and personal productivity, highlighting how these technologies transform business operations and individual workflows.

Exam Essentials

Define AI agents and their components.   Understand what an AI agent is (software that perceives its environment, makes decisions, and takes actions toward goals) and how it differs from traditional applications. Know the four core components: sensors (perceptual inputs), processing engine (computational brain), decision-making component, and actuators (output mechanisms).

Identify different types of AI agents.   Recognize the five primary types of AI agents: simple reflex agents, model-based reflex agents, goal-based agents, utility-based agents, and learning agents. Understand their differences in capabilities and applications.

Understand the Microsoft Copilot ecosystem.   Know how Microsoft has implemented agentic AI across its products, particularly Microsoft 365 Copilot, GitHub Copilot, Dynamics 365 Copilot, and Security Copilot. Recognize how these assistants enhance productivity in specific applications like Word, Excel, PowerPoint, Teams, and Outlook.

Recognize the building blocks of Azure AI agents. Understand the Azure AI Studio framework, how prompt flow orchestrates agent intelligence, how knowledge grounding keeps responses accurate, and how function calling extends agent capabilities.

Know key AI agent use cases. Identify how AI agents transform customer interactions, reveal insights from business data, enhance information management, and improve personal productivity. Understand specific applications like customer support, data analysis, document processing, and workflow automation.

Understand the importance of responsible AI in agent systems. Recognize the ethical considerations, governance practices, and safety measures needed when deploying AI agents, including how to prevent hallucinations and protect sensitive data.

Review Questions

1. Your company wants to implement an AI solution that can understand customer inquiries, make decisions about how to respond, and take appropriate actions like scheduling appointments or providing product information. What type of AI solution would best meet these requirements?

   A. AI agents

   B. Neural networks

   C. Machine learning algorithms

   D. Computer vision systems

2. A retail company wants to use Microsoft's AI capabilities to help their employees draft emails, summarize customer feedback, and generate content for product descriptions. Which Microsoft technology would be most appropriate for this scenario?

   A. Azure Machine Learning

   B. Power BI

   C. Microsoft 365 Copilot

   D. Azure Cognitive Services

3. What is the primary difference between AI agents and traditional software applications?

   A. AI agents require special hardware, unlike traditional applications

   B. AI agents can only be developed using Python, unlike traditional applications

   C. AI agents always use cloud services, while traditional applications run locally

   D. AI agents can perceive their environment, make decisions, and adapt to new situations

4. A healthcare organization is developing an AI agent to assist with medical diagnoses. Which component of an AI agent would be responsible for analyzing patient symptoms and medical history data?

   A. Memory management

   B. Actuators

   C. Processing engine

   D. Sensors

5. Your team is building an AI agent that needs to retrieve company-specific product information to answer customer questions accurately. Which Azure AI capability would help ensure the agent's responses are based on factual company data rather than generic information?

   A. Function calling

   B. Agent memory

   C. Prompt flow

   D. Knowledge grounding

6. Which type of AI agent maintains a model of the world to track changes over time and handle incomplete information?

    A. Utility-based agent

    B. Model-based reflex agent

    C. Simple reflex agent

    D. Goal-based agent

7. A manufacturing company wants to implement an AI solution that can help predict equipment failures before they occur. Which Microsoft AI agent would be most appropriate for this use case?

    A. GitHub Copilot

    B. Security Copilot

    C. Dynamics 365 Copilot

    D. Copilot in Word

8. Your organization is implementing an AI agent that will interact with sensitive organizational data. Which Azure AI Studio component ensures that agents can access this data securely while respecting user permissions?

    A. Retrieval Augmented Generation

    B. Microsoft Entra ID integration

    C. Function calling

    D. Prompt flow

9. Which of the following best describes the relationship between foundation models and AI agents?

    A. AI agents are only useful for simple tasks, while foundation models handle complex scenarios

    B. Foundation models are obsolete technology being replaced by AI agents

    C. Foundation models and AI agents are different terms for the same technology

    D. Foundation models provide the core intelligence, while agents apply these capabilities in specific contexts

10. A developer is creating an AI agent in Azure AI Studio that needs to follow a sequence of steps to process insurance claims. Which component should they use to create a visual workflow that connects language model calls with data processing steps?

    A. Function calling

    B. Agent memory

    C. Prompt flow

    D. Knowledge grounding

11. Your team is building an AI agent that can manage customer service inquiries. During testing, you notice the agent sometimes makes up information about your products. Which Azure AI capability would help prevent this issue?

A. Agent memory

B. Function calling

C. Prompt flow

D. Retrieval Augmented Generation

12. A financial services company is implementing Microsoft Copilot to enhance employee productivity. Which of the following is NOT a capability of Microsoft 365 Copilot in this context?

A. Generating code for financial analysis applications

B. Creating PowerPoint presentations from meeting notes

C. Drafting emails based on previous communications in Outlook

D. Summarizing lengthy financial documents in Word

13. Which component of an AI agent would be responsible for executing actions like sending an email or updating a customer record in a CRM system?

A. Decision-making component

B. Actuators

C. Processing engine

D. Sensors

14. Your company wants to implement an AI assistant that can access and analyze information across your organization's Microsoft 365 environment. Which Microsoft Copilot variant would be most appropriate?

A. Security Copilot

B. Dynamics 365 Copilot

C. GitHub Copilot

D. Microsoft 365 Copilot

15. A developer is building an AI agent that needs to perform actions like booking appointments and checking inventory in external systems. Which Azure AI capability enables this functionality?

A. Prompt flow

B. Agent memory

C. Function calling

D. Knowledge grounding

16. Which type of AI agent would be most appropriate for a scenario where the agent needs to evaluate different possible actions based on their expected outcomes and choose the one with the highest value?

    A. Goal-based agent

    B. Simple reflex agent

    C. Utility-based agent

    D. Model-based reflex agent

17. Your organization is implementing AI agents to help with customer service. Which of the following best represents how a responsible AI approach should be applied to this implementation?

    A. Use the most powerful models available regardless of computational cost

    B. Keep the AI models completely isolated from human oversight

    C. Focus solely on maximizing automation to reduce costs

    D. Implement content filters, role-based access, and continuous monitoring

18. A retail company wants to implement an AI agent that can help employees analyze sales data. Which of the following capabilities would this agent need to be most effective?

    A. Speech recognition to take verbal commands

    B. Natural language understanding to interpret data questions

    C. Computer vision to analyze store layout

    D. Robotics integration to automate inventory

19. Which Azure AI Studio component allows developers to test different versions of agent prompts side by side to compare performance?

    A. Agent memory

    B. Function calling

    C. Prompt flow

    D. Knowledge grounding

20. Your team is developing an AI agent that will help with document processing. Which of the following would be a key consideration to ensure the agent respects organizational data security?

    A. Allowing the agent to access any document without authentication

    B. Integration with Microsoft Purview for data labeling and access control

    C. Making all documents publicly accessible

    D. Storing all document content directly in the agent's memory

Chapter

13

AI Use Cases and Industry Applications

MICROSOFT CERTIFIED: AZURE AI FUNDAMENTALS (AI-900) EXAM OBJECTIVES COVERED IN THIS CHAPTER:

✔ **Domain 1: Describe Artificial Intelligence workloads and considerations**

- Subdomain 1a: Identify features of common AI workloads

  - 1-1 Identify computer vision workloads

  - 1-2 Identify natural language processing workloads

✔ **Domain 3: Describe features of computer vision workloads on Azure**

- Subdomain 3a: Identify common types of computer vision solution

  - 3-1 Identify features of image classification solutions

  - 3-2 Identify features of object detection solutions

  - 3-3 Identify features of optical character recognition solutions

  - 3-4 Identify features of facial detection and facial analysis solutions

✔ **Domain 4: Describe features of Natural Language Processing (NLP) workloads on Azure**

- Subdomain 4a: Identify features of common NLP Workload Scenarios

  - 4-1 Identify features and uses for key phrase extraction

  - 4-2 Identify features and uses for entity recognition

  - 4-3 Identify features and uses for sentiment analysis

  - 4-4 Identify features and uses for language modeling

Previous chapters have covered all the fundamental concepts, and now it's time to see how to apply these concepts in the real world. We will walk through common industries like healthcare, retail, finance, manufacturing, customer service, and education, and show how the same building blocks you already know (data ingestion, model training, deployment, and monitoring) map to Azure services designed for each job. Think of patient-risk models powered by Azure Machine Learning, online stores that use Personalizer for "next best offer," real-time fraud checks built on Cognitive Services, and factory cameras running Custom Vision at the edge.

By the end of the chapter, you should feel ready to read a scenario, pick the right Azure tools, and explain how they fit into a complete solution.

Why Industry Context Matters

When working with technology solutions, especially in fields like artificial intelligence (AI) and cloud computing, it's easy to assume that a one-size-fits-all approach works for every business. But the reality is different. Industries like healthcare, retail, manufacturing, and finance have unique challenges, regulations, and goals. For example, a hospital might need AI tools to analyze patient data while ensuring privacy, whereas a retail company might focus on predicting customer buying patterns. This is why understanding the industry context is critical. It shapes how technology is designed, implemented, and scaled to solve real-world problems. Without this context, even the most advanced tools might fail to deliver meaningful results.

The first step in applying technology effectively is shifting from generic models to industry-specific solutions. Generic AI models are like basic tools. They can perform simple tasks, but they lack the precision needed for specialized scenarios. Imagine using a general weather prediction model to forecast crop yields for a farm. It might give a rough estimate, but it won't account for soil quality, local pests, or irrigation systems. Industry-specific solutions, on the other hand, are tailored to address these nuances. For instance, Microsoft's Azure AI has prebuilt models for healthcare that can analyze medical images, while retail-focused tools might prioritize inventory management. When technology is customized to fit specific industry use cases, businesses can get higher accuracy, efficiency, and value.

This shift is about better algorithms and integrating domain knowledge. Developers and architects need to collaborate with industry experts to understand workflows, compliance requirements, and pain points. For example, a financial institution might require AI models that detect fraud while adhering to strict regulatory standards. A generic model could flag unusual transactions, but a tailored solution would minimize false alarms by learning from historical fraud patterns specific to banking. Ultimately, vertical solutions bridge the gap between raw technology and practical, impactful use cases.

Microsoft has built a complete set of tools that help businesses use AI in practical ways. Their approach combines Azure cloud services with easy-to-use AI tools that don't require a computer science degree to operate. Their ready-made AI building blocks can recognize images, understand speech, and process everyday language, and this is letting businesses add these capabilities to their systems quickly.

Good data is the foundation of any successful AI project, which is why Microsoft has created powerful tools to help companies organize and use their information. Services like Azure Synapse Analytics and Azure Data Factory help businesses gather all their data in one place and prepare it for AI to use. These tools work with all kinds of information from spreadsheets and databases to documents, photos, and even live data from connected devices. Microsoft's Power Platform makes AI accessible to everyone in a company, not just the tech team. Tools like Power BI create easy-to-understand charts and graphs, while Power Apps lets people build their own simple applications without coding. Microsoft has also created special packages for different industries like healthcare, banking, and retail that come preconfigured with the right AI tools and comply with industry rules, saving companies months of setup time.

Across many different industries, certain approaches to building AI systems have proven more successful than others. One common pattern is creating a central place for all company data that breaks down the walls between separate information systems. This typically includes flexible storage for all types of data, organized databases for analysis, and tools that keep track of where data came from and who can access it.

Many effective AI systems use a combination of cloud computing and local processing to balance speed, cost, and practical needs. Retail stores might need AI that instantly recognizes returning customers, while factories need immediate alerts about safety issues. These situations benefit from having some AI processing happen right where the action is, while sending summarized information to the cloud for deeper analysis. Every industry also needs its own approach to security and making AI easy to use. Healthcare systems need strong protections for patient data, banks need fraud detection, and factories need safety protocols. The most successful AI systems are designed with these requirements built in from the start rather than added as afterthoughts. They also make it clear to users why the AI made certain recommendations without overwhelming them with technical details, helping people trust and actually use the AI tools in their daily work.

AI in Healthcare

Smart computers are giving doctors and nurses superpowered helpers that can remember every medical book ever written and spot tiny clues about your health. Azure AI services help find diseases earlier, make checkups easier to schedule, and even help create treatments that work better for you personally. They're like extra brains that make sense of all the health information that would take humans years to read through.

These smart tools handle the boring stuff so the human experts can spend more time with you. Think about how your doctor types notes during your visit instead of looking at you. Azure AI can help by listening and writing those notes automatically. For patients, this means your doctor has time to explain things more clearly and answer your questions instead of staring at a computer screen. Healthcare needs special computer tools because mistakes could hurt people, and your health information needs to stay private. Azure has a toolbox full of healthcare helpers that keep your information safe while helping doctors do their jobs better. These tools follow all the strict rules about medical privacy while still using the latest technology to improve care for everyone.

Predictive Analytics and Population Health

Azure Machine Learning helps hospitals look through patient records to find clues about who might be at risk for conditions like diabetes, heart problems, or mental health issues. These predictive systems look at all kinds of information like lab results, vital signs, medication history, and even lifestyle information. They can help healthcare systems move from reactive care (treating people after they get sick) to proactive care (preventing illness in the first place). For example, Azure Machine Learning might identify patients at high risk for readmission after surgery, allowing care teams to provide extra support and prevent unnecessary hospital stays.

When Azure's data analysis tools look at health information from whole neighborhoods or cities, they can spot bigger trends for population health management. They might notice that kids in one area have more asthma than kids in another area, or that specific demographics aren't getting recommended cancer screenings. This helps hospitals know where to send mobile clinics or where to focus health education efforts.

Medical Imaging and Diagnostics

When you break your arm, your doctor takes an X-ray to see the break. Azure Computer Vision services, including specialized tools like Project InnerEye, help doctors analyze these X-rays and other medical images like MRIs and CT scans. These tools can highlight areas of concern, measure changes in tumors over time, or flag images that need immediate attention from a specialist.

These AI imaging tools support radiologists and other imaging specialists by handling routine cases and drawing attention to potential problems. For example, an AI system might prescreen chest X-rays, sorting them into "likely normal" and "needs review" categories, helping radiologists prioritize their workload. Project InnerEye specifically helps with the time-consuming task of marking boundaries around tumors and organs in 3D scans, turning what used to take hours into minutes.

Conversational Care and Telemedicine

Remember the last time you tried to call your doctor's office and were stuck on hold forever? Healthcare organizations can use Azure's conversational AI tools including Health Bot and Speech services, to make care more accessible and convenient. These technologies power virtual health assistants that can answer patient questions, help schedule appointments, provide medication reminders, and even conduct initial symptom assessments. They're available 24/7, so you don't have to wait until office hours to get simple health information.

Azure Health Bot is specifically designed for healthcare scenarios with built-in medical intelligence. It understands health terminology and can follow clinical protocols for triage and symptom checking. Unlike general chatbots, Health Bot is designed with medical privacy in mind from the ground up. Healthcare organizations can customize the bot with their own protocols and connect it to their scheduling systems and patient records for a more personalized experience.

Azure Speech Services help healthcare providers spend less time on paperwork and more time with patients. Doctors can dictate notes directly into patient records using natural speech, and the AI handles the conversion to text and even organizes information into the right sections of the medical record. This technology continues to improve in understanding medical terminology and the conversational nature of patient–provider interactions, making documentation faster and more accurate during telemedicine visits and in-person appointments.

Genomics and Bioinformatics

Inside every cell in your body, there's a set of instructions called your genome. Genomics, which is the study of this genetic code, generates enormous amounts of data that would be impossible to analyze manually. Azure Synapse Analytics combined with Machine Learning provides the computing power and tools needed to make sense of genomic information. These platforms can help researchers identify genetic factors related to diseases, predict how patients might respond to different medications, and move toward truly personalized medicine.

A single human genome contains about 3 billion base pairs, and analyzing this information requires significant computing resources. Azure has the scalable storage and processing power needed for genomic research, which allows organizations to pay only for what they use rather than building expensive computing infrastructure. This makes advanced genetic research more accessible to smaller research institutions and healthcare providers.

Bioinformatics, which combines biology, computer science, and statistics, helps make sense of complex biological data. Azure Synapse Analytics helps integrate diverse data sources like genomic data, medical records, lifestyle factors, and environmental data while maintaining appropriate security and privacy controls. This approach supports the development of treatments tailored to individual patients based on their unique genetic makeup and health history, potentially making treatments more effective with fewer side effects.

Compliance, Privacy, and Responsible AI

Healthcare organizations must follow strict rules about patient privacy, including regulations like HIPAA (Health Insurance Portability and Accountability Act) and security frameworks like HITRUST. Azure's healthcare solutions are designed with these requirements in mind, and they give you the tools that help organizations maintain compliance while still benefiting from cloud computing and AI. Features like encryption for data both in storage and during transmission help protect sensitive patient information.

Protected Health Information (PHI), which includes details like medical records, billing information, and even appointment schedules, requires special handling. Azure provides specific tools for managing PHI properly, including access controls that ensure only authorized personnel can view sensitive data. Detailed audit logs track who accesses information and when, helping healthcare organizations demonstrate compliance during audits and immediately identify any potential security issues.

Responsible AI is important in healthcare, where algorithm recommendations can influence critical treatment decisions. Microsoft's approach to responsible AI in healthcare focuses on transparency (understanding how AI reaches conclusions), fairness (ensuring systems work equally well for all patient populations), and human oversight (keeping medical professionals in control of decisions). These principles help ensure that AI remains a trustworthy tool that enhances rather than replaces human medical judgment while meeting the highest privacy and security standards.

AI in Retail and e-Commerce

Online stores and physical shops are using AI to transform how they serve customers and run their operations. Azure's AI tools help retailers predict what customers want, keep the right products in stock, prevent fraud, manage complex supply chains, and understand shoppers better than ever before. These technologies are turning the massive amounts of data that retailers collect into useful insights that drive sales and improve customer satisfaction.

AI tools in retail work behind the scenes to make shopping experiences feel more personal and efficient. They help store employees focus on helping customers by handling repetitive tasks like inventory checks and purchase predictions. For shoppers, these technologies mean finding products they actually want more quickly, having items in stock when they need them, and enjoying smoother checkout experiences both online and in physical stores.

The retail industry faces unique challenges that Azure's specialized tools address, including the need to personalize experiences for thousands of customers, predict constantly changing demand patterns, and manage complex supply chains spanning the globe. Let's explore how retailers are using Azure's AI capabilities to stay competitive in today's fast-changing shopping landscape.

Real-Time Personalization

When you visit an online store and see product recommendations that feel like they were picked just for you, that's real-time personalization at work. Azure Personalizer uses reinforcement learning to figure out which products, offers, or content each shopper is most likely to be interested in at that exact moment. Unlike simple systems that just show popular items, Personalizer learns from how customers interact with recommendations and gets smarter over time, increasing the chances you'll find something you actually want to buy.

Real-time personalization goes beyond just product recommendations. Azure OpenAI Service with Retrieval Augmented Generation (RAG) patterns enables retailers to create interactive shopping assistants that understand natural language questions and provide helpful, personalized responses. These systems can pull information from product catalogs, customer reviews, and support documentation to answer complex questions like "What laptop would be good for a college student who also plays games?" with specific, relevant suggestions tailored to the customer's needs.

Azure Personalizer and OpenAI solutions help retailers solve the "discovery problem" by helping customers find products they'll love even when they aren't sure exactly what they're looking for. These tools balance showing customers products similar to what they've liked before with introducing them to new items they might not have discovered on their own. As these systems analyze browsing patterns, purchase history, and even seasonal trends, they create shopping experiences that feel intuitive and helpful rather than random or overly promotional.

Demand Forecasting and Inventory Optimization

One of the biggest challenges for retailers is having the right products in the right places at the right times. Azure AutoML (Automated Machine Learning) helps solve this problem by analyzing historical sales data, seasonal patterns, promotional calendars, and even external factors like weather to predict future demand. This means stores can stock up on swimwear before a heatwave or ensure they have enough holiday items without ending up with excess inventory that needs to be heavily discounted later.

Time-series data is particularly important for retail forecasting, understanding not just what sells but exactly when demand rises and falls. Azure Time Series Insights provides specialized tools for analyzing patterns that occur over time, helping retailers identify weekly shopping patterns, seasonal trends, and even the impact of special events like sports games or concerts on nearby stores. This allows for more granular forecasting, not just predicting monthly sales but understanding which days of the week specific products are most likely to sell and staffing stores accordingly.

Accurate forecasting directly impacts a retailer's bottom line by reducing both stockouts (losing sales because products aren't available) and overstock situations (tying up money in unsold inventory). Azure's machine learning tools help retailers find this balance by automatically adjusting forecasts based on the most recent data. For example, if a product starts selling faster than expected, the system can automatically recommend increasing orders or redistributing inventory from slower-selling locations, ensuring customers can find what they're looking for while retailers maintain healthy profit margins.

Fraud Prevention and Secure Payments

Every day, retailers face sophisticated attempts to commit fraud through stolen credit cards, account takeovers, and fake returns. Azure Cognitive Services help identify suspicious patterns that might indicate fraud like orders shipping to addresses different from billing information, unusual purchase amounts, or transactions from unexpected locations. Microsoft Entra ID Identity Protection adds another layer of security by monitoring signs that customer accounts may have been compromised. The system looks for unusual sign-in locations, impossible travel (logging in from different countries within impossibly short time frames), or sign-ins from infected devices. When suspicious activity is detected, the system can require additional verification like a code sent via text message or email. This protects both customers and retailers from unauthorized purchases without creating unnecessary friction for legitimate shoppers.

Balancing security with convenience is important in retail, where a complicated checkout process can lead to abandoned carts. Azure's fraud prevention tools use adaptive risk scoring that considers the customer's history with the retailer, the specific products being purchased, and real-time signals about the transaction. For loyal customers making typical purchases, the experience remains smooth and seamless. Additional verification steps are only triggered when truly suspicious activity is detected, maximizing security while minimizing disruption to the shopping experience.

Intelligent Supply Chain

Modern retail supply chains are incredibly complex because products move from manufacturers to distribution centers to stores across the globe, with countless opportunities for delays and disruptions. Azure IoT Edge enables "smart shelves" and automated inventory systems that can detect when products are running low and automatically trigger restocking. This technology connects physical stores to digital inventory systems, to ensure that what customers see online accurately reflects what's available in the store they plan to visit.

Azure Digital Twins creates virtual representations of physical retail environments. These could be individual stores or entire distribution networks. These digital models help retailers visualize and optimize their operations, identifying bottlenecks in product flow or simulating how changes to store layouts might impact sales. For example, a retailer could create a digital twin of a store to test different product placement strategies virtually before making physical changes, or model their entire supply chain to identify the most efficient routes for shipping products from warehouses to stores.

Machine learning inference at the edge brings AI capabilities directly to store environments without requiring constant cloud connectivity. This means smart cameras can count customers, detect when lines are forming at checkout, and alert staff to restock empty shelves, all without sending video to the cloud and while respecting customer privacy. These in-store AI systems help retailers bridge their physical and digital operations, creating more responsive stores that can adapt quickly to changing customer needs while providing valuable data that improves the entire supply chain.

Customer 360 Insights

Understanding customers across all their interactions, for example, online browsing, in-store purchases, customer service contacts, and loyalty program participation, is important for modern retailers. Azure Synapse Link connects operational databases with analytical systems in real time, allowing retailers to maintain a complete picture of each customer without disrupting transaction processing. This means a customer's online browsing activity can immediately inform their in-store experience, or a recent support interaction can be considered when personalizing marketing messages.

Dynamics 365 Customer Insights helps retailers turn this connected data into actionable intelligence by identifying patterns in customer behavior and preferences. The platform can automatically segment customers based on their shopping habits, predict which customers are at risk of switching to competitors, and identify opportunities for additional sales based on previous purchases. The real power of Customer 360 insights comes from activating this knowledge across all customer touchpoints. When a loyal customer walks into a store, sales associates equipped with the right information can provide personalized service based on their purchase history and preferences. Marketing teams can create campaigns that respond to specific customer behaviors rather than broad demographic categories. Customer service representatives can see a complete history of interactions across channels. This connected approach helps retailers build stronger customer relationships by providing consistent, personalized experiences no matter how or where customers choose to shop.

AI in Finance and Banking

Banks and financial companies are using smart computer tools to completely change how they do business. Azure's AI tools help them figure out who to lend money to, spot criminals trying to launder money, serve customers day and night, keep financial data super secure, and make faster trading decisions. These tools turn mountains of numbers and transactions into helpful information that makes banking better for everyone.

When you apply for a loan or credit card, banks use Azure Databricks to quickly decide if lending you money is a good idea. These smart systems look at way more than just your credit score—they check your payment history, spending patterns, and even how you use banking apps to get a fuller picture of you as a borrower. This helps more people get loans while keeping banks financially healthy. Banks also use these tools to run "what-if" simulations across their entire loan portfolio, helping them make smarter decisions about which types of loans to offer.

Keeping your money safe from criminals is another huge job for AI in banking. Financial companies process millions of transactions every day, making it impossible for human workers to check each one for signs of fraud. Azure Cognitive Services for Language examines transaction descriptions and customer messages for suspicious patterns, while Azure Anomaly Detector spots unusual activity like someone suddenly making large withdrawals from different branches or a business whose transactions don't match what they claim to do. These tools help banks stop criminal activity without slowing down legitimate transactions, finding the right balance between security and convenience.

Banking whenever and wherever you want is now possible through AI assistants created with Azure Bot Framework Composer. These smart banking helpers can check your balance, transfer money, answer questions about fees, and show your recent transactions, all through websites, mobile apps, messaging platforms, or even smart speakers. Azure Speech Services let you talk to these banking assistants naturally, understanding different accents and filtering out background noise. These bots know their limits too. When you ask about complex products like mortgages or have concerns about possible fraud, they smoothly connect you to a human banker who already has your information ready to go.

Financial companies follow strict rules designed to protect consumers and keep markets stable. Azure Confidential Computing helps banks meet these requirements while still using modern cloud technology. It creates special secure areas where sensitive financial data can be analyzed without ever being exposed, even to Microsoft itself. Azure Confidential Ledger keeps an unchangeable record of financial decisions and transactions. When a loan is approved or denied based partly on AI recommendations, all the factors that influenced that decision are securely stored in a way that can't be altered later. This helps banks prove they're following lending laws and explain decisions to both regulators and customers. In investments, professional traders use algorithms to analyze market data and make trades faster than humans ever could. Azure Event Hubs processes real-time information from stock exchanges worldwide, letting trading systems spot opportunities or risks in milliseconds. Machine learning models find hidden patterns in market behavior, using enormous amounts of historical data to predict how prices might move in the future. While these powerful trading tools were once only available to big Wall Street firms, Azure's technology is making them accessible to smaller investment companies too, potentially creating fairer markets while requiring careful attention to managing risks.

AI in Manufacturing and Industry 4.0

Factories are getting a major upgrade with smart AI tools that help prevent breakdowns, spot defects, simulate production, optimize operations, and keep workers safe. Azure's manufacturing tools connect machines to the cloud, inspect products with computer vision, create virtual copies of entire factories, find the best ways to run production lines through trial and error, and help robots work safely alongside humans. These technologies are helping manufacturers make better products with less waste and fewer accidents.

Catching machine problems before they happen is one of the biggest wins for factory AI. Azure IoT Hub connects manufacturing equipment to the cloud, collecting data from sensors that measure things like temperature, vibration, and power consumption. Stream Analytics processes this information in real time, looking for warning signs of potential failures. Machine Learning models trained on historical breakdown data can predict when a piece of equipment is likely to fail days or even weeks in advance. Instead of waiting for something to break and shutting down the production line, maintenance teams can replace worn parts during scheduled downtime. This predictive maintenance approach saves manufacturers millions in lost production time and extends the life of expensive equipment.

Spotting tiny defects that human eyes might miss is another powerful use of AI in factories. Azure Custom Vision services can be trained to recognize product defects like scratches on metal surfaces, incorrect color patterns, or misaligned components. These vision systems can be deployed directly on edge devices like Azure Percept or industrial cameras on the factory floor, allowing for real-time quality control without sending images to the cloud. Unlike human inspectors who get tired or distracted, these AI vision systems maintain consistent performance 24/7, examining every product with the same careful attention. They can also detect issues that might be invisible to the human eye, like subtle color variations that indicate a chemical process isn't working correctly or microscopic cracks that could lead to product failures later.

Finding the perfect recipe for complex manufacturing processes is where reinforcement learning shines. Many manufacturing processes have hundreds of variables that affect the final product like temperature settings, timing, material mixtures, and more. Azure's reinforcement learning services help discover the perfect combination of these settings through a process similar to how humans learn through trial and error but at a much faster pace. The AI system tries different combinations of settings, learns from the results, and gradually discovers the optimal approach. For example, in chemical manufacturing, reinforcement learning might discover that changing the sequence of mixing ingredients or adjusting temperatures by just a few degrees can significantly improve product quality or reduce energy consumption. These optimizations often find solutions that human engineers might never have considered.

Bringing all these technologies together creates the "smart factory" that forms the heart of Industry 4.0. These connected manufacturing systems share data across previously isolated processes, creating a more responsive and efficient operation. When the quality inspection system identifies an increasing trend in defects, it can automatically notify the predictive maintenance system to check related equipment. The digital twin can simulate the impact of unexpected supplier delays and suggest production schedule adjustments. Reinforcement learning continuously fine-tunes process parameters based on real-time quality data. This connected approach helps manufacturers adapt quickly to changing market demands, maintain consistent quality, reduce waste, and keep workers focused on creative problem-solving rather than repetitive tasks.

The benefits go beyond individual factories to transform entire supply chains. Azure IoT and AI systems help track materials and products through every stage of production and distribution. If a quality problem is discovered, manufacturers can quickly trace affected products to specific production batches and machines. Weather disruptions or shipping delays detected through Azure's systems can trigger automated adjustments to production schedules. The significant efficiency improvements from these technologies aren't just good for business, they're good for the planet too. Smarter manufacturing means less wasted energy, fewer defective products in landfills, and more efficient use of raw materials.

AI for Customer Service and Virtual Assistants

Customer service is being transformed by AI tools that help companies provide faster, more personalized support across multiple channels. Azure's customer service technologies enable businesses to create helpful virtual assistants that understand questions in natural language, recognize and respond to voice commands, analyze customer feelings, power modern contact centers, and continuously improve based on customer feedback. These smart tools are changing how companies connect with their customers, making support available 24/7 while freeing human agents to handle more complex or sensitive issues.

Talking to customers wherever they prefer is now possible through virtual assistants built with Azure Bot Service and Copilot Studio. These smart helpers can answer customer questions, troubleshoot common problems, help with purchases, and hand off to human agents when needed, all across websites, mobile apps, social media, and messaging platforms like Teams, WhatsApp, or Facebook Messenger. What makes these modern bots different from frustrating older versions is their ability to understand natural language. Instead of forcing customers to use exact keywords or navigate confusing menus, Azure bots understand questions asked in everyday language even when there are typos or the question is phrased in different ways. Copilot Studio makes creating these assistants much easier with a visual design tool that doesn't require coding skills, allowing customer service teams to build and update their own bots without waiting for IT help.

Speaking is often easier than typing, which is why voice assistants powered by Azure Speech Services are becoming a key part of modern customer service. These tools convert spoken words into text with remarkable accuracy, understand different accents and dialects, and can even filter out background noise like keyboard clicking or café chatter. For customers with disabilities or those who are multitasking, speaking to a virtual assistant can be much more convenient than navigating a website or app. These same voice technologies also provide real-time transcription during customer calls, automatically documenting important details and action items without agents having to type notes. This helps agents stay focused on the conversation instead of note-taking, while ensuring that no important details get missed. Some companies are even using these transcription services to provide live captions during video support sessions, making their services more accessible.

Understanding how customers really feel goes beyond just hearing their words. Azure Text Analytics for sentiment and Dynamics 365 Customer Insights help companies understand the emotions behind customer interactions. These tools analyze the language customers use in chats, emails, calls, and social media to detect if they're frustrated, confused, satisfied, or delighted. They can spot when seemingly polite language actually indicates a customer is getting increasingly annoyed, helping companies intervene before the customer gives up. The system can also identify common topics that trigger negative reactions or particular product features that consistently generate positive feedback.

Modern contact centers are being reimagined with AI at their core. Azure's contact center reference architecture combines Teams for communication with Cognitive Services for intelligence, creating support centers that are more effective for both customers and agents. When a customer calls or messages, AI tools immediately analyze their history, predict why they're contacting support, and route them to the best available agent with the right skills to help. While the conversation is happening, AI assistants listen in and automatically suggest helpful resources to the agent, like similar solved cases or technical documentation relevant to the customer's issue. After the interaction, the system automatically summarizes the conversation, tags it with relevant categories, and updates the customer record. This helps new agents perform like veterans by putting knowledge at their fingertips, while giving experienced agents the tools to resolve issues faster.

Getting better every day is possible through AI-powered feedback loops using telemetry, customer input, and A/B testing. Azure's tools collect detailed information about how customers interact with virtual assistants, which questions confuse the bot, where customers abandon conversations, or which answers lead to successful resolutions. This telemetry helps identify specific areas for improvement rather than guessing what needs fixing. Companies can then create different versions of responses or conversation flows and test them with real customers to see which performs better. For example, if many customers are abandoning a checkout process at a certain point, the team might test two different approaches to see which helps more customers complete their purchase. This experimental approach, combined with direct customer feedback and AI-generated insights, creates a cycle of continuous improvement that makes virtual assistants more helpful over time.

Blending AI with human touch creates the best customer experiences. The most successful companies don't use AI to replace human agents entirely, but instead create thoughtful handoffs between virtual assistants and people. Azure's tools help identify exactly when a conversation should transition to a human, whether because the issue is too complex, the customer is becoming frustrated, or the topic requires empathy that AI can't provide. The handoff includes a complete summary of what's already been discussed, so customers don't have to repeat themselves. As the human agent works with the customer, AI tools continue to assist behind the scenes, suggesting responses and retrieving relevant information. This collaborative approach combines the consistency and 24/7 availability of AI with the creativity and emotional intelligence of human agents. Personalization at scale becomes possible when companies combine their customer data with AI capabilities. When a customer connects with a virtual assistant built on Azure, the system can instantly access their purchase history, previous support issues, communication preferences, and loyalty status. This allows the assistant to tailor responses specifically to that customer: recommending relevant products, referring to their specific device models, or proactively addressing known issues with products they've purchased. For companies with millions of customers, this level of personalization would be impossible without AI.

AI in Education and Learning Platforms

School is changing in some pretty amazing ways thanks to smart computing tools. These tools help teachers create lessons that fit each student's needs, make learning easier for kids who struggle with reading or speak different languages, give scientists superpowerful computers for big discoveries, keep student information private, and let teachers build their own digital teaching tools without having to be computer experts. Learning at your own speed is now possible with smart systems that figure out what works best for each student. Think of it like having a tutor who notices when you're confused or bored and adjusts the lesson on the spot. These smart learning systems might show one student more pictures, give another more practice problems, or explain things in simpler ways when needed. Teachers get easy-to-read dashboards showing which parts of a lesson the whole class is struggling with or which students need extra help. This personalized approach stops kids from falling behind when they don't understand something important, while letting quick learners move forward without getting bored.

Making lessons work for everyone is another big win for these school technologies. Smart reading tools help students with dyslexia, language barriers, or vision problems by reading text out loud, breaking words into chunks, and highlighting different parts of speech. These tools can even translate lessons into over 70 languages, helping students who are learning English keep up with their classes. For video lessons, smart tools create searchable transcripts and automatically add captions in different languages. Translation tools even allow real-time translation of classroom discussions, so students who speak different languages can all participate. These tools help schools welcome all kinds of learners without needing separate materials for each student who needs help.

Giving scientists superpowered computers opens the door to amazing discoveries while keeping student information safe is super important when using technology in schools. Researchers can run complex simulations, analyze huge amounts of information, or test new ideas without waiting weeks for results. Climate scientists can model environmental changes, geneticists can analyze DNA, and engineers can test new materials at the molecular level. At the same time, smart systems are designed to follow strict privacy laws that protect student records. Schools can control exactly who sees different types of student information, from grades and attendance to health details and family information. These safeguards ensure that while smart tools can suggest personalized learning paths or flag when a student might need extra help, teachers make the final decisions about education.

Creating their own teaching tools is now something teachers can do without needing to be computer programmers. Simple drag-and-drop interfaces let teachers build their own digital activities, feedback forms, grading tools, and classroom management apps. A language teacher might create a pronunciation practice app that listens to students and gives them tips on improving, while a science teacher could build a quiz that automatically grades lab reports by recognizing hand-drawn diagrams. Automatic systems can handle boring tasks like sending reminder emails about assignments or putting together weekly progress reports for parents. When computers handle things like basic grading, tracking progress, and creating practice materials, teachers can spend more time explaining tricky concepts, providing emotional support, and inspiring curiosity.

Getting ready for a future full of AI is perhaps the most important job of these technologies in schools today. As smart computer systems change everything from healthcare to manufacturing, students need to understand not just how to use these tools but how they work and what their limitations are. Schools are teaching AI literacy, helping students think critically about how algorithms work, understand data privacy, and consider the ethical questions that come with automated decisions. Some learning platforms even let students experiment with building their own simple AI models, making this technology less mysterious for kids who will use it throughout their lives. When schools make AI part of learning from an early age, they are preparing students for a world where working with smart computer systems will be as basic as using a smartphone is today.

Cross-Industry Patterns and Best Practices

No matter what business you're in, healthcare, retail, banking, or education, some AI building blocks and best practices work everywhere. These shared approaches help companies use AI in ways that are trustworthy, keep systems running smoothly, work in places with poor internet, give regular employees AI superpowers, and organize huge amounts of data.

Making sure AI behaves itself is a top priority for every organization. When computers make decisions that affect people's lives, like who gets a loan, which medical treatment to try, or who gets hired, those decisions need to be fair, explainable, and respectful of privacy. Tools like Azure's AI governance toolkit help companies create guardrails that prevent AI from discriminating against certain groups, ensure systems can explain their reasoning in human terms, and protect sensitive information. Companies are creating clear rules about what their AI systems can and can't do, then using technical tools to enforce those rules automatically. For example, a healthcare system might set up checks to make sure its diagnosis recommendations work equally well for all patient groups, while a bank might require that loan decisions always come with clear explanations of the factors involved. These responsible AI practices are essential for building trust with customers and staying on the right side of increasing regulations.

Getting AI from idea to reality used to be a messy process with lots of handoffs between different teams. Now companies are adopting MLOps (Machine Learning Operations) that treat AI development more like software development. These systems create a smooth pipeline from collecting and storing data in data lakes, to building and tracking models with tools like MLflow, to testing and deploying them through Azure DevOps, to running them in containers on services like AKS (Azure Kubernetes Service). This approach means less time wasted on manual work, fewer errors when moving from testing to production, and the ability to update AI systems quickly as needs change. It also makes it easier for different people to collaborate. Data scientists can focus on creating great models while IT teams handle the infrastructure, all working together with shared tools and clear handoffs. Companies that adopt these practices can go from "Hey, we should try using AI for this problem" to having a working solution in weeks instead of months or years.

Taking AI to the edge is changing how companies handle situations where internet connections are slow, unreliable, or non-existent. With Azure Arc–enabled ML, organizations can run AI directly on local devices without needing a constant cloud connection. An oil rig in the middle of the ocean can use computer vision to spot safety issues, a delivery vehicle can optimize routes while driving through areas with no cell service, or a grocery store can track inventory even when the internet goes down. These edge systems can make quick decisions locally while still syncing with cloud systems when connections are available, getting the benefits of both approaches. They're also great for situations where data is sensitive or huge in volume. A factory might generate terabytes of sensor data that would be expensive to send to the cloud but can be processed locally with only the important insights sent back for central analysis. This hybrid approach gives companies flexibility to run AI wherever it makes the most sense (cloud, edge, or both) while managing everything from a single control center.

Giving everyone AI superpowers, not just technical experts, is revolutionizing how companies solve problems. Tools like Power Apps and Microsoft Copilot let regular employees with no coding experience create their own AI-powered apps and automations through simple, visual interfaces. A retail store manager might build an app that uses computer vision to check if shelves are properly stocked, a HR team member could create a system that summarizes job applications, or a marketing person might set up a tool that generates social media content ideas based on current trends. These "citizen developers" understand their business problems intimately and can now create solutions directly instead of trying to explain their needs to technical teams. The best part is that these tools connect to enterprise systems and follow company security policies, unlike random apps people might download.

Organizing massive amounts of data is a challenge every company faces, and new approaches are making this much easier. Modern patterns like data fabric and lakehouse combine the best features of different data systems, the flexibility of data lakes with the reliability of traditional warehouses, in platforms like Microsoft Fabric and OneLake. These systems let companies store all kinds of data (from structured database tables to unstructured text, images, and videos) in standard formats like Delta that work with many different tools. Instead of having information trapped in separate systems that don't talk to each other, these approaches create a connected web of data that can be accessed from anywhere while still maintaining security and governance. A company might keep customer information, product details, manufacturing data, and marketing analytics all in this unified system, which makes it much easier to get a complete picture of what's happening in the business. When new AI projects come up, the data is already organized and ready to use instead of requiring months of preparation work. This approach doesn't directly solve your problems, but it makes solving them much faster and easier.

Summary

This chapter covered how AI and Azure services are applied across various industries. It explored healthcare applications like predictive analytics for patient risk, medical imaging with Computer Vision, virtual assistants with Health Bot, and genomics using Azure

Synapse Analytics. In retail, AI enables personalization with Azure Personalizer, demand forecasting with AutoML, fraud prevention, and supply chain optimization via IoT Edge and Digital Twins. Financial services benefit from AI through credit decisioning, fraud detection, virtual assistants, and regulatory compliance tools. Manufacturing uses AI for predictive maintenance, quality control with Custom Vision, and process optimization through reinforcement learning. Customer service is transformed by omnichannel bots with Azure Bot Service and Copilot Studio, voice assistants, and sentiment analysis. Education applications include personalized learning, accessibility tools, and teacher-friendly development platforms. The chapter concluded with cross-industry best practices like responsible AI governance, MLOps for smoother deployment, edge computing with Azure Arc, citizen development with Power Apps, and unified data management through fabric and lakehouse architectures.

Exam Essentials

Understand industry-specific AI applications.   Learn how AI solutions are tailored to different vertical markets like healthcare, retail, finance, manufacturing, customer service, and education rather than using generic models.

Know healthcare AI use cases.   Understand how Azure services support predictive analytics for patient risk, medical imaging with Computer Vision, conversational care with Health Bot, and genomics research while maintaining HIPAA compliance.

Recognize retail and e-Commerce AI patterns.   Know how Azure Personalizer drives real-time recommendations, AutoML enables demand forecasting, and IoT Edge with Digital Twins optimizes supply chains and inventory management.

Understand financial services AI implementations.   Learn how Azure supports credit decisioning, fraud detection, virtual assistants for banking, and confidential computing for regulatory compliance.

Know manufacturing and Industry 4.0 solutions.   Understand how predictive maintenance with IoT Hub, quality control with Custom Vision, and process optimization through reinforcement learning transform factory operations.

Master customer service AI capabilities.   Learn how Azure Bot Service and Copilot Studio enable omnichannel bots, Speech Services power voice assistants, and sentiment analysis improves customer experiences.

Recognize cross-industry AI patterns.   Understand common best practices including responsible AI governance, MLOps for deployment pipelines, edge computing with Azure Arc, low-code development with Power Apps, and unified data management with fabric architecture.

Review Questions

1. A healthcare organization wants to analyze thousands of radiology images to assist radiologists in identifying potential areas of concern more efficiently. Which Azure service would be most appropriate for this scenario?

   A. Azure Power BI

   B. Azure Computer Vision

   C. Azure Personalizer

   D. Azure IoT Hub

2. A retail company wants to provide personalized product recommendations to customers in real time based on their browsing behavior and purchase history. Which Azure service would best support this requirement?

   A. Azure Anomaly Detector

   B. Azure Personalizer

   C. Azure Digital Twins

   D. Azure Time Series Insights

3. A manufacturing company wants to prevent unexpected machine failures by predicting when maintenance will be needed before breakdowns occur. Which combination of Azure services would best support this predictive maintenance scenario?

   A. Azure IoT Hub and Azure Machine Learning

   B. Azure Digital Twins and Azure Personalizer

   C. Azure Bot Service and Azure Cognitive Services

   D. Azure Computer Vision and Azure Speech Services

4. A financial institution needs to develop a system that can automatically detect potentially fraudulent transactions in real time without significantly impacting legitimate customer transactions. Which Azure service would be most appropriate?

   A. Azure Health Bot

   B. Azure Anomaly Detector

   C. Azure Custom Vision

   D. Azure OpenAI Service

5. A customer service department wants to implement a solution that allows customers to get immediate help through multiple channels including their website, mobile app, and social media platforms. Which Azure service would be the foundation of this solution?

   A. Azure IoT Hub

   B. Azure Bot Service and Copilot Studio

   C. Azure Digital Twins

   D. Azure Synapse Analytics

6. An educational institution wants to provide personalized learning experiences that adapt to each student's learning pace and style. Which Azure AI approach best addresses this need?

   A. Industrial IoT implementation

   B. Fraud detection systems

   C. Adaptive learning platforms with Azure Machine Learning

   D. Real-time inventory management

7. A retailer wants to reduce both stockouts and excess inventory by better predicting future product demand. Which Azure service would be most effective for analyzing seasonal sales patterns and forecasting future needs?

   A. Azure Time Series Insights

   B. Azure Custom Vision

   C. Azure Health Bot

   D. Azure Confidential Computing

8. A hospital needs to ensure that all of its AI solutions for patient data analysis comply with healthcare privacy regulations. Which Azure feature is specifically designed to support this requirement?

   A. Azure IoT Edge

   B. Azure Confidential Computing

   C. Azure Personalizer

   D. Azure Digital Twins

9. A factory wants to implement quality control systems that can detect product defects in real time on the production line without sending images to the cloud. Which Azure technology would best support this requirement?

   A. Azure Custom Vision deployed on Azure IoT Edge devices

   B. Azure Digital Twins

   C. Azure Bot Framework

   D. Azure Synapse Analytics

10. A multinational company wants to create a virtual assistant that can understand and respond to customer inquiries in multiple languages. Which Azure service is specifically designed to support this multilingual requirement?

    A. Azure Speech Services

    B. Azure Translator

    C. Azure Personalizer

    D. Azure Digital Twins

11. A bank is developing an AI system that helps make lending decisions. To ensure compliance with financial regulations, the bank needs to be able to explain exactly why each application was approved or denied. Which Azure AI principle does this requirement most closely align with?

   A. Fairness

   B. Privacy

   C. Transparency

   D. Security

12. A retail company wants to use AI to optimize their supply chain by creating virtual representations of their stores and distribution network. Which Azure service would be most appropriate for this scenario?

   A. Azure IoT Hub

   B. Azure Digital Twins

   C. Azure Bot Service

   D. Azure Computer Vision

13. A healthcare organization wants to enable patients to check symptoms, schedule appointments, and get medication reminders through a conversational interface. Which Azure service is specifically designed for healthcare conversational AI?

   A. Azure Health Bot

   B. Azure Personalizer

   C. Azure IoT Hub

   D. Azure Digital Twins

14. A company wants to develop AI solutions but lacks staff with extensive coding expertise. Which Azure service would best enable non-technical staff to create AI-powered applications?

   A. Azure Kubernetes Service

   B. Azure Machine Learning

   C. Power Apps with AI Builder

   D. Azure DevOps

15. A manufacturing company wants to optimize a complex production process with hundreds of variables affecting product quality. Which Azure AI approach would be most effective for discovering the optimal combination of settings?

   A. Computer Vision

   B. Natural Language Processing

   C. Reinforcement Learning

   D. Sentiment Analysis

16. A financial services company needs to analyze transaction descriptions to identify potential money laundering activities. Which Azure Cognitive Service would be most appropriate for this text analysis task?

    A. Azure Computer Vision

    B. Azure Cognitive Services for Language

    C. Azure Speech Services

    D. Azure Personalizer

17. A retail company wants to implement "smart shelves" that can automatically detect when products are running low and trigger restocking. Which Azure service would be the foundation of this solution?

    A. Azure IoT Edge

    B. Azure Bot Service

    C. Azure Personalizer

    D. Azure Confidential Computing

18. A genomics research organization needs to analyze enormous amounts of genetic data. Which Azure service combination would best support this computational requirement while maintaining data security?

    A. Azure IoT Hub and Azure Digital Twins

    B. Azure Synapse Analytics and Azure Machine Learning

    C. Azure Bot Service and Azure Cognitive Services

    D. Azure Personalizer and Azure Anomaly Detector

19. A company is implementing AI solutions across multiple departments but wants to ensure consistent governance, security, and deployment practices. Which Azure pattern addresses this need?

    A. Digital Twins

    B. MLOps (Machine Learning Operations)

    C. Reinforcement Learning

    D. Edge Computing

20. A school district wants to implement AI tools that help students with dyslexia or language barriers access educational content. Which Azure service would best support this accessibility requirement?

    A. Azure Personalizer

    B. Azure Cognitive Services for Speech and Language

    C. Azure IoT Hub

    D. Azure Digital Twins

Conclusion

Congratulations! You've made it through your journey into the world of artificial intelligence with Azure. From the basic building blocks of AI to specialized areas like computer vision and natural language processing, you now have a solid foundation to build upon. Remember that AI combines technical ideas with real-world solutions that solve problems and make life easier for everyone.

Throughout this guide, you've seen how Azure makes AI more accessible for various applications working with images, processing text, and creating new content with generative AI. The Azure OpenAI Service has powerful tools previously available only to specialized researchers. Azure's AI agents enable systems that understand people's needs and respond appropriately, without requiring advanced technical expertise.

What makes Azure special is how it balances innovation with responsibility. As you've learned, Microsoft takes ethical AI seriously, ensuring that these powerful tools help rather than harm. This balance is important as AI becomes more common in our everyday lives, from healthcare and education, to business and entertainment. The real-world applications we discussed show that AI is already making a difference today.

As you move forward with your AI-900 certification and beyond, keep an open and curious mind. The field constantly evolves, with new tools and capabilities emerging regularly. The core concepts in this guide will serve as your compass. Feel free to experiment, make mistakes, and learn from them. This mirrors how AI systems improve over time.

Though this book ends here, your journey with AI is just beginning. Good luck on your exam! I hope this guide has prepared you well and sparked your imagination about the possibilities when human creativity combines with Azure's AI capabilities. I can't wait to see what you build!

Appendix

Answers to the Review Questions

Chapter 1: Overview of AI Concepts and Workloads

1. B. Predictive Analytics is designed to use historical data to forecast future events. In this scenario, the system would analyze previous sales data and seasonal patterns to predict future demand. This approach falls under discriminative AI, which classifies and predicts outcomes based on learned patterns. The explanation here shows that while generative AI creates new content and NLP deals with language, predictive analytics is the best fit for making forecasts based on existing trends.

2. A. Knowledge Mining transforms unstructured data, such as research papers and feedback, into organized and searchable information. This helps the university identify patterns and gaps in its curriculum. The process involves using services that can extract meaningful details from large sets of text and multimedia content, which is essential for data-driven improvements in education.

3. D. Azure AI Personalizer is designed for personalization tasks and uses reinforcement learning to dynamically adjust recommendations based on user interactions. This service can analyze user behavior, such as viewing history, to suggest movies that fit their tastes. While Azure Machine Learning provides a broad platform for model development, Azure AI Personalizer specifically targets the challenge of personalization with dynamic learning from real-time user data.

4. C. Reinforcement Learning enables an agent, in this case the self-driving car, to learn by interacting with its environment. It takes actions, receives rewards or penalties, and adjusts its decisions based on feedback. This method helps the car gradually learn the best routes and maneuvers in real time. The explanation clarifies that while deep learning is used for pattern recognition and expert systems rely on predefined rules, reinforcement learning is best for dynamic decision-making in changing environments.

5. A. Generative AI is focused on creating new content, such as text, images, or music, by learning from existing data. In this scenario, the system needs to generate creative marketing copy that reflects human language and style. The explanation points out that while NLP is used to understand and process language, generative AI has the capability to produce new content, making it the ideal choice.

6. B. The workload in this case involves extracting meaningful information from unstructured data sources such as market reports and news articles. This process helps the firm identify patterns and trends that inform financial decisions. The goal is to convert vast amounts of text into structured information that can be used for analysis, rather than generating new data or directly controlling trading.

7. A. This application uses Expert Systems since it leverages predefined rules from domain experts to provide recommendations. The system does not adapt based on new data, but it consistently applies expert knowledge to assist farmers.

8. A. Knowledge Mining is used to transform unstructured data, like viewer comments and social media feedback, into organized information. This helps the media company identify trends and patterns in audience behavior. Through knowledge mining, the company can better understand what content resonates with viewers and adjust its strategy accordingly. Although recommendation systems also analyze user behavior, knowledge mining is more comprehensive for understanding diverse types of feedback.

9. B. A hybrid cloud model enables an organization to maintain sensitive data on-premises for tighter security and control while using cloud services to scale and manage less sensitive workloads. This approach balances the benefits of cloud computing, such as flexibility and scalability, with the need for data privacy and security, which is particularly important in regulated industries.

10. B. Separating heavy computational tasks from the user interface means that the complex processing, such as data analysis and model training, occurs on a centralized server. This approach simplifies system updates and maintenance, as improvements can be made on the server without affecting the client.

11. A. Computer Vision is focused on enabling computers to interpret and understand visual data. For tasks such as image tagging, it uses algorithms to recognize features in images and assign appropriate labels.

12. A. The smart home system involves multiple tasks, including language understanding, prediction, and decision-making. To design such a system, you must understand the broad concept of artificial intelligence, which includes machine learning, deep learning, natural language processing, and reinforcement learning. This comprehensive understanding will help you integrate various AI techniques to meet the system's requirements.

13. B. NLP is specifically for understanding, interpreting, and generating human language. It is the most suitable technology for a customer support chatbot that must handle a wide variety of queries and provide accurate responses in plain language.

14. C. Predictive Analytics is designed to use historical data, such as maintenance logs and sensor readings, to forecast future events like equipment failures.

15. B. Azure Machine Learning is a comprehensive service that provides tools for building, training, and deploying custom machine learning models. It is well-suited for organizations needing to develop models that address unique, industry-specific challenges.

16. B. Cloud computing provides the flexibility to scale computing resources up or down based on demand. This means that as more users interact with the AI system, additional resources can be allocated to maintain performance and responsiveness without the need for significant upfront investments in hardware.

17. B. Knowledge Mining is used to transform unstructured data into organized, searchable information. Azure AI Search supports this process by indexing content, extracting key information, and making it easily searchable, which is ideal for managing large sets of diverse data.

18. C. A hybrid model that integrates both cloud computing and edge devices allows the company to take advantage of the scalability and powerful processing of the cloud while keeping sensitive data on local devices for security.

19. B. The troubleshooting tool uses Expert Systems because it applies a collection of fixed rules and expert knowledge to diagnose and suggest fixes. Unlike machine learning models, it does not learn from new data but follows a set program.

20. B. Reinforcement Learning is best suited for this task because it allows an AI agent to learn from trial and error. The system receives feedback from the environment (traffic conditions) and adjusts its decisions accordingly to optimize outcomes in real time.

Chapter 2: Responsible AI in Azure

1. A. Fairness ensures that the AI system treats everyone equally and does not favor one group over another.

2. B. InterpretML provides model interpretability, making it easier to understand and communicate the factors that influenced each decision, thus enhancing transparency.

3. B. Reliability ensures that the system handles various inputs consistently. By enhancing error handling, the chatbot can better manage ambiguous queries and ask for clarification.

4. C. Inclusiveness involves ensuring that the AI system caters to diverse user needs. By broadening product recommendations, the system avoids narrow filter bubbles.

5. A. The Responsible AI Dashboard helps integrate tools that explain how the AI system reaches its decisions. This added transparency makes the system's processes clearer to users, thereby improving overall understandability.

6. A. Reliability focuses on ensuring that the system operates consistently under different conditions. Improving the training data and conducting thorough testing can reduce sensitivity to minor changes and prevent false alarms.

7. B. Audit trails and version control allow the company to track every modification made to the AI model. This documentation is essential for accountability, troubleshooting, and ensuring that the system remains aligned with ethical guidelines.

8. D. InterpretML provides clear visualizations and explanations for model decisions, which can help the marketing team understand the factors that drive discount offers and build trust in the system.

9. B. Regular AI impact assessments, along with maintaining version control, enable the team to systematically track how updates affect the system's performance and ensure that changes align with responsible AI practices.

10. B. Fairlearn is designed to detect and mitigate bias in AI models. By using Fairlearn, the development team can assess the extent of bias in the content filtering system and implement corrective measures to ensure fair treatment of all content.

11. C. Audit trails and a dashboard for transparency allow the public to see how decisions are made, increasing accountability and trust.

12. B. Improving the training data and testing under varied conditions strengthens the system's reliability.

13. A. Updating the model with rare scenarios improves its reliability and ensures consistent performance.

14. B. InterpretML enhances transparency by explaining how different inputs lead to specific energy recommendations.

15. B. Improving reliability by integrating real-time information helps the AI system make better and more consistent routing decisions.

16. A. Enhancing inclusiveness ensures that the system is designed to cater to diverse cultural and language needs, providing relevant recommendations for all users.

17. C. Presidio is built to detect and anonymize sensitive information, making it ideal for handling confidential patient data in compliance with privacy regulations.

18. A. Microsoft Purview enables unified data governance, helping organizations manage, discover, and classify data across hybrid environments, ensuring compliance.

19. B. PyRIT is an open-source toolkit that helps teams assess risks in generative AI systems by simulating adverse scenarios and identifying potential vulnerabilities.

20. A. AI Red Teaming involves simulating attacks on the system to find weaknesses and ensure that the AI is resilient against real-world misuse.

Chapter 3: Core Concepts of AI Models and Solutions

1. B. Pretrained models like ResNet can be fine-tuned with domain-specific data (e.g., X-rays), saving time and resources.

2. C. Unsupervised models like clustering are used when there are no labels, such as for customer segmentation.

3. B. Custom models allow full control over architecture and transparency, important in regulated industries like banking.

4. B. AKS provides auto-scaling and high availability, ideal for production-grade, real-time applications.

5. D. Testing involves evaluating the model's behavior in real-world or edge-case scenarios, including adversarial inputs.

6. C. Reinforcement learning is designed for interactive environments where agents learn by rewards and penalties.

7. C. Azure Monitor tracks performance metrics and can alert teams to slowdowns or high error rates.

8. B. Dropout randomly disables neurons during training, helping the model generalize better and prevent overfitting.

9. B. Overfitting occurs when a model memorizes training data and fails to generalize.

10. C. ONNX allows models to run across different frameworks and environments consistently.

11. B. Quantization simplifies numerical precision, reducing model size and power usage on edge devices.

12. C. Custom models are ideal for niche tasks where high accuracy and control are needed.

13. B. Recall focuses on identifying all true positives, crucial in medical settings where false negatives are harmful.

14. A. Model drift occurs when data patterns shift over time, requiring updates to the model.

15. C. Vision models work with image data, typically unstructured.

16. C. Synthetic data helps in scenarios where real data is limited or sensitive, like healthcare.

17. B. Azure Pipelines automates workflows like retraining and deployment.

18. C. Testing how the model performs under unusual but possible conditions is edge-case testing.

19. D. Pretrained models reflect the biases in their training data, which can lead to unfair results.

20. B. Dropout helps the model avoid relying too heavily on specific neurons, improving generalization.

Chapter 4: Introduction to Machine Learning Concepts

1. C. The hospital has labeled outcomes (readmitted or not), which is a classification task suitable for supervised learning.

2. A. Clustering is an unsupervised method used when labels aren't available.

3. D. The test set evaluates the model's final performance on unseen data.

4. C. Data cleaning helps eliminate duplicates and inconsistencies.

5. C. Precision is concerned with the proportion of predicted positives that are actually positive.

6. A. Linear regression is used to predict continuous numeric outcomes.

7. A. Reinforcement learning involves learning by interacting with an environment to maximize rewards.

8. A. Algorithms like KNN are sensitive to feature scale, so standardization is necessary.

9. C. Hyperparameter tuning adjusts model configurations for optimal performance.

10. B. One-hot encoding creates a binary column for each unique category.

11. B. Recall helps catch all true positives, minimizing false negatives.

12. B. Labeled outcomes and prediction tasks are suited for supervised learning.

13. A. Dropout randomly deactivates neurons during training to prevent overfitting.

14. C. High variance shows the model is too sensitive to training data.

15. B. Stratified splitting maintains class ratios in all splits.

16. B. PCA is a dimensionality reduction method that preserves important variance.

17. B. The validation set helps in model selection and hyperparameter tuning.

18. D. F1 Score balances both precision and recall, ideal for imbalanced datasets.

19. B. Dropout prevents overfitting by encouraging redundancy in learned features.

20. C. Min-max scaling compresses feature values to 0–1; unseen values outside this range affect model predictions.

Chapter 5: Machine Learning in Azure

1. C. AutoML helps users build models without needing deep data science knowledge by automating model selection, training, and evaluation.

2. B. Model versioning allows tracking and reverting to older versions of trained models.

3. C. MLOps pipelines support automation and scheduling, enabling regular retraining and deployment.

4. B. The prediction involves categorical outcomes (pass or fail), which is a classification problem.

5. C. Deep learning workloads require high-performance compute, and GPU clusters are optimized for such tasks.

6. C. AutoML requires the user to define the target column to understand what to predict or classify.

7. C. Model registration tracks model metadata, supports version control, and prepares the model for deployment.

8. B. Data drift detection monitors incoming data to identify distribution changes that could affect model performance.

9. C. AKS supports scalable, real-time inference for deployed machine learning models.

10. C. Time-series forecasting is used when predictions are based on data over time, like weekly sales.

11. A. Pipelines organize machine learning steps into reusable, automated workflows.

12. B. Auto-shutdown settings help reduce costs by stopping clusters when they are idle.

13. C. File datasets are used for unstructured data and act as references without duplicating files.

14. C. PyTorch is a popular deep learning framework supported in Azure ML.

15. B. Dataset versioning tracks changes in training data to support reproducibility and audits.

16. C. Azure Machine Learning abstracts infrastructure management while supporting end-to-end ML development.

17. C. Deep learning is optimized for unstructured data using layered neural networks.

18. C. Azure ML Designer has a drag-and-drop interface for building ML models without writing code.

19. C. MLOps brings structure to ML projects, making them easier to manage, scale, and audit.

20. B. A Python script using the requests library can send test payloads to the endpoint URL to verify deployment.

Chapter 6: Introduction to Computer Vision

1. B. Image classification labels the entire image based on content, which fits this use case.

2. C. Object detection identifies and locates multiple items within a scene, such as products on a shelf.

3. A. Form Recognizer extracts structured text, including handwriting, from forms using OCR.

4. C. Facial analysis interprets expressions like smiles or emotions from detected faces.

5. C. Bounding boxes provide coordinates to locate each object in the image.

6. C. Facial analysis extracts traits, while facial recognition matches identities.

7. A. OCR, a branch of computer vision, is used to digitize handwritten content.

8. C. Object detection identifies and labels multiple items in real-time scenes.

9. B. Facial analysis is used to interpret and respond to facial features.

10. C. It classifies parts of the field (e.g., "dry" or "healthy") based on image features.

11. C. Diverse data helps the model recognize more varied real-world examples.

12. D. Dim lighting or blurry images reduce accuracy due to unclear visual data.

13. C. It filters redundant bounding boxes by keeping the most confident ones.

14. C. Facial recognition identifies individuals by matching their features to known faces.

15. C. Biased training data can cause the model to underperform on underrepresented examples.

16. B. Pedestrian detection is an object detection task, not OCR.

17. B. Image classification labels the entire image, not individual objects.

18. B. The car needs to locate and classify multiple objects simultaneously.

19. C. CNNs process images layer by layer to identify features like shapes and textures.

20. C. OCR transforms visual text into editable, machine-readable content.

Chapter 7: Azure Tools for Computer Vision

1. B. The Computer Vision API provides image description and tagging features out of the box, making it ideal for auto-captioning scenarios. Custom Vision is for domain-specific classification, Video Indexer handles video content, and Content Moderator filters inappropriate content.

2. B. The Read API uses modern neural-network models to handle multi-column layouts and cursive handwriting with better accuracy than the legacy OCR endpoint.

3. C. Object detection returns bounding boxes around individual objects like sofas and televisions, whereas tagging only provides labels without locations.

4. B. Selecting the North Europe region ensures data residency compliance and lower latency for European users; a paid tier supports production workloads.

5. B. The domain-specific landmark model identifies famous monuments like the Eiffel Tower; Custom Vision would require you to train your own model.

6. D. The Verify operation performs one-to-one face comparison, confirming if two face images belong to the same person.

7. B. First detect faces to obtain face IDs, then use Identify against a trained person group (one-to-many) to find the matching individual.

8. C. Regularly deleting unused face IDs and person groups ensures compliance with data minimization and deletion requests.

9. C. Custom Vision lets you train bespoke object detection models with your own labeled images for domain-specific tasks like defect detection.

10. B. Exporting as a Docker container enables offline, on-premises inference without cloud connectivity.

11. B. mAP summarizes how well the model balances precision and recall across all object classes.

12. C. Video Indexer automates video ingestion, encoding, and AI pipelines for speech-to-text, scene detection, OCR, and more.

13. B. Video Indexer's embed widget provides an interactive player with indexed scene thumbnails and timestamps.

14. B. The brand detection model spots known logos from its global database without requiring custom training.

15. B. Using a managed identity keeps secrets out of code and lets Azure rotate credentials automatically.

16. D. Azure's asynchronous endpoints let you submit jobs in batches and poll for results, fitting large-scale offline workloads.

17. A. Precision shows correct positive predictions rate, and recall shows how many true positives were found. Together they reflect overall detection quality.

18. B. The GPU container variant leverages the device's GPU for faster inference when available.

19. B. The Read API supports multiple languages and can auto-detect scripts for accurate transcription.

20. C. Security scenarios require near-instant face detection and identification to respond immediately when a known face is seen.

Chapter 8: Introduction to Natural Language Processing (NLP)

1. **A.** Azure Text Analytics sentiment API uses a prebuilt, machine learning–based model that requires no custom training and delivers high accuracy for common domains, making it ideal for near-real-time negative review detection.

2. **A.** Sentence segmentation correctly identifies sentence boundaries (handling "Dr." and abbreviations) so downstream tasks operate at the sentence level. Tokenization breaks text into tokens but not full sentences.

3. **D.** The prebuilt NER model in Azure Text Analytics recognizes common entity types like Person, Date, and Quantity out-of-the-box, reducing development effort.

4. **D.** TF-IDF down-weights common words and up-weights rare words that carry more significance, improving classifier focus on informative terms.

5. **C.** Recall measures the proportion of actual positives (fraud) detected. In imbalanced scenarios, high recall ensures most frauds are caught, even if some false positives occur.

6. **B.** Lexicon-based methods sum sentiment scores and often misinterpret negations like "can't say … is bad," leading to incorrect net sentiment.

7. **A.** Azure Translator Text uses transformer-based NMT under the hood, delivering fluent translations and handling long-range dependencies better than rule-based or statistical methods.

8. **C.** Dialogue management or state tracking maintains context (e.g., destination, dates) so the bot can handle follow-up questions reliably.

9. **A.** Noise reduction algorithms clean the audio waveform to improve phoneme detection accuracy in noisy environments.

10. **B.** Contextual embeddings generate different vectors based on surrounding text, correctly disambiguating "bank" in each scenario.

11. **B.** High recall (Model B) ensures fewer false negatives, which is crucial when missing a positive case carries high cost.

12. **D.** METEOR accounts for synonyms and structure, and human (extrinsic) evaluation captures fluency and appropriateness beyond n-gram overlap.

13. **A.** Azure Speech Service's Text-to-Speech API generates neural TTS audio with natural prosody for custom voice assistants.

14. C. Key-phrase extraction surfaces important multi-word expressions from text without requiring specific entity definitions.

15. C. Semantic search uses contextual embeddings to measure meaning similarity beyond simple term matching.

16. B. Few-shot examples demonstrate the desired format and improve consistency in generated responses.

17. D. Training a custom NER model on annotated legal text will teach it to recognize domain-specific entities accurately.

18. A. Speech Service's ASR pipeline transcribes audio into text, which can then be displayed as real-time captions.

19. C. Raising the classification threshold typically increases precision (fewer false positives) at the expense of recall.

20. B. Incorporating accented speech into a custom acoustic model helps the ASR pipeline better recognize diverse pronunciations.

Chapter 9: Azure Tools for NLP Workloads

1. C. Azure AI Language Service with custom text classification allows you to train models to categorize text into predefined classes like "Billing," "Technical," or "General." This is perfect for automating support ticket classification based on the content. Document Intelligence focuses on extracting structured data from documents, Speech Service handles spoken language, and Cognitive Search is for creating searchable indexes.

2. B. Azure AI Document Intelligence (formerly Form Recognizer) specializes in extracting structured data from forms and documents. It can identify fields like claim numbers, names, and dates from scanned forms, which is exactly what the insurance company needs. Speech Service handles audio, Translator Service handles language translation, and sentiment analysis evaluates emotional tone rather than extracting structured data.

3. C. Sentiment analysis evaluates whether text is positive, negative, or neutral, making it the perfect choice for analyzing patient feedback. Entity recognition identifies named entities like people or places, key phrase extraction pulls important phrases from text, and PII detection finds personal information, none of which directly assess sentiment.

4. A. For multilingual call processing, the company should first convert speech to text using Azure AI Speech Service's transcription capabilities, then translate that text to a common language using Azure Translator Service. This combination allows processing calls in any supported language. The other options don't address the speech-to-text and translation requirements needed for multilingual call processing.

5. D. Key phrase extraction identifies the main points or important phrases in text, making it ideal for summarizing large product reviews. Sentiment analysis evaluates emotional tone, entity recognition identifies named entities, and PII detection finds personal information, none of which focus on extracting important phrases from text.

6. B. Containerized Cognitive Services allows the company to run Azure AI services like Translator in their own infrastructure (on-premises or in their own cloud environment), ensuring data privacy while maintaining the same API functionality. Azure Functions, Logic Apps, and REST API all require sending data to Azure's cloud for processing.

7. A. Azure AI Speech Service's pronunciation assessment evaluates language learners' accuracy, fluency, and intonation, providing feedback similar to a human tutor. This is exactly what a language learning app would need. The other options don't provide pronunciation evaluation capabilities.

8. B. PII (Personally Identifiable Information) detection specifically locates and can redact sensitive data like social security numbers, credit card information, and email addresses. This makes it the appropriate choice for detecting and removing sensitive financial information from transcripts. The other options don't focus on identifying sensitive personal information.

9. B. Batch transcription is designed for processing large audio files asynchronously with high accuracy, making it perfect for converting an archive of audio interviews into text. It optimizes for throughput rather than latency. Real-time transcription is for live scenarios, conversation transcription separates speakers, and custom speech models improve accuracy but don't address the batch processing need.

10. C. Semantic search uses deep learning to understand the intent and context behind queries, not just matching keywords. This allows the search system to return results based on meaning rather than exact word matches. Vector search represents text as numerical vectors, AI enrichment pipelines process raw data, and custom analyzers modify how text is processed during indexing, none of these specifically focus on understanding query intent.

11. A. Custom named entity recognition allows the company to train a model to identify specific medical conditions mentioned in text, which is exactly what they need to categorize scientific papers. The model can be trained to recognize specialized medical terminology. Sentiment analysis evaluates emotional tone, PII detection finds personal information, and text summarization condenses content, none of which help with identifying specific medical conditions.

12. C. Conversation transcription is designed for multi-speaker scenarios such as meetings or phone calls. It transcribes the dialogue in real time and separates what each speaker says, making it ideal for customer service environments. Batch transcription is used for processing pre-recorded audio, real-time transcription does not separate speakers, and custom speech models improve recognition accuracy but don't provide speaker separation.

13. C. Phrase lists boost recognition of specific words or phrases, making them ideal for improving a voice assistant's accuracy with industry-specific terminology. Neural voices are for text-to-speech output quality, speech translation converts between languages, and conversation transcription handles multi-speaker conversations, none of which specifically improve recognition of industry terms.

14. D. A custom glossary allows specific terms (like brand names) to be translated in a particular way or left untranslated, which is exactly what's needed to preserve brand-specific terms. Neural machine translation is the underlying technology, document translation API handles file formats, and custom translator is for domain-specific training, but a glossary specifically addresses preserving selected terms.

15. C. Managed identities allow applications running on Azure services like App Service to authenticate to Azure resources without managing credentials. The system automatically handles token acquisition, renewal, and authentication. This is more secure than API keys or service principals that require secret management, and SAS tokens are used primarily for Azure Storage, not Cognitive Services.

16. A. For translating speech from one language to another, the process requires: (1) Converting speech to text using Azure AI Speech Service's speech-to-text, (2) Translating the text using Azure Translator Service, and (3) Converting translated text back to speech using Azure AI Speech Service's text-to-speech. This is the complete workflow for speech translation as described in the chapter.

17. B. To analyze customer reviews effectively, the company should use key phrase extraction to identify the main topics mentioned, and sentiment analysis to determine whether reviews are positive, negative, or neutral. This combination provides insights into what customers are talking about and how they feel. The other combinations don't address both aspects of the requirement.

18. B. Containerized deployment allows Azure AI services to run locally without requiring constant internet connectivity. This makes it ideal for environments with unreliable connections, as the container runs the complete service on local infrastructure. Azure Functions, REST API calls, and Logic Apps all require internet connectivity to reach Azure's cloud.

19. C. Azure Cognitive Search with AI enrichment pipelines is designed to process documents (including PDFs), extract text and structure, apply AI enrichments (like entity recognition or key phrase extraction), and create searchable indexes with metadata. This is exactly what's needed to make PDFs searchable with AI-enhanced metadata. The other services don't provide the document processing and search indexing capabilities required.

20. A. Azure AI Speech Service's pronunciation assessment feature evaluates how accurately users pronounce words, providing scores on accuracy, fluency, and completeness. This is specifically designed for language learning applications. The other services don't provide pronunciation evaluation capabilities.

Chapter 10: Introduction to Generative AI

1. B. Generative AI is designed to create new content based on patterns learned from training data. For generating product descriptions, you need a system that creates original text content, which is exactly what generative AI is designed to do. Discriminative AI would classify content rather than generate it, supervised learning typically focuses on classification/prediction, and unsupervised clustering groups similar items but doesn't create new content.

2. B. Transformer-based Large Language Models excel at understanding context in conversations and generating coherent, contextually appropriate responses. They can maintain conversation history and provide detailed troubleshooting steps, making them ideal for chatbot applications. GANs and diffusion models are primarily for image generation, while VAEs are less suitable for the complex reasoning needed in customer support scenarios.

3. B. Diffusion models excel at generating high-quality, photorealistic images from text prompts. They gradually transform random noise into structured images, making them ideal for text-to-image generation tasks like creating furniture visualizations from descriptions. Systems like DALL·E, Midjourney, and Stable Diffusion use diffusion techniques for precisely this type of application.

4. C. Retrieval-Augmented Generation (RAG) combines generative models with the ability to retrieve information from external knowledge sources. This approach helps ground the model's responses in factual information rather than relying solely on parametric knowledge, which is crucial for healthcare applications where accuracy is paramount. Higher temperature would increase creativity but potentially reduce factual accuracy, and simply increasing model size doesn't necessarily improve factual grounding.

5. B. Transformer architectures use self-attention mechanisms that allow them to analyze relationships between all words in a text simultaneously, rather than processing text sequentially as recurrent neural networks do. This parallel processing enables transformers to capture long-range dependencies more effectively, which is one of the main reasons they have become dominant in text generation tasks.

6. C. Generating synthetic data that maintains statistical properties of the original dataset requires models that can learn the underlying distribution of the data. VAEs and diffusion models are specifically designed to learn probability distributions of training data, enabling them to generate new samples that share statistical properties with the original data. RLHF and instruction tuning are more focused on aligning model outputs with human preferences rather than learning statistical distributions.

7. D. ROUGE (Recall-Oriented Understudy for Gisting Evaluation) is specifically designed for evaluating summaries by measuring how many of the reference summary's phrases are captured in the generated summary. It focuses on recall of key information, making it particularly well-suited for summarization tasks. BLEU is more suited for translation, FID is for image quality assessment, and perplexity measures the model's confidence but not summary quality.

8. D. Reinforcement Learning from Human Feedback (RLHF) is specifically designed to align model outputs with human values and preferences. By having humans rank different model responses and using these rankings to train a reward model, RLHF helps steer the model toward generating helpful, harmless, and honest responses that align with company values. The other options don't directly address alignment with specific values or safety concerns.

9. B. Temperature controls randomness in the generation process. Higher temperature settings produce more diverse and creative outputs by increasing the probability of selecting lower-ranked tokens. This makes higher temperatures ideal for creative tasks like brainstorming marketing ideas, where novelty and diversity are valuable. For factual, technical, or structured outputs where accuracy and consistency are priorities, lower temperature settings would be more appropriate.

10. A. Continual learning workflows allow models to acquire new information and adapt to changing circumstances over time without forgetting previously learned knowledge. For a financial services assistant that needs to stay current with evolving regulations, continual learning provides a way to update the model with new information as it becomes available, ensuring responses reflect the latest policies.

11. B. Diffusion models have demonstrated strong capabilities in 3D content generation by either directly generating 3D structures or creating consistent multi-view images that can be converted to 3D representations. They've proven particularly effective for architectural visualization tasks because they can generate detailed, realistic 3D models with fine-grained control based on text descriptions or other inputs.

12. A. The context window refers to the maximum number of tokens (words, subwords, or characters) that a language model can process and consider simultaneously when generating responses. This limitation affects how much previous conversation or document content the model can reference when responding to queries, with longer context windows allowing the model to consider more information at once.

13. D. Transformer-based Large Language Models fine-tuned on programming data have demonstrated exceptional capabilities in code generation from natural language descriptions. Models specifically trained on code repositories can understand programming concepts, generate syntactically correct code in various languages, and follow detailed development requirements. Diffusion models and GANs are primarily for image generation, while VAEs aren't typically used for sequence generation tasks like coding.

14. D. Chunk-and-summarize approaches help overcome context window limitations by breaking large documents into smaller sections (chunks) that fit within the model's context window, processing each chunk individually, and then combining the results. This technique allows the model to effectively process documents that would otherwise exceed its context window capacity, making it suitable for summarizing large documents.

15. B. Fine-tuning is the process of further training a pretrained model on a smaller, more specific dataset representing the target application. For adapting a general-purpose language model to generate content in a specific brand voice, fine-tuning on examples of the brand's existing content (product descriptions, marketing materials, etc.) would efficiently adapt the model to match the desired style and terminology without requiring extensive computational resources.

16. C. Human evaluation remains the gold standard because humans can assess subjective qualities like creativity, coherence, helpfulness, and cultural appropriateness that automated metrics struggle to capture. While automated metrics provide objective and reproducible measurements, they often fail to capture the nuanced aspects of quality that matter to end users. Human evaluators bring contextual understanding and judgment that automated systems lack.

17. B. Retrieval-Augmented Generation (RAG) enhances generative models by connecting them to external knowledge sources (like educational databases or textbooks). This approach allows the model to look up relevant information before generating responses, significantly improving factual accuracy compared to relying solely on parametric knowledge. For educational content where accuracy is critical, RAG provides a way to ground the generation process in verified information.

18. C. Denoising objectives train models to recover clean data from corrupted or noisy inputs. This approach is particularly central to diffusion models, which learn by gradually adding noise to training data until it becomes pure random noise (forward diffusion process) and then learning to reverse this process to generate new content (reverse diffusion). This technique teaches the model robustness and attention to detail in reconstructing original data patterns.

19. B. For medical applications where accuracy is critical, human-in-the-loop evaluation ensures that generated images maintain the specific diagnostic features that medical professionals would use for assessment. Medical experts can provide feedback on whether synthetic images accurately represent disease characteristics, anatomical structures, and other clinically relevant features. This expert guidance helps refine the generative models to produce more medically accurate and useful training data.

20. C. Tool use and function calling capabilities allow generative AI systems to interact with external systems and data sources, such as company knowledge bases, product catalogs, or customer records. This enables the assistant to retrieve accurate, up-to-date company-specific information rather than relying solely on what was in its training data. For customer service applications, the ability to look up exact product details, policies, or account information is crucial for providing accurate responses.

Chapter 11: Azure OpenAI Service

1. C. Azure OpenAI Service keeps prompts, outputs, embeddings, and fine-tuning data within Microsoft-controlled infrastructure, is operated under Microsoft Product Terms, and provides compliance features that help organizations meet regulatory requirements like GDPR and HIPAA, making it appropriate for enterprises with strict governance needs.

2. D. Azure OpenAI includes a content filtering system that checks both prompts and responses for inappropriate content. Healthcare organizations can customize these thresholds to permit medical descriptions that might otherwise be flagged while maintaining safety in other categories.

3. C. Output constraints are a key component of effective prompt engineering that specifies the required structure, length, or format of the response. By clearly defining output constraints, developers can guard against rambling responses and ensure the answer is in a machine-readable format.

4. B. The text-embedding-3 model in Azure OpenAI is specifically designed to convert text into numeric vectors (embeddings) that capture semantic meaning, making it ideal for implementing semantic search functionality.

5. A. For creative concept generation in marketing, DALL·E integration would be most efficient as it allows the team to generate visual concepts based on text descriptions, which is particularly valuable for product campaigns that require both textual and visual creative elements.

6. D. The primary advantage of Azure OpenAI for enterprises is its enhanced security features, compliance certifications (like GDPR and HIPAA compliance), and seamless integration with other Azure services and identity management systems, which are critical for enterprise governance requirements.

7. A. Azure Machine Learning is the service that helps with developing, training, and deploying custom machine learning models, which can be combined with Azure OpenAI to create highly specialized AI solutions that leverage both foundation models and custom-trained models.

8. C. Role framing is an essential component of well-crafted prompts that casts the model in a specific persona (e.g., "You are a bilingual tech-support agent"). This primes the model's internal attention toward the right tone and domain knowledge, helping it understand its purpose.

9. B. Retrieval-Augmented Generation (RAG) is the pattern where Azure AI Search retrieves relevant passages from company documentation based on a customer query, and then Azure OpenAI uses those passages to generate a relevant, grounded response with citations to the source documents.

10. D. Azure AI Studio (formerly OpenAI Studio) is a unified platform that brings together Azure OpenAI, Cognitive Services, and Machine Learning into a single workspace where developers can experiment, build, and deploy AI solutions without switching between tools.

11. A. For a retail chatbot that must adhere to brand guidelines, a clear task description with specific output constraints is most important. This ensures the model knows exactly what to do (answer product queries) and how to format responses (following brand tone and style) while maintaining consistency.

12. C. GPT-3.5-Turbo is a mid-tier model that trades some reasoning depth for speed and price, making it ideal for high-volume, cost-sensitive chatbot applications that don't require the deeper reasoning capabilities of GPT-4 or the o-series models.

13. B. DALL·E's in-context edits with masks allow for targeted modifications to specific portions of an image while keeping the rest unchanged. This is ideal for generating product packaging variations where only certain elements (like colors or text) need to be altered while maintaining the base design.

14. A. GPT-4o is a multimodal model that can process images and short audio clips in addition to text, which is a capability that earlier GPT models did not have. This allows it to understand content across different modalities.

15. C. Azure OpenAI provides regional deployment options that allow organizations to specify in which geographic region their model and data will be hosted, helping them meet data residency requirements mandated by regulations.

16. B. The correct endpoint for generating images using DALL·E in Azure OpenAI is / images/generations, which follows the same OpenAI-style API format but with traffic and data confined to Microsoft data centers.

17. D. For financial summaries of earnings calls, output constraints are crucial to ensure the model provides structured information including risk assessments, which are particularly important in financial contexts where regulatory compliance and accurate risk communication are required.

18. A. Azure AI Search is the service that should be integrated with Azure OpenAI to connect an internal knowledge base for employee queries. It provides vector search capabilities that can retrieve relevant documents based on semantic meaning rather than just keywords.

19. B. Azure OpenAI includes a content filtering system that scans both prompts and responses for violence, self-harm, sexual imagery, hate speech, and other disallowed material, helping prevent the generation of harmful content.

20. C. For code completion tasks, the most important capability is the model's ability to understand the context of the code and follow project-level style conventions, ensuring that generated code is consistent with existing codebase practices.

Chapter 12: AI Agents in Azure

1. A. AI agents are software programs designed to perceive their environment (understand customer inquiries), make decisions (determine appropriate responses), and take actions to achieve specific goals (schedule appointments, provide information). This perfectly matches the requirement, while neural networks, machine learning algorithms, and computer vision systems are components or specific AI technologies but don't inherently have the complete perceive-decide-act loop that defines agents.

2. C. Microsoft 365 Copilot is specifically designed to enhance productivity within Microsoft's productivity applications by drafting content, summarizing information, and generating text-based outputs. This makes it the ideal solution for the described scenario of helping employees with email drafting, summarizing feedback, and generating product descriptions, all of which are text-generation tasks in the workplace context.

3. D. The fundamental difference between AI agents and traditional applications is that AI agents possess awareness of their environment, can interpret ambiguous instructions, make decisions, and adapt their responses based on changing circumstances. Traditional applications, in contrast, function within tightly defined parameters and follow predetermined paths without genuine understanding of context or purpose.

4. C. The processing engine is the computational brain of an AI agent that makes sense of incoming data. In the case of a healthcare diagnostic assistant, the processing engine would analyze the patient symptoms and medical history data to help formulate potential diagnoses. Sensors would collect the data, actuators would communicate the results, and memory management would store information but not perform the analytical processing.

5. D. Knowledge grounding ensures that AI agents stay tethered to reality by connecting them to knowledge bases containing accurate, up-to-date information (like company product data). This prevents agents from hallucinating or providing generic answers by ensuring responses are anchored in factual organizational data. While agent memory stores past interactions, function calling enables actions, and prompt flow orchestrates components, knowledge grounding specifically addresses the need to base answers on company-specific information.

6. B. Model-based reflex agents add an internal "model" of the world to handle incomplete information and track changes over time. Unlike simple reflex agents that only react to the current input, model-based reflex agents maintain a representation of the world that allows them to make decisions based on both current and historical information, making them better at handling uncertainty.

7. C. Dynamics 365 Copilot is designed for business applications, including manufacturing and operations scenarios. It can analyze operational data, recognize patterns, and predict events like equipment failures. Copilot in Word is for document creation, GitHub Copilot is for software development, and Security Copilot focuses on cybersecurity threats, making Dynamics 365 Copilot the most appropriate choice for manufacturing equipment monitoring.

8. B. Microsoft Entra ID integration (formerly Azure AD) enables secure organizational data access by allowing AI agents to authenticate through the same identity provider that employees use. This "run-as-user" model ensures agents inherit a user's existing permissions rather than requiring new credentials, enforcing least privilege automatically and maintaining security when accessing sensitive organizational data.

9. D. Foundation models serve as the "brains" behind AI agents, providing the knowledge and adaptability needed to handle diverse scenarios. The relationship is symbiotic. Agents rely on foundation models for core intelligence, while foundation models depend on agents to apply their capabilities in real-world contexts with specific business needs.

10. C. Prompt flow is Azure AI Studio's visual orchestrator that allows developers to drag and drop LLM calls, Python scripts, and data connectors onto a canvas and link them with arrows showing execution order. This is the ideal component for creating a visual

workflow that processes insurance claims through a sequence of steps, connecting language model calls with data processing.

11. D. Retrieval Augmented Generation (RAG) helps prevent AI hallucinations (making up facts) by having agents fetch real-time data from trusted sources before answering questions. This ensures responses are grounded in accurate organizational information rather than generated solely based on the model's training data, directly addressing the issue of the agent making up product information.

12. A. While Microsoft 365 Copilot can draft emails, create presentations, and summarize documents, generating code for financial analysis applications is more aligned with GitHub Copilot's capabilities, which is specifically designed for software development. Microsoft 365 Copilot focuses on enhancing productivity in Office applications rather than specialized code generation for financial analysis.

13. B. Actuators or output mechanisms carry out the chosen actions in the environment. These might generate text responses, control physical devices, update databases, or trigger other systems. In the given scenario, sending an email or updating a CRM record would be the responsibility of the actuators component of the AI agent.

14. D. Microsoft 365 Copilot is specifically designed to work within the Microsoft 365 environment, including applications like Word, Excel, PowerPoint, Outlook, and Teams. It can access and analyze information across these applications, making it the most appropriate choice for an assistant that needs to work with Microsoft 365 data. The other variants are specialized for different environments like software development, business applications, or security operations.

15. C. Function calling allows AI agents to trigger actions in external systems, such as booking appointments or checking inventory. This capability enables agents to bridge between natural language understanding and concrete actions by invoking predefined functions that developers integrate with external systems and APIs.

16. C. Utility-based agents introduce the concept of "quality" to decision-making. Instead of just achieving a goal, they aim for the best outcome based on a utility function (a mathematical measure of success). This makes them ideal for scenarios requiring evaluation of different possible actions based on their expected outcomes to select the highest-value option.

17. D. A responsible AI approach to implementing customer service agents should include content filters to prevent harmful responses, role-based access to control who can modify the agents, and continuous monitoring to track agent performance and detect issues. This balanced approach addresses safety, security, and quality concerns, unlike focusing solely on automation, avoiding human oversight, or prioritizing power over responsibility.

18. B. For an AI agent helping employees analyze sales data, natural language understanding is essential to interpret questions about the data (like "How did our holiday promotion affect sales?"). This allows non-technical staff to query data using everyday language rather than technical query languages. While computer vision, speech recognition, and robotics might be useful in retail, they don't directly address the core need of analyzing sales data.

19. C. Prompt flow in Azure AI Studio allows developers to clone a branch, tweak a system prompt, and run both versions side by side to see which produces fewer hallucinations or lower cost. The studio records metrics for every run (tokens, latency, custom scores) so evidence replaces guesswork when deciding which version to deploy. This capability is essential for testing and comparing different versions of agent prompts.

20. B. Microsoft Purview integration is crucial for secure document processing, as it labels sensitive files, applies encryption, and audits access. When an agent requests document content, Purview's Data Security Posture Management layer checks policy first, ensuring the agent receives only the allowed view based on permissions. This properly addresses organizational data security concerns, unlike the other options which would create security risks.

Chapter 13: AI Use Cases and Industry Applications

1. B. Azure Computer Vision and specialized tools like Project InnerEye are designed to help analyze medical images such as X-rays, MRIs, and CT scans. These tools can highlight areas of concern, measure changes in tumors over time, and flag images that need immediate attention from specialists, making them ideal for assisting radiologists in analyzing radiology images.

2. B. Azure Personalizer uses reinforcement learning to determine which products, offers, or content each shopper is most likely to be interested in at that exact moment. Unlike simple systems that just show popular items, Personalizer learns from how customers interact with recommendations and gets smarter over time, making it the ideal choice for real-time personalization in retail.

3. A. For predictive maintenance, Azure IoT Hub would collect sensor data from manufacturing equipment (temperature, vibration, power consumption), while Azure Machine Learning would use this data to create models that predict when equipment is likely to fail based on historical breakdown patterns. This combination allows maintenance to be performed before failures occur, preventing costly downtime.

4. B. Azure Anomaly Detector is designed to spot unusual patterns in data streams, making it ideal for identifying unusual financial transactions that may indicate fraud. It can detect when activity deviates from normal patterns, such as someone suddenly making large withdrawals from different branches or a business whose transactions don't match its claimed activities, while minimizing disruption to legitimate transactions.

5. B. Azure Bot Service and Copilot Studio enable the creation of virtual assistants that can answer customer questions, troubleshoot common problems, and help with purchases across multiple channels including websites, mobile apps, and social media platforms. Copilot Studio's visual design tools also make it easier for customer service teams to build and update their own bots without extensive coding experience.

6. C. Adaptive learning platforms powered by Azure Machine Learning can analyze student performance data to tailor educational content to individual learning styles and paces. These systems can identify when students are struggling with specific concepts, provide additional practice or alternative explanations, and allow faster learners to advance more quickly, creating a personalized educational experience.

7. A. Azure Time Series Insights provides specialized tools for analyzing patterns that occur over time, making it ideal for identifying seasonal trends, weekly shopping patterns, and the impact of special events on retail sales. This allows for more accurate demand forecasting, helping retailers maintain appropriate inventory levels and reduce both stockouts and overstock situations.

8. B. Azure Confidential Computing helps healthcare organizations meet strict privacy requirements while still leveraging modern cloud technology. It creates secure enclaves where sensitive data (like Protected Health Information) can be analyzed without being exposed, even to Microsoft itself, helping hospitals maintain compliance with regulations like HIPAA while benefiting from AI capabilities.

9. A. Azure Custom Vision can be trained to recognize specific product defects, and when deployed on Azure IoT Edge devices like industrial cameras on the factory floor, it can perform real-time quality inspection without sending images to the cloud. This edge deployment allows for immediate detection of defects while maintaining consistent performance 24/7 without cloud connectivity requirements.

10. B. Azure Translator is designed to provide real-time translation capabilities across over 70 languages, making it the ideal service for creating multilingual virtual assistants. When combined with other Cognitive Services like Language Understanding, it allows virtual assistants to understand and respond to customer inquiries in multiple languages, supporting global customer service operations.

11. C. Transparency in AI refers to the ability to explain how AI systems reach their conclusions. For lending decisions, this means being able to provide clear explanations of which factors influenced the AI's recommendation to approve or deny a loan application. Azure's responsible AI tools support this by maintaining records of decision factors and providing explainable AI features that help financial institutions meet regulatory requirements for transparent decision-making.

12. B. Azure Digital Twins creates virtual representations of physical environments like stores or distribution networks. These digital models help retailers visualize and optimize their operations by identifying bottlenecks in product flow or simulating changes to store layouts before implementing them physically. This service is specifically designed for creating the virtual representations needed for supply chain optimization.

13. A. Azure Health Bot is specifically designed for healthcare scenarios with built-in medical intelligence. It understands health terminology and can follow clinical protocols for triage and symptom checking. Unlike general chatbots, Health Bot is designed with medical privacy in mind from the ground up, making it the ideal choice for patient-facing conversational interfaces in healthcare.

14. C. Power Apps with AI Builder enables "citizen developers" with limited coding experience to create AI-powered applications through visual, low-code interfaces. This allows business experts to directly create solutions for their domain-specific problems without extensive technical knowledge, while still connecting to enterprise systems and following company security policies.

15. C. Reinforcement Learning is specifically suited for optimization problems with many variables. It works through a process similar to trial and error, trying different combinations of settings, learning from the results, and gradually discovering the optimal approach. For complex manufacturing processes with hundreds of variables, reinforcement learning can discover solutions that human engineers might never have considered.

16. B. Azure Cognitive Services for Language is designed to analyze text, making it ideal for examining transaction descriptions for patterns that might indicate money laundering. It can identify suspicious language patterns, recognize entities mentioned in descriptions, and categorize transactions based on their text content, helping financial institutions detect potentially illegal activities.

17. A. Azure IoT Edge enables "smart shelves" by connecting shelf sensors to the cloud, allowing them to detect when products are running low and automatically trigger restocking. This technology bridges physical stores with digital inventory systems, ensuring accurate inventory tracking and timely replenishment without requiring constant human monitoring.

18. B. Genomic analysis requires processing enormous amounts of data (a single human genome contains about 3 billion base pairs). Azure Synapse Analytics provides the scalable storage and processing power needed for this volume of data, while Azure Machine Learning offers the tools to identify patterns and relationships within genetic information, all with appropriate security controls for sensitive research data.

19. B. MLOps (Machine Learning Operations) treats AI development like software development, creating consistent pipelines from data collection to model deployment. This approach ensures governance policies are consistently applied, reduces manual work and errors when moving from testing to production, and facilitates collaboration between data scientists and IT teams, making it ideal for organizations implementing AI across multiple departments.

20. B. Azure Cognitive Services for Speech and Language includes tools that can read text aloud, break words into chunks, highlight different parts of speech, and translate content into different languages. These capabilities are essential for making educational content accessible to students with dyslexia or language barriers, helping them participate fully in the classroom regardless of their learning differences.

Index

Note: Page numbers in *italics* and **bold** refers to figures and tables respectively.

Printed and bound by CPI Group (UK) Ltd, Croydon, CR0 4YY

21/12/2025

14796421-0001